Using TRILL, Fab and VXLAN

Sanjay Hooda
Shyam Kapadia
Padmanabhan Krishnan

Cisco Press

800 East 96th Street

Indianapolis, IN 46240

Using TRILL, FabricPath, and VXLAN

Designing Massively Scalable Data Centers with Overlays

Sanjay Hooda
Shyam Kapadia
Padmanabhan Krishnan

Published by:
Cisco Press
800 East 96th Street
Indianapolis, IN 46240 USA

Printed in the United States of America

First Printing January 2014

Library of Congress Control Number: 2013957519

ISBN-13: 978-1-58714-393-9

ISBN-10: 1-58714-393-3

Warning and Disclaimer

Trademark Acknowledgments

Special Sales

For information about buying this title in bulk quantities, or for special sales opportunities (which may include electronic versions; custom cover designs; and content particular to your business, training goals, marketing focus, or branding interests), please contact our corporate sales department at corpsales@pearsoned.com or (800) 382-3419.

For government sales inquiries, please contact governmentsales@pearsoned.com.

For questions about sales outside the U.S., please contact international@pearsoned.com.

Feedback Information

At Cisco Press, our goal is to create in-depth technical books of the highest quality and value. Each book is crafted with care and precision, undergoing rigorous development that involves the unique expertise of members from the professional technical community.

Readers' feedback is a natural continuation of this process. If you have any comments regarding how we could improve the quality of this book, or otherwise alter it to better suit your needs, you can contact us through e-mail at feedback@ciscopress.com. Please make sure to include the book title and ISBN in your message.

We greatly appreciate your assistance.

Publisher: Paul Boger	**Business Operation Manager, Cisco Press:** Jan Cornelssen
Associate Publisher: Dave Dusthimer	**Executive Editor:** Brett Bartow
Development Editor: Eleanor C. Bru	**Copy Editor:** Apostrophe Editing Services
Managing Editor: Sandra Schroeder	**Technical Editors:** Narbik Kocharians, Ryan Lindfield
Project Editor: Seth Kerney	**Proofreader:** Megan Wade-Taxter
Editorial Assistant: Vanessa Evans	**Indexer:** Tim Wright
Cover Designer: Mark Shirar	**Composition:** Bronkella Publishing, LLC

Americas Headquarters	Asia Pacific Headquarters	Europe Headquarters
Cisco Systems, Inc.	Cisco Systems (USA) Pte. Ltd.	Cisco Systems International BV
San Jose, CA	Singapore	Amsterdam, The Netherlands

Cisco has more than 200 offices worldwide. Addresses, phone numbers, and fax numbers are listed on the Cisco Website at **www.cisco.com/go/offices.**

CCDE, CCENT, Cisco Eos, Cisco HealthPresence, the Cisco logo, Cisco Lumin, Cisco Nexus, Cisco StadiumVision, Cisco TelePresence, Cisco WebEx, DCE, and Welcome to the Human Network are trademarks; Changing the Way We Work, Live, Play, and Learn and Cisco Store are service marks; and Access Registrar, Aironet, AsyncOS, Bringing the Meeting To You, Catalyst, CCDA, CCDP, CCIE, CCIP, CCNA, CCNP, CCSP, CCVP, Cisco, the Cisco Certified Internetwork Expert logo, Cisco IOS, Cisco Press, Cisco Systems, Cisco Systems Capital, the Cisco Systems logo, Cisco Unity, Collaboration Without Limitation, EtherFast, EtherSwitch, Event Center, Fast Step, Follow Me Browsing, FormShare, GigaDrive, HomeLink, Internet Quotient, IOS, iPhone, iQuick Study, IronPort, the IronPort logo, LightStream, Linksys, MediaTone, MeetingPlace, MeetingPlace Chime Sound, MGX, Networkers, Networking Academy, Network Registrar, PCNow, PIX, PowerPanels, ProConnect, ScriptShare, SenderBase, SMARTnet, Spectrum Expert, StackWise, The Fastest Way to Increase Your Internet Quotient, TransPath, WebEx, and the WebEx logo are registered trademarks of Cisco Systems, Inc. and/or its affiliates in the United States and certain other countries.

All other trademarks mentioned in this document or website are the property of their respective owners. The use of the word partner does not imply a partnership relationship between Cisco and any other company. (0812R)

About the Authors

Sanjay Hooda, CCIE No. 11737, is currently a principal engineer at Cisco, where he works with embedded systems and helps define new product architectures. His current passion is to design the next-generation campus architecture, and he is focused on simplifying the design and deployment of wired and wireless infrastructure. Over the last 17 years, Sanjay's experience spans various areas including high availability; messaging in large-scale distributed systems; Supervisory Control and Data Acquisition (SCADA); large-scale software projects; and enterprise campus and LAN, WAN, and data center network design.

Shyam Kapadia, Ph.D., is currently a technical leader in the Data Center Group at Cisco. He graduated from the University of Southern California with Ph.D. and master's degrees in computer science in 2006. His research interests broadly lie in the area of networking systems including wired, wireless, ad-hoc, vehicular, and sensor networks. He has co-authored several conference and journal publications in these areas including a book chapter in the relatively nascent area of intermittently connected wireless networks (http://anrg.usc.edu/~kapadia/publications.html).

At Cisco, for the first few years, he was an integral part of the team that delivered the next-generation Catalyst 6500 Sup 2T platform. During the past few years, he has been intrinsically involved in developing solutions for data center environments with more than 25 submitted patents in this area. Over the past 12 years, Shyam has been the speakers chair for a premiere Open Source conference, Southern California Linux Exposition (SCALE), hosted in the Los Angeles area. In his spare time, he loves watching international movies and is passionate about sports like cricket, basketball, and American football.

Padmanabhan Krishnan is a software engineer in the Data Center Group at Cisco. He joined Cisco 7 years ago and has more than 12 years of experience in various areas of networking and telecommunication. He obtained his master's degree in computer science from the University of Missouri, Kansas City, and his bachelor's degree in engineering from Madras University, India. His research work for the master's degree included Diffserv, MPLS traffic engineering, and QOS routing/Connection Admission Control in ad-hoc wireless networks.

Padmanabhan has worked in many overlay technologies in Cisco such as 802.1ah, TRILL, FabricPath, and VPLS. He was responsible for the design and development of the core infrastructure used by the forwarding drivers and many Layer 2 features in the next-generation Catalyst 6500 Sup 2T Platform. Prior to joining Cisco, Padmanabhan worked in ATM signaling and DVB-RCS, an interactive on-demand multimedia satellite communication system specification.

About the Technical Reviewers

Jeevan Sharma, CCIE No. 11529, is a technical marketing engineer at Brocade, where he works with the Enterprise Networking Group focusing on Enterprise Switching Business. He has more than 16 years of worldwide work experience in data center and wide area network technologies, focusing on routing, switching, security, content networking, application delivery, and WAN optimization. During this period, Jeevan has held various technical roles in which he has worked extensively with customers all around the world to help them design and implement their data center and campus networks, in addition to helping them troubleshoot their complex network issues. Working internally with engineering teams, Jeevan has been instrumental in driving several new features and product enhancements, making products and solutions work better for customers. Prior to Brocade, Jeevan worked for Riverbed Technologies, Cisco Systems, HCL Technologies, and CMC Limited. He holds a bachelor's degree in engineering and an MBA degree from Santa Clara University. In his spare time, Jeevan enjoys spending time with family and friends, hiking, playing tennis, traveling, and photography.

Dedications

Sanjay Hooda: First of all, I would like to dedicate this book to my father (Satbir Singh) for being an inspiration and support. I would like to thank my mother (Indrawati), wife (Suman), and children (Pulkit and Apoorva) for their support during the writing of the book.

Shyam Kapadia: I dedicate this book to my family, especially my wife Rakhee and my mother who have provided and continue to provide their undying love and support.

Padmanabhan Krishnan: I would like to dedicate this book to my wife Krithiga and daughter Ishana. It would not have been possible without their understanding and support in spite of all the time it took me away from them. I would also like to dedicate this book to my parents and sister for their support and encouragement in all aspects of my life.

Acknowledgments

Sanjay Hooda: First of all, I would like to thank my co-authors, Shyam Kapadia and Padmanabhan Krishnan, who have been very supportive during the course of writing. In addition, I would like to thank my great friends Muninder Singh Sambi and Sanjay Thyamagundalu. Both of them have been a source of inspiration and thought-provoking insights into various areas.

Thanks as well to Brett Bartow, Ellie Bru, and all the folks at Cisco Press for their support, patience, and high quality work.

Shyam Kapadia: Special thanks to my co-authors, Padmanabhan and Sanjay, for putting in a great deal of effort in ensuring that we came up with a quality deliverable that we can all be proud of. Special acknowledgment goes to my wife Rakhee without whose help I would not have been able to complete this book on time. And last but certainly not least, special thanks to the reviewers and editors for their tremendous help and support in developing this publication.

Padmanabhan Krishnan: First and foremost, I would like to thank the editors Ellie and Brett for their helpful reviews, patience, and understanding our work-related priorities. I would like to sincerely acknowledge Rajagopalan Janakiraman for many of our technical discussions. His insights and deep technical expertise in networking helped me immensely. I would like to thank Sridhar Subramanian for sharing his expertise and materials in TRILL deployment, which were extremely helpful. A special thanks to the technical reviewer Jeevan Sharma for his thorough reviews and providing comments that added value to the chapters. I would like to express my sincere gratitude to my co-authors, Shyam and Sanjay, for their invaluable comments and support. Last, but not the least, I would like to thank my manager, Milton Xu, for giving me the opportunity to work in different overlay technologies, which gave me the needed practical exposure.

Contents at a Glance

Contents

Icons

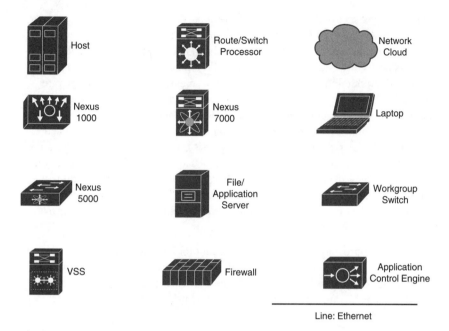

Line: Ethernet

Command Syntax Conventions

The conventions used to present command syntax in this book are the same conventions used in the IOS Command Reference. The Command Reference describes these conventions as follows:

- Boldface indicates commands and keywords that are entered literally, as shown. In actual configuration examples and output (not general command syntax), boldface indicates commands that are manually input by the user (such as a show command).

- Italics indicate arguments for which you supply actual values.

- Vertical bars (|) separate alternative, mutually exclusive elements.

- Square brackets [ ] indicate optional elements.

- Braces { } indicate a required choice.

- Braces within brackets [{ }] indicate a required choice within an optional element.

Introduction

Over the past few years, virtualization and the cloud have become exceedingly popular. The recognition that server resources including memory, CPU, and so on are severely underutilized in large data centers has led to virtualized data center deployments. Physical servers now constitute a number of virtual servers that each cater to different application needs. Architectures are sought for deployment of public clouds, private clouds, and more recently hybrid clouds. Network architects are thus faced with challenges in the design and implementation of massive scale data centers that serve these challenging requirements. To address the requirements, this book describes data center deployments using overlay technologies with emphasis on the three most popular ones: FabricPath, TRILL, and VXLAN. Data center architects are looking for innovative solutions to (a) simplify their data centers vis-à-vis, (b) retain the functionality to add new PODs without making large-scale changes to their existing DC network, and (c) ensure data center designs allow for scalability, mobility, agility, extensibility, and easier management and maintenance.

Because the book's approach is to deploy these technologies in MSDCs, the focus is to divide the chapters in the book based on understanding the overlay technology, followed by a description of some representative deployments. The final chapter is dedicated toward interconnecting two or more data centers using overlay technologies.

Goals and Methods

The goal of this book is provide a resource for readers who want to get familiar with the data center overlay technologies. The main goal is to provide a methodology for network architects and administrators to plan, design, and implement massive scale data centers using overlay technologies such as FabricPath, TRILL, and VXLAN. Readers do not have to be networking professionals or data center administrators to benefit from this book. The book is geared toward the understanding of current overlay technologies followed by their deployment. Our hope is that all readers from university students to professors to networking experts benefit from this book.

Who Should Read This Book?

This book has been written with a broad audience in mind. Consider CTOs/CIOs who want to get familiar with the overlay technologies. This book helps them by providing information on all the major overlay technology options for data centers. For the network professional with the in-depth understanding of various networking areas, this book serves as an authoritative guide explaining detailed control and data plane concepts with popular overlays, specifically, FabricPath, TRILL, and VXLAN. In addition, detailed packet flows are presented covering numerous deployment scenarios.

Regardless of your expertise or role in the IT industry, this book has a place for you; it takes various overly technology concepts and and explains them in detail. This book also provides migration guidelines as to how today's networks can move to using overlay deployments.

How This Book Is Organized

Although you could read this book cover-to-cover, it is designed to be flexible and allow you to easily move between chapters and sections of chapters to cover only the material you need. The first two chapters target the CTO/CIO–level executives and describe the need for overlays and provide a brief description of the existing overlay technology options. Chapter 3 forms the foundation for the subsequent FabricPath and TRILL chapters and describes Layer 2 IS-IS with an emphasis on the extensions for supporting Layer 2 multipath overlay schemes. Chapter 4 through Chapter 9 describes the design, innerworkings, and deployment of the most popular data center overlay technologies; namely, FabricPath, TRILL, and VXLAN.

Chapters 1 through 9 cover the following topics:

- **Chapter 1, "Need for Overlays in Massive Scale Data Centers"**: This chapter describes the major requirements of massive scale data centers and the associated deployment challenges. Popular data center architectures are introduced, and the case for overlays in data center networks is firmly established.

- **Chapter 2, "Introduction to Overlay Technologies"**: This chapter provides a brief survey of various overlay technologies employed in data center environments.

- **Chapter 3, "IS-IS"**: This chapter provides a brief introduction to IS-IS. It ex-plains in detail the extensions that were introduced in IS-IS to support TRILL.

- **Chapter 4, "FabricPath"**: This chapter introduces FabricPath, a novel Cisco overlay solution, and provides details of the architecture and innerworkings of FabricPath, both from the point of view of control plane and data plane. Detailed end-to-end packet flows are presented in a FabricPath network.

- **Chapter 5, "TRILL"**: This chapter introduces TRILL, an IETF standard, and provides details of the architecture and innerworkings of TRILL. Both control and data plane aspects are described. This chapter also covers in detail the different areas of development in the TRILL community as of this writing. Detailed end-to-end packet flows are presented in a TRILL network.

- **Chapter 6, "VXLAN"**: This chapter provides a detailed description of VXLAN, a popular MAC over IP/UDP overlay deployed in data center environments. Details of the VXLAN architecture are presented coupled with step-by-step packet flows covering unicast, multicast, and broadcast cases in VXLAN clouds. Both multicast as well as multicast-less VXLAN deployment options are presented.

- **Chapter 7, "FabricPath Deployment, Migration, and Troubleshooting":** This chapter covers the different deployment possibilities with FabricPath along with representative examples. Migration strategies to FabricPath including (Classical Layer 2 to FabricPath and vPC to vPC+) are covered. In addition, some common FabricPath deployment topologies are presented. The chapter concludes with a brief description of troubleshooting and monitoring tools for FabricPath networks.

- **Chapter 8, "TRILL Deployment, Migration and Troubleshooting":** This chapter explains how current data center deployments can be migrated to TRILL. Various deployment scenarios along with some case studies are explained in detail. A brief introduction to troubleshooting in TRILL networks is also provided.

- **Chapter 9, "Interoperability of Other Technologies":** This chapter describes some specific deployments where multiple overlay technologies may be employed to realize an end-to-end solution in data center environments. Three representative case studies are presented that cover both intra-DC and inter-DC deployments.

Chapter 1

Need for Overlays in Massive Scale Data Centers

This chapter covers the following objectives.

- **Evolution of the data center:** This section provides a brief description of how data centers have evolved in the past few years highlighting some major paradigm shifts.

- **Changing requirements of data centers:** This section highlights some of the major requirements of modern data centers.

- **Data center architectures:** This section provides a survey of popular data center architectures.

- **Need for overlays:** This section firmly establishes the need for overlays to meet the requirements of massive scale data centers.

This chapter serves as an introduction to the modern-day data center (DC). It provides a listing of the changing data center requirements and the different architectures that are considered to meet these requirements. With scale as the prime requirement, the case for overlays in massive scale data centers (MSDCs) is firmly established.

Evolution of the Data Center

The last 5 years or so have popularized the paradigm of cloud computing and virtualization. The general expectation has now become the ability to have secure access to your data from the *cloud* anytime, anywhere, and anyhow (that is, from any device). Perhaps Amazon.com's EC2 cloud[1] was the first of its kind to provide this capability all the way to the consumers. Enterprise and service-provider data centers have also rapidly moved toward the cloud deployment model. As Gartner indicated in its 2012 study[2] on data center trends, the "new data center" is here and will continue to grow and evolve (see Figure 1-1). The data center evolution has enabled IT departments to keep pace with the rapidly changing business requirements. Data centers are designed to exhibit flexibility, scalability, modularity, robustness, easy operability and maintenance, power efficiency, and above all enhanced business value.

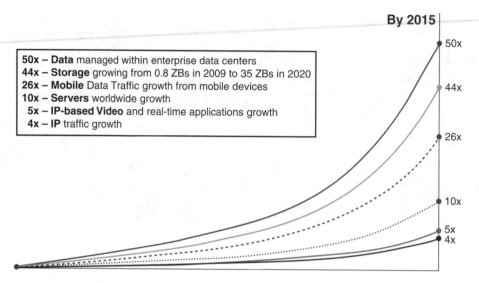

By 2015

50x – **Data** managed within enterprise data centers
44x – **Storage** growing from 0.8 ZBs in 2009 to 35 ZBs in 2020
26x – **Mobile** Data Traffic growth from mobile devices
10x – **Servers** worldwide growth
 5x – **IP-based Video** and real-time applications growth
 4x – **IP** traffic growth

Figure 1-1   *Data Center Trends[2]*

The notions of Software-as-a-Service (SaaS), Platform-as-a-Service (PaaS), Infrastructure-as-a-Service (IaaS), and Cloud-as-a-Service (CaaS) are all central data center cloud offerings, each commanding different levels of security considerations[3]. Various providers deliver one or more offerings in the areas of IaaS, SaaS, and PaaS; see Figure 1-2 for a nonexhaustive listing of some of the major players. SaaS refers to application services delivered over the network on a subscription basis such as Google Docs or Cisco Webex. PaaS provides a software development framework typically aimed at application developers such as the Google Apps Engine. IaaS refers to delivery of a combination of compute, storage, and network resources much like what Amazon Web Services offers on a pay-as-you-go basis. This cloud computing value chain has resulted in a push toward building large scale multitenant data centers that support a variety of operational models where compute, storage, and network resources are unified and can be holistically managed.

Figure 1-2   *Cloud Computing Offerings*

Traditionally, the majority of the traffic in data center deployments was north-south, aka from the Internet into the data center, adhering to the traditional client-server model for web and media access. However, the combination of IT budgets being cut and the realization that often servers were operated at 30 percent to 40 percent of their capability for computation and memory utilization has led to a rapid rise in adoption of virtualization. Server virtualization enables multiple operating system (OS) images to transparently share the same physical server and I/O devices. This significantly improves the utilization of the server resources because it enables workloads to be evenly spread among the available compute nodes. The traditional application deployment models of having separate database, web, and file physical servers were transformed into equivalent virtual machines. With a proliferation of virtual machines inside the data center, the east-to-west server-to-server traffic started dominating the north-south traffic from the Internet. Cloud service offerings of SaaS, PaaS, IaaS, and so on have resulted in more services being deployed within the data center cloud, resulting in a rapid rise in the intra-DC traffic. An incoming request into the data center would result in various resources being accessed over the intra-DC network fabric such as database servers, file servers, load balancers, security gateways, and so on. Memcache-based[4] applications popularized by Facebook, Big Data, and Hadoop-based[5] applications popularized by Google have also resulted in a heavy rise in the intra-DC traffic.

Virtualization has brought about a number of new requirements to data center networks. To name a few, this includes the following:

- Ability to support local switching between different virtual machines within the same physical server

- Ability to move virtualized workloads, aka virtual machines, between physical servers on demand

- Rapid increase in the scale for managing end hosts

- Increase in the forwarding-table capacity of the data center network switches

- Operability in hybrid environments with a mix of physical and virtual workloads.

The next section covers these and other data center requirements in detail.

Software defined networks (SDNs) built on the popular paradigm of Openflow[6] provide yet another paradigm shift. The idea of separating the data plane that runs in the hardware ASICs on the network switches, from the control plane that runs at a central controller has gained traction in the last few years. Standardized Openflow APIs that continue to evolve to expose richer functionality from the hardware to the controller are a big part of this effort. SDNs foster programmatic interfaces that should be supported by switch vendors so that the entire data center cluster composed of different types of switches can be uniformly programmed to enforce a certain policy. Actually, in its simplest form, the data plane merely serves as a set of "dumb" devices that only program the hardware the hardware based on instructions from the controller.

Finally, for completeness, a mention must be made on how storage[7] has evolved. With network-attached storage (NAS) and storage area networks (SANs) being the norm, especially in data centers, the network switches have needed to support both Fibre Channel (FC) and Ethernet traffic. The advent of Fibre Channel over Ethernet (FCoE) strives to consolidate I/O and reduce switch and network complexity by having both storage and regular traffic carried over the same physical cabling infrastructure that transports Ethernet. However, Big Data-related[8] applications based on Hadoop[5] and MapReduce[9] have reversed the NAS/SAN trend by requiring direct attached storage (DAS). As the name implies, Big Data constitutes handling truly large amounts of data in the order of terabytes to multipetabytes. This requires the underlying data center network fabric to support traditional and virtualized workloads with unified storage and data networking with the intent of supporting seamless scalability, convergence, and network intelligence.

Changing Requirements of Data Centers

Traditional requirements of data centers include low cost, power efficiency, and high availability. In addition, with the evolving data center, additional requirements have risen that have resulted in a rethink of the data center architecture. This section briefly describes these requirements (see Figure 1-3).

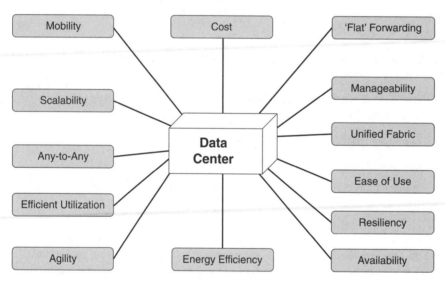

Figure 1-3 *Data Center Requirements and Design Goals*

■ **Scalability:** With virtualization, the number of end hosts in data center environments has increased tremendously. Each virtual machine behaves like an end-host with one or more virtual network interface cards (vNICs). Each vNIC has a unique MAC address and potentially can have one or more IP addresses (with IPv4 and IPv6 dual-stack support). Although previously the physical server connected to the upstream access switch was the only host that the network switch needed to cater for on that port, suddenly the network switch needs to now accommodate multiple hosts on the same port. With a 48-port switch and assuming 20 virtual machines per physical server, the number of hosts has increased from approximately 50 to 1000, that is, 20-fold. With Fabric-Extender (FEX[10]) based architectures, the number of hosts below a switch goes up even further. This means that the various switch hardware tables (namely Layer 2 MAC tables, Layer 3 routing tables, and so on) also need to increase by an order of magnitude to accommodate this increase in scale.

■ **Mobility:** Server virtualization enables decoupling of the virtual machine image from the underlying physical resources. Consequently, the virtual machine can be "moved" from one physical server to another. With VMware vMotion, live migration is possible; that is, a running virtual machine can be migrated from a physical server to another physical server while still retaining its state. The physical servers may even reside in different data centers across geographical boundaries. This imposes significant challenges on the underlying networking infrastructure. For starters, the bandwidth requirements to support live migration are fairly high. If both storage and compute state need to be migrated simultaneously, the network bandwidth requirements go further up.

VM movement can take can take place within the same access switch or to another access switch in the same or a different data center. The consequences of this new level of mobility on the network are nontrivial, and their effects may go beyond just the access layer, as, for example, some of the services deployed in the aggregation layer may need to be modified to support virtual machine mobility. Even in terms of pure Layer 2 switching and connectivity, mobility of virtual machines, implemented by products such as VMware vMotion, poses fairly stringent requirements on the underlying network infrastructure, especially at the access layer. For example, it requires that both the source and destination hosts be part of the same set of Layer 2 domains (VLANs). Therefore, all switch ports of a particular virtualization cluster must be configured uniformly as trunk ports that allow traffic from any of the virtual LANs (VLANs) used by the cluster's virtual machines, certainly not a classic network design best practice.

■ **Agility:** Agility by definition means an ability to respond quickly. Within the context of data centers, this stands for a number of things: the ability to "elastically" provision for resources based on changing demands, the ability to adapt so that any service can be mapped to any available server resource, and above all the ability to rapidly and efficiently execute the life cycle from request to fulfillment. This includes the ability to rapidly orchestrate a cloud for a new customer or add network segments for an existing customer together with network services such as load-balancer, firewall, and so on. Orchestration entities such as VMware vCloud Director (vCD[11]), System Center Virtual Machine Manager (SCVMM[12]), Openstack[13], and more strive to provide rapid provisioning of multiple virtual data clouds on a shared physical network data center cluster.

- **Flat forwarding:** From a flexibility and mobility point of view, having a flat architecture for a data center is appealing so that any server can have any IP address. This doesn't imply that all the hosts should be put in the same broadcast domain because such an approach can never scale. What this does imply is that any host (physical or virtual) should be able to communicate with any other host within a couple of fabric hops (ideally only one).

- **Any-to-any:** The domination of east-to-west traffic in data centers along with end-host mobility supported by virtualization, has rapidly changed the communication model to any-to-any. What this means is that any host (virtual or physical) should should be able to communicate with any other host at any time. Clearly, as the number of hosts in the data center cluster goes up, a naïve approach of installing all host entries in the Layer 2 or Layer 3 tables of the access or aggregation switches is not going to work. Moreover, recall that there is a push toward commoditizing Top-of-Rack (ToR), aka access switches, so these switches cannot be expected to have huge table capacities.

- **Manageability:** With data centers getting virtualized at a rapid rate, now there is a mix of workloads that the IT department must manage. Appliances such as firewall, load balancer, and so on can be physical or virtual. A large number of distributed virtual switches such as the Nexus 1000v, IBM's Nexus 5000, or the VMware VDS may be present in a large data center cluster, which need to be configured, managed, and maintained. Moreover, there will still be some physical bare-bone servers (nonvirtualized) needed to support older operating systems and older (also known as legacy) applications. This brings interoperability challenges to provision the heterogeneous workload in the same network. Although there is a substantial capital investment needed for building a large data center cluster, including incremental costs in buying more servers and switches to meet demands of higher scale, the operational costs associated with maintaining the data center can be significant.

- **Energy efficiency:** Power is a big ingredient in driving up data center operational costs, so it's imperative to have energy-efficient equipment with sufficient cooling along with efficient data center operational practices. Data center architects, managers, and administrators have become increasingly conscious of building a green data center, and the energy efficiency of operational data centers is periodically measured based on standardized metrics.[14]

Data Center Architectures

Today, data centers are composed of physical servers arranged in racks and multiple racks forming a row. A data center may be composed of tens to thousands of rows and thereby composed of several hundred thousand physical servers. Figure 1-4 shows the classical three-tier architecture employed by data centers. The three layers are composed of the following:

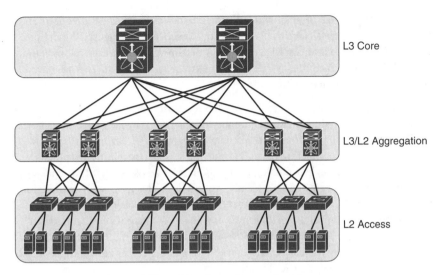

Figure 1-4   *Traditional Three-Tier Data Center Architecture*

- **Core layer:** The high-speed backplane that also serves as the data center edge by which traffic ingresses and egresses out of the data center.

- **Aggregation layer:** Typically provides routing functionality along with services such as firewall, load balancing, and so on.

- **Access layer:** The lowest layer where the servers are physically attached to the switches. Access layers are typically deployed using one of the two models:

  - **End-of-Row (EoR) Model:** Servers connect to small switches one (or a pair) per rack, and all these terminate into a large, modular end-of-row switch, one per row.

  - **ToR Model:** Each rack has a switch (or a pair of switches for redundancy purposes) that provides connectivity to one or more adjacent racks and interfaces with the aggregation layer devices.

- Blade server architectures have introduced an embedded blade switch that is part of the blade chassis enclosure. Although these may also serve as access layer switches, typically, blade switches are connected to another layer of access switches, thereby providing an additional networking layer between access layer switches and compute nodes (blades).

Typically the access layer is Layer 2 only with servers in the same subnet using bridging for communication and servers in different subnets using routing via Integrated Bridged and Routing (IRB) interfaces at the aggregation layer. However, Layer 3 ToR designs are becoming more popular because Layer 2 bridging or switching has an inherent limitation of suffering from the ill effects of flooding and broadcasting. For unknown unicasts or broadcasts, a packet is sent to every host within a subnet or VLAN or broadcast domain. As the number of hosts within a broadcast domain goes up, the negative effects caused by flooding packets because of unknown unicasts, broadcasts (such as ARP requests and DHCP requests) or multicasts (such as IPv6 Neighbor Discovery messages) are more pronounced. As indicated by various studies,[15-19] this is detrimental to the network operation and limiting the scope of the broadcast domains is extremely important. This has paved the way for Layer 3 ToR-based architectures.[20]

By terminating Layer 3 at the ToR, the sizes of the broadcast domains are reduced, but this comes at the cost of reduction in the mobility domain across which virtual machines (VMs) can be moved, which was one of the primary advantages of having Layer 2 at the access layer. In addition, terminating Layer 3 at the ToR can also result in suboptimal routing because there will be hair-pinning or tromboning of across-subnet traffic taking multiple hops via the data center fabric. Ideally, what is desired is to have an architecture that has both the benefits of Layer 2 and Layer 3 in that (a) the broadcast domain and floods should be reduced; (b) the flexibility of moving any VM across any access layer switch is retained; and (c) both within and across subnet traffic should still be optimally forwarded (via one-hop) by the data center fabric[21]; (d) all data center network links must be efficiently utilized for data traffic. Traditional spanning tree-based Layer 2 architectures have given way to Layer 2 multipath-based (L2MP) designs where all the available links are efficiently used for forwarding traffic.

To meet the changing requirements of the evolving data center, numerous designs have been proposed. These designs strive to primarily meet the requirements of scalability, mobility, ease-of-operation, manageability, and increasing utilization of the network switches and links by reducing the number of tiers in the architecture. Over the last few years, a few data center topologies have gained popularity. The following sections briefly highlight some common architectures.

CLOS

CLOS-based[31] architectures have been extremely popular since the advent of high-speed network switches. A multitier CLOS topology has a simple rule that switches at tier x should be connected only to switches at tier x-1 and x+1 but never to other switches at the same tier. This kind of topology provides a large degree of redundancy and thereby offers a good amount of resiliency, fault tolerance, and traffic load sharing. Specifically, the large number of redundant paths between any pair of switches enables efficient utilization of the network resources. CLOS-based architectures provide a huge bisection bandwidth; the bisection bandwidth is the same at every tier so that there is no oversubscription, which may be appealing for certain applications. In addition, the relatively simple topology is attractive for traffic troubleshooting and avoids the added burden of having a separate core and aggregation layer fostered by the traditional three-tier architecture. Figure 1-5 shows a sample two-tier CLOS network where a series of aggregation switches (called *spines*) connects to a series of access switches (called *leafs*). In the figure, 32 spine switches are attached to 256 48-port leaf-switches, thereby realizing a data center CLOS fabric that is capable of servicing 12,288 edge devices. CLOS-based architectures represent perhaps the most favorable option for modern data center networks.[18]

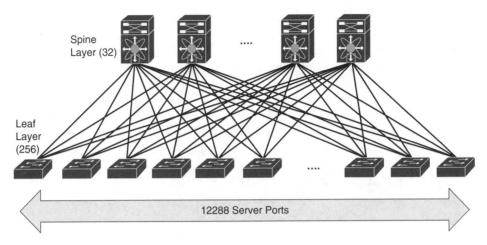

Figure 1-5 *CLOS-Based Data Center Architecture*

Fat-Tree

A special instance of a CLOS topology is called a fat-tree, which can be employed to build a scale-out network architecture by interconnecting commodity Ethernet switches.[22] Figure 1-6 shows a sample a k-ary fat-tree with k = 4. In this topology, there are k pods, each containing two layers of k/2 switches. Each k-port switch in the lower layer is directly connected to k/2 hosts or servers. Each of the remaining k/2 ports connects to k/2 of the k ports in the aggregation layer of the hierarchy. Each core switch has one port connected to each of k pods via the aggregation layer. In general, a fat-tree built with k-port switches supports $k^3/48$ ports. A big advantage of the fat-tree architecture is that all the switching elements are identical and have cost advantages over other architectures with similar port-density.[23] Fat-trees retain the advantages of a CLOS topology in providing a high bisection bandwidth and are rearrangeably nonblocking. However, they do impose an overhead of significant cabling complexity, which can be somewhat amortized by intelligent aggregation at the lower layers. Another advantage of this architecture is that the symmetric topology ensures that every switch, port, and host has a fixed location in the topology that allows them to be hierarchically addressed, similar to how IP addresses work. Therefore, this architecture is popular in academic systems research and has been endorsed by various studies such as Portland,[15] Dcell,[16] and so on.

Single Fabric

Another popular data center architecture includes ToR switches connected via a single giant fabric as has been productized by Juniper for its QFabric[24] offering. Figure 1-7 shows a schematic of a sample single fabric-based architecture. In this simple architecture, only the external access layer switches are visible to the data center operator. The fabric is completely abstracted out, which enables a huge reduction in the amount of cabling required. Not only ToRs, but other devices such as storage devices, load balancers, firewalls, and so on can be connected to the fabric to increase its "richness." The single fabric enables a natural sharing of resources after they are connected somewhere in the fabric. Even from a management point of view, such an architecture is inherently appealing because the number of devices that require external configuration and management reduces drastically. Having a giant single fabric does have the downside that the system has a certain finite capacity beyond which it cannot scale. Moreover, this design does not have the same level of fault tolerance as a CLOS architecture.

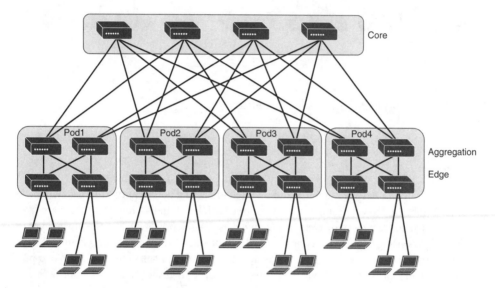

Figure 1-6   *Fat-Tree–Based Data Center Architecture*

Need for Overlays

The previous sections introduced the "new" data center along with its evolving requirements and the different architectures that have been considered to meet these requirements. The data center fabric is expected to further evolve, and its design should be fluid enough in that it can amalgamate in different ways to meet currently unforeseen business needs. Adaptability at a high scale and rapid on-demand provisioning are prime requirements where the network should not be the bottleneck.

Overlay-based architectures[25] provide a level of indirection that enables switch table sizes to *not* increase in the order of the number of end hosts that are supported by the data center. This applies to switches at both the access and the aggregation tier. Consequently, among other things, they are ideal for addressing the high scale requirement demanded by MSDCs. In its simplest form, an overlay is a dynamic tunnel between two endpoints that enables frames to be transported between those endpoints. The following classes of overlay deployments have emerged in data center deployments (see Table 1-1 for a succinct summary of these classes):

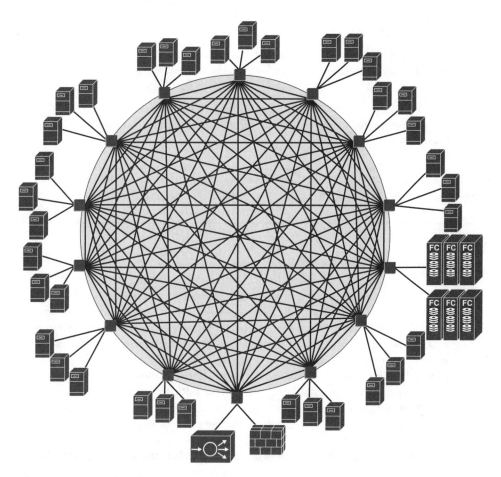

Figure 1-7   *Single Fabric-Based Data Center Architecture*

Table 1-1   *Comparison of Switch-Based Overlays and Host-Based Overlays*

Switch-Based Overlays	Host-Based Overlays
Overlay begins at the access layer (typically ToR) switch.	Overlay begins at the virtual switch residing on the server.
Aggregation switch tables need to scale in the order of the number of switches at the access layer.	Access switch tables need to scale in the order of number of virtualized servers.
Only access switch tables need to be programmed on an end-host coming up/move event.	End host coming up or move events do not require any programming of forwarding entries in the network switches (both access and aggregation).
Since fabric overlay is terminated at the access layer, physical to virtualized workloads can be transparently supported.	Requires specialized gateway devices for traffic between virtualized and legacy workloads.
Aggregation switches forward traffic based only on the overlay header.	Underlying physical network infrastructure (both access and aggregation switches) forward traffic based only on the overlay header.

- **Network-based overlays (or switch-based overlays):** The overlay begins at the access layer switch that is the ingress point into the data center fabric (see Figure 1-8). Similarly, in the egress direction, the overlay terminates at the egress switch when the packet leaves the fabric to be sent toward the destination end host. With network-based overlays, the aggregation layer switches now don't need to be aware of all the end hosts in the data center, and their tables need to scale only in the order of the number of access layer switches to which they connect. In the topology composing the aggregation and the access layer switches (see Figure-1-8), each switch is given a unique identifier. An individual ToR switch serves as the unique advertisement point for all the end hosts below it. Whenever an end host (say, VM-A) below a ToR (say, ToR1) needs to talk to another end-host (say, VM-B) below another ToR switch (say, ToR2), ToR1 takes the original packet and encapsulates that with an overlay header where the source and destination fields in the header are set to ToR1 and ToR2 identifiers, respectively. This encapsulated packet is then dispatched to one of the aggregation switches. The switches in the aggregation layer need to only direct the packet toward ToR2 that can be done based on the overlay header. In this way, the aggregation layer switches can be made lean and are completely unaware of the end hosts.

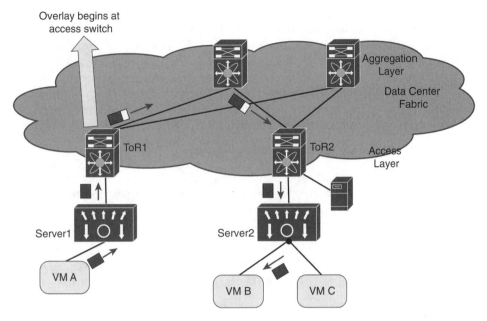

Figure 1-8 *Network-Based Overlays*

- In addition to the high scale, overlays have the following benefits:

  - Better utilization of the network resources by employing multipathing so that different flows can exploit the many different redundant paths available between the source and destination switches.

  - Better resiliency and faster convergence because an aggregation switch going down or a link down event between an access and aggregation switch does not require a large number of end host entries to be reprogrammed in the switches at the access layer. Instead, just the overlay connectivity tables need to be updated to reflect the updated topology.

  - Easily satisfy the east-to-west any-to-any communication requirement in data center environments because the topology maintenance control plane needs to keep tracks of endpoints in terms of switches (access and aggregation layer), which are typically in the order of tens to a few hundreds rather than end hosts that could be in the order of hundreds to millions.

- Common examples of network-based overlays include TRILL,[26] FabricPath,[27] and so on.

■ **Host-based overlays:** The overlay originates at the hypervisor virtual switch (see Figure 1-9). For cloud-based deployments, the emergence of the software-defined data center[28] has resulted in a complete end-to-end overlay architecture. This option is suitable for completely virtualized architectures where the entire physical network topology is abstracted out and viewed as a mere transport network (typically IP-based) for delivering encapsulated frames. A variety of overlay options are available with different combinations of transport and payload options where Layer 2 payloads may be carried in Layer 3 packets, or vice versa.

■ Host-based overlays have the following advantages:

  ■ By moving the overlay at the virtual switch, now all the benefits that apply to the aggregation layer switches for network-based overlays are now inherited by the access layer switches. The forwarding tables at the access layer switches need to scale only in the order of the number of physical server endpoints rather than the number of end hosts, aka VMs.

  ■ Any VM coming up or VM move event does not result in any reprogramming of forwarding table entries at either the aggregation or access layer switches.

  ■ Rapid and agile provisioning of tenant network resources in a cloud does not require any additional configuration on the underlying physical network infrastructure.

  ■ No termination or initiation of overlays is required on the access or aggregation layer network switches.

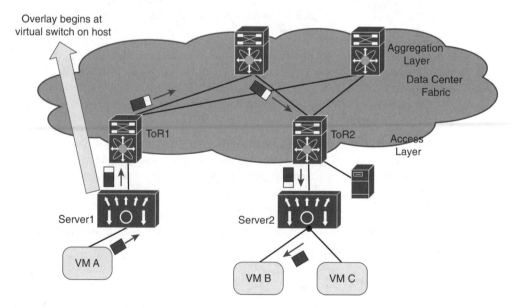

Figure 1-9 *Host-Based Overlays*

Host-based overlays do come with a set of caveats in that while they are attractive from a rapid provisioning and agility point of view, the lack of knowledge of the underlying network topology can result in suboptimal traffic forwarding resulting in multiple redundant hops through the data center fabric. Moreover, for legacy workloads that are still not virtualized and incapable of parsing the overlay header, specialized gateway devices that terminate the overlay and act as a liaison between the virtualized and legacy workloads are required. In addition, there is a school of thought that the ToR ASICs that have been designed to support tunnel traffic at high speed are the right place to originate and terminate overlay headers rather than virtual switches, which can never match the performance of the former. Popular choices for host-based overlays include VXLAN,[29] NvGRE,[30] and so on.

Finally, for completeness, consider *hybrid overlays*, which are a combination of both host-based and switch-based overlays. With a large number of overlay headers, to provide the most flexibility, an architecture that supports any combination of host-based and network-based overlays enables the most flexibility. The idea is that the host overlay from the virtual switch is terminated at the directly attached access layer switch (aka ToR) and another overlay that has fabricwide significance is initiated. At the egress access layer switch connected to the destination, the reverse operation is performed, that is, the network-based overlay is terminated and the host-based overlay (if applicable) is stamped before sending the packet toward the destination server. Such an architecture serves to address some of the disadvantages of pure host-based overlays while at the same time retain its salient features. At the time of this writing, there are no solutions or products that have such streamlined overlay architectures, but this is likely to change in the near future.

Summary

This chapter introduced the recent advances in data center designs and the different requirements that they seek to serve. Some popular data center network architectural topologies were described briefly, and the need for overlays in massive scale data centers was confirmed. The rest of this book serves to provide a comprehensive primer for overlay-based architectures in data centers.

References

1. http://aws.amazon.com/ec2/.

2. http://www.gartner.com/technology/topics/cloud-computing.jsp.

3. http://www.cisco.com/web/offer/emea/14181/docs/Security_in_the_Green_Cloud.pdf.

4. Rajesh Nishtala, Hans Fugal, Steven Grimm, Marc Kwiatkowski, Herman Lee, Harry C. Li, Ryan McElroy, Mike Paleczny, Daniel Peek, Paul Saab, David Stafford, Tony Tung, and Venkateshwaran Venkataramani, "Scaling Memcache at Facebook," in proceedings of the 10th USENIX conference on networked systems design and implementation (NSDI 2013), Nick Feamster and Jeff Mogul (Eds.). USENIX Association, Berkeley, CA, USA, 385–398.

5. http://hadoop.apache.org/.

6. http://www.openflow.org/.

7. Troppens, Ulf, Rainer Erkens, Wolfgang Mueller-Friedt, Rainer Wolafka, and Nils Haustein, "Storage Networks Explained: Basics and Application of Fibre Channel SAN, NAS, iSCSI, infiniband and FCoE," Wiley.com, 2011.

8. http://www.cisco.com/en/US/solutions/collateral/ns340/ns857/ns156/ns1094/ critical_role_network_big_data_idc.pdf.

9. http://research.google.com/archive/mapreduce.html.

10. http://www.cisco.com/en/US/netsol/ns1134/index.html.

11. https://www.vmware.com/products/vcloud-director/overview.html.

12. http://www.microsoft.com/en-us/server-cloud/system-center/datacenter-management.aspx.

13. http://www.openstack.org/.

14. http://www.thegreengrid.org/en/Global/Content/white-papers/ WP49-PUEAComprehensiveExaminationoftheMetric.

15. Radhika Niranjan Mysore, Andreas Pamboris, Nathan Farrington, Nelson Huang, Pardis Miri, Sivasankar Radhakrishnan, Vikram Subramanya, and Amin Vahdat, "PortLand: A Scalable Fault-Tolerant Layer 2 Data Center Network Fabric," SIGCOMM Comput. Commun. Rev. 39, 4 (August 2009), 39-50.

16. Chuanxiong Guo, Haitao Wu, Kun Tan, Lei Shi, Yongguang Zhang, and Songwu Lu, "Dcell: A Scalable and Fault-Tolerant Network Structure for Data Centers." SIGCOMM Comput. Commun. Rev. 38, 4 (August 2008), 75–86.

17. Albert Greenberg, Parantap Lahiri, David A. Maltz, Parveen Patel, and Sudipta Sengupta, "Toward a Next Generation Data Center Architecture: Scalability and Commoditization," in proceedings of the ACM workshop on programmable routers for extensible services of tomorrow (PRESTO '08). ACM, New York, NY, USA, 57–62.

18. Albert Greenberg, James R. Hamilton, Navendu Jain, Srikanth Kandula, Changhoon Kim, Parantap Lahiri, David A. Maltz, Parveen Patel, and Sudipta Sengupta, "VL2: A Scalable and Flexible Data Center Network," in proceedings of the ACM SIGCOMM 2009 conference on data communication. ACM, New York, NY, USA, 51–56.

19. http://tools.ietf.org/html/draft-dunbar-arp-for-large-dc-problem-statement-00.

20. http://tools.ietf.org/html/draft-karir-armd-datacenter-reference-arch-00.

21. http://www.cisco.com/en/US/solutions/ns340/ns517/ns224/ns945/dynamic_ fabric_automation.html.

22. Mohammad Al-Fares, Alexander Loukissas, and Amin Vahdat, "A Scalable Commodity Data Center Network Architecture," in proceedings of the ACM SIGCOMM 2008 conference on data communication. ACM, New York, NY, USA, 63–74.

23. Farrington, N., Rubow, E., Vahdat, A., "Data Center Switch Architecture in the Age of Merchant Silicon," 17th IEEE Symposium on High Performance Interconnects, HOTI 2009, pp.93–102, 25–27.

24. http://www.juniper.net/us/en/products-services/switching/qfx-series/qfabric-system/.

25. https://datatracker.ietf.org/doc/draft-ietf-nvo3-overlay-problem-statement/.

26. "Routing Bridges (RBridges): Base Protocol Specification" – RFC 6325.

27. http://www.cisco.com/en/US/netsol/ns1151/index.html.

28. http://tools.ietf.org/html/draft-pan-sdn-dc-problem-statement-and-use-cases-02.

29. http://tools.ietf.org/html/draft-mahalingam-dutt-dcops-vxlan-00.

30. http://tools.ietf.org/html/draft-sridharan-virtualization-nvgre-00.

31. C. Clos, "A Study of Non-Blocking Switching Networks," Bell Syst. Tech. J., Vol. 32 (1953), pp. 406-424.

Chapter 2

Introduction to Overlay Technologies

This chapter covers the following objectives:

- **FabricPath:** This section starts with an introduction to FabricPath and its high-level architecture followed by frame format details and then delves into data plane operations with FabricPath. For in-depth details on FabricPath, refer to Chapter 4, "FabricPath."

- **Transparent Interconnection of Lots of Links (TRILL):** This section provides an overview of the requirements and benefits of TRILL along with the frame format and high-level data plane operations. For more details on TRILL refer to Chapter 5, "TRILL."

- **Locator/ID Separation Protocol (LISP):** This section provides an overview of LISP frame format details and LISP high-level data plane operations, and discusses LISP mobility.

- **Virtual Extensible LAN (VXLAN):** This section provides an overview of VXLAN along with frame format followed by a brief description of VXLAN operation. For more details, refer to Chapter 6, "VXLAN."

- **Network Virtualization using Generic Routing Encapsulation (NVGRE):** This section provides an overview of NVGRE along with the frame format followed by NVGRE data plane operations.

- **Overlay Transport Virtualization (OTV):** This section provides an overview of OTV followed by frame format details and data plane operations.

- **Provider Backbone Bridging (PBB):** This section provides an overview of IEEE 802.1ah followed by frame format details and data plane operations.

■ **Shortest Path Bridging (SPB):** This section provides an overview of SPB (including Shortest Path Bridging VID [SPBV] and Shortest Path Bridging - MAC [SPBM]) and data plane operations.

This chapter covers the various overlay technologies, which have become extremely popular in data center and enterprise networks. Because the underlying control protocol for both FabricPath and TRILL is IS-IS[1], if you want an in-depth understanding of IS-IS, refer to Chapter 3, "IS-IS," for details on IS-IS. This chapter, in addition to providing an executive-level overview of the different overlay technologies, also enables you to get a quick grasp of each of these technologies. This chapter builds the foundation for further discussion of these technologies in subsequent chapters.

Overlay Technologies Overview

Table 2-1 gives an overview of the different overlay technologies along with their benefits.

Table 2-1   *Different Overlay Technologies Overview*

Technology	Description	Benefit
FabricPath	FabricPath is a Layer 2 technology that provides Layer 3 benefits such as multipathing to the classical Layer 2 networks by using link state protocol (IS-IS) at Layer 2. This enables the network to be free of the spanning tree protocol, thereby avoiding its pitfalls especially in a large Layer 2 topology.	Provides plug-and-play features of classical Ethernet Networks. Multipath Support (ECMP) provides high availability to Ethernet networks. Conversational MAC learning provides MAC scalability. Enables larger Layer 2 domains because it doesn't run spanning tree.
TRILL	TRILL is an IEEE standard that, like FabricPath, is a Layer 2 technology, which also provides the same Layer 3 benefits as Fabric Path to the Layer 2 networks by using the link state protocol (IS-IS) over Layer 2 networks.	Provides plug-and-play features of classical Ethernet networks. MAC-in-MAC encapsulation enables MAC address scalability in the TRILL networks.

Technology	Description	Benefit
LISP	LISP separates the location and the identifier (EID) of the network hosts thus allowing virtual machine mobility across subnet boundaries while keeping the endpoint identification (IP address for IP networks).	Optimal shortest-path routing. Support for both IPv4 and IPv6 hosts. There is a draft for Layer 2 LISP that supports MAC addresses as well. Load balancing and multi homing support.
VXLAN	Virtual Extensible LAN (VXLAN) is a LAN extension over a Layer 3 network. This encapsulation with its 24-bit segment-ID enables up to 16 million VLANs in your network.	Large number of Virtual LANs (16 million). The extension of the VXLAN across different Layer 3 networks, while enabling communication at Layer 2 enables elastic capacity extension for the cloud infrastructure. Enables VM mobility at Layer 2 across Layer 3 boundaries.
NVGRE	NVGRE, like VXLAN, is an encapsulation of a Layer 2 Ethernet Frame in IP, which enables the creation of virtualized Layer 2 subnets. With an external IP header, these virtualized Layer 2 subnets can span physical Layer 3 IP networks.	Compatible with today's data center hardware infrastructure because it doesn't require an upgrade of data center hardware because GRE support is common. Like VXLAN the Tenant Network Identifier (TNI) in the GRE frame enables 16 million logical Layer 2 networks. Enables VM mobility at Layer 2 across Layer 3 boundaries.
OTV	Overlay transport virtualization (OTV) is a Cisco-proprietary innovation in the Data Center Interconnect (DCI) space for enabling Layer 2 extension across data center sites.	OTV, being an overlay technology, is transparent to the core network and the sites. Failure boundary and site independence are preserved in OTV networks because OTV uses a control plane protocol to sync MAC addresses between sites and avoIDs any unknown unicast floods.

Technology	Description	Benefit
Shortest Path Bridging (SPB)	Like TRILL, SPB uses IS-IS to advertise topology information. SPB is an IEEE counterpart to TRILL but differs in the use of the tree structures. At the edge devices, the packets are either encapsulated in MAC-in-MAC (802.1ah) or tagged (802.1Q/802.1ad) frames.	The benefits are similar to FabricPath and TRILL networks including: ■ Multipath support (ECMP) provides high availability for Ethernet networks. ■ Failure/recovery is handled by standard IS-IS behavior.

FabricPath

The trend toward virtualization of physical servers especially in large data centers began a few years ago. VMware became the leader on the server virtualization front; the benefits from server virtualization and commodities of scale led to the emergence of "mega data centers" hosting applications running on tens of thousands of servers. This required support for distributed applications at a large scale and having the flexibility to provision them in different zones of data centers. This necessitated the need to develop a scalable and resilient Layer 2 fabric enabling any-to-any communication. Cisco pioneered the development of FabricPath to meet these new demands. FabricPath provides a highly scalable Layer 2 fabric with a required level of simplicity, resiliency, and flexibility.

FabricPath Requirements

The evolution of large data centers with more than 1000 servers, with a design that enables scaling in size and computing capacity aka Massively Scalable Data Centers (MSDC) and virtualization technologies, has led to the need for large Layer 2 domains. The well-known Spanning Tree Protocol (STP) on which Layer 2 switching relies introduces some limitations, which led to the evolution of technologies such as TRILL and FabricPath. Before delving into further details, you need to consider the limitations of current Layer 2 networks based on STP, which were the drivers for FabricPath:

■ **No multipathing support:** STP creates loop-free topologies in the Layer 2 networks by blocking redundant paths. To achieve this, STP uses the well-known root election process. After the root is elected, all the other switches build shortest paths to the root switch and block other ports. This yields a loop-free Layer 2 network topology. The side effect of this is that all redundant paths are blocked in the Layer 2 network. Although some enhancements were done specially with the use of Per VLAN Spanning Tree Protocol (PVSTP), PVST enables per VLAN load balancing, but it also suffers from multipathing support limitations.

- **STP leads to inefficient path selection:** As the shortest path is chosen for the root bridge, the available path between switches depends upon the location of the root bridge. Hence, the selected path is not necessarily a shortest path between the switches. As an example, consider two access switches that connect to the distribution and to each other. Now if the distribution switch is the STP root bridge, the link between the two access switches is blocked, and all traffic between the two access layer switches takes the suboptimal path through the distribution switch.

- **Unavailability of features like Time-To-Live (TTL):** The Layer 2 packet header doesn't have a TTL field. This can lead to a network meltdown in switched networks because a forwarding loop can cause a broadcast packet to exponentially duplicate thereby consuming excessive network resources.

- **MAC address scalability:** Nonhierarchical flat addressing of Ethernet MAC addressing leads to limited scalability as MAC address summarization becomes impossible. Also, all the MAC addresses are essentially populated in all switches in the Layer 2 network leading to large requirements in the Layer 2 table sizes.

These shortcomings of Layer 2 networks are resolved by the Layer 3 routing protocols, which provide multipathing and efficient shortest path among all nodes in the network without any limitations. Although the Layer 3 network design solves these issues, it has the side effect of making the network design static. As the static network design limits the size of the Layer 2 domain, it limits the use of virtualization technologies. FabricPath marries the two technologies to provide flexibility of Layer 2 networks and scaling of the Layer 3 networks.

FabricPath Benefits

FabricPath is a new technology that enables the data center architects and administrators to design and implement a scalable Layer 2 fabric. FabricPath offers the following benefits:

- **Preserves the plug-and-play features of classical Ethernet:** Because the configuration requirements are minimal and the administrator needs to include the interfaces belonging to the FabricPath core network, it significantly reduces the administrative effort to configure the network. FabricPath also uses a single control protocol (IS-IS) for unicast forwarding, multicast forwarding, and VLAN pruning. In addition, ping and trace route are now available in FabricPath operations, administration, and management (OAM), enabling the network administrators to debug problems in the Layer 2 FabricPath network similar to common troubleshooting techniques employed for Layer 3 networks.

- **Provides high performance using multipathing:** The N-way (more than one paths) multipathing enables the data center network architects to build large, scalable networks. It also enables network administrators to incrementally add additional devices to the existing network topology as the need arises. This enables the MSDC networks to have flat topologies, enabling the nodes to be separated by a single hop.

The N-way multipathing has an additional benefit that a single node failure just leads to a reduction by 1/Nth of the fabric bandwidth.

■ **High availability:** The enhancements to Layer 2 networks with the combination of Layer 3 capabilities enables the replacement of STP, which blocks all paths except a single path, enabling multiple paths between the endpoints. This enables the network administrator to incrementally add network bandwidth as the bandwidth needs increases.

■ **Forwarding efficiency:** FabricPath enables the traffic to be forwarded across the shortest path to the destination, thus reducing latency in the Layer 2 network. This is more efficient when compared to Layer 2 forwarding based on the STP.

■ **Small Layer 2 table size:** Conversational MAC learning in the FabricPath solution enables selective learning of the MAC addresses based on the active flows. This reduces the need for the large MAC tables.

FabricPath Architecture

Figure 2-1 shows the high-level addressing scheme employed by FabricPath.

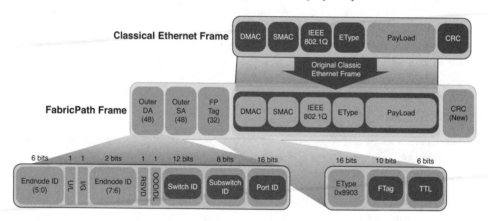

Figure 2-1 *FabricPath High-Level Architecture*

The following sections start with a brief description of the encapsulation employed by FabricPath[2] followed by a sample packet walk-through of a FabricPath network.

FabricPath Encapsulation

To forward the frames, FabricPath employs hierarchical MAC addresses that are locally assigned. FabricPath encapsulates the original Layer 2 frame with a new source and destination MAC address, a FabricPath tag, the original Layer 2 frame, and a new CRC (refer to Figure 2-1). To forward the frames in the FabricPath network, the outer source and destination MAC addresses contain a 12-bit unique identifier called a SwitchID. The SwitchID is the field used in the FabricPath core network to forward packets to the right destination switch. Chapter 4 describes each of these fields.

FabricPath Data Plane Operation

You can use Figure 2-2 as a reference to describe the high-level FabricPath data-path operation.[3]

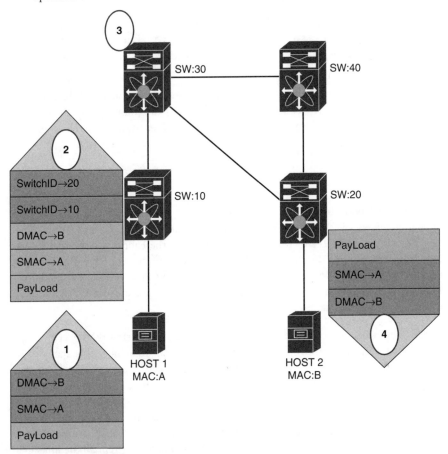

Figure 2-2 *FabricPath Data Path*

To describe the data path from Host 1 to Host 2, you can assume that all the control plane information has already been learned. Host 1 and Host 2 already know about each other's MAC addresses. The basic steps involve the encapsulation of the frame with a FabricPath header at the ingress switch, followed by switching the frame using the outer header in the FabricPath network and then finally decapsulation of the frame at the egress switch. The following steps provide more details on this operation.

1. Host 1 uses its MAC address A as a source MAC (SMAC) and sends a classical Ethernet frame, which is destined to Host 2 with a destination MAC (DMAC) address B. On receiving this frame, the ingress FabricPath switch does a standard layer lookup based on VLAN and DMAC.

2. The lookup result points to the destination SwitchID 20 as the egress switch for this frame. So the ingress switch encapsulates this frame in a FabricPath header and sends it out on an appropriate FabricPath core port. The source and destination switch IDs in the FabricPath header are set as 10 and 20, respectively.

3. The fabric path switch 30 forwards the frame based on the best path to the destination switch 20. Here there are two paths, but the best path is a directly connected link, and therefore the packet is forwarded over the directly connected interface to switch 20.

4. The destination switch 20 receives this frame. As the destination switch ID is itself, it removes the FabricPath header. On decapsulation of the frame, it uses the inner DMAC for a Layer 2 lookup and, based on the lookup result, forwards the frame toward Host 2.

TRILL

Transparent Inter-Connection of Lots of Links (TRILL) is a technology that addresses the same requirements as the FabricPath and has almost the same benefits as FabricPath. The requirements and benefits of FabricPath were given in the FabricPath section of this chapter. The chapter on TRILL discusses all the limitations of current Layer 2 networking in detail and how TRILL addresses them. TRILL, as of this writing, is an IETF standard. With the changes happening in the data center environments, the current STP has lots of disadvantages as outlined here:

- **Inefficient utilization of links:** To avoID loops in a Layer 2 network, the STP ensures that there's only one path from a source to a destination. To achieve this, many of the links in a switch are put in a blocked state so that data traffic doesn't flow through the links. With the rapID increase in server-to-server communication, referred to as east-west traffic, blocking many of the links can cause congestion in the links that are in an unblocked state. Shutting down or blocking the links in a switch reduces the value of a switch that has the capacity to host many ports capable of carrying high-bandwidth traffic. A Layer 3-like behavior is required, wherein all the links in a switch can be used and that provides a loop-free mechanism.

- **Long time to converge:** STP is not designed for topologies such as MSDC. The time taken for all the nodes in a network to go to a steady state is high. Traffic is disrupted until the steady state is reached. Whenever there is a change in the topology because of a link going up or down or when new nodes are added or removed, spanning tree recalculation results in traffic disruption. Clearly, a loop prevention mechanism is required that can scale well in an MSDC environment. Again, a Layer 3 behavior is required, wherein the routing protocol takes care of avoiding loops and can also scale to a large number of nodes.

- **Scaling the MAC table:** With the emergence of virtual machines, with each VM assigned a MAC address, the size of the Layer 2 table can grow by a big margin, especially at the core of the data center network that learns the MAC address of all the VMs. The cost of the hardware may increase with the increase in the size of the hardware Layer 2 table. It's preferable to have a clear separation of the overlay network and the end host access network such that the core network can have a Layer 2 table whose size can be better quantified by the number of switches in the overlay network than trying to quantify the number of end host VMs in the entire network, which may not be a trivial task. If the size of the Layer 2 table at the core is less, it may result in some entries not being learned. This can result in a Layer 2 lookup miss, which can result in a flood in the network. Flooding can consume unnecessary network bandwidth and may consume the CPU resources of the server because the server may also receive the flood frames. Clearly, a tunneling protocol such as MAC-in-MAC is required so that all the core switches do not need to learn all the end host MAC addresses.

TRILL Requirements

Some of the design criteria and requirements of TRILL follow:

- **Control protocol:** TRILL uses Layer 2 IS-IS as its control protocol. The idea is to take the advantages of a Layer 3 routing protocol and at the same time maintain the simplicity of a Layer 2 network. Every node in a TRILL network is referred to as RBridge, aka Router-Bridge. Every RBridge is identified by its nickname. In other words, a nickname is the routable entity in a TRILL network, just like an IP address in an IP network. Unlike Layer 3, there are no separate protocols for unicast and multicast. The Layer 2-IS-IS protocol takes care of populating the routing table for unicast traffic, thereby ensuring multiple shortest equal cost paths (ECMPs) for all the RBridges and also creating trees for multicast traffic. Needless to say, Layer 2 IS-IS also ensures loop-free routing. But at the same time, TRILL inherits the TTL field from the Layer 3 world to ensure traffic due to intermittent loops eventually expires out.

- **Preserve plug-and-play features of classical Ethernet:** One of the main advantages of a Layer 2 network is its plug-and-play nature, and the administrator is relieved of heavy configuration unlike in a Layer 3 network. TRILL achieves this with its Dynamic Resource Allocation Protocol (DRAP), where every node derives its own nickname and the protocol ensures there's no duplicity. The configuration requirement of TRILL is minimal.

- **Layer 2 table scaling:** TRILL uses a MAC-in-MAC encapsulation, where the traffic from the host is encapsulated by the ingress RBridge. The core RBridges see only the outer MAC header, which has the MAC address of the source and destination RBridge. Consequently, the MAC table at the core RBridges will not be polluted with all the end host MAC addresses.

The following section starts with the TRILL frame format and then delves into the high-level data plane architecture:

TRILL Frame Format

To forward frames, TRILL uses a MAC-in-MAC encapsulation format, as shown in Figure 2-3. The ingress RBridge encapsulates the original Layer 2 frame with a new source and destination MAC, which are the MAC addresses of the source RBridge and the next-hop RBridge respectively; a TRILL Header, which has the Ingress and Egress nickname that identifies the source and destination RBridge, respectively; and the original Layer 2 frame with a new CRC. The incoming 802.1q or q-in-q tag needs to be preserved in the inner header. Chapter 5 covers all these fields in greater depth. Egress RBridge removes the headers added by the ingress RBridge and will forward based on the inner frame.

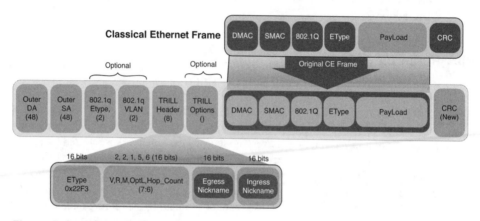

Figure 2-3 *TRILL Frame Format*

TRILL Data Plane Operation

To describe the high-level data path operation, use the network shown in Figure 2-4. By now you would have already figured out that the forwarding is similar to FabricPath.

To describe the data path from Host 1 to Host 2, assume that all the control plane information has already been learned. Host 1 and Host 2 already know about each other's MAC addresses. The basic steps involve the encapsulation of the frame with the TRILL header at the ingress RBridge, followed by switching using the TRILL header in the TRILL network and then finally decapsulation of the frame at the egress RBridge. The following steps provide more details on this operation.

1. Host 1 uses its MAC address of A as the source MAC (SMAC) and sends a classical Ethernet frame, which is destined to Host 2 with a destination MAC (DMAC) address of B. On receiving this frame, the ingress RBridge (Nickname 10) does a (VLAN, DMAC) lookup.

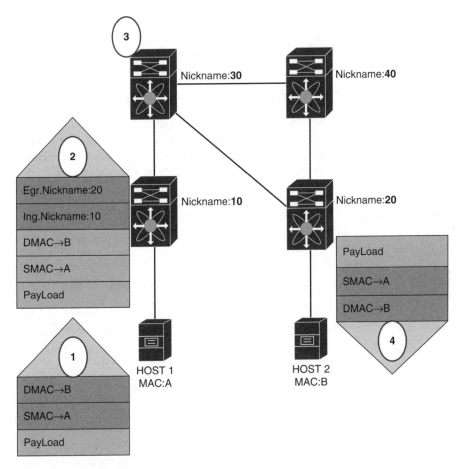

Figure 2-4   *TRILL Data Path*

2. The MAC lookup points to the destination (Nickname 20) as the egress RBridge for this Ethernet frame. So the ingress switch encapsulates this frame using the TRILL header for forwarding the frame to the TRILL core port. The source and destination nicknames are set as 10 and 20, respectively. The outer DMAC is the MAC address of the next-hop RBridge, and the outer SMAC is the MAC address of the source RBridge.

3. The core RBridge (Nickname 30 in this example) forwards the frame based on the best path to the destination RBridge Nickname 20. In this case there are two paths to reach the egress RBridge with Nickname 20, but the best path is a directly connected link; therefore, the packet is forwarded over the directly connected interface to the switch with Nickname 20. The TTL is decremented, and the outer SMAC and DMAC are rewritten with the MAC address of this RBridge and RBridge 20's MAC address. Just like regular IP routing, the TRILL header is not modified, but at each hop the outer DMAC and SMAC are rewritten along with a TTL decrement.

4. The destination RBridge 20 receives this frame. Because the incoming frame is destined to this RBridge, it removes the outer MAC and the TRILL header. It then forwards the frame to Host 2 based on the inner (DMAC and VLAN) lookup.

Locator ID/Separator Protocol

Locator ID/Separator Protocol (LISP) as the name suggests separates the location and the identifier of the network hosts, thus making it possible for virtual machines to move across subnet boundaries while retaining their IP address. LISP is composed of a network architecture and a set of protocols that enable new semantics for IP addressing by creating two namespaces:

- **Endpoint Identifiers (EIDs):** EIDs are assigned to end hosts.

- **Routing Locators (RLOCs):** RLOCs are assigned to routers that make up the global routing system.

The creation of these separate namespaces provides several advantages, including the following:

- Topologically aggregated RLOCs enable improved routing system scalability.

- IP portability.

- Easier IPv6 transition.

- IP mobility, the host EIDs can move without changing the IP address of the host or virtual machine; only the RLOC changes on a host move.

LISP integrates well into the current network infrastructure and requires no changes to the end host stack. It fosters a simple, incremental, network-based implementation with most of the deployment at the network edge devices.

LISP Frame Format

Figure 2-5 shows the various fields in the LISP header.

A LISP frame's outer encapsulation is a UDP frame where the destination and source IP addresses are the addresses of the Ingress Tunnel Router (ITR) and Egress Tunnel Router (ETR), respectively. For Layer 3 LISP, the destination UDP port number is 4341. The LISP header has the Locator reachability bits and the nonce fields.

LISP Routing

As a host transmits a packet, if the destination of the packet is in another LISP domain, it reaches the LISP ITR. The ITR maps the destination endpoint ID (EID) to an RLOC by looking up the destination in a map server. As shown in Figure 2-6, using this information the ITR encapsulates the packet with an outer header. The destination RLOC is ETR behind which the destination host exists.

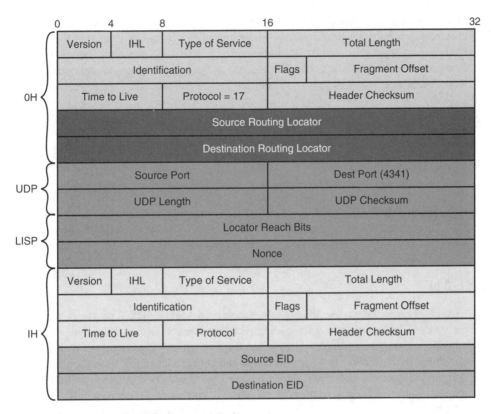

Figure 2-5 *LISP Frame Format*

When the destination ETR is known, the ITR encapsulates the packet, setting the destination address to the RLOC of the destination ETR returned by the mapping infrastructure. Refer to Figure 2-6 to see the flow of traffic in a LISP-enabled network.

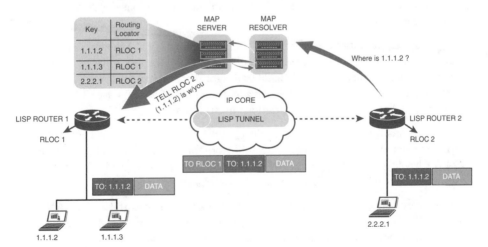

Figure 2-6 *LISP Routing*

In addition to LISP routing, the location and EID separation provides flexible and unmatched mobility for IP endpoints without any subnet boundary limitation allowing IP endpoints, regardless of their IP addresses, to be deployed anywhere. These EIDs can freely move within and across data center racks and across geographical and organizational boundaries. The LISP Mobility solution has the following characteristics:

- Optimal shortest path routing.

- Both IPv4 and IPv6 addresses are supported.

- Support for load balancing and multihoming.

- Provides a solution that is transparent to both EIDs and the core network.

By allowing IP endpoints to change location while maintaining their assigned IP address, the LISP mobility solution enables the IP endpoints to move between different subnets, while guaranteeing optimal routing to the IP endpoint.

VXLAN

Cloud service providers, specifically Infrastructure as a Service (IaaS) providers, require a network segmentation solution that supports a large number of network segments. The advent of server virtualization has increased the demand on the physical network infrastructure. As the number of VMs attached to the network increases, there is an increased demand in the number of MAC address table entries in switches. In addition, the VMs may be grouped according to their VLAN with the current limitation of number of VLANs being 4096. Server virtualization especially in service provider data center environments has exposed the limitation of a limited number of VLANs. This limitation has introduced challenges for the IP address management.

In addition, VM mobility requires a Layer 2 extension from the old physical host to the new host where the VM is moving. As the data center architects strive to remove this limitation of native Layer 2 extension, they are looking for solutions that don't bind them to physical infrastructure.

The network segmentation, server virtualization, and Layer 2 VM Mobility require an overlay that can carry Layer 2 (MAC) frames. VXLAN is a Layer 2 overlay mechanism that addresses these needs. VXLAN stands for the Virtual eXtensible Local Area Network and provides a way to implement a large number of virtual Layer 2 networks on top of today's networking and virtualization infrastructure.

VXLAN encapsulates a MAC frame within a User Datagram Protocol packet (MAC-in-UDP). A 24-bit virtual segment identifier in the form of a VXLAN ID (VNI) is part of the VXLAN header that enables the VLANs to scale up to 16 million. In addition, the UDP encapsulation enables each VLAN to span across a Layer 3 routed network.

In its simplest form, for broadcast, multicast, and unknown unicast traffic, VXLAN employs IP multicast. After a virtual machine joins a VXLAN segment, the physical host on which the VM resides joins the multicast group associated with that segment.

VXLAN uses a multicast tree to send broadcast/multicast/unknown-unicast packets to all the servers in the same multicast group. When the learning is complete, the unicast packets are encapsulated and sent directly to the destination physical host. On each virtualized host, there resides an entity called the Virtual Tunnel End-Point (VTEP). This entity is responsible for suitably encapsulating and decapsulating the VXLAN header as it is sent to or received from the upstream network.

VXLAN Frame Format

Figure 2-7 shows the VXLAN frame format.[4] Each of the components of the frame is also described:

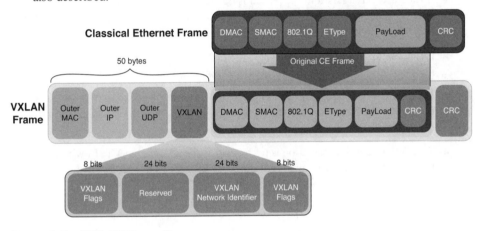

Figure 2-7 *VXLAN Frame Format*

- Outer Ethernet header

- Outer IP header

- Outer UDP header

- VXLAN header

- Inner Ethernet header

The different fields in the VXLAN header,[5] of size 8 bytes, include 8 bits of VXLAN flags, 24 bits of VXLAN identifier (VNI), and reserved flags.

- **VXLAN flags:** Reserved bits set to 0 except bit 3, the I bit, which is set to 1 to indicate a valID VNI

- **VNI:** 24-bit field that is the VXLAN network identifier

- **Reserved:** A set of fields, 24 bits and 8 bits, that are reserved and set to zero

VXLAN Data Path Operation

Figure 2-8 shows a sample VXLAN packet flow;[6] now consider a packet being sent by a virtual machine on one of its vNICs. As the virtual switch (that is, vSwitch) receives the packet from the vNIC, it knows the VXLAN Network ID (VNI) for this packet. The vSwitch performs two lookups on the packet:

- The vSwitch uses the ingress interface (vNIC) to determine which VNI the packet belongs to.

- vSwitch does a (VNI and DMAC) lookup.

- If the lookup is a HIT and the packet is destined to a remote VM, the packet is suitably encapsulated by the source VTEP with a VXLAN header with the Destination IP (DIP) set to the physical host on which the destination VM resides.

- If the lookup is a MISS, the packet is VXLAN encapsulated, but the DIP is set to the multicast group associated with the corresponding VNI.

- The vSwitch then does a second lookup, this time on the encapsulated packet, and dispatches the packet toward the IP core that delivers the packet to the DIP in the overlay header.

- VXLAN header decapsulation is performed at the destination VTEPs where the inner SMAC is learned against the source VTEP's IP in the overlay header and the packet is switched as per the (VNI, inner_DMAC) lookup.

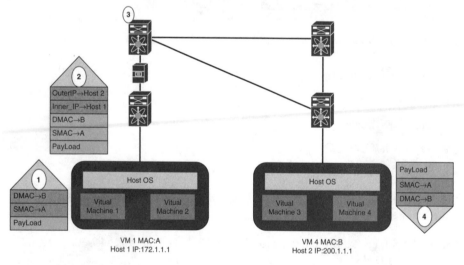

Figure 2-8   *VXLAN Data Path*

The following list describes a sample packet flow in a VXLAN network (refer to Figure 2-8).

1. VM1 (MAC=A) tries to communicate with VM4 (MAC=B). Assume that VM1's and VM4's MAC addresses are known on Host 1 and Host 2 whose VTEP IP addresses are 172.1.1.1 and 200.1.1.1, respectively. VM1 sends out a frame with SMAC=A, and DMAC=B. vSwitch on Host 1 performs a lookup based on (VNI, B).

2. The lookup result yields destination Host 2 as the egress endpoint for this frame. Hence, the ingress vSwitch encapsulates this frame with a VXLAN header for forwarding the frame through the core network. The outer source and destination IP addresses are set as 172.1.1.1 and 172.1.1.2, respectively. The outer DMAC is the MAC address of the next-hop router, and the outer SMAC is the MAC address of the source Host 1.

3. The intermediate routers or switches (for example, 3) do a routing lookup on the outer header and forwards the frame based on the best path to the destination 200.1.1.1. The TTL is decremented, and the outer SMAC and DMAC are rewritten as per regular Layer 3 routing semantics.

4. The destination Host 2 receives this frame. Because the destination IP address points to itself, it decapsulates the packet by removing the outer headers. The packet is forwarded to VM4 based on a Layer 2 lookup on the inner frame, which in this example is (VNI, B).

NVGRE

Network Virtualization using Generic Routing Encapsulation (NVGRE),[7] like VXLAN, is an encapsulation of a Layer 2 Ethernet Frame in IP, which enables the creation of virtualized Layer 2 segments. These virtualized Layer 2 segments, because of the external IP header, can span across Layer 3 networks. NVGRE is based on Generic Routing Encapsulation (GRE), which is a tunneling protocol developed by Cisco. For detail on GRE, refer to www.cisco.com.[8]

As NVGRE creates a connection between two or more Layer 3 networks, it makes them appear as Layer 2 accessible. The Layer 2 accessibility enables VM migrations across Layer 3 networks and inter-VM communication. During these transactions, the VMs operate as if they were attached to the same VLAN (Layer 2 segment).

NVGRE's use of the GRE header enables it to be backward compatible with many stacks because GRE has been there for many years in the switching arena where hardware support is needed for tunnels. Because of this current support of a GRE header in many vendor switches, supporting NVGRE on these platforms is likely to be much simpler than other overlay encapsulations.

All-in-all like VXLAN, NVGRE provides a Layer 2 overlay over an IP network.

NVGRE Frame Format

Figure 2-9 shows the NVGRE frame format. Each of the components of the frame is also described:

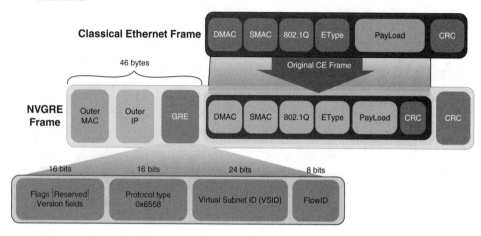

Figure 2-9   *NVGRE Frame Format*

- Outer Ethernet header

- Outer IP header

- NVGRE header

- Inner Ethernet header

NVGRE Data Path Operation

Figure 2-10 shows a sample NVGRE packet flow. At a high level, the NVGRE packet flow is almost identical to that employed by VXLAN except for the different encapsulation header. NVGRE, being a Layer 2 overlay, considers a packet sent by the VM out of one of its vNICs. As the vSwitch receives the packet from the vNIC, it knows the 24-bit Virtual Subnet ID, aka Tenant Network ID (TNI), for this packet. Basically, the vSwitch does two lookups on the packet:

- The vSwitch uses the ingress interface (vNIC) to determine which TNI the packet belongs to.

- vSwitch uses Destination MAC (DMAC) in the packet to determine which NVGRE tunnel the packet should be sent on.

- If DMAC is known, the packet is sent over a point-to-point GRE tunnel.

- If the DMAC is unknown, the packet is sent over a multipoint GRE tunnel with the destination IP being a multicast address associated with the TNI that the packet ingresses on.

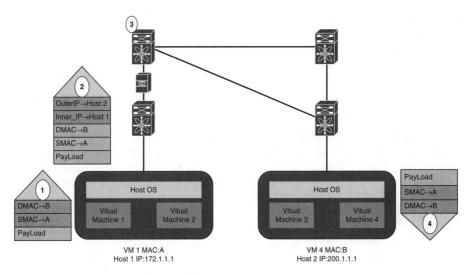

Figure 2-10 *NVGRE Data Path*

Refer to Figure 2-10 to see a high-level flow for a packet traversing the NVGRE network. NVGRE, like VXLAN, is an IP encapsulation, so the data path operation is similar to the VXLAN. The only difference is the GRE header is carried inside the outer IP frame.

1. VM 1 uses its MAC address of A as source MAC (SMAC) and sends a classical Ethernet frame, which is destined to VM 4 with a destination MAC (DMAC) address of B. On receiving this frame, the vSwitch on Host 1 does a Layer 2 lookup based on (VLAN and DMAC).

2. Now consider a case where the destination VM's address is known resulting in a hit in the Layer 2 table. The lookup points to the destination Host 2 as the egress endpoint for this Ethernet frame. The ingress vSwitch encapsulates this frame using the GRE header for forwarding the frame through the core network. The outer source and destination IP addresses are set as 172.1.1.1 and 172.1.1.2, respectively. The outer DMAC is the MAC address of the next-hop router, and the outer SMAC is the MAC address of the source Host 1.

3. The core router or switch (Router/Switch 3 in this example) forwards the frame based on the best path to the destination IP address of Host 2. In this case, there are two paths, but the best path is a single hop away; therefore, the frame is forwarded based on the outer IP address. The TTL is decremented and the outer SMAC and DMAC are rewritten as per regular routing semantics.

4. The destination Host (2) receives this frame. Because the destination IP address in the packet points to itself, Host 2 decapsulates the packet thereby stripping off the outer MAC and the GRE header. It then forwards the frame to VM 4 based on the inner DMAC, VLAN lookup.

Overlay Transport Virtualization

Overlay Transport Virtualization (OTV), also called Over-The-Top virtualization, is a Cisco-proprietary innovation in the Data Center Interconnect (DCI) space enabling Layer 2 extension across data center sites. It was introduced to address the drawbacks of other DCI technologies such as Virtual Private LAN Service (VPLS), Ethernet over MPLS (EoMPLS), Layer 2 over GRE (L2oGRE), and so on.

In OTV, the spanning tree domains remain site-local, and an overlay protocol is employed to share site-local unicast and multicast information with other sites that are all considered part of the same overlay network. OTV employs a MAC in IP encapsulation. One or more edge devices per site that interface with the provider core network are configured with OTV configuration. Each such device has two types of interfaces:

- **Internal interfaces:** It serves as a regular switch or bridge for packets entering and leaving these interfaces. In other words, it does regular SMAC learning based on incoming traffic and DMAC lookup for forwarding the traffic toward the appropriate destination.

- **Overlay interface:** This is a logical interface that faces the provider or core network. It has an IP address in the provider or core address space. All the MAC addresses within a site are advertised to remote sites against this IP address by the overlay control plane.

In OTV, there is no data plane learning. All unicast and multicast learning between sites is facilitated via the overlay control plane that runs on top of the provider/core network. The provider/core network may be Layer 2 or Layer 3. In its most common form, Layer 2 IS-IS is the control protocol of choice for the overlay. All edge devices belonging to the same VPN join the same provider multicast group address thereby allowing peering with each other. The multicast group is employed both for exchange of information in the control plane and sending multicast or broadcast frames in the data plane. A set of multicast group addresses in the provider or core network is made available for OTV usage.

As mentioned earlier, for scalability reasons, spanning tree Bridge Protocol Data Units (BPDUs) are never sent over the overlay interface. Unknown unicast lookups at the edge device are never flooded over the overlay interface but are instead dropped. OTV relies on the concept that hosts or nodes are not silent, and after they speak they will be discovered at a site locally. Then this information will be shared with the remote sites, thereby reducing the probability of unknown unicast lookups at remote sites for existing hosts. Internal Group Management Protocol (IGMP)/Multicast Listener Discovery (MLD) snooping on the internal edge interfaces enables learning about multicast sources, receivers, and group information that, in turn, triggers appropriate joins or leaves on the overlay interface.

To prevent loops and duplicate packets, OTV introduces the concept of an authoritative edge device (AED). A site may have multiple OTV edge devices, and they can either be statically or dynamically configured as AEDs at the granularity of a VLAN or potentially a (VLAN, MAC) combination. An AED is the chosen edge device that is responsible for encapsulating and decapsulating packets to and from the remote sites over the overlay interface for the chosen VLAN or (VLAN, MAC) pair. OTV also supports active-active multihoming to leverage multiple equal-cost paths between edge devices across the provider or core network. Finally, because the functionality of OTV is only on the edge boxes, no changes are required to any core or customer boxes.

OTV Frame Format

OTV employs a MAC in IP frame format, as shown in Figure 2-11 that adds a 42-byte header to each frame transported across the overlay. The source and destination IP addresses are set to that of the source overlay interface and remote overlay interface behind which the destination MAC is located, respectively. The Don't Fragment (DF) flag in the IP header is set to prevent fragmentation of the OTV packet. The OTV header contains an overlay ID and an instance of the ID. The overlay ID is for control plane packets belonging to a particular overlay. The instance ID field provides the option for using a logical table ID for lookup at the destination edge device. For completeness, OTV may also employ an optional UDP encapsulation where the UDP destination port is set to a well-known IANA reserved value of 8472 [13].

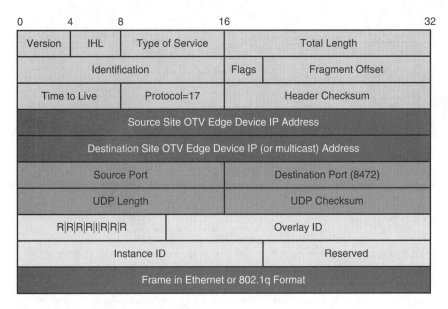

Figure 2-11   *OTV Frame Format*

OTV Operation

In its simplest form, an edge device appears as an IP host with respect to the provider or core network. It learns about (VLAN and uMAC) and (VLAN, mMAC, and mIP) bindings on the internal interfaces (where uMAC is a unicast MAC address, mMAC is a multicast MAC address, and mIP is the multicast group IP address) and distributes it to the remote edge devices via the overlay control plane. The remote devices learn about these bindings against the IP address of the advertising AED. Suitable extensions have been introduced in the Layer 2 IS-IS protocol to enable this information to be carried. including introduction of appropriate TLVs and sub-TLVs. For more information on this, refer to reference [12] at the end of this chapter.

Figure 2-12 shows that MAC1, MAC2, and MAC3 represent hosts in data centers 1, 2, and 3, respectively. Based on the exchange of learned information on the overlay control plane, an edge device on data center 1 has its MAC table appropriately populated. This enables dynamic encapsulation of packets destined from data center 1 to MAC2 and MAC3.

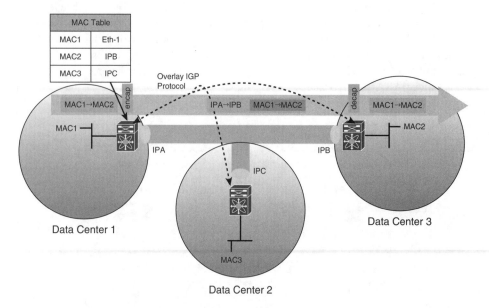

Figure 2-12   *OTV Illustration*

OTV enables quick detection of host mobility across data centers. This is facilitated by the control plane advertisement of a metric of 0 for the moved host. All remote sites update their MAC table on reception of an advertisement with metric 0. In addition, the old site on reception of such an advertisement can detect a host move event and withdraw its original advertisement.

Provider Backbone Bridges (PBB)

802.1ah[9] is an IEEE standard developed for addressing the scalability concerns in carrier Ethernet. It is a MAC-IN-MAC encapsulation scheme that addresses the limitation of 4KVLANs and MAC address table explosion at the metro-Ethernet provider. Figure 2-13 shows the historical evolution of Ethernet tagging.

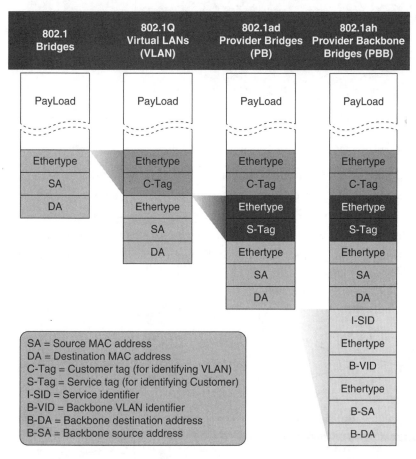

Figure 2-13 *802.1 Frame Formats*

802.1Q defines the customer frames to be differentiated using a 2-byte TAG. The Tag consisted of a 12-bit VLAN field, which enables roughly 4 K services to be provided. The 802.1ad (also called QinQ) enables the customer and provider tags to be separated. The idea is to separate the customer and provider space. The frame consists of a customer tag (C-TAG) along with a service tag used at the service provider core (called S-TAG). The 4 K limitation of service instances was to an extent addressed by 802.1ad, but the MAC table explosion still remained at the core. The 802.1ah defines bridge protocols for the interconnection of provider bridged networks (PBN). An 802.1ah frame is shown in Figure 2-14.

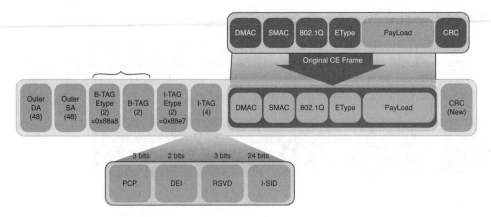

Figure 2-14   *802.1ah Frame Formats*

Figure 2-14 shows an 802.1ah header, which consists of the following:

> **Outer DA:** This is the Destination Backbone Edge Bridge's MAC Address.
>
> **Outer SA:** This is the Source Backbone Edge Bridge's MAC Address.
>
> **BTAG:** This field prefixed with the Ether Type represents the Backbone VLAN.
>
> **ITAG:** This field prefixed with the Ether Type represents the service identifier.

The header fields will become clear after you go through a packet flow. Consider the topology shown in Figure 2-15:

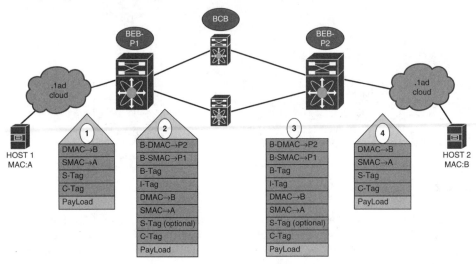

Figure 2-15   *IEEE 802.1ah Data Path*

Figure 2-15 shows a customer frame, after it arrives at the Backbone Edge Bridge (BEB), is encapsulated with an 802.1ah header. The customer frame is associated with a service instance. The S-VLAN or C-VLAN or a combination of both can be used to derive a service instance. The 802.1ah enables a provider to support up to 2^24 service instances (16 million). The Backbone VLAN is used at the provider core to form different bridge domains. The outer B-SA and B-DA are the source and destination MAC addresses of the BEBs. The Backbone Core Bridge (BCB) does regular Layer 2 bridging and doesn't need to be 802.1ah-aware. At the egress, a BEB learns the inner MAC address and associates it with the BEB's MAC address present at the outer header. In this way, the provider core needs to learn only all the BEB's MAC addresses. It's true that this doesn't solve the BEB's MAC address table explosion problem. The egress BEB then removes the outer 802.1ah header, derives the service instance of the frame based on the I-SID, and then forwards the frame to the destination host.

This example assumes that the MAC addresses are already learned. Of course, the source BEB initially does not know the B-DA for the destination host's MAC address (MAC:B). Therefore, the destination host's MAC address is not present in the Layer 2 table; the frame is flooded to all the BEB's in the network. There are optimizations that require the frame to be sent to only the BEBs that are part of the Backbone VLAN, or a special multicast address is used that allow the frames to be sent to the BEBs that have hosts in the service instance.

Shortest Path Bridging

Shortest Path Bridging (SPB) is an IEEE standard (802.1aq). It tries to solve the same problems as TRILL and FabricPath do, namely inefficient utilization of links and scalability concerns due to Spanning Tree, MAC table explosion in the MSDC environment, but still retaining the simplicity of a Layer 2 network.

SPB used Layer 2-IS-IS with some specific extensions[10] as the control protocol. Every SPB switch computes a number of shortest path trees with every other SPB switch as the root. SPB comes in two flavors, SPBM and SPBV. SPBM uses an IEEE 802.1ah format, whereas SPBV uses an IEEE 802.1ad format.

Shortest Path Bridging MAC

The overlay header and the data path for Shortest Path Bridging MAC (SPBM) are similar to that of 802.1ah, described in the previous section. Now consider an example for unicast traffic. A sample topology is shown in Figure 2-16. Layer 2-IS-IS distributes the Backbone MAC (BMAC) of all the SPB nodes. Every node has a link state database of all the nodes in the SPB network identified uniquely by its BMAC, and the shortest path is computed for every node.

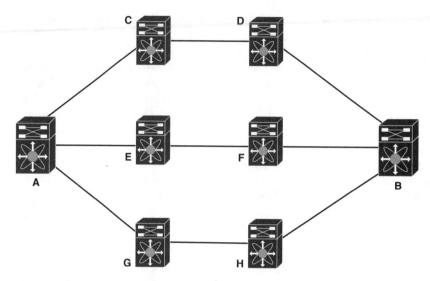

Figure 2-16   *IEEE 802.1aq Data Path*

In the figure, from node A to B, there are three different equal cost shortest paths available. Each path is assigned a different B-VID. B-VID is the backbone VLAN ID, which is a subfield in the B-TAG field of the 802.1ah frame shown in Figure 2-14. The path that has the lowest node ID is chosen among the different equal cost paths (Low Path ID). Alternately, the path with the highest node ID can also be chosen among the different equal cost paths. All the nodes in the SPB network use the same tie-breaking mechanism. The exact tie-breaking mechanism used is advertised in the IS-IS TLV to ensure all nodes use the same tie-breaking mechanism to guarantee symmetric lookup results for traffic forwarding. Node ID, here, is the MAC-Address of the bridge. So, assuming Low Path ID is used, the frames from A to B traverse the path A - C - D - B.

The reverse path can also flow through the same set of nodes. When a native frame arrives at the ingress node of the SPB network, a look up is done in the Layer 2 table to find the egress node of the SPB network behind which the host is located. In the example, say, the look up result indicates B as the egress node. Node A then encapsulates the frame into an 802.1ah header. The B-VID information for the corresponding path is exchanged through the Layer 2 IS-IS. The B-MAC is the MAC address of egress node, which is B. The appropriate I-SID is used based on the classification of the frame. Then, another lookup is performed in the forwarding table to find the outgoing interface for B-MAC - 'B'. This is where SPBM differs from 802.1ah. The802.1ah operates like a regular Layer 2 switch in terms of learning and forwarding of the BMAC, BVID in the 802.1ah header. In SPB-M, the topology information of all nodes, identified by its B-MAC, is distributed through IS-IS and a shortest path is computed for every BMAC. BMAC is the routable entity in SPB-M, and the result of the lookup for BMAC, BVID is the interface to reach the next hop obtained through shortest path computation. Switch A, after a lookup in the forwarding table, chooses the interface connecting to Switch C as the outgoing interface. Switch C does a lookup based on the outer 802.1ah header (B-MAC and

B-VID and optionally ISID, as will be explained subsequently) and forwards the frame
to node D. Node D forwards the frame to the egress node B. Node B decapsulates the
frame; it learns the source MAC address of the sending host (inner source MAC address)
against the ingress SPB node, which in this example is A. Then, the original frame is forwarded using the traditional way based on the Layer 2/Layer 3 header.

The key points to note here are that the data traffic between two SPB nodes is symmetri-
cal and no learning on B-MAC happens at the SPB network.

There are further optimizations proposed for load balancing the traffic. One mechanism
picks the path among the different set of ECMP paths based on the I-SID. As can be
recalled from the preceding section on 802.1ah, I-SID is the service instance to which the
frame belongs. So, traffic belonging to different services takes different paths, thereby
achieving load balancing. To illustrate this, a simple mechanism consists of employing a
modulo-operation of I-SID with the total number of equal cost paths to yield the path to
be taken.

The example described in this section is for unicast traffic, where in the destination
host MAC was already present in the Layer 2 table of the ingress node. Therefore, the
look up for the inner DMAC is a miss; a special multicast address is used as the destination B-MAC. The multicast address is derived based on the I-SID, to which the frame
belongs to and the source node ID from where the traffic is rooted, which is node A in
this example. So, there is per-source, per-service multicast forwarding and the multicast
address uses a special format to achieve this. The low-order 24 bits represent the service
ID and the upper 22 bits represent a network-wide unique identifier. The I/G bit is set and
the U/L bit is also set to mark it as a nonstandard OUI address. To achieve this forwarding behavior, Layer 2 IS-IS carries information about which nodes are members of a given
service. Because all nodes compute the tree rooted at every SPB node, they populate the
forwarding table with the different multicast addresses along with the outgoing interfaces.

Shortest Path Bridging VID

Shortest Path Bridging VID (SPBV) is wanted when there is no need to separate the customer and core address spaces. The control plane operation in SPBV is similar to that of
SPBM. A SPBV frame is single (one 802.1q tag) or double (that is, q-in-q) tagged. There's
no overlay header added for SPBV unlike the SPBM case. SPBV limits the number of
VLANs in the network.

The 802.1q[11] tag is overloaded to carry both the VLAN ID and the Tree ID. Each node
computes a shortest path tree to all other nodes. Consequently, SPBV is suitable for
deployments in which Number_of_VLAN's * Number_of_Nodes < 4K. A VLAN or
802.1q tag translation happens at the ingress. The translated tag is called the SPVID, Now
consider a simple example with SPBV for a bidirectional traffic flow. A sample topology
is shown in Figure 2-17 where the Node ID of each node is listed in parenthesis. Layer 2
IS-IS distributes the SPVID of all the SPB nodes. Every node has a link state database of
all the nodes in the SPB network, and the shortest path tree is computed for every node.

For example, Node E would have computed a number of shortest path trees with nodes A to H as the root.

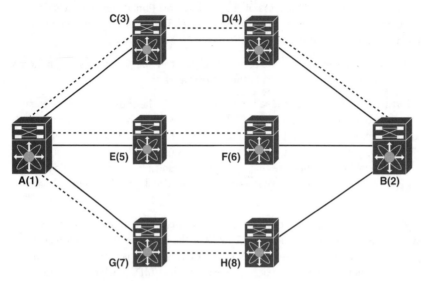

Figure 2-17   *SPBV Data Path*

SPVID is calculated as Base VID + Node ID. For example, if there's a VLAN 100, there will be 8 different node IDs, as shown in Figure 2-17, starting from 101 to 108, where 1 to 8 are the node IDs. Forwarding in SPBV works as follows: Broadcast, multicast, and unknown unicast frames are forwarded out of the Shortest Path Tree (SPT) with the ingress as the root. IS-IS already would have propagated the tree information along with its appropriate SPVID, which also identifies the tree. Known unicast frames are forwarded based on the lookup result. The key for the lookup and the learning mechanism employed is HW-specific, and that dictates how this forwarding behavior is achieved.

Now walk through a conceptual packet flow. When a frame arrives at ingress node A, an 802.1q tag translation or encapsulation is done on the frame based on whether the original frame arrived with a 802.1q tag or was untagged. The tag translation is done based on the VLAN to which the outgoing frame is associated with and the node ID of the ingress. For example, if the frame arrives at A and the outgoing frame is associated with VLAN 100, the SPVID in the frame will have the value of 101. Initially, when the frame arrives at A, a lookup on destination B will be a miss in its forwarding table. Lookup is done based on VLAN and the MAC address of B. Because it's a miss, the frame is forwarded along the SPT corresponding to SPVID 101, which are interfaces connecting to C, E, and G. The outgoing interfaces are a part of the shortest path tree computed by A. The tree with node A as the root is shown in dotted lines in Figure 2-17.

When the frame arrives at C, E, and G, each derives the interfaces corresponding to the tree (SPVID of 101) because the lookup is a miss. Each node can also do a reverse path check to ensure that the frame arrived at a valID interface and is a part of the computed shortest path to the node ID, carried in the SPVID. The frame is forwarded to destination

B and follows the path shown in Figure 2-17 (A -> C -> D -> B). Nodes F and H terminate the frame and don't forward the frame to B because the tree for SPVID 101 does not include the links F - B and H - B. Node B learns the <MAC address of A, VLAN (value of 100)> against the incoming interface. An important thing to note is learning does not happen on the incoming SPVID (value of 101). The reason will become clear when you trace the packet flow for the reverse traffic.

When reverse traffic arrives at B, an 802.1q tag translation is done, as explained previously, and the SPVID will have the value of 102 because the node ID of B is 2. A lookup in the forwarding table for destination MAC address of" and VLAN ID of 100 points to the interface connecting to D. The reverse traffic follows the path B -> D -> C -> A. If learning had happened on just SPVID 101 instead, a lookup for the reverse traffic would have been a miss, which is not wanted. The basic idea is that learning happens by ignoring the node ID.

To summarize, shared VLAN learning is employed for unicast traffic and node ID-specific entries are installed in the forwarding table for broadcast and multicast traffic.

Summary

In this chapter, you learned about the various Layer 2 and Layer 3 overlay technologies including Cisco Fabric path, TRILL, LISP, VXLAN, NVGRE, OTV, PBB, and Shortest Path Bridging. Each of these technologies tries to address various limitations of today's networks including mobility across networks which are Layer 3 apart. Layer 2 LISP, VXLAN, NVGRE, PBB, and Shortest Path Bridging also address the current limitation of 4094 Virtual LANs by providing 16 million logical Layer-2 segments in the network.

References

IS-IS for Layer 2 Systems:

1. http://www.ietf.org/rfc/rfc6165.txt

FabricPath:

2. http://www.cisco.com/en/US/docs/switches/datacenter/nexus5000/sw/fabric-path/513_n1_1/fp_n5k_switching.html#wp1790893

3. http://www.cisco.com/en/US/prod/collateral/switches/ps9441/ps9402/white_paper_c11-687554.html

VXLAN:

4. http://tools.ietf.org/html/draft-mahalingam-dutt-dcops-vxlan-02

5. http://www.techmahindra.com/Documents/WhitePaper/VXLAN2011.pdf

6. http://www.borgcube.com/blogs/2011/11/vxlan-primer-part-1/

NVGRE:

   7. http://tools.ietf.org/html/draft-sridharan-virtualization-nvgre-01

GRE:

   8. http://www.cisco.com/en/US/tech/tk827/tk369/tk287/tsd_technology_support_sub-protocol_home.html

802.1ah:

   9. http://www.ieee802.org/1/pages/802.1ah.html

SPB:

   10. http://tools.ietf.org/html/rfc6329

   11. http://www.ieee802.org/1/pages/802.1aq.html

   12. http://www.cisco.com/en/US/docs/solutions/Enterprise/Data_Center/DCI/whitepaper/DCI3_OTV_Intro_WP.pdf

OTV:

   13. http://tools.ietf.org/html/draft-hasmit-otv-04

Chapter 3

IS-IS

This chapter covers the following objectives:

- **Concepts:** This section discusses the general concepts of a link state protocol. An overview of the different stages in a link state protocol is given.

- **IS-IS architecture details:** This section discusses the high level IS-IS architecture details.

- **TRILL and FabricPath relevant changes:** This section covers in detail the changes specific to TRILL and FabricPath.

Introduction to IS-IS

This chapter provides a brief explanation of Intermediate Systems – Intermediate Systems (IS-IS[1]) Intra Domain Routing Protocol. Both TRILL and FabricPath use IS-IS as their control protocol. Consequently, you must be familiar with the inner workings of IS-IS. This chapter, by no means, provides comprehensive details on IS-IS. Many good resources and books are dedicated to IS-IS. Some of them are listed in the "References" section at the end of the chapter. The purpose of this chapter is to provide the necessary details on IS-IS so that you can get started. This chapter also explains in detail the extensions that were done to IS-IS to support TRILL. The extensions to IS-IS for TRILL and FabricPath are also referenced in the respective chapters. Although there is some redundancy, this has been done for added convenience to address both class of readers, those who want to understand the IS-IS specific details and those who may be interested in knowing only enough about IS-IS that is necessary to understand TRILL and FabricPath.

- IS-IS is an ISO standard and like Open Shortest Path First (OSPF)[2] is a link state protocol. IS-IS was originally designed as a dynamic routing protocol for ISO's

Connectionless Mode Network Protocol (CLNP) in 1987. It was later extended by IETF to carry IP addresses in 1990. IS-IS operates over the link layer. Though it was originally developed for the OSI protocol stack, all its messages are easily extendable (unlike OSPF, which is primarily written for IPV4). IS-IS uses a generic Type Length Value (TLV) format for its message exchange. Supporting any new protocol can be done elegantly in IS-IS by adding new extensions without modifying the base infrastructure. For this reason, TRILL and FabricPath chose IS-IS with some extensions as their control protocol.

Concepts

This section explains the fundamental concepts behind link state protocols. Routing protocols can be classified in to Distance Vector Protocols such as Routing Information Protocol (RIP),[3] Enhanced Interior Gateway Routing Protocol (EIGRP)[4], and so on and as Link State Protocols such as Open Shortest Path First (OSPF)[2] and IS-IS. The basic idea behind link state protocols is that each node is made aware of the entire network topology. The protocol ensures that all the nodes have accurate information of the entire topology. Then, all the nodes independently run the same Shortest Path First (SPF) algorithm to compute the shortest route between each node. Because the topology information is the same, the route computation will also be the same at all the nodes. Synchronizing the topology database with the neighbors and computing the routes are independent operations and can be done in parallel. The mechanism by which this is achieved is left to the details of the individual protocol. Now consider a simple topology, as shown in Figure 3-1, to illustrate neighbor discovery, topology exchange, and synchronization in an IS-IS network. Assume that a new node (labeled as "G" in Figure 3-1) is connected to the network. A typical link state protocol has multiple stages.

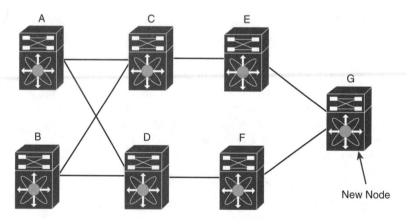

Figure 3-1   *IS-IS Network*

Neighbor Discovery

Neighbor discovery is the first stage of the protocol in which a node discovers its neighbors. Every node sends a multicast packet on all the interfaces configured for the link state protocol to run. This packet contains the properties of the protocol. The other routers respond to this packet with their capabilities. After processing the information, the router accepts or rejects the adjacent nodes as neighbors. The next section on IS-IS goes into the specifics that detail the packet format, the three-way hand shake, and so on. Every node also sends a periodic keepalive packet. When the keepalive packet is not heard for a specific duration, the corresponding neighboring router is considered unreachable and not taken into consideration for computing routes. For the topology shown in Figure 3-1, after the neighbor discovery phase, node G would have established nodes E and F as its neighbors and vice versa.

Topology Exchange

As stated previously, every node has the complete topology information. This means that the amount of data exchanged between the nodes is large and, needless to say, it increases with the increase in the number of nodes in the topology. During every topology change, such as link failures, the node going down triggers topology updates. The obvious intention of any routing protocol is to minimize the number of times the route computation algorithm is run, minimize the number of topology updates, and reduce the size of the topology updates whenever possible.

After the neighbor discovery is done, the nodes exchange in short packets, describing the revision of the topology information it has. If both the nodes have the same information, no exchange of topology is needed. Otherwise, the node having the latest information sends only the portion of the topology database, which is out of date in the neighbor node. In this way, topology information is exchanged only when needed. Considering the topology shown in Figure 3-1 because node G's topology database is empty, it can request nodes E and F to send the entire database.

Flooding

Information about new nodes or network changes is propagated to all the nodes in the network through flooding. The idea behind flooding is simple. A change picked up by a node is transmitted on all the links where the link state protocol is configured. The other nodes, after receiving the flood packet, in turn send it out on all its links, except the link through which the packet arrived. This process continues until all the nodes have obtained the packet. It is normal for a node to receive multiple copies of the same packet. Usually, the classic split horizon rule is employed, wherein a node will not transmit the packet back to the neighbor from which it received the announcement. There are other optimizations employed like having a hold-down timer, wherein after receiving a flood packet, it is not transmitted immediately but transmitted after waiting for a small random time. There are numerous optimizations proposed for flooding that include limiting the number of duplicate packets, corruption detection, versioning of the flooded packets, and so on. You see how IS-IS handles some of these in the subsequent sections. For a deep dive on this, refer to the reference for IS-IS.[1] Refer to the topology shown in Figure 3-1. As soon as the nodes E and F detect the new neighbor G, they will flood the topology change information to their neighbors. In this example, node E sends the information to node C, and node F sends the information to node D. Nodes C and D in turn flood the information to both the nodes A and B. In this way, all the nodes in the network have the same topology information.

Route Computation

After a node has built its database, it calculates the shortest path to all the other nodes in the network. Usually Dijkstra's shortest path first (SPF) algorithm is employed. This algorithm was originally proposed for Graph Theory, wherein each vertex is treated as a node, and the edges connecting the vertices are the links connecting the nodes. The cost of the edges is the metric associated with the link. When the network topology is redrawn by only considering the path computed by SPF algorithm, it forms a spanning tree with itself as the root. The tree is composed of the shortest path from the root to all the other nodes in the network. Because a tree is an acyclic graph, there are no loops. This plays an important role in how TRILL and FabricPath support forwarding of multidestination frames. For the topology shown in Figure 3-1, every node computes a shortest path to reach the new node G. In this topology, node A has two equal cost paths to reach node G, assuming the metric of all the links are the same. The two equal cost paths are A-C-E-G and A-D-F-G.

Link State Protocol Scaling

Scaling poses a big threat especially to link state protocols. Recall that all the nodes maintain the topology of the entire network. The higher the number of nodes, the higher the size of the database maintained by each node and the higher the time spent by each CPU to compute the routes. Because flooding is the mechanism used to propagate the database, any topology change can trigger a flood, the effects of which will be severe for a larger network. The higher the floods, the higher the network traffic and time spent by the CPU in processing the messages. To address the scalability concern, link state protocols usually divide the network into areas. Flooding is limited to an area. Flood packets originated within an area are not sent to other areas. Flood packets terminate at the area boundary. Each area has a border router that synchronizes the database with the border router of the adjacent area. The database that gets synchronized between the border routers and later on distributed inside an area is summarized and not the complete database of the other area. Limiting the scope of flooding and the size of the database can improve the scalability by a big factor.

Link State Protocol in a Local Area Network

Figure 3-1 has routers connected to each other through point-to-point links. But it is not uncommon for multiple routers to be connected through a shared media or a local-area network (LAN) as shown in Figure 3-2.

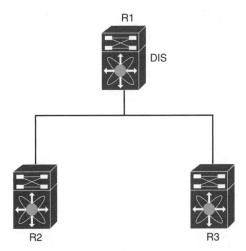

Figure 3-2   *IS-IS LAN Network*

In this example, Routers R1, R2, and R3 that are running a link state protocol have one of their ports connected to the LAN. R1, R2, and R3 can see each other as neighbors. Even though they are part of the LAN, neighbor discovery, topology exchange, and flooding of information happen between every peer (or neighbor pairs). When the number of routers connected to the LAN increases, the number of peers increases, and this increases the number of messages seen in the network, the redundant information in the messages leading to increased CPU utilization in the routers to process extra messages and compute the routes. To get around this issue, the concept of designated router (DR in OSPF) or designated intermediate-system (DIS in IS-IS) was introduced. A DR or DIS is elected among all the routers in the LAN during the neighbor discovery phase. Figure 3-2 shows R1 as the DIS. A DR or DIS has the following additional functionality:

- All the routers synchronize their database only with the DR or DIS.

- The DR or DIS synchronizes the topology database information with the rest of the LAN.

- All the routers in a network form a neighbor relationship only with the DR in OSPF. In IS-IS, a full mesh of adjacencies is established.

This scalability issue is seen not only within the LAN, but also in the routers that are not a part of the LAN but are directly connected to the routers in the LAN, as shown in Figure 3-3.

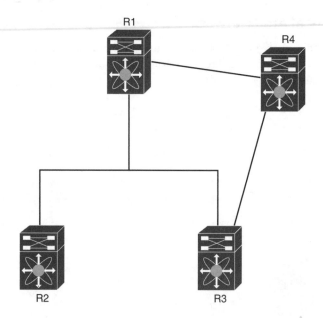

Figure 3-3   *IS-IS LAN Connected to an External Router*

In Figure 3-3, an external Router R4 is connected to both R1 and R2 but is not a part of the LAN. If every router in the LAN includes all the nodes in its topology database as a part of its topology database advertisement to the external router, this can lead to a lot of redundant information being carried, and a single topology advertisement can become big. So, the concept of pseudo-node was introduced, wherein a special message is sent with the pseudo-node as the source of the advertisement that includes reachability to all the other nodes in the LAN with a cost of zero. The DR or DIS sends this special advertisement. When the routers in the LAN advertise their topology database to the external routers, they just advertise the reachability to the pseudo-node (or virtual node) with the actual cost of the broadcast link rather than advertising their reachability to all the other nodes in the LAN. The logical topology as viewed by the external routers after processing the topology advertisements from the routers in the LAN is shown in Figure 3-4. There is no pseudo-node in the actual physical topology. The pseudo-node will be seen as another router connected to all the routers in the LAN. Running a link state protocol in a LAN environment introduces a lot of additional complexities as discussed in this section. A link state protocol in a LAN environment is a detailed topic and you are encouraged to refer to IS-IS[1] and OSPF[2] for additional details.

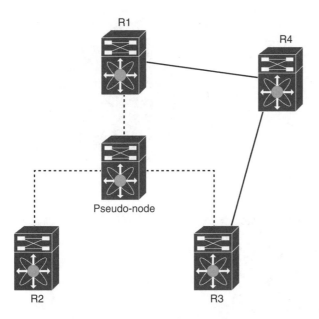

Figure 3-4   *IS-IS Pseudo-Node*

IS-IS Architecture Details

IS-IS has the concept of areas for the purpose of scalability, security, and network separation. IS-IS, being a link state protocol, uses a flooding mechanism to synchronize its databases. As stated previously, when the IS-IS network grows, the number of packets in the network due to flooding increases. This results in the following:

- Increase in the memory consumption in each of the switches.

- Higher number of SPF calculations or recalculations and therefore an increase in the CPU processing time. This affects the network convergence leading to network instability.

- Reduced throughput in the links for data traffic.

Consequently, the IS-IS network is divided into domains. Every domain is identified using an Area Identifier. There are two levels in IS-IS. Level L1 refers to all the switches in an area. Level L2 refers to the backbone, which is for switches connecting two different areas. Switches connected to other switches in the same area are L1 switches. Switches connected to both the switches in the same area and different areas are L1/L2 switches. Switches that are connected only to switches in different areas are L2 switches (see Figure 3-5).

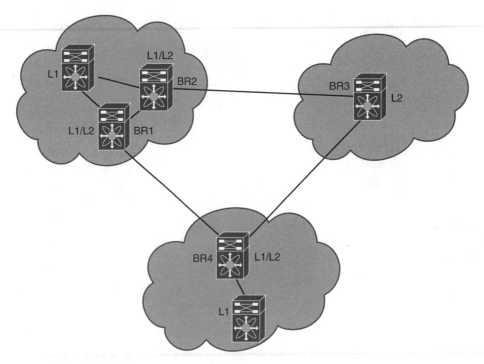

Figure 3-5 *IS-IS Area*

If a switch is connected to another switch in the same area, it is configured as an L1 link (not shown in the Figure 3-5). If the switch is connected to another switch belonging to a different area, it is configured as an L2 link. LAN links (links connected to a shared media, for example, a bridge), are configured as L1/L2, which means both because it is possible that the shared media has switches connected from the same area as well as different areas. For example, in Figure 3-5, the links connecting the border routers are configured as L2 links. The links connecting the routers within the same area (represented as a cloud in the figure) are configured as L1 links. Figure 3-5 shows four border routers (BR1 to BR4) for their respective areas. As explained previously, the IS-IS flood packets originated in an area do not cross the border routers. The border routers summarize the information of its area before synchronizing it with the border router of another area.

TRILL and FabricPath Specific Changes in IS-IS

This section explains the changes that are done in IS-IS for supporting TRILL and FabricPath. IS-IS uses Type Length Value (TLV) objects to exchange information. A TLV can have sub-TLVs. The TLVs and Sub-TL's introduced or modified for TRILL are explained in this section. This section starts with a short introduction to TRILL and FabricPath by listing the salient points for your convenience. The general frame format of

IS-IS is followed by a short description of the TLVs in IS-IS that are used by TRILL and FabricPath for carrying out its information. Then this section explains the TRILL-specific changes that are done in different stages of the IS-IS protocol such as neighbor discovery, topology exchange, and route computation. The packet format of the sub-TLVs introduced by TRILL for every stage in IS-IS is also explained. Finally, the changes done in IS-IS to support TRILL-specific concepts such as Nickname Resolution, multidestination pruning, and Fine Grained Labeling are also explained. The TLV-specific changes done in IS-IS to support FabricPath are not detailed because the changes are proprietary and internal to a Cisco implementation.

Overview of TRILL and FabricPath

This section summarizes the key points in TRILL and FabricPath so that you can understand the context when reading the subsequent sections that detail the changes in IS-IS for TRILL and FabricPath. For a detailed reading on TRILL/FabricPath, refer to Chapter 4, "FabricPath," and Chapter 5, "TRILL."

- TRILL and FabricPath are overlay technologies in which the ingress switch adds the overlay header and the egress switch removes the overlay header. The core switches forward the frame based on the TRILL and FabricPath header.

- TRILL identifies each switch by a unique Nickname, and FabricPath identifies each switch using a unique SwitchID.

- RBridge is a switch that has TRILL implemented.

- Layer-2 IS-IS[5] is used as the control protocol in TRILL and FabricPath. All the RBridges in the TRILL network belong to the Level-1 (L1) IS-IS area.

- The control protocol in TRILL and FabricPath assigns a unique random Nickname and SwitchID, respectively, to each switch.

- TRILL switches forward the frame primarily using the Nickname field present in the TRILL overlay header. FabricPath switches forward the frame primarily using the SwitchID and FTAG field present in the FabricPath overlay header.

- Apart from the unicast routing table, the TRILL and FabricPath switches also compute a number of trees for forwarding multidestination frames. The tree includes all the nodes in the TRILL and FabricPath network. Every tree can be rooted at different nodes. When forwarding a multidestination frame for TRILL, the Nickname identifies the tree along with another bit in the header. For FabricPath, the FTAG field along with the outer multicast destination address is used for forwarding a multidestination frame.

- The egress switches after removing the overlay header learn the inner source MAC address and associate it with the Nickname or SwitchID for TRILL or FabricPath, respectively.

IS-IS Frame Formats

Some changes have been introduced to IS-IS to specifically support TRILL and FabricPath. TRILL and FabricPath uses an extension of IS-IS[6] as its routing protocol. The IS-IS implementation for TRILL and FabricPath runs separately and is different from the L3-IS-IS. The packet processing behavior for IS-IS in TRILL and FabricPath is not different from other routing protocols in the sense that they are never forwarded by a TRILL and FabricPath switch and are consumed and processed locally on receipt. The packet format of TRILL and FabricPath IS-IS frames is shown in Figure 3-6. The TRILL and FabricPath IS-IS frames are identified by their L2-IS-IS ether-type as well as the reserved outer multicast destination address (ALL-IS-IS-RBridges). Even though the header format specifies All-IS-IS-RBridge, FabricPath also uses the same multicast destination address. The IS-IS common header and the fixed PDU header for TRILL are the same as a level-LAN IS-IS HELLO PDU.[5]

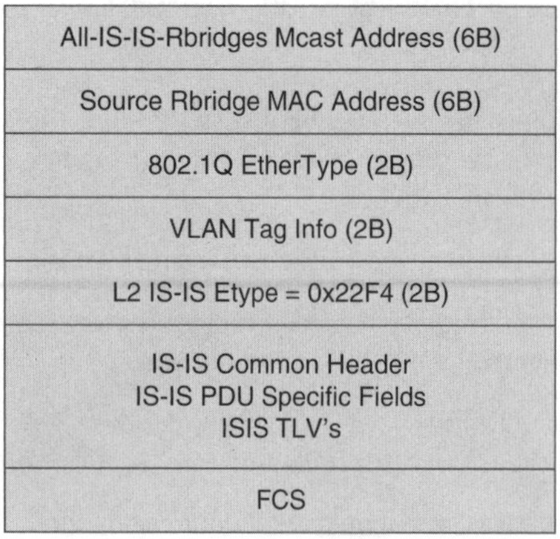

All-IS-IS-Rbridges Mcast Address (6B)
Source Rbridge MAC Address (6B)
802.1Q EtherType (2B)
VLAN Tag Info (2B)
L2 IS-IS Etype = 0x22F4 (2B)
IS-IS Common Header IS-IS PDU Specific Fields ISIS TLV's
FCS

Figure 3-6   *TRILL and FabricPath IS-IS Packet*

In TRILL, all RBridges participating in IS-IS are configured in a Level-1 IS-IS area. The Outer VLAN tag is optional and depends on the configuration of the interface. TRILL and FabricPath use the Layer 2 IS-IS frame format. As mentioned earlier, IS-IS uses TLV (Type Value Length) objects to carry the information. An IS-IS frame has many TLVs. A TLV can carry many sub-TLVs. Refer to IS-IS[1], Layer 2 IS-IS[5] for a comprehensive listing of all TLVs and sub-TLVs used in IS-IS. TRILL has introduced TLVs and sub-TLVs to carry its information. The sub-TLVs are carried under the Router Capability TLV and Multi-Topology (MT)-aware Port Capability TLV. Similarly, FabricPath also has introduced different sub-TLVs and TLVs to carry its information, and these are not covered in this chapter because these are proprietary to Cisco. A brief description of the Router Capability TLV and MT-Aware Port Capability TLV along with the list of sub-TLVs that are introduced for TRILL follow.

Router Capability TLV

Switches announce their capabilities in an IS-IS area or the entire domain through this TLV. Router capability TLV has multiple sub-TLVs. It consists of one octet for Type (value of 242), one octet for length of the value field in bytes, and the actual contents of the TLV. The contents start with a 32-bit Router ID followed by a one octet flags field and optional sub-TLVs. Refer to IS-IS extensions[7] for more information on this TLV. The subsequent sections explain the following sub-TLVs in detail along with the packet formats. The sub-TLVs introduced by TRILL are as follows:

- TRILL Version Sub-TLV

- Nickname Sub-TLV

- Trees Sub-TLV

- Tree Identifier Sub-TLV

- Trees Used Identifier Sub-TLV

- Interested VLAN's and Spanning Tree Roots Sub-TLV

- VLAN Group Sub-TLV

- MTV Sub-TLV

- TRILL Neighbor Sub-TLV

Multitopology-Aware Port Capability TLV

This TLV is introduced for technologies that use Layer 2 addresses to perform routing. TRILL, FabricPath, IEEE 802.1aq, and OTV are some of the technologies that use this TLV. This has multiple sub-TLVs. It consists of one octet for Type (value of 143), one octet for length of the value field in bytes, and the actual contents of the TLV. The value field has a 12-bit topology identifier. Refer to Layer 2 IS-IS[7] for more information on this TLV. The subsequent sections explain the following sub-TLVs in detail along with the packet formats. The sub-TLVs introduced by TRILL are as follows:

- Special VLAN and Flags Sub-TLV

- Enabled VLANS Sub-TLV

- Appointed Forwarders Sub-TLV

TRILL IS-IS Neighbor Discovery

This section covers the TRILL-specific changes done in IS-IS during the neighbor discovery phase followed by the description and packet format of the TLVs and sub-TLVs introduced by TRILL for this phase. IS-IS discovers its neighbors using the HELLO protocol.

An IS-IS interface is configured as a point-to-point interface if it is directly connected to another router through a direct or point-to-point link. An IS-IS interface is configured as a LAN interface if it is connected to a shared media. An example of a shared media deployment includes a switch connected to a hub to which multiple other switches are connected, and all of them are running IS-IS. Following are the different kinds of HELLO Packets for TRILL:

■ Point-to-Point (P2P) HELLO, sent on point-to-point links

■ TRILL HELLO sent on LAN interfaces

TRILL HELLOs

When the switches running IS-IS are connected using a shared media, like, for example, using a Layer 2 bridge, TRILL HELLOs are used to discover the neighbors. There may be multiple switches running IS-IS connected to the same bridge. When a node comes up, it sends a TRILL HELLO frame on the LAN describing its capabilities. The destination MAC address of the TRILL HELLO frame is set to ALL-IS-IS-RBridge multicast address. The purpose of the TRILL LAN HELLO is as follows:

■ To elect a unique Designated RBridge (DRB) on the LAN link.

■ To identify the RBridge neighbors on the LAN link to establish the topology.

■ To determine the MTU for communication with the neighbors. This is an optional test to determine if data frames can be passed between two RBridges.

Designated RBridge

A Designated RBridge (DRB) is elected among all the RBridges in the LAN link. In TRILL, the DRB election process is based only on the MAC address and priority of the IS-IS running switches. In a shared media environment, there can clearly be only one DRB and one appointed forwarder for any given VLAN, as shown in Figure 3-7. Some of the functionality of the DRB is as follows:

■ Assign a designated VLAN to be used in the link for all TRILL encapsulated data frames and IS-IS frames, except for some HELLO frames. This designated VLAN refers to the VLAN tag in the optional outer 802.1q header of the TRILL encapsulated data frames.

■ For each VLAN (say, "a") on the LAN link, elect an appointed VLAN-a forwarder on the link. The DRB can choose itself as the appointed forwarder. This is the VLAN of the native data frames. A single RBridge can serve as the appointed forwarder for a group of VLANs.

■ A DRB has other functionalities in case of pseudo-nodes, which are covered in the respective section.

Some of the functionality of the appointed VLAN-a forwarder follows:

- For any traffic on VLAN-a from the end host that is destined to go over the TRILL cloud, perform the TRILL encapsulation.

- For any TRILL encapsulated traffic from the cloud with the inner VLAN tag of "a," perform the decapsulation and forward the inner frame to the end host.

- Perform remote source MAC address learning for VLAN-a apart from regular source MAC address learning on the LAN link.

- Send TRILL HELLO frames on VLAN-a, if configured to do so.

- Snoop IGMP frames belonging to VLAN-a, if configured to do so.

- Listen to BPDUs on the common spanning tree to learn the root bridge if any, and report it in its Link State Packets (LSP) during topology exchange phase.

Figure 3-7 shows RBridge-1 as the DRB and RBridge-3 acting as the appointed forwarder for a set of VLANs.

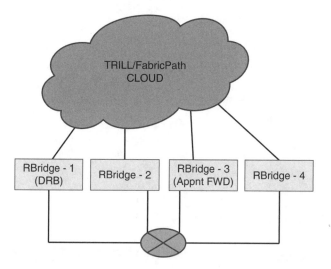

Figure 3-7   *TRILL RBridges in a LAN*

Neighbor Adjacency

In a LAN environment, an adjacency is formed between two RBridges only if a two-way hand-shake has occurred. A two-way adjacency is established with another switch only if the switch receives a HELLO frame with its information present. Now consider an example. In Figure 3-7, RBridge-2 comes online and sends a HELLO frame. RBridge-1 receives the frame and in its next HELLO message includes RBridge-2's information. RBridge-2 on receiving this frame establishes a two-way adjacency with RBridge-1. A fundamental scaling problem is with the choice of the VLAN tag to be used in the HELLO message.

The interface can be configured as a trunk with only certain VLANs enabled, or it can be an access interface with only a specific VLAN enabled. Therefore, it becomes necessary to send HELLO packets on multiple VLAN tags. Sending the HELLO packet on all 4K VLANs is a possibility, but when every RBridge connected to the shared media does this, it causes a serious performance degradation. A choice can be made to have only the DRB send multiple HELLO packets on all its enabled VLANs, and the other switches can send its HELLO only on a limited set of VLANs. Another important thing to note is that a two-way adjacency is not required for electing a DRB. It is possible that a switch can receive HELLOs from another switch even though a two-way connectivity is not formed. This can happen, if a switch (say, "a") continues to receive HELLOs from another switch (say, "b") without its information listed in the received HELLO packet. In such a scenario, switch "a" will not have switch "b" in its topology database and will not announce "b" as its neighbor. But it will take switch "b" into account for DRB election. This is because in a Layer 2 environment such as TRILL and FabricPath, it is extremely critical that there can be only one DRB and appointed forwarder (per vlan) as otherwise looping of Layer 2 frames can occur. The packet format of the common header and PDU specific portion in the IS-IS TRILL LAN HELLO is shown in Figure 3-8.

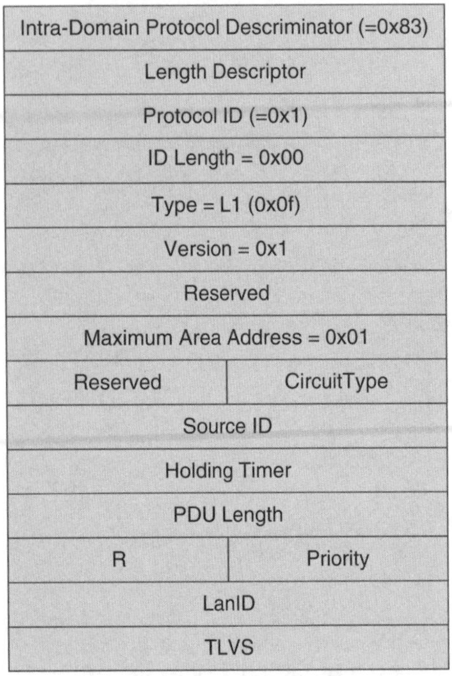

Intra-Domain Protocol Descriminator (=0x83)	
Length Descriptor	
Protocol ID (=0x1)	
ID Length = 0x00	
Type = L1 (0x0f)	
Version = 0x1	
Reserved	
Maximum Area Address = 0x01	
Reserved	CircuitType
Source ID	
Holding Timer	
PDU Length	
R	Priority
LanID	
TLVS	

Figure 3-8 *IS-IS TRILL LAN HELLO Common and PDU-Specific Header*

The Source ID is the Unique ID of the sending switch or referred to as Intermediate System (IS). A value of 16 for the Type field indicates that this is a TRILL or LAN IS-IS HELLO packet. Please refer to IS-IS[1] for details about the other fields.

P2P HELLOs

When two switches are connected through a point-to-point link, P2P HELLOs are used to discover each other. On a P2P link, no DRB or appointed forwarded election is necessary. No end station service such as encapsulation or decapsulation is done for frames on a P2P link. TRILL and FabricPath usually do a three-way handshake procedure to discover their neighbors and establish adjacencies on a P2P link. When a switch (say, "A") starts up, it sends a TRILL HELLO frame on all its IS-IS–enabled interfaces. The destination MAC address in a P2P HELLO packet is set to an ALL-IS-IS-RBridge multicast address. The neighbor (say, "B") responds back with the identity of the sending switch ("A") in the HELLO contents. The sending switch ("A") in its next HELLO includes the identity of the switch ("B") from which it received the unicast HELLO message. The three-way handshake is complete and switches A and B would have formed an adjacency. The common and PDU-specific header for an IS-IS point-to-point HELLO frame is shown in Figure 3-9.

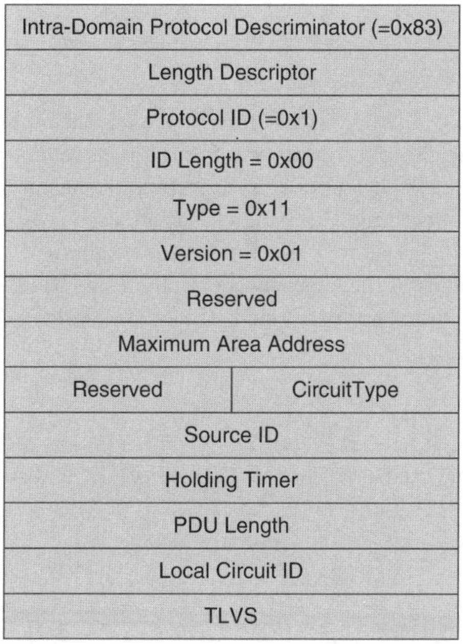

Intra-Domain Protocol Descriminator (=0x83)	
Length Descriptor	
Protocol ID (=0x1)	
ID Length = 0x00	
Type = 0x11	
Version = 0x01	
Reserved	
Maximum Area Address	
Reserved	CircuitType
Source ID	
Holding Timer	
PDU Length	
Local Circuit ID	
TLVS	

Figure 3-9   *IS-IS P2P HELLO Common and PDU-Specific Header*

The value of the Type field (=0x11) differentiates a P2P HELLO from a TRILL HELLO. The Source ID is the unique ID of the sending switch or referred to as Intermediate System (IS). The Local Circuit ID is the circuit identifier of the P2P link, and the lower SourceID of the connecting switches is used as the Local Circuit ID. Please refer to IS-IS[1] for details about the other fields. The TRILL specific TLVs and sub-TLVs for the HELLO protocol are described in the next section.

TRILL Neighbor TLV

This TLV appears in the IS-IS HELLO packet for both TRILL HELLOs and P2P HELLOs. This TLV is introduced for TRILL and carries the neighbor information. Adjacency between RBridges using either two-way or three-way handshake is established based on the neighbor contents of this TLV. Its format is shown in Figure 3-10.

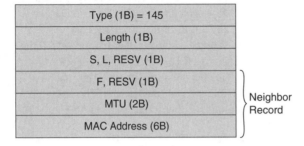

Figure 3-10   *TRILL Neighbor TLV*

The value of the Type field is 145. The Length of this TLV is 1 + n * 9, where n is the number of neighbor records and the size of each neighbor record is nine. S and L flags represent the smallest and largest flags and indicate if the neighbor records include the neighbor with the smallest and largest MAC address, respectively. The S and L flags are used mostly for DRB election in case of LAN links. The F flag is set to a value of 1 if the neighbor failed the MTU test. The 2-byte MTU field indicates the largest successfully tested MTU size for this neighbor. It is set to 0 if the MTU test is not performed. The MAC address field carries the MAC address of the neighbor.

Router Capability Sub-TLVs

Next, is a brief description of the sub-TLVs that are part of Router Capability TLV and are sent in the HELLO message.

Nickname Sub-TLV

This sub-TLV is specific to TRILL and carries the Nickname of the originating RBridge. This sub-TLV appears in the IS-IS HELLO packets and in the topology exchange packets. The discussion of this TLV is deferred to later sections of topology exchange where it is more appropriate.

Multitopology-Aware Port Capability Sub-TLVs

The sub-TLVs that are part of the Multitopology-aware Port-Capability TLV and that are sent in a TRILL HELLO message are detailed further in the following sections, which include

- Special VLANs and Flags Sub-TLV
- Enabled VLANs Sub-TLV

- Appointed Forwarders Sub-TLV

- Area Address TLV

Special VLANs and Flags Sub-TLV

This TRILL specific TLV is used in TRILL-LAN HELLOs, and its packet format is shown in Figure 3-11.

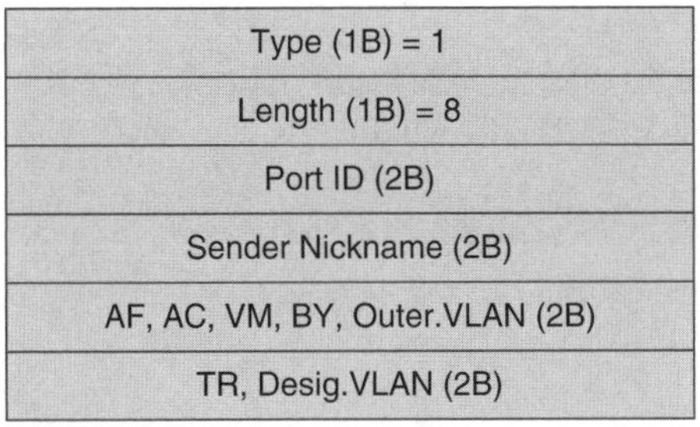

Type (1B) = 1
Length (1B) = 8
Port ID (2B)
Sender Nickname (2B)
AF, AC, VM, BY, Outer.VLAN (2B)
TR, Desig.VLAN (2B)

Figure 3-11 *Special VLAN and Flags Sub-TLV*

The fields in the sub-TLV are explained as follows:

- Port ID is a unique 16-bit value assigned to the port on which the TRILL LAN HELLO is sent.

- The Sender Nickname, as the name implies, is the Nickname of the RBridge sending the HELLO.

- The AF bit is set to 1 if the sending RBridge believes that it is the appointed forwarder for the VLAN and port on which the HELLO is sent.

- The AC bit is set to 1 if the port in which HELLO is sent is configured as an access port. No IS-IS frames or TRILL encapsulated traffic is sent on the access ports except for HELLO frames. Only end station service is supported on such ports. When an RBridge sets this bit, it means it has TRILL disabled for this port.

- Outer.VLAN is the VLAN ID of the frame, which carries this sub-TLV. Usually, this is the same as the VLAN ID of the Ethernet header that carries this IS-IS frame. If it is not the same, this means VLAN mapping has occurred at the sending RBridge.

- The receiving RBridge, if it is a non-DRB, sets the VM bit in all its HELLO packets and frames for a period of two * Holding Time. The DRB on seeing this flag or on detecting a VLAN mapping ensures that there is only one appointed forwarder on that link for all VLANs.

- The BY bit indicates a Bypass Pseudo-node for generating HELLOs.

- The TR bit indicates that the port on which this HELLO is sent is configured as a trunk port. This means all end station services such as native frame encapsulation to

TRILL frames and sending a native frame after decapsulation of a TRILL frame are disabled on this port.

- Desig.VLAN indicates the designated VLAN to be used for this port for all TRILL data traffic, IS-IS traffic, and End Station Address Distribution Information (ESADI) traffic. This VLAN is announced by the DRB. ESADI is explained in later sections of this chapter and in Chapter 5.

Enabled VLANs Sub-TLV:

This is an optional TLV that specifies the list of VLANs for which end station service is enabled on that link. This sub-TLV appears only in TRILL LAN HELLOs. The sub-TLV format is shown in Figure 3-12.

Type (1B) = 2
Length (1B)
RESV, Start VLAN ID (2B)
VLAN Bit MAP (Variable)

Figure 3-12 *Enabled VLANs Sub-TLV*

The length of this sub-TLV depends on the size of the VLAN bit map field. The minimum value of the length field is 3. The Start VLAN ID indicates the starting value of the VLAN ID for which the end station service is enabled. The VLAN bit map field along with the Start VLAN ID indicates the list of VLANs for which the end station service is enabled. The highest-order bit indicates the starting VLAN ID, the next highest-order bit indicates the starting VLAN ID + 1, and so on.

Appointed Forwarders Sub-TLV

This sub-TLV is used by the DRB to inform the other switches about the identity of the appointed forwarder for a group of VLANs. This sub-TLV appears only in TRILL LAN HELLOs. The contents of this sub-TLV are illustrated in Figure 3-13.

Figure 3-13 *Appointed FWD Sub-TLV*

There can be multiple appointee information in a sub-TLV. The length field will be 6 *
n, where n is the number of appointee records and the size of each appointee record is
6. The start VLAN and end VLAN represent the continuous VLAN range for which the
switch identified by the Appointee Nickname field is the appointed forwarder.

Area Address TLV

This TLV is carried in IS-IS HELLO packets, and the content of this TLV specifies the
area that the RBridge originating the HELLO packet belongs to. Usually, all nodes in an
area have the same area address. In TRILL, all RBridges belong to the same Level-1 (L1)
IS-IS area, and the value of the area address is set to zero. Each HELLO packets in TRILL
must have the Area Address TLV listing only the single Area Zero. If an RBridge receives
a HELLO packet from a neighbor with the area address not equal to zero, an adjacency is
not established with that neighbor.

Protocols Supported TLV

This TLV appears in the IS-IS HELLO packets and signifies the network layer protocol
supported by the switches running IS-IS. This TLV carries the Network Layer Protocol
Identifiers (NLPID) field that identifies the protocol supported. The value of NLPID for
TRILL is 0xC0. If an RBridge receives a HELLO packet from a neighbor with a different
NLPID value (not equal to 0xC0), an adjacency is not established with the neighbor.

TRILL and FabricPath Topology Exchange

After the neighbors are identified, the switches start to synchronize their databases.
TRILL and FabricPath do not introduce any changes in this procedure. This section gives
enough details on the topology exchange to understand the complete flow. For additional
details, refer to the IS-IS[1] documentation provided in the "References" section.

The IS-IS database consists of Link State PDUs (LSP) as the fundamental building block,
which the switch has either originated for its adjacencies or has heard from other switches. After an adjacency is established with a neighbor, the two switches exchange information to find out how to effectively synchronize their databases. Exchanging the complete
database does not scale well. So the switches begin by exchanging the description of
their LSPs. Complete Sequence Number PDUs (CSNP) are used for this purpose. The
packet format of the common and PDU specific portion in a CSNP is shown in
Figure 3-14.

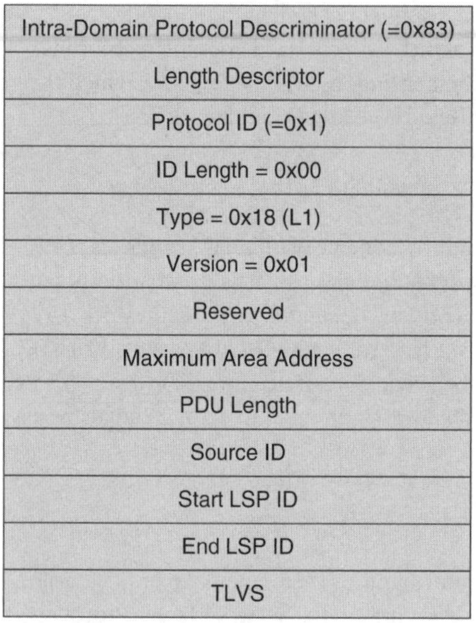

Intra-Domain Protocol Descriminator (=0x83)
Length Descriptor
Protocol ID (=0x1)
ID Length = 0x00
Type = 0x18 (L1)
Version = 0x01
Reserved
Maximum Area Address
PDU Length
Source ID
Start LSP ID
End LSP ID
TLVS

Figure 3-14   *CSNP Format*

Every LSP is assigned a unique ID (LSP ID). After the common header, the PDU-specific header in the CSNP frame consists of the starting and ending LSP ID described in this CSNP. The LSP ID is 8 bytes long. The LSP entries TLV and Authentication TLV are the TLVs that can be carried in a CSNP frame. Every LSP is described by the LSP entry TLV. The LSP entries TLV contains the LSP ID, remaining Lifetime, checksum, and the LSP sequence number. The LSP ID and current sequence number together uniquely identify each LSP. The sequence number starts with zero and is incremented for successive LSPs sent by the originator of the LSP. The number of these TLVs in a CSNP message depends on the number of described LSPs. When a switch receives a CSNP, it finds out if it has a newer, older, or the same version of the LSP as that of the other switch. The starting and ending LSP IDs in the CSNP frame helps the switch to determine the missing LSPs. If the switch does not have an LSP or if it has an older version of an LSP, it requests the other switch to send the complete LSP record. Partial Sequence Number PDU (PSNP) is used to request the other switch for an LSP. PSNP is also used for acknowledgment, as seen in the next section. If the switch has a newer version of the LSP compared to what it received in the CSNP from the adjacent switch, it sends out the complete LSP to the other switch. There are state machines and timers for the loss of CSNP and PSNP messages. After the database synchronization, both the switches have the recent copy of all the LSPs. The packet format of the common and PDU-specific portion in a PSNP is shown in Figure 3-15.

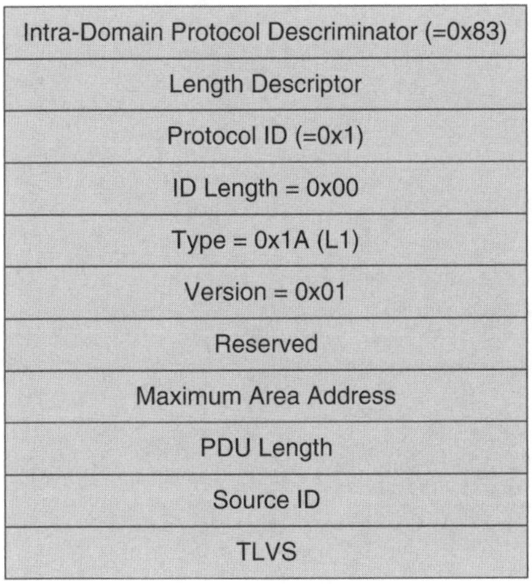

Intra-Domain Protocol Descriminator (=0x83)
Length Descriptor
Protocol ID (=0x1)
ID Length = 0x00
Type = 0x1A (L1)
Version = 0x01
Reserved
Maximum Area Address
PDU Length
Source ID
TLVS

Figure 3-15 *PSNP Frame Format*

Like a CSNP, the TLVs that can be carried in a PSNP are the LSP entries TLV and Authentication TLV. Even for a broadcast network, when a new switch gets attached to the network, the Designated RBridge or switch ensures that the new node has the latest information about all the LSPs. Some modifications are necessary in case of broadcast networks to limit the number of messages sent for database synchronization as given in the IS-IS[1] documentation.

Flooding

After the CSNP/PSNP exchange, the LSPs are exchanged between the switches. The LSP packet format is shown in Figure 3-16.

When a switch receives an LSP that is either not present in its database or is newer than its locally stored version, the received LSP is flooded to all its neighbors except the neighbor from which it was received. After receiving an LSP, a PSNP is sent by a switch as an acknowledgment. A switch can choose to generate a new LSP when any of the following events happen:

- Any of the switch's adjacency information is added, deleted, or modified.
- The metric associated with any of the switch's link changes.
- Any of the switch attributes such as the hostname, System ID, and so on are modified. System ID is a unique value assigned to every switch in an IS-IS network.

After the database exchange happens and when a switch has all the information it needs, it computes the topology and the shortest path to all the other switches in the network. In TRILL and FabricPath, apart from computing the shortest paths, it also needs to do a Nickname or SwitchID resolution and multicast tree computation.

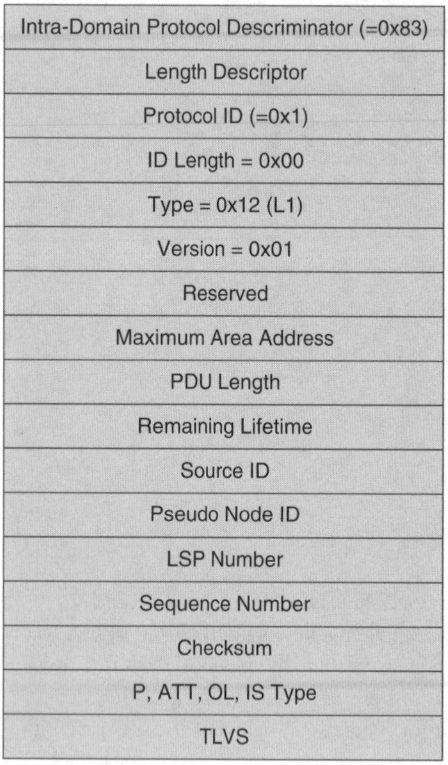

Intra-Domain Protocol Descriminator (=0x83)
Length Descriptor
Protocol ID (=0x1)
ID Length = 0x00
Type = 0x12 (L1)
Version = 0x01
Reserved
Maximum Area Address
PDU Length
Remaining Lifetime
Source ID
Pseudo Node ID
LSP Number
Sequence Number
Checksum
P, ATT, OL, IS Type
TLVS

Figure 3-16   *LSP Frame Format*

Nickname or SwitchID Resolution

In TRILL, every RBridge is uniquely identified by its Nickname. In FabricPath, every switch is uniquely identified by its SwitchID. The control protocol in TRILL and FabricPath ensures that every switch is assigned a unique random Nickname or SwitchID, respectively. Chapter 4 and Chapter 5 detail this procedure of Nickname/SwitchID assignment to some extent. We will concentrate more on the role that IS-IS plays in selecting the Nickname or SwitchID. Every node chooses a random Nickname or SwitchID for itself. You can use the term NodeID from here onward with the understanding that it may represent either a Nickname or a SwitchID. To reduce the probability of collisions, every node after picking a random NodeID, first checks if any of the switches in the network already have the same NodeID. It does this by comparing its selected NodeID with that of the NodeIDs of all the switches in the network present in its locally stored LSP database. After it picks a unique NodeID that is not present in its LSP database, the node announces it to the network using IS-IS. The NodeID can also be configured statically in which case the administrator should ensure that it is unique. In either case, IS-IS announces the NodeID and associates a priority for holding that NodeID. In case of collisions and a tie in the priority, the node with the numerically higher IS-IS

System ID implicitly has more priority to hold the Nickname. A node can have more than one NodeID. The sections on multicast and pseudo-node indicate why this is required. The IS-IS sub-TLVs used by TRILL for distributing this information is the Nickname Sub-TLV. This Sub-TLV falls under the Router Capability TLV and is a part of the LSP. The format of this TLV is shown Figure 3-17.

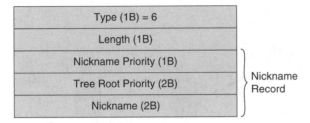

Figure 3-17   *Nickname Sub-TLV*

A node may have more than one Nickname in which case there will be more than one Nickname Record. The fields of the Nickname Record are the self-assigned or configured Nickname, its priority to hold that Nickname, and the tree root priority, which is detailed in the multicast section. The length field will be 5 * n where n is the number of Nickname Records in this Sub-TLV, and the length of each nickname record is 5.

Shortest Path Computation

Every RBridge is identified by its Nickname, which also serves as the addressable entity. In FabricPath, every switch is identified by its SwitchID, which is the addressable entity. After the database exchange happens, a switch will have the complete details of the entire topology. IS-IS Extended ID Reachability TLV is used to announce the neighbor and the cost to reach that neighbor. Every switch runs the shortest path algorithm to compute the shortest paths to all the nodes in the network. Both TRILL and FabricPath support ECMP, which is the capability to support multiple equal cost paths to the destination. The routing table, in its simplest form, consists of a destination switch identified by its Nickname or Switch ID and the set of next-hop switches and the interface through which the next hop switch can be reached.

Distribution Trees Computation

One of the significant features of TRILL and FabricPath is its capability to use IS-IS for multicast routing and not having a separate protocol for multicast. Multicast routing refers to the forwarding of multidestination traffic, which can be broadcast, multicast, or unknown unicast. Because IS-IS is a link state protocol, every node has the complete topology of the network. Apart from computing the shortest paths from itself to every other node, a node can also compute the shortest distribution tree from any node in the network. The computed distribution tree includes all the nodes in the network. The example topology shown in Figure 3-18 has two distribution trees: rooted at nodes RB and RD.

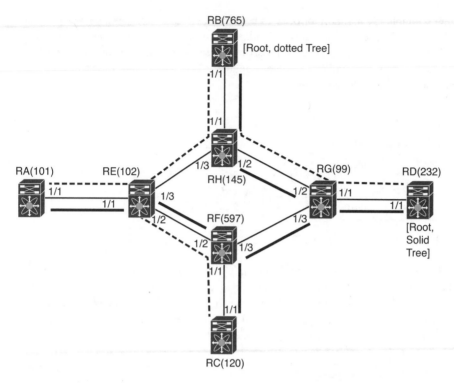

Figure 3-18 *Distribution Tree*

Every node needs to be aware of the number of distribution trees it has to compute
and the root node for each distribution tree. The identity for each tree also needs to be
known and associated for data traffic. The node that informs all the other nodes of such
information (number of trees, root node for each tree, and so on) is the root node for the
entire network. The root node is the node that has advertised the highest value of the
Tree root priority in the Nickname Sub-TLV, as discussed in the earlier sections. The Sub-
TLV is again given in Figure 3-19 for easier reference.

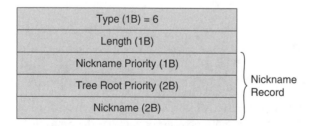

Figure 3-19 *Nickname Sub-TLV*

If all the nodes in the network have advertised the tree root priority as zero or if there's a tie-break in the tree root priority, the node with the numerically highest System ID followed by the Nickname is chosen as the root node. Each node advertises the maximum number of trees it can compute and the number of distribution trees it wants the other nodes in the network to compute. After the root node is elected, the number of distribution trees that will be computed by every node is what had been previously advertised by the root node. This information appears in the Trees Sub-TLV of the Router Capability TLV, as shown in Figure 3-20.

Type (1B) = 7
Length (1B)
Number of Trees to Compute (2B)
Maximum Trees able to Compute (2B)
Number of Trees to Use (2B)

Figure 3-20   *Trees Sub-TLV*

When the number of trees to compute are known, each node needs to know the root for each distribution tree for it to compute the distribution tree. There are two ways in which this information is made available to all the nodes. One is the explicit way in which the root node announces this information in its TLV, and the other is the implicit way in which each node computes this information independently. The elected root node explicitly announces in its Tree Identifiers Sub-TLV about the list of Nicknames where each tree is rooted. The Tree identifiers Sub-TLV is illustrated in Figure 3-21.

Type (1B) = 8
Length (1B)
Starting Tree Number (2B)
Nickname-1 (2B)
Nickname...

Figure 3-21   *Tree Identifiers Sub-TLV*

The Length of this Sub-TLV is 2 * n, where n is the number of Nicknames that appear in this Sub-TLV and the size of each Nickname field is 2 bytes. The starting tree number, as the name suggests is the tree number of the tree that is rooted at the first nickname field in this sub-TLV. The Nickname field refers to the Nickname of the RBridge where the distribution tree is rooted. There can be multiple Nickname fields in this Sub-TLV. For example, if the Starting Tree Number is 1, and there are three Nickname fields, the first distribution tree rooted at the first Nickname will have tree number 1, the second distribution tree rooted at the second Nickname will have tree number 2, and so on.

In the absence of this Sub-TLV, each node computes this information independently as follows. Based on the Trees Sub-TLV, each node knows the number of trees to compute using the locally stored LSP database of all the nodes in the network. Each node numerically orders the following information and comes up with a sorted list.

1. Highest numerical value of Tree Root Priority as given in the Nickname Sub-TLV

2. Highest numerical value of System ID (in case of a tie-break in step 1)

3. Highest numerical value of Nickname (in case of a tie-break in step 2)

After this is done, trees are computed and numbered in the order of priority from this sorted list. The first element in the sorted list (highest numerical priority) is taken, and tree will be computed with the corresponding Nickname as the root. The tree number will be given a value of 1. Then the second element from the sorted list is taken, and the same procedure will be followed and so on. Recall from Nickname Sub-TLV that it is possible for a single node to have multiple Nicknames in which case multiple equal cost distribution trees will be computed from the same node, if possible.

Sometimes, both the approaches need to be applied. This is the case in which the number of Nicknames in the Tree Identifiers Sub-TLV (say, "s") is less than the number of trees to compute field in the Trees Sub-TLV (say, "k"). In such a case, the first "s" trees will be computed and numbered based on Trees Identifiers Sub-TLV as advertised by the root. Then the remaining k − s trees will be computed independently as previously described with tree numbering beginning from s + 1.

Because the distribution tree computation is independently done based on the link state information, it is extremely critical that all the nodes compute an identical distribution tree. The high likelihood of multiple equal cost links results in multiple equal cost paths that, in turn, yield multiple equal cost path trees. In such a scenario, an identical tie-breaking scheme should be used so that all the nodes compute an identical distribution tree. For example, when building a tree number "t" and if a node has "p" equal cost parents, the parents are ordered in numerically ascending order of their System ID's and numbered starting at 0. Then the parent chosen for that node for the tree "t" will be t modulo p.

Sometimes, an RBridge can also announce the tree it will use when sending multidestination traffic. The Trees Used Identifiers Sub-TLV is used for this purpose. This Sub-TLV has the same format as that of Trees Identifiers Sub-TLV except for the Type field, which has the value of 9. The information in this Sub-TLV corresponds to the trees that will be used by the RBridge for multidestination traffic that is injected into the L2MP network from that node.

Pruning the Distribution Tree

The data frames that are sent on the distribution trees are non-unicast frames like broadcast frames, native multicast frames, and unknown unicast frames, that is, frames that yielded a destination MAC address lookup miss in the Layer 2 table. Each distribution tree should be pruned per VLAN. If there are no potential listeners (or receivers) for multidestination traffic downstream, the traffic should be pruned. Further, native Layer 2 and Layer 3 multicast frames should be pruned based on whether there are interested receivers for the multicast frames. The interested receivers for the Layer 3 multicast frames is based on IGMP joins originated by the receiver or if there's a multicast router downstream. Figure 3-22 shows an example of multidestination pruning. The dashed line indicates the tree rooted at node RB, and the X indicates the branches of the tree that are pruned because of the absence of interested receivers.

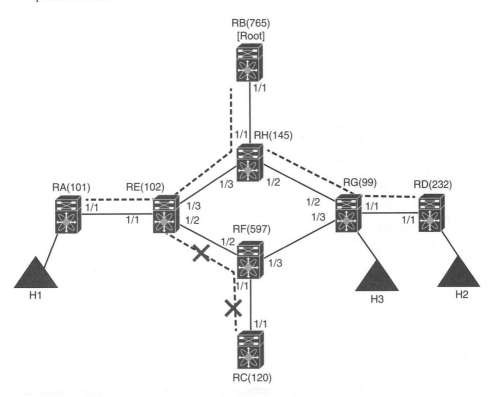

Figure 3-22 *Multicast Pruning*

The edge switches advertise the VLANs and multicast group address it is interested in receiving to the TRILL and FabricPath network using IS-IS TLVs. This information is used by the TRILL and FabricPath switches to prune the multidestination traffic. The information about the interested VLANs and multicast group address is specified in Interested VLANs and Spanning Tree Roots Sub-TLV and Group Address TLV, respectively. The Group Address TLV is a new TLV introduced by TRILL, as shown in Figure 3-23. The value field in this TLV has sub-TLVs that carry the multicast listeners' information.

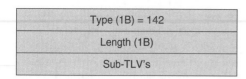

Figure 3-23 *Group Address TLV*

This TLV has a sub-TLV called the Group MAC address Sub-TLV. This sub-TLV lists the multicast group MAC address and if applicable, the source of the multicast traffic. This sub-TLV is used by the other RBridges for pruning the Layer 2 multicast traffic. When this Sub-TLV is originated by a RBridge, this means there are interested receivers for this traffic destined to this Layer 2 multicast group. The format of the Group MAC Address sub-TLV is shown in Figure 3-24.

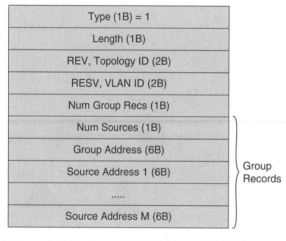

Figure 3-24 *Group MAC Address Sub-TLV*

The Topology ID is not used in TRILL. The VLAN ID field represents the VLAN corresponding to the MAC addresses in this sub-TLV. Num Group Recs denotes the number of group records. Each group record carries the number of sources. If the Num Sources field is zero, it indicates a (*, G) entry, which implies there are receivers for the group address irrespective of the source of the multicast traffic. Otherwise, the group record has the group MAC address and a list of source MAC addresses of the multicast traffic. For pruning the Layer 3 multicast traffic, there are other Sub-TLVs proposed such as Group IPV4 address Sub-TLV and Group IPV6 address Sub-TLV that have not yet been standardized. The formats of these Sub-TLVs are similar and carry the IPV4 or IPV6 Group and source addresses.

The Interested VLANs and Spanning Tree Roots Sub-TLV is included in the Router Capability TLV. It consists of a set of VLANs for which the originating switch is the appointed forwarder. This Sub-TLV also has information about whether the originating switch has any IPV4 or IPV6 multicast routers connected to it. The format of this Sub-TLV is shown in Figure 3-25.

Type (1B) = 10
Length (1B)
Nickname (2B)
M4, M6, VLAN_Start, VLAN_End (4B)
Appointed Forwarder Status Lost Counter (4B)
Root RBridges (6*nB)

Figure 3-25 *Interested VLAN and Spanning Tree Roots Sub-TLV*

The Nickname field is used to associate a Nickname with the group of VLANs specified in this Sub-TLV. The reason for this field is that it is likely for an RBridge to have more than one Nickname, and it can associate different Nicknames for different VLAN ranges. M4, M6 flags specify if the RBridge has any multicast IPV4, IPV6 routers, respectively, connected to it. If an RBridge has multicast routers connected to it, Layer 3 multicast frames belonging to the VLAN as well as IGMP and MLD membership reports should be sent to this RBridge so that it can be forwarded to the multicast router. The other fields indicate the number of times an RBridge has lost the appointed forwarder status and the spanning tree Root Bridges IDs for this VLAN range.

The Interested VLAN Sub-TLV can be used for pruning unknown unicast traffic from going to all the egress RBridges. The Group Address Sub-TLV can be used to prune the multicast traffic based on if there are potential listeners behind an egress RBridge.

FabricPath follows a similar procedure for multicast. It uses the FTAG field in the header to identify the multicast tree. It has similar Sub-TLVs that achieve the previously described multicast functionalities.

ESADI

ESADI is specific to TRILL and is detailed in Chapter 5. ESADI stands for end station address distribution information protocol. This is a means for statically distributing the end host's MAC address and associating it with an RBridge. By statically distributing such information, flooding in the TRILL cloud because of destination lookup miss in the Layer 2 table is minimized. The general frame format of ESADI is shown in Figure 3-26.

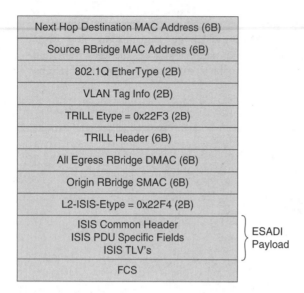

Next Hop Destination MAC Address (6B)
Source RBridge MAC Address (6B)
802.1Q EtherType (2B)
VLAN Tag Info (2B)
TRILL Etype = 0x22F3 (2B)
TRILL Header (6B)
All Egress RBridge DMAC (6B)
Origin RBridge SMAC (6B)
L2-ISIS-Etype = 0x22F4 (2B)
ISIS Common Header ISIS PDU Specific Fields ISIS TLV's
FCS

ESADI Payload

Figure 3-26 *ESADI Payload*

ESADI frames are regular IS-IS frames encapsulated in a TRILL header. The ESADI information can be sent to all participating ESADI RBridges in which case the outer destination MAC address will be an all-RBridges multicast address. If the ESADI information is sent to only a specific RBridge, the outer destination MAC address will be the next-hop RBridge's MAC address. The ESADI PDU consists of a list of end station MAC addresses reachable through the RBridge that originates the ESADI frame along with the confidence level in this information. The confidence level may be used by the receiving RBridge to decide whether to use the information learned through the ESADI frame for forwarding.

MAC Reachability TLV

This TLV specifies the list of end station MAC addresses reachable through the originating RBridge. The content of this TLV is shown in Figure 3-27.

Type (1B) = 147
Length (1B)
Topology ID/Nickname (2B)
Confidence (1B)
RESV, VLAN ID (2B)
MAC 1 (6B)
...
MAC n (6B)

Figure 3-27 *MAC Reachability TLV*

The length field is set to 5 + 6 * n bytes where n is the number of MAC addresses appearing in this TLV. When the Topology ID field is zero, it refers to the MAC address being reachable from all topologies. Confidence field refers to the confidence level in the information, and the value assigned to it is implementation-specific. VLAN ID specifies the VLAN corresponding to all the MAC addresses listed in this TLV. The list of MAC address refers to the end station MAC addresses. As of this writing, there aren't many TLVs defined for ESADI. Refer to the publications of the IETF TRILL working group for up-to-date information.

Fine Grained Labeling

Fine Grained Labeling (FGL) is a concept in TRILL that enables the number of service instances to go beyond 4 K. This is done by introducing a new Ethertype (0x893b) in the inner payload and having a 4-byte value to represent the service instance. This is a work in progress as of this writing. During data packet forwarding, the inner payload is examined for both unicast and multidestination traffic. For unicast traffic, the core RBridges examine the inner payload for computing the hash to be used for ECMP. For multidestination traffic, the inner payload is examined for pruning purposes. If an RBridge does not understand the new Ethertype introduced for FGL, it can drop the frame. For this reason, FGL traffic should never go through RBridges that have not implemented FGL because the behavior is unpredictable. It is essential for every RBridge to advertise through IS-IS if it supports FGL (called FGL-Safe RBridges). When that is done, the FGL safe RBridge advertises the cost of the link connecting to an FGL-unsafe RBridge to a high value ($2^{24} - 2$). Then, the path through the FGL Safe – FGL Unsafe link will be taken only if there are no alternative paths. In addition to advertising this high cost, if a frame still arrives at an FGL safe RBridge to be forwarded out of the FGL safe – FGL unsafe link, the FGL safe RBridge drops the frame if it tries to egress out to the FGL unsafe RBridge. If the RBridge does not have the capability to drop such frames, it blocks the FGL Safe – FGL unsafe link by advertising the cost to be $2^{24} - 1$. This is detailed in Chapter 5. The method proposed by which an RBridge advertises if it is FGL safe is through the TRILL version Sub-TLV. This can be present in either Router Capability TLV or MT Capability TLV. The format of TRILL Version Sub-TLV[8] is shown in Figure 3-28.

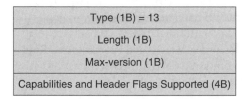

Figure 3-28 *TRILL Version Sub-TLV*

The max-version field indicates the maximum version supported by this RBridge. The capabilities and header flags are 32-bits wide. Bits 0 through 13 indicate the support of optional capabilities. If the bit is 1, it indicates that particular capability is supported. A proposal was made to have an FGL-safe bit in this 4-byte field; however, its position is still unknown as of this writing. Bits 14 through 31 indicate the TRILL extended header flags.

An FGL-safe RBridge should also indicate the list of FGLs that it is interested in receiving. This means the RBridge has hosts that belong to this mapped instance. Similarly, for multicast traffic, an RBridge should also indicate the FGL of the multicast group address it is interested in receiving. This information is mainly used for pruning the multidestination traffic by an FGL-safe RBridge. For VLANs (or non-FGL), such information was carried in IS-IS using Interested VLANs and Spanning Tree Root Sub-TLV and GMAC Address Sub-TLV. For FGL, Interested Labels and Spanning Tree Root Sub-TLV[8] and Group Labelled MAC-address Sub-TLV[8] are introduced that carry this information. The format of Interested Labels and Spanning Tree Root Sub-TLV is shown in Figure 3-29.

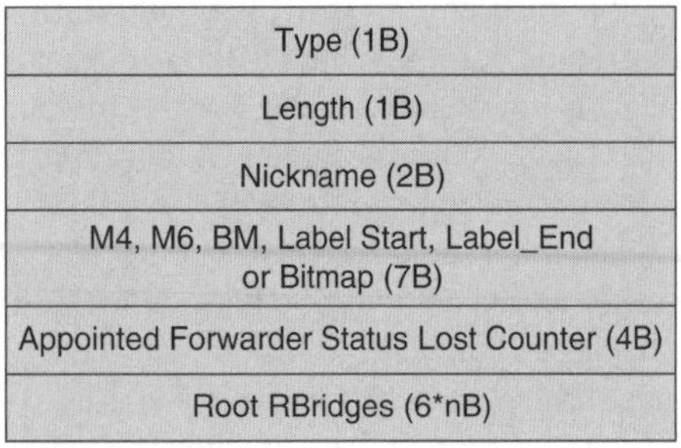

Type (1B)
Length (1B)
Nickname (2B)
M4, M6, BM, Label Start, Label_End or Bitmap (7B)
Appointed Forwarder Status Lost Counter (4B)
Root RBridges (6*nB)

Figure 3-29   *Interested Labels and Spanning Tree Roots Sub-TLV*

The Label Start field indicates the starting value of the label that the RBridge is interested in receiving. The "BM" bit indicates if the Label End field is a numerical value or a bit map. If the BM bit is 0, the starting and ending values of the interested labels are specified in Label Start and Label End, respectively. If the BM bit is 1, Label_End is represented as a bit map. The starting label specified in Label_Start, when added with the bit number in the bitmap field that has a 1 gives the list of interested labels. For example, if bit number 10 is 1, and starting label is 100, then the RBridge is interested in label 110. The other fields convey the same meaning as Interested VLANs and Spanning Tree Root Sub-TLV except that the scope is label instead of the VLAN. The packet format of Group Labeled MAC-address Sub-TLV is shown in Figure 3-30.

The fine grained label field indicates the label or service instance of all the MAC address fields in this Sub-TLV. The other fields were already described in GMAC Address Sub-TLV.

Type (1B)
Length (1B)
RESV, Topology ID (2B)
Fine Grained Label (3B)
Num Group Recs (1B)
Num Sources (1B)
Group Address (6B)
Source 1 Address (6B)
....
Source M Address (6B)

Figure 3-30   *Group Labeled Address Sub-TLV*

Pseudo Node

TRILL supports Link-aggregation in which multiple RBridges can be connected to a source. Chapter 5 details the problem and solution. Here, the issues and the role IS-IS plays in the solution are briefly discussed. This is a work in progress as of this writing. Consider the sample topology illustrated in Figure 3-31.

Both RB1 and RB2 are connected to the source S through a LAG. The issues and solutions for this follow:

1. **MAC Move Issue:** Source S can send a frame to either RB1 or RB2. When RB1 and RB2 encapsulate the frame, it uses its own Nickname in the source Nickname field in the TRILL header. For some flow, the traffic could ingress through RB1, and for others it could ingress through RB2. When the Egress RBridge performs source Mac address learning after decapsulating the frame, it appears as a MAC Move because for the same end host address, the source Nickname field can alter between RB1 and RB2. To solve this, both RB1 and RB2 chose a common pseudo Nickname and use it as the source Nickname when encapsulating the native frame. Each RBridge uses the Nickname Sub-TLV to announce the pseudo Nickname apart from its regular Nickname. Nickname Sub-TLV was already discussed in the earlier sections.

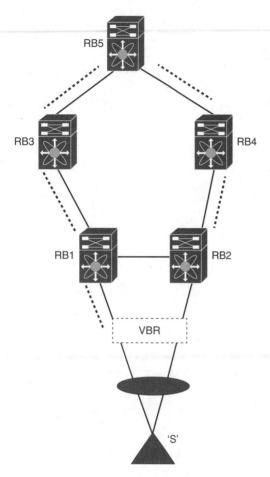

Figure 3-31 *Pseudo-Node*

2. **Reverse Path Forwarding Check Issue:** By choosing a common Nickname, the MAC move issue is solved. But this introduces another issue wherein for multidestination frames, the RPF check fails. Consider Figure 3-31 because the pseudo-node (VBR) also appears as a node with a Nickname, the distribution tree also includes it as a node. In this example, RB5 can receive a multidestination frame with the source Nickname as VBR only through RB3 because otherwise the RPF check will fail. The way this issue is resolved is by associating different trees to different member RBridges. Because in TRILL there can be multiple multidestination trees, RB1 and RB2 can independently choose trees such that the trees chosen by RB1 and RB2 are different. For example, if there are four trees, RB1 can choose tree number 1 and 3, and RB2 can choose tree number 2 and 4. When sourcing a multidestination frame, RB1 uses only trees 1 and 3, and RB2 uses only trees 2 and 4. Refer to Chapter 5 for more details regarding how this information can be computed independently without overlapping. After this is computed, both RB1 and RB2 announce using IS-IS their

affinity toward a tree. Then, when other RBridges receive this information, they store this information in the relevant hardware or software tables so that the RPF check does not fail when multidestination frames arrive from a pseudo-node with the right affiliated tree. RBridges use the Affinity Sub-TLV[8] that falls under Router Capability TLV for this purpose. The content of this Sub-TLV is shown in Figure 3-32. There can be multiple affinity records, and the length field includes the size of all affinity records. The Nickname field specifies the association of the multidestination trees listed in this Sub-TLV through the originating RBridge. The Affinity flags are reserved for future use. The Number of trees field, as the name suggests specifies the number of trees for which affinity is announced in this Sub-TLV. The tree num of roots field gives the tree number of the distribution tree for which affinity is announced.

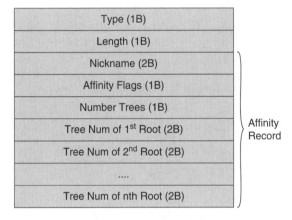

Figure 3-32 *Affinity Sub-TLV*

Multi Topology Routing

The concept of Multi Topology Routing (MTR) is to construct multiple logical topologies to achieve service differentiation. To support MTR, it is required to construct a separate forwarding table for each topology. A frame is classified into a topology at the ingress, and some extensions are proposed in TRILL to carry the topology information in the TRILL overlay header. FabricPath has had support for MTR since the beginning, and its header (through FTAG field) has provisions to carry the topology information. Based on the topology information in the header, a lookup is done in the appropriate forwarding table. To construct a separate forwarding table for each topology, the RBridges should advertise the topology that they want to be a part of. Refer to Chapter 5 on TRILL for more details on MTR. There should be a provision in IS-IS to exchange the topology information, the tag associated with each topology, and if an RBridge is capable of Multi Topology Routing. As of this writing, there's no standard or work in progress that details how this information is carried in IS-IS for TRILL. Refer to the publications from the IETF TRILL working group for the latest information.

Summary

This chapter covered the control plane aspects of TRILL and FabricPath. Both TRILL and FabricPath use IS-IS with some extensions as their control protocol. A brief overview of IS-IS was given followed by a detailed description of the changes that were made in IS-IS to support TRILL. This chapter focused primarily on the IS-IS–related changes including the packet format of the newly introduced TLVs for TRILL. The forwarding and architecture concepts in TRILL and FabricPath were touched upon briefly to give some context. Study Chapters 4 and Chapter 5 to get a thorough understanding of the architecture and forwarding concepts.

References

1. "OSI IS-IS Intra-Domain Routing Protocol" – RFC 1142.

2. "OSPF Version 2," RFC 2328.

3. "RIP Version 2," RFC 2453.

4. "Introduction to EIGRP," http://www.cisco.com/en/US/tech/tk365/technologies_tech_note09186a0080093f07.shtml.

5. "Extensions to IS-IS for Layer 2 Systems," RFC 6165.

6. "Use of OSI IS-IS for Routing in TCP/IP and Dual Environments," RFC 1195.

7. "IS-IS Extensions for Advertising Router Information," RFC 4971.

8. "TRILL Use of IS-IS," http://datatracker.ietf.org/doc/draft-ietf-isis-rfc6326bis/ (Status – Requested for publication).

Additional Resources

- "RBridges Base Protocol Specification," RFC 6325.

- "RBridges Adjacency," RFC 6327.

- "TRILL Use of IS-IS," RFC 6326.

- *OSPF and IS-IS: Choosing an IGP for Large-Scale Networks* by Jeff Doyle.

- "Extensions to IS-IS for Layer-2 Systems," RFC 6165.

Chapter 4

FabricPath

This chapter has the following objectives.

- **FabricPath overview:** This section provides an overview of the requirement and benefits of FabricPath.

- **FabricPath architecture:** This section starts with FabricPath encapsulation details and then delves into the architectural details including control protocols and Layer 2 learning in a FabricPath network.

- **FabricPath STP interaction:** This section describes the interactions with Spanning Tree Protocol (STP) when a legacy Layer 2 network is connected to a FabricPath network.

- **FabricPath packet forwarding:** This section provides details of sample unicast, multicast, and broadcast packet flows in a FabricPath network.

- **FabricPath basic configuration:** This section outlines the steps required to enable FabricPath on a Nexus 7000/6000/5000 switch.

This chapter covers the architecture and implementation techniques of deploying FabricPath in a data center. The first section provides an overview of FabricPath. The subsequent sections cover in detail the architecture, forwarding, configuration, and verification of data forwarding in FabricPath networks. Finally, after you go through different aspects of FabricPath, the chapter covers its main benefits to the Layer 2 networks.

The FabricPath architecture section is the most important section and describes FabricPath operation, so you should cover this section before moving on to the configuration section.

FabricPath Overview

The increase in the adoption of virtualization in data centers has changed the way the data center networks are deployed. The latest data center network trend is not only toward the hosting of more-and-more applications, but also moving the users' computational load to the virtual machines in the data centers. This has led to the evolution of Massively Scalable Data Centers (MSDCs). This evolution of huge data centers; the requirement of virtual machine mobility; and the need to have any-to-any communication between the different workloads, both physical and virtual, necessitates a scalable and resilient data center fabric. So the evolution of MSDC and virtualization technologies has led to the need for large Layer 2 domains. The existing STP-based Layer 2 switching has some limitations that has led to the evolution of technologies such as TRILL and FabricPath. These limitations include

- **No multipathing support:** STP protocol creates loop-free topologies in the Layer 2 networks by blocking redundant paths. To achieve this, STP uses a root election process. After the root is elected, all the other switches build shortest paths to the root switch and block other ports. This enables the Layer 2 network to achieve a loop-free topology. The side effect of this is that all redundant paths are blocked in the Layer 2 network. Although, some enhancements were done, especially with the use of Per VLAN Spanning Tree Protocol (PVSTP), it has its own limitations where the load balancing is per VLAN-based-only.

- **STP leads to inefficient path selection:** As the shortest path is computed from the root bridge, the available path between switches depends upon the location of the root bridge; therefore, the path available is not necessarily a shortest path between the switches. For example, consider two access switches that are connected to a distribution switch and to each other. Now if the distribution switch is the STP root bridge, the link between the two access switches will get blocked and all traffic between the two access layer switches takes, the suboptimal path through the distribution switch.

- **Unavailability of features such as Time-To-Live (TTL):** The Layer 2 packet header doesn't have fields like TTL. This can pose serious problems if loops are formed in the network, where the frames can loop forever. This can lead to network meltdown in switched networks because a forwarding loop can cause a broadcast packet to be exponentially duplicated.

- **MAC address scalability:** Nonhierarchical flat addressing of the Ethernet MAC address leads to limited scalability as MAC address summarization becomes impossible to achieve. Moreover, the any-to-any requirement results in all the MAC addresses being essentially populated in all switches in the Layer 2 network leading to a large requirement for Layer 2 table sizes.

These shortcomings of Layer 2 networks are resolved by Layer 3 routing protocols, which provide multipathing and efficient shortest path from among all nodes in the network without any limitations. Although the Layer 3 network design solves these issues, it makes the network design static. The static network design limits the use of virtualization technologies. FabricPath marries the two technologies together to provide flexibility of Layer 2 networks and scaling of the Layer 3 networks.

FabricPath has pioneered to solve this problem in the MSDC space by employing a Layer 2 fabric overlay. Cisco introduced FabricPath technology in Cisco Nexus OS Software Release 5.1(3). It started with the idea of bringing the benefits provided by the routing protocols in Layer 3 networks to the Layer 2 Ethernet environments. The FabricPath technology was introduced on Nexus 7000 line cards and as of this writing Nexus 7000/6000/5000 switches support FabricPath technology. FabricPath has been in existence for a couple years and is a mature technology. By using the best characteristics of traditional Layer 2 and Layer 3 technologies, FabricPath provides a new control plane and data plane implementation.

Like spanning tree, FabricPath provides an operational plug-and-play deployment model along with the stability, convergence, and Equal Cost Multi-Pathing (ECMP), which are typical of a Layer 3 routed environment. This is achieved with Layer 2 Intermediate-System-to-Intermediate-System (IS-IS) protocol. This results in a scalable, flexible, and highly available Ethernet fabric suitable for even the most demanding data center environments. The following sections outline the benefits of enabling FabricPath.[1]

FabricPath Architecture

This section starts with the high-level architecture followed by delving into its details, including

- FabricPath encapsulation

- FabricPath control plane protocols (IS-IS)

- FabricPath Dynamic Resource Allocation Protocol (DRAP)

- FabricPath address learning

From a high-level architecture perspective, FabricPath enables administrators to incrementally upgrade their classical Layer 2 network to FabricPath mode. This enables the switch to operate some ports in the classical Ethernet mode and other ports in FabricPath mode.

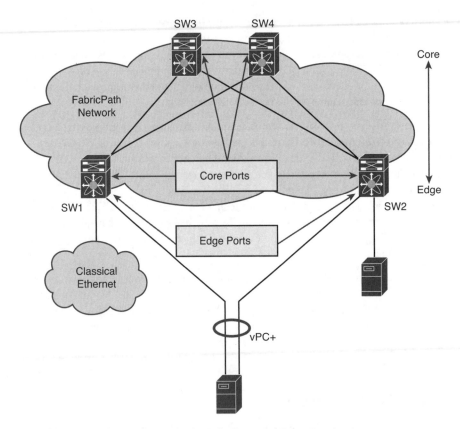

Figure 4-1   *FabricPath Network with Core and Edge Devices*

Core and Edge

Figure 4-1 shows a FabricPath network with core edge devices with Sw1, Sw2 as the edge devices and Sw3 and Sw4 as the core devices. FabricPath networks have two types of switch functionalities: core and edge. This functionality is based on the where the switch is placed:

- **Edge devices:** As the name suggests these devices are connected to the edge of the FabricPath network and have two kinds of ports: (a) connected to Classic Ethernet devices including servers, routers, and other compute devices and (b) ports connected to the FabricPath core. The edge devices also map the MAC addressed to the destination Switch-ID. These are the only devices that have knowledge of the host MAC addresses.

- **Core devices:** Core devices interconnect edge devices or other core devices. These devices switch traffic based on the destination Switch-ID and FTAG in the FabricPath header.

Addressing Concepts

Each of the switches in the FabricPath networks has a unique identifier called Switch-ID. Even though manual configuration of Switch-IDs is allowed, to enable plug-and-play functionality, the Switch-IDs are dynamically assigned using the Dynamic Resource Allocation Protocol (DRAP). Switch-id has global significance within a given FabricPath cluster making Switch-ID common to all forwarding instances on the FabricPath network. FabricPath builds the Layer 2 forwarding tables by learning the end hosts MAC addresses against the Switch-ID. Another forwarding table of Switch-IDs is built using the modified Layer 2 IS-IS control protocol.

VLANs

Because the FabricPath header does not have the provision to carry the VLAN, it is mandatory for the inner payload to carry the 802.1q header so that the destination switch can associate the frame with the correct VLAN. The 802.1Q tag has the original VLAN ID of the frame. So from the perspective of VLAN, the FabricPath ports act like trunks.

vPC+

A virtual PortChannel (vPC) was introduced on the Nexus switches to enable links physically connected to two different switches to appear as a single PortChannel. As shown in Figure 4-1, a host or classical Ethernet switch can be connected to two FabricPath edge switches by using an ether channel. This is achieved using the concept of an emulated switch (vPC+). The emulated switch configuration enables Layer 2 multipathing by emulating a virtual switch. The Switch-ID of the virtual switch is used as the outer source address in the FabricPath network enabling the return traffic to be load balanced. For details on vPC+, refer to Chapter 7, "FabricPath Migration, Deployment, and Troubleshooting."

Figure 4-1 also depicts the core and edge ports in the FabricPath network along with a vPC+ connection to a host device.

On the core ports IS-IS is the control plane of choice that runs on FabricPath-enabled switches. Using FabricPath IS-IS, the switches build their forwarding table, which is similar to building the forwarding table in Layer 3 networks. FabricPath IS-IS maintains a complete link state database enabling the switches or nodes to compute pair-wise multiple equal cost optimal paths for unicast traffic. In contrast to Layer 3 networks, where typically Protocol Independent Multicast (PIM) is used to support multicast, in FabricPath multiple forwarding trees routed at different nodes are computed using the same control protocol (IS-IS).[1]

Figure 4-2 shows the unicast shortest paths from Switch Sw1 to Switch Sw3, where there are three equal cost paths available through Switches Sw4, Sw5, and Sw6, respectively.

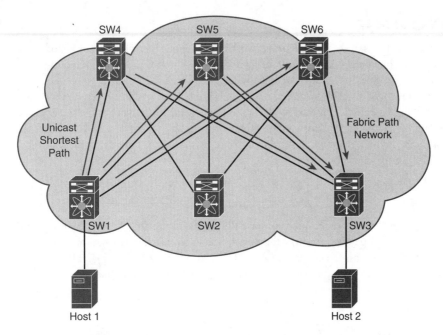

Figure 4-2   *FabricPath Unicast Equal Cost Paths*

Figure 4-3 shows two multicast distribution trees rooted at Sw4 and Sw6 for the same example topology. Multicast traffic is load balanced using the two multicast trees. The system uses a hash function to load balance multicast traffic across the two trees.

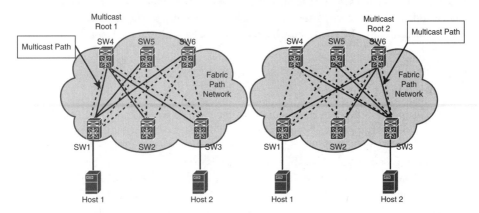

Figure 4-3   *FabricPath Multicast Tree*

The FabricPath header has hop count as one of the fields, which mitigates temporary loops in the Layer 2 FabricPath networks. When a packet enters a FabricPath network, it is prepended with a FabricPath header at the ingress switch. This FabricPath header is stripped off when the packet leaves the FabricPath network at the egress switch. Figure 4-4 shows the encapsulation and decapsulation in the FabricPath network.

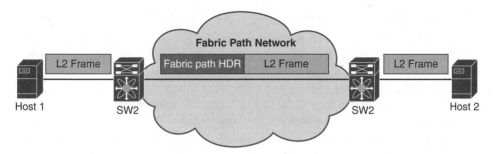

Figure 4-4 *FabricPath Encapsulation and Decapsulation*

In the FabricPath network the frame is switched using the FabricPath tag (FTAG) and Switch-ID in the FabricPath header. (See the subsequent section for details of the FabricPath header.) In a FabricPath network a set of VLANs that have the same forwarding behavior are mapped to a forwarding instance. FabricPath enables different topologies to be constructed for different VLANs. For example, if an enterprise has three sets of VLANs, that is, a VLAN group, gold consists of VLANs 1–10, VLAN group bronze consists of VLANs 11–20, and VLAN group silver consists of VLANs 21–30. The enterprise can map each group gold, bronze, and silver to different topologies (FTAG defines a topology) in the FabricPath network. The different topologies for VLANs could be used by the administrator for traffic engineering, security, or other administrative purposes.

FabricPath Encapsulation

The FabricPath header uses locally assigned hierarchical MAC addresses for forwarding frames in the FabricPath network. As shown if Figure 4-5, the original Layer 2 frame is encapsulated with a FabricPath header that consists of a new outer source MAC address, destination outer MAC addresses, and FTAG. A new CRC is appended to the existing packet. In the FabricPath network for unicast, the 12-bit destination Switch-ID and FTAG are used for forwarding.

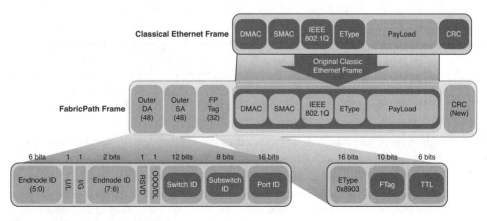

Figure 4-5 *FabricPath Header*

The various fields in the FabricPath header along with description follow:

Switch-id: Each of the switches in a FabricPath network has a unique identifier called the Switch-ID. The Switch-ID could be allocated manually or dynamically through the Switch-ID allocation protocol. Switch-id is unique for a FabricPath switch and has global significance within a given FabricPath cluster making Switch-ID common to all forwarding instances on the FabricPath switch, whereas other hierarchical fields including sub-Switch-ID, port-id/local-id, and endnode-ID are local to the switch.

Sub-Switch-ID: The sub-Switch-ID is an 8-bit value introduced for vPC+ (for details on vPC+ refer to Chapter 7) and must be unique within each vPC+ virtual switch domain. FabricPath switches running vPC+ use sub-Switch-ID field (optionally) to identify vPC+ PortChannel.

port-id/Local-id: As the name suggests, the port-id/local-id was introduce to iden- tify a port to which a host is connected. This identifier can be used at the ingress switch to make a forwarding decision and output the frame to the correct edge-port without doing any additional MAC address table lookup at the destination switch. The destination switch can ignore this field; in this case the destination switch has to do an additional MAC lookup to forward the frame on to the right egress port. This field is used in a special way for frames sourced or destined from the vPC+ PortChannel; the port-id field is set to a common value shared by both vPC+ peer switches; and the sub-Switch-ID is used to select the outgoing port.

Endnode-id: Hierarchical MAC addresses reduce the MAC address table size require- ments. Each end-host located behind a single edge-port can be assigned a hierarchi- cal MAC address, whereas the Local-id and Switch/Sub-Switch-ID are the same, but the Endnode-id is different and identifies the host connected to the port.

U/L bit: This bit is set by FabricPath switches in the outer unicast source and desti- nation MAC address fields. This bit indicates that the MAC address is locally admin- istered and is not universally unique. This bit is needed to indicate that the outer source and destination fields are not standard MAC addresses.

OOO/DL: This can be used in a FabricPath network to specify that the frames with this bit set can be load balanced across multiple paths without taking the flow of the packet into account. Typically, a flow is identified by the standard 5-tuple, namely SourceIP, DestIP, TransportProtocol, SrcPort, and DestPort. This bit enables per- packet load balancing. In a typical network, to avoid reordering, frames from the same flow are sent on the same path. Reordering of frames can reduce the efficiency of high-level protocols such as TCP, but for protocols that are agnostic to reordering of frames, better load balancing can be achieved by transporting frames across mul- tiple paths on a per-packet basis.

Ethertype: FabricPath uses 0x8903 as the ether type to convey that the frame is not a standard Ethernet frame but is a FabricPath frame.

FTAG: Forwarding tag is a 10-bit identifier that together with the type of destination address (unicast, broadcast, or multicast) selects the path through a set of possible links along which the frame is forwarded. In essence, the FTAG identifies the topol- ogy along which the frame is forwarded (tree for multidestination frames). The decision of which topology or tree along which a frame is forwarded via the FabricPath network is typically done by the ingress switch based on the selected FTAG. In the FabricPath network, after the FTAG is assigned at the ingress switch, it is honored by all subsequent switches.

Time-To-Live: Like traditional IP forwarding, the TTL field serves the same purpose in FabricPath. Each switch decrements the TTL by 1, and if the TTL becomes "0", the frames are discarded. The TTL setting prevents Layer 2 frames from looping endlessly in case of any intermittent loops.

FabricPath Control Plane Protocols

To exchange reachability information for both unicast and multicast traffic, FabricPath uses IS-IS as the control protocol. The choice of IS-IS was driven mainly by two factors:

1. IS-IS is flexible and enables extensions through new TLVs.

2. IS-IS runs directly over the link layer, thereby obviating the need for any underlying Layer 3 protocol like IP to work.

Several extensions to standard IS-IS are introduced for FabricPath support. FabricPath Layer 2 IS-IS is used to build shortest path trees for all kinds of traffic including unicast, broadcast, and multicast traffic. These were covered in detail in Chapter 3, "IS-IS." Following is a brief summary of the main IS-IS extensions for the FabricPath networks.[2]

- Unlike the IS-IS standard implementation, FabricPath devices are in a single Layer 1 IS-IS area without any hierarchical Layer 1 or Layer 2.

- FabricPath Layer 2 IS-IS uses a different MAC address from the Layer 3 IS-IS instances.

- New nonstandard sub-TLVs have been added including the one that carries Switch-ID, FTAG, and so on.

- In FabricPath, Layer 2 IS-IS is a link-state protocol to compute the shortest path by all devices to all other devices using the shortest-path first (SPF) algorithm.

- To provide ECMP, the standard IS-IS functionality is used by FabricPath Layer 2 IS-IS and populates up to 16 routes.

- Multiple distribution trees can be constructed in FabricPath to forward multidestination traffic. The root for each of these trees is announced the Router Capability TLV in IS-IS. The FTAG in the FabricPath header identifies the tree. The ingress switch in a FabricPath network can load balance the multidestination traffic by picking different trees.

In today's Layer 2 networks, VLANs play a key role in subnet management. In FabricPath the topologies are built using the Layer 2 IS-IS, and after the administrator configures the mode FabricPath under the VLAN, it is assigned to a topology. By default all the VLANs configured in FabricPath mode are assigned the default IS-IS topology 0, but for traffic engineering purposes, the administrator can create multiple topologies and can group FabricPath VLANs to different topologies. Figure 4-6 shows the multiple topologies in a FabricPath network.

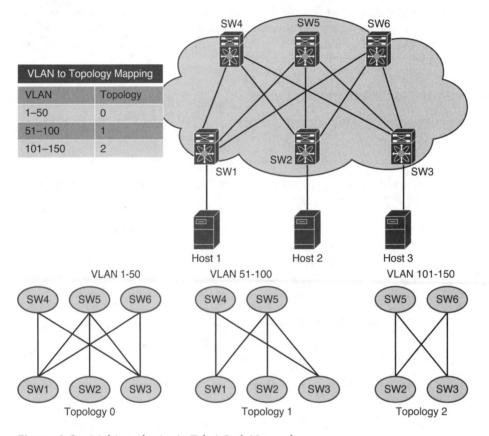

Figure 4-6 *Multitopologies in FabricPath Network*

As of this writing FabricPath creates two distribution trees to forward multidestination frames and uses the first tree with FTAG 1 to carry unknown unicast, multicast, and broadcast traffic. The second tree is used for load-balanced multicast traffic. The switch with the configurable highest priority becomes the root of the first tree. When multiple switches have the same priority, the system ID in the IS-IS header and further the Switch-ID of a switch is used to resolve the tie. The Figure 4-7 shows the broadcast graph for topology where Switch Sw4 is the broadcast root (FTAG1).

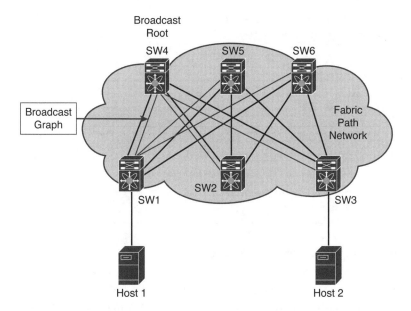

Figure 4-7   *Broadcast Graph in FabricPath Network*

After the root for the first tree with FTAG1 is elected, this node or switch identifies another switch, which becomes the root of the second multidestination tree. Figure 4-8 shows the FabricPath topology with Switch Sw4 and Switch Sw6 as the multicast roots of the two multicast trees. The figure also shows their corresponding multicast graphs.

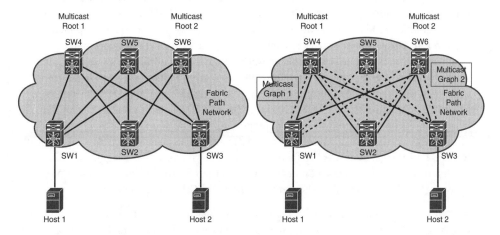

Figure 4-8   *FabricPath Network with Corresponding Multicast Graphs*

From the best practices perspective, it is recommended that the two roots are chosen by the administrator to make the root of these trees deterministic. Example 4-1 shows the configuration on core for root choice.

Example 4-1   *Core Switch Configuration for Root*

```
/* To make  SW4 (Core) as root of first tree */
SW4# conf t
SW4(config)# fabricpath domain default
SW4(config-fabricpath-isis)# root-priority 64
SW4(config-fabricpath-isis)#


/* To make SW 5 (Core) as root of second tree */
SW6#conf t
SW6(config)# fabricpath domain default
SW6(config-fabricpath-isis)# root-priority 63
SW6(config-fabricpath-isis)#
```

IGMP Snooping in FabricPath Multicast Networks

In IPv4 multicast networks, the Ethernet switch uses Internet Group Management Protocol (IGMP) snooping to restrict multicast traffic to the portions of the network that have interested receivers. In IPv6 multicast networks, the Ethernet switch uses Multicast Listener Protocol (MLD) snooping to restrict multicast traffic to the portions of the network that have interested receivers. IGMP snooping keeps track of the edge ports that have multicast hosts and routers. IGMP snooping also keeps track of the groups that the hosts are interested in.

The FabricPath network appears as a single switch to the hosts connected to it via edge ports, so IGMP snooping is done at the edges of the FabricPath network, and the information learned through this snooping process is relayed to IS-IS. IS-IS in turn distributes this information to all the switches in the FabricPath network using the Group membership LSP. Using this information, each switch in the FabricPath network builds the multicast forwarding state. Using this forwarding state, the FabricPath switches know to which multicast tree to send the frames related to a given multicast group. In addition, the switch uses the pruning information that it had learned from the group membership LSP to decide the outgoing interfaces so that the FTAG selected multicast tree at the ingress can be appropriately and optimally pruned to avoid sending traffic to a portion of the network where there are no interested receivers. The primary benefit of using IS-IS to build multicast state in a FabricPath network is that it appears as a single switch to the rest of the network. This prevents the need to run multiple protocols such as MLD snooping, PIM snooping, and so on in the core of the FabricPath network.

Routed unicast and multicast is not considered in this chapter because it has no implication on how the FabricPath network works. For Layer 3 unicast and multicast deployment with FabricPath, refer to Chapter 7.

FabricPath Dynamic Resource Allocation Protocol

For unicast or unidestination traffic, a FabricPath network uses two key identifiers for the data packet forwarding:

■ Switch-ID

■ FTAG

For multidestination traffic, FTAG is used to select the appropriate multicast tree along which the packet should be forwarded. In a FabricPath network, Switch-ID uniquely identifies a switch, and FTAG uniquely identifies a forwarding graph. To keep the classic Ethernet's plug-and-play philosophy in FabricPath networks, these identifiers are allocated dynamically using the DRAP. DRAP enables FabricPath to have zero configurations for allocation of these resources. DRAP provides automatic configuration for these resources using a distributed algorithm. Each switch announces its own information using IS-IS reliable flooding. The switches in the FabricPath network take action based on the information they have seen from rest of the switches. Using the information received over IS-IS, each switch maintains a database of all the resources that have been allocated throughout the network.

Allocation of Resources by DRAP

To allocate a resource Switch-ID or FTAG, DRAP uses the MAC address as a key to first pick out a random value for Switch-ID. Using the switch IS-IS local database, DRAP compares the resources of other switches in the local database with the generated random value. In case there is no collision, this resource is marked as "tentative," and then IS-IS includes this resource in its new database record announcement. The marking of the resource as "tentative" is needed to make sure that if two switches try to allocate a resource at the same time, they can resolve the conflict. Only after making sure that there are no conflicts, the resource is marked as "confirmed."

The marking from "tentative" to "confirmed" is based on a timeout, which enables the resource allocation to be propagated across the FabricPath network. In case of a collision, the switch receives another record with the same allocated resource value; this kicks off a collision resolution phase. During the collision resolution phase, different parameters such as System ID and resource state are taken into account to resolve the tie. The tie is resolved by the switch based on the tiebreaker parameters; if it loses the tie, the switch allocates another resource value, and the whole process is repeated. Although FabricPath ensures the Switch-ID in a network is unique, a configuration command is still provided to statically assign a Switch-ID to the FabricPath switch. In case the network administrator chooses to manually configure the Switch-IDs, the administrator needs to make sure every switch in the FabricPath network has a unique value. In case there is a conflicting Switch-ID, the switch with the conflicting Switch-ID moves to a suspended state and does not forward data on its interfaces.

FTAG follows a predefined scheme for allocation. The first multidestination tree uses FTAG1, and the second multidestination tree uses FTAG2. FTAG tree usage follows:

FTAG1: In a FabricPath topology the highest-priority switch becomes the root for FTAG1. This FTAG is used for unknown unicast, broadcast, and multicast. In a FabricPath domain if the default priority is unchanged, the switch system-id determines the switch with the highest root priority.

FTAG2: In a FabricPath topology the second highest-priority switch becomes the root for FTAG2. This FTAG is used only for multicast traffic.

The factors that can elect the root for FTAG1 and FTAG2 follows

- Highest root priority
- Highest system-id
- Highest Switch-ID

FabricPath MAC Address Learning

In a FabricPath network learning happens through two mechanisms:

- Control plane learning
- Data plane learning

Control Plane Learning

IS-IS control plane is responsible for learning, propagating, and populating the Switch-ID based on forwarding entries in the FabricPath network. The core of the FabricPath uses the Switch-ID to forward the unicast frames, and all the forwarding in the FabricPath core uses IS-IS control plane.

Data Plane Learning

At the core of the FabricPath network, forwarding is done based on the Switch-ID for unidestination or unicast traffic. But the frame coming from the host is a classical Ethernet frame. At the edge of a FabricPath network, switches needs to maintain a mapping between the classical MAC address and the corresponding Switch-ID. This mapping is built using data plane learning.

When the host sends a frame and if the destination MAC address is "unknown," the frame will be flooded using the broadcast graph. The flooding enables the frame to reach all the edge switches and finally the destination host. In this process, the following happens:

- **Learning at the Ingress edge switch:** This is the normal Layer 2 learning from a host or classical Ethernet port.

■ **Learning at the Egress edge switches:** In this case, the packet was received from one of the "core ports" of the FabricPath network. The edge switch decapsulates the FabricPath encapsulated packet and learns the inner source MAC address against the remote Switch-ID.

FabricPath by default performs conversational MAC learning. What this means is that for packets to be received from the core ports, the SMAC in the inner packet is learned against the remote Switch-ID only if the DMAC is a hit. Otherwise, no learning is performed for packets received from the core port. This enables a switch to learn only those remote MACs involved in active bidirectional communication or conversation.

Conversational MAC address learning leads to the population of only the interested hosts' MAC addresses, rather than all MAC addresses in the domain. Each forwarding engine in the switch learns only those MAC addresses that the hosts under its interface are actively communicating with. In essence, conversational MAC learning requires a three-way handshake. This selective learning, or conversational MAC address learning, enables you to scale the network beyond the limits of individual switch MAC address tables.[2]

Figure 4-9 illustrates the conversational learning. In this topology there are three hosts—Host A, Host B, and Host C—that connect to interface E1/0 on Switch Sw1, Sw3, and Sw2, respectively. Host A and Host B have an active conversation, whereas there is no active conversation with Host C.

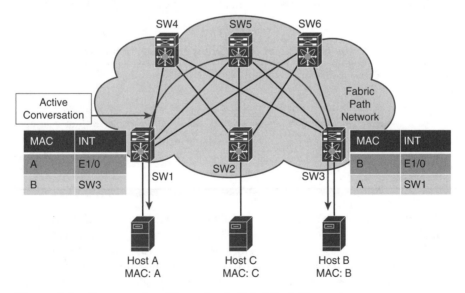

Figure 4-9 *Conversational Learning in FabricPath Network*

Figure 4-9 shows there is no MAC learning for end hosts on Switches Sw4, Sw5, and Sw6. Switch Sw1 has learned the MAC address against its interface E1/0 and MAC address B against remote Switch Sw3. Similarly, Switch Sw3 has learned MAC address B against its interface E1/0 and MAC address A against remote Switch Sw1. SW2 does not learn any of the addresses of the end host because there is no host behind SW2 in active conversation with other hosts. In FabricPath, any unknown unicast packet flooded through the broadcast graph doesn't participate in address learning. The concept of conversational learning is that a switch does not learn the inner MAC address of the FabricPath encapsulated frame received from the core unless the inner destination MAC address exists in its Layer 2 table. This ensures that the frame is indeed destined to a host behind this switch and possibly the two hosts are in active conversation with each other.

Assuming that Host A and Host B know each other's MAC addresses and Host A wants to communicate to Host B, following are the steps in the conversational learning:

1. Host A wants to start a communication with Host B. Assume that each of the hosts know each other's MAC addresses. Host A forms a unicast packet and sends the frame with the destination MAC 0000.0000.000B and source MAC 0000.0000.000A of Host A.

2. This frame reaches the directly attached FabricPath edge Switch Sw1 on port Eth1/0. This switch is configured with FabricPath and the port E1/0 is in VLAN 10, with VLAN 10 in mode fabricpath. A Layer 2 forwarding lookup is performed on the frame. A source lookup for {VLAN=10, MAC=0000.000.000A} results in a miss, and therefore a classical Layer 2 learning is performed with (VLAN=10, MAC=0000.0000.000A)-> Eth1/0. The destination MAC being unknown results in a flood for the frame on VLAN 10. Example 4-2 shows the MAC address table at Sw1.

Example 4-2 *MAC Address Table on Sw1 After Receiving Frame from Host A*

```
SW1# show mac address-table dynamic
Legend:
          * - primary entry, G - Gateway MAC, (R) - Routed MAC, O -Overlay MAC
          age - seconds since last seen,+ - primary entry using vPC Peer-Link
    VLAN     MAC Address     Type      age     Secure NTFY Ports/SWID.SSID.LID
-------------+-----------------+---------+-------+------+----+------------------
* 10        0000.0000.000a    dynamic   30       F      F     Eth1/0
```

3. To forward the unknown unicast frame, FabricPath Switch Sw1 selects the first multidestination tree (Tree 1) to forward all broadcast frames. Except for vPC+, FabricPath switches use the Tree 1 to forward all broadcast, non-IP multicast, and unknown unicast traffic. After encapsulating the frame in the FabricPath header, it is transmitted over the interfaces that are part of Tree 1. The FTAG in the FabricPath header signifies the first tree selected.

4. While traversing over Tree 1 the intermediate switches use the FTAG value to forward the frame. The FabricPath encapsulated frame reaches the Switch Sw3.

5. The frames arrive in Switch Sw3 on the input interface on Tree 1. Because there are edge ports in VLAN 10, Switch Sw3 removes the FabricPath header and does a destination MAC lookup based on the inner frame. The lookup result is a miss, so Sw1 forwards the frame to all ports on VLAN 10. At this time, Sw3 doesn't learn the source MAC 0000.0000.000A because the destination MAC lookup has resulted in a miss.

6. Host B receives the frame destined to it. It replies to this frame with a source MAC 0000.0000.000B and destination MAC 0000.0000.000. This frame reaches the directly attached FabricPath edge Switch Sw1 on port Eth1/0. This switch is configured with FabricPath and the port E1/0 is in VLAN 10, with VLAN 10 in mode fabricpath. A Layer 2 forwarding lookup is performed on the frame. Because the source lookup results in a miss for {VLAN=10, MAC=0000.000.000B}, a classical Layer 2 learning is performed with (VLAN=10, MAC=0000.0000.000B)-> Eth1/0. The destination MAC being unknown results in a flood for the frame on VLAN 10. Example 4-3 shows the MAC address table at Switch Sw3.

Example 4-3 *MAC Address Table on Sw3 After Receiving Frame from Host A*

```
SW3# show mac address-table dynamic
Legend:
        * - primary entry, G - Gateway MAC, (R) - Routed MAC, O -Overlay MAC
        age - seconds since last seen,+ - primary entry using vPC Peer-Link
   VLAN     MAC Address     Type      age     Secure NTFY Ports/SWID.SSID.LID
------------+---------------+---------+-------+------+----+------------------
* 10        0000.0000.000b   dynamic  30        F      F    Eth1/0
```

7. To forward the unknown unicast frame, FabricPath Switch Sw3 selects the first multidestination tree (Tree 1) to forward all broadcast frames. Except for vPC+, FabricPath switches use the Tree 1 to forward all broadcast, non-IP multicast, and unknown unicast traffic. After encapsulating the frame in the FabricPath header, it is transmitted over the interfaces that are part of Tree 1. The FTAG in the FabricPath header signifies the first tree selected.

8. While traversing over Tree 1, the intermediate switches use the FTAG value to forward the frame. The FabricPath encapsulated frame reaches the Switch Sw1.

9. The frames arrives in Switch Sw1 on the input interface on Tree 1. Because there are edge ports in VLAN 10, Switch Sw3 removes the FabricPath header and does a destination MAC lookup based on the inner frame. The lookup result is a hit. Sw1 forwards the frame on interface Eth1/0, which was learned for (VLAN=10, MAC=0000.0000.000A).

10. Because the inner destination MAC 0000.0000.000a is already known as local to Switch Sw1, it learns the inner source MAC (0000.0000.000b, VLAN=10) against the remote Switch-ID corresponding to Sw3. Optionally, the remote sub-switch-id may also be learned.

11. Host A receives the frame destined to it. Host A forms a unicast packet and sends the frame with the destination MAC 0000.0000.000B and source MAC 0000.0000.000A of Host A.

12. This frame reaches the directly attached FabricPath edge Switch Sw1 on port Eth1/0. This switch is configured with FabricPath and the port E1/0 is in VLAN 10, with VLAN 10 in mode fabricpath. A Layer 2 forwarding lookup is performed on the frame. First, the source lookup results in a hit for {VLAN=10, MAC=0000.000.000A}; this MAC is already learned against Eth1/0. Switch Sw1 just resets the inactivity timer. Because the destination MAC is known, the destination MAC lookup results in a hit.

13. Sw1 encapsulates the frame in a FabricPath header. This frame has destination Switch-ID set as Sw3 in the outer header. The frame travels over the FabricPath core to reach the Switch Sw3.

14. On Switch Sw3, after the frames arrives, as the outer MAC points to it, Switch Sw3 removes the FabricPath header and does a destination MAC lookup based on the inner frame. The lookup result is a hit. So Sw1 forwards the frame on interface Eth1/0, which was learned for (VLAN=10, MAC=0000.0000.000B).

15. Because the inner destination MAC 0000.0000.000b is already known as local to Switch Sw1, it learns the inner source MAC (0000.0000.000a, VLAN=10) against the remote Switch-ID corresponding to Sw1. Optionally, the remote sub-switchid may also be learned.

This completes the conversational learning in the FabricPath network. Conversational learning in FabricPath is enabled by default but can be optionally disabled on per-VLAN basis.

FabricPath STP Interaction

Classical Ethernet uses STP to form a loop-free Layer 2 forwarding topology, whereas FabricPath uses IS-IS for building appropriate FTAG-associated trees. A mechanism is needed when a classical Layer 2 Ethernet network running STP is connected to a FabricPath network. Figure 4-10 shows a topology where a FabricPath network is connected to a classical Ethernet network that has a physical loop.

To avoid forming a loop when a regular Ethernet network is connected to a FabricPath network, a FabricPath network appears like a single switch with the STP root located in the virtual FabricPath switch. All edge switches need to derive the same STP root information. This enables FabricPath edge switches to send the superior bridge protocol data unit (BPDU) toward classical Ethernet network, thus eliminating loops within the classical Ethernet network. FabricPath reserves a MAC address for STP so that a common root bridge-id could be advertised by each of the FabricPath edge switches.

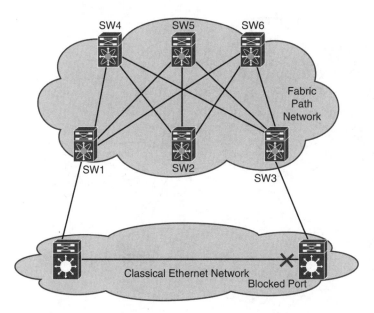

Figure 4-10 *FabricPath and Classical Ethernet Forming a Loop*

In classical Ethernet, STP root bridge-id has two parts:

- Bridge priority

- MAC address

For a FabricPath network to appear as a single switch, all the FabricPath edge switches need to announce the same priority. In the FabricPath network, the default priority for this virtual root bridge is set to 32768. To make sure the FabricPath edge ports are always forwarding, the user can lower the priority on each edge switch. This way only the blocking responsibility is on the classical Ethernet side.

By default, FabricPath switches participate in building the Spanning Tree Protocol forwarding topology by sending and receiving STP BPDUs on FabricPath edge ports. This behavior can be modified by using features such as BPDU guard, BPDU filter, and so on. Thus FabricPath switches participate in building the STP topologies in different traditionally connected STP domains. Each of the different STP domains connected with FabricPath network acts completely independent of the others.

Figure 4-11 shows a FabricPath and classical Ethernet network when there is a physical loop. Switch Sw1, Sw2, and Sw3 are FabricPath edge switches. These edge switches send BPDUs to announce a common virtual STP root to a classical Ethernet network. For the STP root, the MAC address used on the edge devices is c84c.75fa.6000; this MAC address is chosen from a pool of reserved MAC addresses.

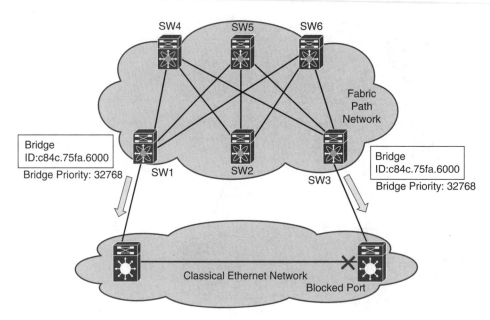

Figure 4-11   *Layer 2 Gateway Spanning Tree Protocol*

In Figure 4-12 one of the switches becomes the STP root in the classical Ethernet network due to lower bridge priority, so the edge switch Sw1 blocks the edge port on receiving superior BPDUs from the classical Ethernet side.

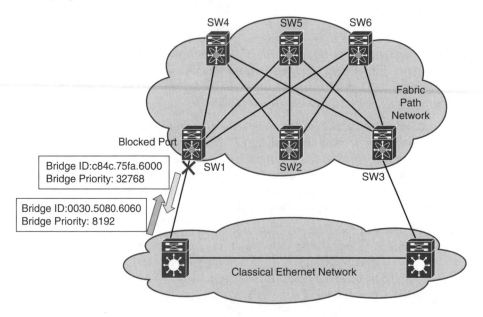

Figure 4-12   *STP Root in Classical Ethernet*

To avoid the STP root in the classical Ethernet part of the network, you can manually configure the FabricPath edge devices to set the bridge priority lower than any STP bridge or enter the commands shown in Example 4-4.

Example 4-4 *Changing Bridge Priority on edge Switches*

```
Sw1#config t
Sw1(config)# spanning-tree VLAN <x> root primary
/* Example to configure primary root for VLAN 1 to 50 */
Sw1(config)# spanning-tree VLAN 1-50 root primary
Sw1(config)#
```

Topology Change Notifications Forwarding

No BPDUs are sent over FabricPath core ports. BPDUs, like topological change notification (TCN), are never sent over the FabricPath core network ports (until configured to be forwarded). By default any topology changes in one STP domain are not propagated to STP domains connected to the same FabricPath network.

However, a configuration option is available to enable FabricPath edge switches to forward TCNs through the FabricPath network to support certain topologies. Figure 4-13 illustrates why certain topologies need the TCNs to be forwarded across FabricPath network.

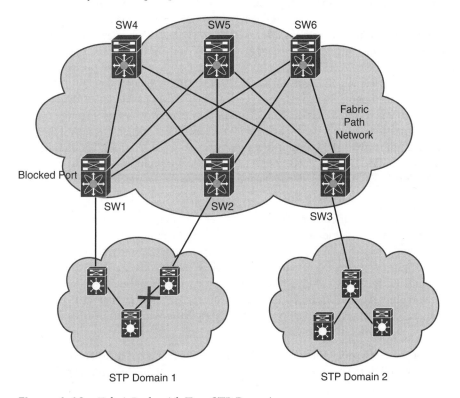

Figure 4-13 *FabricPath with Two STP Domains*

The global configuration command **spanning tree domain id** can optimize reconvergence when connecting extended STP domains to a FabricPath core. This command must be configured on the FabricPath edge switches.

As shown in Figure 4-13, initially the port on Sw1 connected to STP domain 1 is blocked. Now suppose because of a link failure in STP domain 1, a topology change event occurred in STP domain 1, resulting in the generation of an STP topology change notification BPDU. Referring to Figure 4-13, say that Switch Sw2 receives a TCN from one of its edge ports. On receiving the TCN, Switch Sw2 should forward this to Switch Sw1 so that Sw1 can flush its MAC address tables. Now Switch Sw1 also needs to propagate this TCN back to Spanning Tree domain 1 so that other switches on the classical Ethernet side of STP domain 1 can also flush their MAC address tables. In this case, the FabricPath edge switches connected to STP domain 2 need to receive the TCN so that they can flush any MAC entries associated with STP domain 1, but there is no need to forward such TCNs to the STP domain 2 classical Ethernet side of the network. The FabricPath edge Switches Sw1 and Sw2 are connected to same spanning tree network. So to make this scenario work properly, these edge switches are configured with same domain id using the command **spanning-tree domain 1**.

FabricPath Packet Forwarding

Like any other Layer 2 network, four possible types of packets can be forwarded through a FabricPath network: unicast packets (known unicast), multicast packets, broadcast packets, and unknown unicast packets. As discussed, "known unicast" implies that address learning has already happened for the (DMAC, VLAN) pair. For edge ports, classical MAC learning happens where (SMAC, VLAN) is learned against the edge port along which the MAC is learned. For core ports, post decapsulation (inner-SMAC, VLAN) is learned against the remote Switch-ID. As a prerequisite for data packet forwarding and MAC learning, it is required that the FabricPath IS-IS core network enables remote MAC learning and has already computed the Switch-ID reachability for each of the switches in the FabricPath network. FTAG identifies a unicast topology for unidestination traffic and a tree for multidestination traffic. For unicast traffic, for multiple equal cost paths to the destination switch, flow-based load balancing is done for the traffic destined to that switch.

For multidestination (multicast) traffic, multicast trees computed by IS-IS are used for traffic forwarding, The multicast trees are rooted at specific multicast roots, which are advertised by the broadcast root. The multicast traffic follows these multicast trees to reach the destination switches that are attached to interested receivers. To further optimize IP multicast traffic forwarding, IGMP snooping data at the FabricPath edge switches prunes the multicast graphs/trees. By using multicast receiver information, IS-IS is used to propagate multicast receiver locations, so the FabricPath switches prune off subtrees of the graph that do not have downstream receivers.

Figure 4-14 shows a FabricPath network with three hosts (Host A, Host B, and Host C), and each of them communicate to each other. This figure also shows the multidestination trees. Tree 1 (FTAG1) is drawn with a solid line; Tree2 (FTAG2) is drawn with dashed lines.

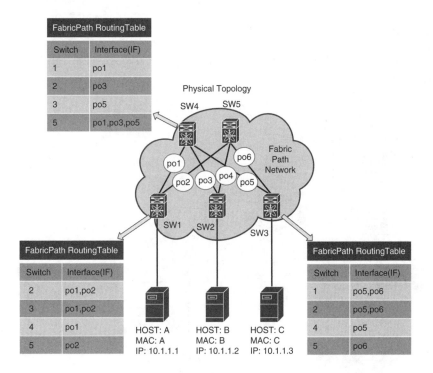

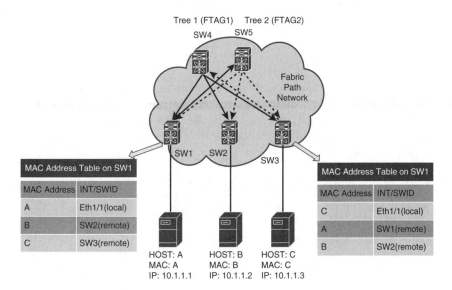

Figure 4-14 *MAC Learning and Multidestination Trees in FabricPath*

The broadcast tree, which was computed by IS-IS, is used to forward both broadcast and unknown unicast. With this basic understanding, now consider some of the packet flows.

Broadcast: ARP Request

Figure 4-15 shows the packet walk-through for an ARP packet through a FabricPath network from Host A to Host B.[3]

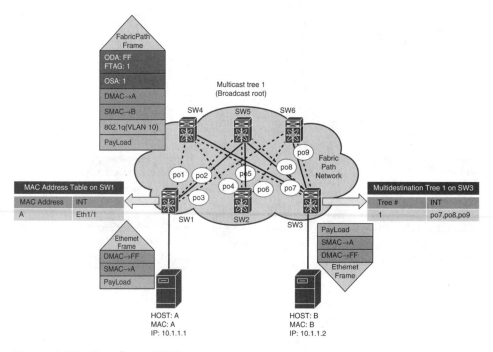

Figure 4-15   *Broadcast ARP Request*

The solid lines in Figure 4-15 show the multidestination tree 1 with Sw5 as the root of the tree. The ARP request follows this tree to reach the destination. The figure also shows the port-channel interfaces marked as po1 to po9. Before going through the steps of ARP packet, take a look at the multidestination tree from Sw1's perspective, as shown in Example 4-5.

Example 4-5   *FabricPath Multidestination Forwarding Tree on Sw1*

```
SW1# show fabricpath multicast trees ftag 1

(ftag/1, topo/0, Switch-id 5) uptime 15:20:15, isis
 Outgoing interface list: (count 1, '*' is the preferred interface)
* Interface port-channel2, [admin distance/115] uptime: 15:20:15, isis
```

```
(ftag/1, topo/0, Switch-id 6) uptime 15:20:15, isis
 Outgoing interface list: (count 1, '*' is the preferred interface)
* Interface port-channel2, [admin distance/115] uptime: 14:20:25, isis

(ftag/1, topo/0, Switch-id 4) uptime 15:20:15, isis
 Outgoing interface list: (count 1, '*' is the preferred interface)
* Interface port-channel2, [admin distance/115] uptime: 14:20:25, isis

(ftag/1, topo/0, Switch-id 2) uptime 12:19:15, isis
 Outgoing interface list: (count 1, '*' is the preferred interface)
* Interface port-channel2, [admin distance/115] uptime: 11:29:28, isis

(ftag/1, topo/0, Switch-id 3) uptime 12:19:15, isis
 Outgoing interface list: (count 1, '*' is the preferred interface)
* Interface port-channel2, [admin distance/115] uptime: 11:27:15, isis

Found total 5 route(s)

Sw1#
```

Following are the steps for the ARP request:

1. Host A wants to start a communication with Host B in the same IP subnet, so it sends the ARP request to determine the IP-MAC binding associated with Host B. Because Host A doesn't know the MAC address of Host B, it sends the frame with the broadcast destination MAC (FFFF.FFFF.FFF) and source MAC 0000.0000.000A of Host A.

2. This frame reaches the directly attached FabricPath edge Switch Sw1 on port Eth1/1. This switch is configured with FabricPath, and the port e1/1 is in VLAN 10, with VLAN 10 in mode fabricpath. A Layer 2 forwarding lookup is performed on the frame. First, the source lookup results in a miss for {VLAN=10, MAC=0000.000.000A}; therefore, the classical Layer 2 learning is performed with (VLAN=10, MAC=0000.0000.000A)-> Eth1/1, as shown in Example 4-6. The destination MAC being all FFs results in a flood result for the frame on VLAN 10.

Example 4-6 *MAC Address Table on Sw1 After Receiving ARP Request from Host A*

```
SW1# show mac address-table dynamic
Legend:
        * - primary entry, G - Gateway MAC, (R) - Routed MAC, O -Overlay MAC
        age - seconds since last seen,+ - primary entry using vPC Peer-Link
   VLAN     MAC Address     Type      age     Secure NTFY Ports/SWID.SSID.LID
-------------+--------------------+----------+-------+------+----+------------------
* 10       0000.0000.000a     dynamic  30       F        F      Eth1/1
```

3. To forward the broadcast frame, FabricPath Switch Sw1 selects the first multides-tination tree (Tree 1) to forward all broadcast frames. Except for vPC+, FabricPath switches use the Tree 1 to forward all broadcast, non-IP multicast, and unknown unicast traffic.

4. After the tree is selected, Switch Sw1 does a multidestination lookup for Tree 1; this lookup results in the selection of the interfaces the frame must be forwarded on. Tree 1 on the Switch Sw1 consists of a single interface (po2). After encap-sulating the frame with an appropriate FabricPath header, it is flooded over this interface. The FabricPath header for the broadcast frame consists of the following parameters:

- **Outer DA (ODA):** The outer destination address for a broadcast frame is the same destination MAC address as the inner frame (ODA: FFFF.FFFF.FFFF).

- **Outer SA(OSA):** The outer source address identifies the FabricPath source Switch-ID, sub-Switch-ID, and port ID (or local ID). The source Switch-ID is set to Sw1's Switch-ID of 1, sub-Switch-ID is set to 0, and port Eth 1/1 has a local port ID of 0.

- **FabricPath tag (FTAG):** As the frame is a broadcast frame, it uses the first multi-destination tree with an ID of 1. So the FTAG is 1.

5. The FabricPath encapsulated ARP frame reaches the neighbor Switch Sw5, and a forwarding table lookup is done by this switch. Because the outer destination address (ODA) corresponds to a special value that indicates that this is a multides-tination frame, specifically a broadcast frame, the FTAG in the packet header for-wards the frame over the right multidestination tree (Tree 1 in this case). On Switch Sw5, although there are three interfaces on Tree 1 but because the frame arrives on interface po2 (RPF check), the frame is flooded on the remaining two interfaces toward Switch Sw2 and Sw3, respectively.

6. Switch Sw2 and Sw3 receive the FabricPath encapsulated frame. As on Switch Sw2, there are no interfaces that belong to Tree 1, so it doesn't forward over the tree, but if there are some edge ports in VLAN 10, the switch removes the FabricPath header and performs a lookup on the inner payload. Because the DMAC is all FFs, the Switch Sw2 forwards the frame over the edge ports in VLAN 10 (if any).

7. On Switch Sw3, after the frame arrives on Tree 1, given that it is the transit node for Tree 1, it has the responsibility of forwarding the frame toward two interfaces: one toward Sw4 and another toward Switch Sw6. In addition, Switch Sw3 decap-sulates the frame and performs a lookup on the inner payload. Because the DMAC is all FFs, it floods a copy of the ARP packet along all its edge ports in VLAN 10. Because DMAC is unknown, no SMAC learning for 0000.0000.0000a in VLAN 10 happens on Sw3 for the ARP request packet received from the core port.

8. After switch Sw3 forwards the ARP request over edge ports in VLAN 10, Host B receives the ARP request from Host A.

Throughout this process, the only switch that learned about MAC A based on the broadcast frame was Switch Sw1.

Unicast: ARP Reply

Figure 4-16 shows the packet walk-through for an ARP reply packet through a FabricPath network from Host B to Host A.

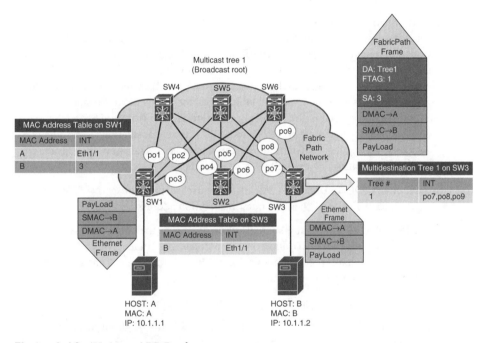

Figure 4-16   *Unicast ARP Reply*

Following are the steps for the ARP:

1. After the broadcast ARP request is received by Host B from Host A, Host B replies with a unicast ARP response with source MAC of Host B (0000.0000.000b) and destination MAC of Host A (0000.0000.000a).

2. This frame reaches the FabricPath Switch Sw3 on Ethernet port Eth1/1 in VLAN 10. A Layer 2 forwarding lookup is performed on the frame. First, the source lookup ends in a miss for {VLAN=10, MAC=0000.0000.000b}; therefore, the forwarding engine learns this MAC in VLAN 10 against port Eth1/1, as shown in Example 4-7.

Example 4-7   *MAC Address Table on Sw3 After Receiving ARP Response from Host B*

```
SW3# show mac address-table dynamic
Legend:
        * - primary entry, G - Gateway MAC, (R) - Routed MAC, O -Overlay MAC
        age - seconds since last seen,+ - primary entry using vPC Peer-Link
   VLAN     MAC Address     Type      age     Secure NTFY Ports/SWID.SSID.LID
-------------+-----------------+----------+-------+------+----+------------------
* 10       0000.0000.000b    dynamic   30        F       F      Eth1/1
```

3. The destination MAC address lookup for {VLAN=10, MAC=0000.0000.000a} results in a miss. This is treated as an unknown unicast case. The frame is locally flooded on the edge ports that are part of VLAN 10 and forwarded toward the core on the multidestination tree. To forward the unknown unicast frame, FabricPath Switch Sw3 selects the first multidestination tree (Tree 1). After the tree is selected, Switch Sw3 does a multidestination lookup for Tree 1; this lookup results in the selection of the interfaces the frame must be flooded on. Tree 1 on Switch Sw3 consists of three interfaces: po7, po8, and po9. After encapsulating the frame in the FabricPath header, it is transmitted over these interfaces. The FabricPath header for the broadcast consists of the following parameters:

   ■ **Outer DA (ODA):** Unknown unicast frame uses a special reserved MAC address (MC1: 010F.FFC1.01C0) as the outer destination address.

   ■ **Outer SA(OSA):** The outer source address identifies the FabricPath source Switch-ID, sub-Switch-ID, and port ID (or local ID). Source Switch-ID is set to the Sw3's Switch-ID of 1; sub-Switch-ID is 0; and port Eth 1/1 has a local port ID of 0.

   ■ **FabricPath tag (FTAG):** FTAG is 1, which identifies topology 1.

4. The FabricPath encapsulated ARP reply frame reaches the neighbor Switches Sw4, Sw5, and Sw6. Each of the switches does a forwarding table lookup based on the FabricPath header. The switches use the FTAG value to identify the multidestination tree that this frame should be sent on. Except for Switch Sw5, other switches (Sw4 and Sw6) discard the frame because no other interface except the incoming interface is part of the multidestination Tree 1. Moreover, there are no edge ports in VLAN 10 on these switches. On the root Switch Sw5, two other interfaces (in addition to interface po8 on which the frame came) are part of the multidestination Tree 1. Therefore, the Switch Sw5 forwards this frame over these links after the RPF check.

5. Switches Sw1 and Sw2 receive the FabricPath encapsulated frame and perform a forwarding lookup. On Switch Sw2, no other interfaces belong to Tree 1, so it doesn't forward the FabricPath frame on the tree.

6. On Switch Sw1, after the frames arrives on the input interface on Tree 1, no more interfaces on Tree 1 need to forward the frame back out toward the core. In other words, Sw1 is not the transit for this tree. Because there are edge ports in VLAN

10, Switch Sw1 removes the FabricPath header and does a destination MAC lookup based on the inner frame. The lookup result is a hit and the result yields port Eth1/1. So Sw1 forwards the frame to Host A on port Eth1/1.

7. Because the inner destination MAC 0000.0000.000a is already known as local to Switch Sw1, it learns the inner source MAC (0000.0000.000b, VLAN=10) against the remote Switch-ID corresponding to Sw3. Optionally, the remote sub-switchid may also be learned.

At the end of the ARP exchange, the MAC 0000.0000.000a is learned on Sw1 and 0000.000.000b is learned on both Switches Sw1 and Sw3. The subsequent data packet flow described in the next packet flow ensures that MAC 0000.0000.000a is also learned at Sw3, completing the three-way handshake.

Unicast: Data

Figure 4-17 shows the packet walk-through for a unicast packet through a FabricPath network after Host A has received an ARP reply from Host B.

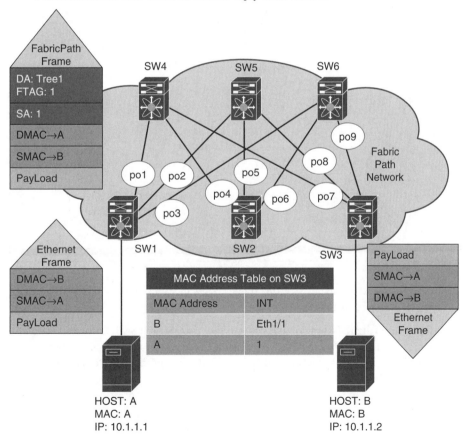

Figure 4-17   *Unicast Data Flow*

Following are the steps for a unicast data packet flow from Host A to Host B:

1. Host A now transmits a standard IP packet with SMAC=0000.0000.000a and DMAC=0000.0000.000b.

2. Switch Sw1 receives the frame from Host A on the FabricPath edge port E1/1 in VLAN 10. The Layer 2 forwarding lookup is performed on the frame. First, the source lookup ends up in a hit for {VLAN=10, MAC=0000.0000.000a}; therefore, the forwarding engine updates the related aging timer. The destination MAC address lookup {VLAN=10, MAC=0000.0000.000b} also results in a hit, which returns the result as Switch-ID Sw3 (3).

3. From Sw1, Sw3 is reachable via three equal cost paths through Sw4, Sw5, and Sw6, respectively. Thus, the switch routing table entry related to Sw3 has an ECMP count of 3, and based on an appropriate hash computed based on the frame contents, one of the three entries is selected. Example 4-8 shows the routing table on Switch Sw1 for Switch Sw3. Sw3 is reachable via interfaces po1, po2, and po3 with the same cost along topology 0.

Example 4-8   *Routing Table on Sw1 for Reaching Sw3*

```
SW1# show fabricpath route topology 0 switchid 3
FabricPath Unicast Route Table
'a/b/c' denotes ftag/Switch-ID/subSwitch-ID
'[x/y]' denotes [admin distance/metric]
ftag 0 is local ftag
subSwitch-ID 0 is default subSwitch-ID

FabricPath Unicast Route Table for Topology-Default

1/3/0, number of next-hops: 3
        via Po1, [115/40], 0 day/s  10:12:15, isis_fabricpath-default
        via Po2, [115/40], 0 day/s  10:12:15, isis_fabricpath-default
        via Po3, [115/40], 0 day/s  10:12:15, isis_fabricpath-default
SW1#
```

Now assume that the hash for this frame results in selection of the interface po2, which is toward Switch Sw5.

4. Upon receiving the frame on ingress interface po2, Switch Sw5 performs a route table lookup based on the outer FabricPath header. The routing table lookup is based on the destination Switch-ID, with FTAG present in the FabricPath header.

This results in an adjacency pointing to next-hop interface po8. This is because from Sw5, Sw3 is reachable via po8, and this is the only least cost path. Example 4-9 shows the routing table on Switch Sw5 for Switch Sw3.

Example 4-9 *Routing Table on Sw5 for Reaching Sw3*

```
SW5# show fabricpath route topology 0 switchid 3
FabricPath Unicast Route Table
'a/b/c' denotes ftag/Switch-ID/subSwitch-ID
'[x/y]' denotes [admin distance/metric]
ftag 0 is local ftag
subSwitch-ID 0 is default subSwitch-ID

FabricPath Unicast Route Table for Topology-Default

1/3/0, number of next-hops: 1
        via Po8, [115/40], 0 day/s  10:12:10, isis_fabricpath-default

SW5#
```

Sw5 being the core performs a TTL check and decrements the TTL before forwarding the frame to the next hop, Switch 3.

5. Upon receiving the frame, Sw3 determines based on the outer header that the frame is indeed destined to itself. Therefore, it decapsulates the outer FabricPath header, and the forwarding of the packet is based on whether it honors the result in the outer header or performs a local lookup based on the inner payload. For the former, Switch Sw3 uses the sub-Switch-ID and local ID to determine the edge port along which the frame should be forwarded. In this case, in the sub-Switch-ID, local ID is zero, and a forwarding lookup is performed on the inner frame to determine the interface along which the frame should be sent. The egress or destination switch is likely to have more up-to-date information about its locally attached host MACs, and it may be desirable to always rely on an egress lookup on the destination switch to forward the packet.

6. On the egress port E1/1, as the inner destination MAC B address is already learned, the inner source MAC address A is also learned with Switch-ID of 1.

At this point, the local and remote MAC addresses are learned on both Switches Sw1 and Sw3. Example 4-10 shows the entries on both switches at this point.

Example 4-10 *MAC Address Table on Sw1 and Sw3*

```
SW3# show mac address-table dynamic
Legend:
          * - primary entry, G - Gateway MAC, (R) - Routed MAC, O -Overlay MAC
          age - seconds since last seen,+ - primary entry using vPC Peer-Link
    VLAN      MAC Address      Type       age     Secure NTFY Ports/SWID.SSID.LID
-------------+-------------------+----------+-------+------+----+-----------------
    10        0000.0000.000a    dynamic  0          F        F       1
*   10        0000.0000.000b    dynamic  30         F        F       Eth1/1
SW3#


/* On Switch Sw3 */


SW1# show mac address-table dynamic
Legend:
          * - primary entry, G - Gateway MAC, (R) - Routed MAC, O -Overlay MAC
          age - seconds since last seen,+ - primary entry using vPC Peer-Link
    VLAN      MAC Address      Type       age     Secure NTFY Ports/SWID.SSID.LID
-------------+-------------------+----------+-------+------+----+-----------------
    10        0000.0000.000b    dynamic  80         F        F       3
*   10        0000.0000.000a    dynamic  0          F        F       Eth1/1
SW1#
```

FabricPath supports ECMP. Now if the costs of the paths are unequal, the frames are sent only over the lowest cost equal paths. The high-cost paths can be used as a backup when the lower-cost paths fail.

IP Multicast Forwarding

For IP multicast, at the ingress FabricPath edge switch, a hash function selects an appropriate multidestination tree along which the multicast frame should be forwarded. For better load balancing the IP multicast frames the Layer 3 and Layer 4 information from the IP multicast packet, which is used as an input to hash function.

On receiving an IP multicast frame, a FabricPath edge switch picks a symmetric per flow hash function combining both Layer 3 and Layer 4 information along with the VLAN ID. The hash input is programmable with the following available options:

- **Source:** Use only Layer 3 source IP address and Layer 4 source TCP and UDP port number as parameters.

- **Destination:** Use only destination IP address and Layer 4 destination TCP and UDP port number as parameters.

- **Source-destination:** Use Layer 3 (Source and Destination IP) and Layer 4 (Source and Destination TCP and UDP port numbers) as source and destination parameters.

- **Symmetric:** This is a default option, and it forces to sort source and destination tuples before entering them in the hash function. This enables the flows from the source-to-destination and destination-to-source to select the same path/tree in the FabricPath network.

- **XOR:** Perform an exclusive OR operation on the source and destination tuples before entering them in the hash function.

- **Include-VLAN:** This is a default option that includes the VLAN ID of the frame for hash calculations.

- **Rotate-amount:** This specifies the number of bytes to rotate the hash string before entering it in the hash function.

To determine the edge ports on which the IP multicast packets needs to be delivered, FabricPath edge switches use IGMP snooping. The IGMP snooping works exactly the same way on FabricPath switches as any other switches. The IGMP packets will be tunneled over the FabricPath network toward the multicast routers.

The edge switches track the IP multicast group memberships on the edge ports. Using FabricPath Layer 2 IS-IS group-membership link-state (GM-LSP) protocol data units, group interest on the edge switches is advertised to the FabricPath network. This advertisement using GM_LSP is used to restrict multicast traffic flow in the core to the edge switches that have multicast receivers.[4]

The FabricPath switches combine the information learned from Layer 2 IS-IS GM-LSPs and IGMP snooping (core switches don't see IGMP packets) to create an output interface list for a multicast group. So this output interface list is a combination of

- Interfaces learned through IGMP snooping.

- Interfaces leading to other FabricPath switches; these interfaces are tracked on a per-multidestination tree basis.

Using the exchanged information using FabricPath IS_IS, a pruned tree is created, so that the multicast frames are constrained to FabricPath switches that have interested receivers.

Before looking at IP multicast packet flow, you need to know that each switch has a core functionality and an edge functionality. Core means it honors FTAG, decrements TTL, and forwards frames toward the core interfaces. There is always FTAG pruning and VLAN pruning. Only if both pass then the frame is sent out over the remaining interfaces. Edge functionality is to learn the source MAC address from the inner payload and forward based on the destination MAC address. Figure 4-18 shows the source and receiver for an IP multicast group G1 (239.0.0.20) with a corresponding Layer 2 multicast MAC :0100.5300.0014.

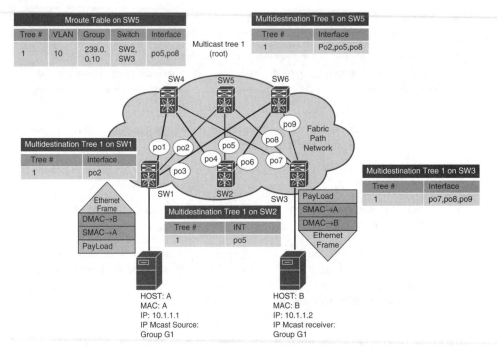

Figure 4-18   *IP Multicast Flow for Group G1*

Following are the steps of a sample IP multicast flow from the source of Group G1 (239.0.0.20) to its receivers:

1. For IP multicast Group G1(239.0.0.20), Host A connected to Switch Sw1 is the multicast source.

2. The FabricPath Switch Sw1 receives the standard Ethernet frame with an SMAC address A of Host A and IP multicast destination MAC address (0100.5300.0014).

    The source lookup triggers unconditional new learning or updates {VLAN=10, MAC=0000.0000.000a} for the MAC of Host A in VLAN 10.

    The destination MAC address lookup indicates that the frame is IP multicast. Because the destination is an IP multicast, the forwarding engine on Switch SW1 uses a hash function to select a multidestination tree (in this case Tree 1) on which to forward the frame.

    The forwarding engine performs a FabricPath mroute lookup because the mroute table has combined information populated by IGMP and FabricPath IS-IS GM-LSPs. The forwarding entry contains the output interface list containing any edge port with receivers on this Switch Sw1 and core port in Tree 1 through which other receivers in FabricPath network can be reached.

The Switch Sw1 forwards the frame based on this list. On the edge ports, a standard Ethernet frame is transmitted. On the FabricPath, core ports the original IP multicast frame is encapsulated in a FabricPath header and only one copy of the frame is sent toward the core ports. As Tree 1 is selected, an FTAG of 1 is used in the FabricPath header before transmitting the frame.

3. Switch Sw5 receives the FabricPath encapsulated frame on its core ports. Because the frame is IP multicast, it has a special destination address in the ODA; the switch uses the FTAG value in the FabricPath header for selecting the forwarding tree. The Switch Sw5 does an RPF check to validate the reception of the frame on the interface. After the corresponding tree (Tree 1) is selected, the Switch Sw5 does an mroute lookup for the frame in VLAN 10. In this case, there is a single output interface list (po8) because po5 is pruned because there are no interested receivers for G1 on Sw2.

4. The forwarding continues in the FabricPath network along Tree 1 until the frame reaches Switch Sw3. Using the FabricPath header, Switch Sw3 performs a lookup. Because the frame is IP multicast, the switch uses an FTAG value in the FabricPath header for selecting the forwarding tree. After selecting Tree 1, Switch Sw3 does an mroute lookup for the frame in VLAN 10.

    Although, in this case, there are additional interfaces for Tree 1, which are po7 and po9 toward Switch Sw4 and Switch Sw6, respectively, the frame is pruned because there are no interested receivers for group G1 behind Switches Sw4 and Sw6.

    In addition, there is also an edge port E1/1 on this output interface list where a receiver for IP multicast group G1 is attached. The Switch Sw3 decapsulates the outer FabricPath header and forwards the standard Ethernet frame toward this receiver.

FabricPath Basic Configuration

This section provides the minimal steps for enabling FabricPath on Nexus 7000 switch.[5]

From the prerequisite perspective before configuring FabricPath, you need to make sure that

- To run FabricPath on the switches, an Enhanced Layer 2 license is required.

- The correct hardware modules that support FabricPath switching are deployed.

After FabricPath switching is enabled on the device, IS-IS starts by default and learning occurs automatically. Example 4-11 enables basic FabricPath on Sw1.

Example 4-11   *FabricPath Configuration Example*

```
/* 1. Enable FabricPath feature set */
SW1# conf t
SW1(config)# install feature-set fabricpath
SW1(config)# feature-set fabricpath
SW1(config)#

/* 2. Enable FabricPath configuration on VLAN */
SW1(config)# VLAN 10
SW1(config-VLAN)# mode fabricpath
SW1(config-VLAN)#exit

/* 3. Enable FabricPath configuration on a core interface */
SW1(config)# interface e1/1
SW1(config-if)# switchport
SW1(config-if)# switchport mode fabricpath
SW1(config-VLAN)#exit


/* 4. Config MAC address learning mode (optional), Enabled by default
      Command given here only to be explicit*/

SW1(config)# mac address learning-mode conversational VLAN 1-100
SW1(config)#

/* 5. Configure switch id (optional) */

SW1(config)# fabric-path Switch-ID 1
SW1(config)#

/* 6. Finally save the config */

SW1(config)# save running-config startup-config
SW1(config)#
```

If the FabricPath network is connected to an STP network behind the edge switches, one important piece of configuration required is the STP configuration. Example 4-12 gives the sample STP configuration.

Example 4-12   *STP Configuration Example (FabricPath Switches)*

```
! Generally either the VLANs in the network are in Rapid PVST+ or mst mode
 So either step 1 or step 2 will be required. */
/* 1. If VLANs are Rapid PVST+ */
SW1# conf t
SW1(config)# spanning-tree VLAN 10-100 priority 8192
SW1(config)#

/* 2. If VLANs are in mst mode */
SW1(config)# spanning-tree mst 1-5 priority 8192
SW1(config)#

/* 3. If the Lead switch connects to STP instances below */
/*Give a domain <id> */
SW1(config)# spanning-tree domain 1
SW1(config)#exit

/* 4. Finally save the config */

SW1(config)# save running-config startup-config
SW1(config)#
```

FabricPath Benefits

Now that you understand FabricPath, consider the benefits that FabricPath offers to data center architects and administrators to design and implement a scalable Layer 2 fabric:

- **Preserves the plug-and-play features of classical Ethernet:** The configuration requirements for FabricPath are minimal. The administrator just needs to specify which interfaces are connected to the FabricPath network. FabricPath uses a single control protocol (IS-IS) for unicast forwarding, multicast forwarding, and VLAN pruning, which provide an integrated forwarding paradigm. In addition, ping and trace route are now available in FabricPath with OAM extensions allowing the network administrators to debug problems in the network.

- **Provides high performance using multipathing:** The N-way multipathing enables the data center network architects to build large, scalable networks by incrementally adding to the existing network topology. This enables MSDC networks to have flat topologies, enabling the nodes to communicate with each other optimally via a single hop. The 16-way multipathing has an additional benefit that a single switch failure just leads to a reduction of 1/16th in the fabric bandwidth.

- **High availability:** The enhancements for Layer 2 networks combined with Layer 3 capabilities enable the replacement of STP, which blocks all paths except one, enabling multiple paths between endpoints. This enables the network administrator to incrementally add network bandwidth to address increased demand.

■ **Small Layer 2 table size and forwarding efficiency:** FabricPath enables traffic to be forwarded to the destination along one of several shortest paths, thus reducing latency in the Layer 2 network. This is more efficient when compared to the Layer 2 forwarding based on the STP. Conversational learning in the FabricPath solution enables selective learning of the MAC addresses based on bidirectional traffic. This reduces the need for large table sizes.

Summary

This chapter covered FabricPath in detail. Various aspects of FabricPath were covered including its architecture, encapsulation details, interaction with classical Ethernet networks, control plane details, enhanced or conversational MAC learning, and data packet forwarding for various unidestination and multidestination flows. This was followed by a sample set of configuration required for enabling FabricPath on a Cisco Nexus 7000 switch. The basic configuration is simple and is shown in Example 4-7.

References

1. http://www.cisco.com/en/US/docs/switches/datacenter/nexus5000/sw/fabricpath/513_n1_1/fp_n5k_forwarding.html.

2. http://www.cisco.com/en/US/docs/switches/datacenter/sw/5_x/nx-os/fabricpath/configuration/guide/fp_switching.html#wp1790893.

3. *FabricPath Design Guide*: http://www.cisco.com/en/US/prod/collateral/switches/ps9441/ps9670/guide_c07-690079.html.

4. http://www.cisco.com/en/US/prod/collateral/switches/ps9441/ps9402/white_paper_c11-687554.html#wp9000376.

5. *Configuration Guide*: http://www.cisco.com/en/US/docs/switches/datacenter/sw/6_x/nx-os/fabricpath/configuration/guide/fppreface.html.

Chapter 5

TRILL

This chapter has the following objectives:

- **Need for TRILL:** This section discusses the drawbacks of the current networks with different scenarios and the need for TRILL.

- **Architecture and concepts:** This section covers the architecture and working concepts in TRILL.

- **Frame format:** This section explains the TRILL overlay header.

- **Control plane:** This section gives a high-level overview of the TRILL control plane without getting into a lot of IS-IS details. For IS-IS, refer to Chapter 3, "IS-IS."

- **Data plane:** This section explains the TRILL forwarding behavior in detail for unicast and multicast.

- **MAC address learning:** This section discusses the data path learning and out-of-band learning in TRILL networks.

- **Work in progress:** This section discusses in detail the different developments going on in the TRILL community as of this writing.

- **Case study:** This section goes through packet flow case studies over a TRILL network.

This chapter covers the working aspects of Transparent Interconnection of Lots of Links (TRILL) in detail. Many case studies and examples are provided that can help you to completely understand the TRILL architecture and the forwarding behavior. TRILL has a control plane, data plane, and management plane. This chapter explains all the nitty-gritty details of the data plane. The functionality of the control plane is discussed at the appropriate places without going into much detail. This gives you an idea to as to where the control plane fits in and how it complements the data plane. You are encouraged to go through Chapter 3 to get an in-depth understanding on the control plane.

This chapter can be useful for those who want to understand the basic working of TRILL, its architecture, and in-depth data flow. It provides a solid foundation for Chapter 8, "TRILL Deployment, Migration, and Troubleshooting," which includes the details on deployment and migration strategies for TRILL. Chapter 8 also discusses the management plane employed by TRILL.

Need for TRILL

This section discusses the shortcomings of today's networks and lays the foundation for the need for TRILL. This section uses the hierarchical network model as a reference to how networks are deployed today. The hierarchical network model has access switches at the lowest level for connecting to the end hosts. The access switches in turn are connected to aggregation or distribution switches for redundancy and load balancing purposes. The distribution switches are connected to core switches for interpod or inter-DC traffic and for Internet connectivity. Typically, Layer 2 (L2) is employed between access and distribution switches and Layer 3 (L3) is employed between distribution and core switches. The Layer 2 or Layer 3 boundary for the hosts is at the distribution layer, which routes traffic across VLANs. You can also connect the access and distribution switches using Layer 3, which mitigates many of the issues seen in Layer 2 networks. But deploying Layer 3 between access and distribution has other drawbacks discussed toward the end of this section. This section starts with the issues found in a typical Layer 2 network and how Spanning Tree Protocol (STP) addresses them. Then the drawbacks of STP are discussed and how combining multiple distribution switches addresses these issues to some extent followed by the issues in combining multiple distribution switches.

Spanning Tree in Layer 2 Networks

Consider a packet flow for a regular three-level hierarchical Layer 2 network, as shown in Figure 5-1, when there are no control protocols running to prevent loops in the network. The network has four access switches (AS1–AS4), two distribution switches (DS1–DS2), and a core switch (CS-1).

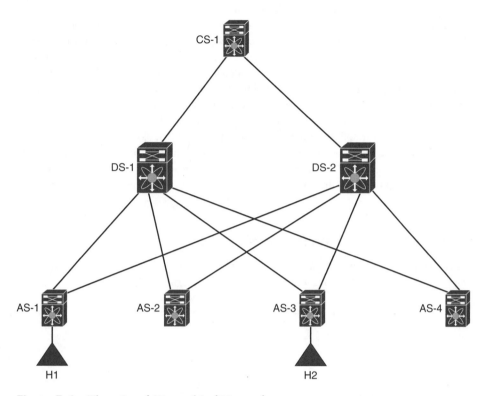

Figure 5-1 *Three-Level Hierarchical Network*

The packet flow between a source (for example, H1) and a destination (for example, H2) in the topology shown in Figure 5-1 is as follows: Assume H1 and H2 are hosts within the same VLAN:

- H1 connected to AS-1 originates a packet destined to H2, which is connected to AS-3. Initially, the Layer 2 table is empty in all the switches.

- AS-1 learns the source address of H1 and installs it in its Layer 2 table.

- AS-1 does a destination lookup in its Layer 2 table and finds that the destination address H2 does not exist there. AS-1 floods the packet to DS-1 and DS-2.

- DS-1 also floods the packet to AS-2, AS-3, and AS-4. Because Layer 2 is terminated at the distribution, the frame is not sent toward the core.

- DS-2 floods the packet to AS-2, AS-3, and AS-4.

- The access switches (AS-2, AS-3, and AS-4) after receiving the packet flood it back to the distribution switches and to the hosts connected to it.

- The destination host H2 receives the packet through AS-3. But the flooding process continues as the Layer 2 header does not have any provision to terminate the flood (like the Time-To-Live [TTL] field in the IP header).

- All the hosts including H2 receive multiple copies of the packet.

This necessitates the need for a protocol that prevents the packets from looping in the network. STP was designed for this purpose of loop prevention for Layer 2 traffic. The basic essence of STP is to elect a root node in the network. A spanning tree is computed from the root, and the tree includes all the nodes in the network. A tree by definition is an acyclic graph that has no loops. The interfaces connecting the links that are a part of the spanning tree are put in a forwarding state. The other interfaces connecting the links that are not a part of the spanning tree are put in a blocked state. Regular data flow happens only across the links in the forwarding state. A protocol is certainly needed for proper forwarding and preventing loops in the network. The lack of a TTL field in the Ethernet header made this scenario worse. Even in the presence of a control protocol, intermittent loops may occur, and having a TTL field prevents the network from a flood storm.

Issues with Spanning Tree Protocol

After STP is run, the network becomes as shown in Figure 5-2. Here, assume that distribution switch DS-1 is elected as the root of the spanning tree.

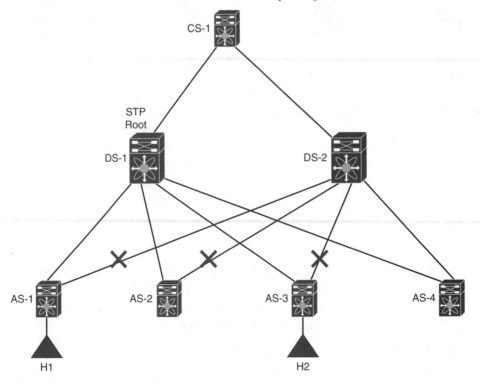

Figure 5-2 *Hierarchical Layer 2 Network after STP Is Run*

Basically all the links connecting the access switches (AS-1, AS-2, and AS-3) to the distribution switch DS-2 are put in blocked state. Regular spanning tree takes a long time to converge (approximately 15 seconds) and underutilizes the available resources (links) in the network, as shown in Figure 5-2. To reduce the convergence time, Rapid Spanning Tree Protocol (RSTP,)[1] was developed, which reduces the convergence time to approximately 2 seconds. Even though RSTP is often claimed to reduce the convergence time to less than 2 seconds, this is not true in all scenarios, especially when there are many redundant paths in the network.[2] Even though the convergence time in RSTP is reduced drastically as compared to the traditional STP, it still does not improve the link utilization. With RSTP, multiple links in the network are still blocked, as shown in Figure 5-2. Even if the network provides alternative routes between two switches with equal cost, the spanning tree protocols (both STP and RSTP) blocks them, thereby making it impossible to achieve Equal Cost Multi-Path (ECMP), a key improvement in IP networks. To overcome the link utilization issue, Multiple VLAN Spanning Tree (MVST[3]) protocol was introduced. MVST runs multiple spanning tree instances, each for a group of VLANs. The spanning tree computed by each instance of the protocol is different, thereby achieving better link utilization. MVST was certainly better than the standard STP for link utilization, but it increases the configuration and the administrator has to carefully plan and allocate VLANs to each spanning tree instance to efficiently use all the available links.

The MSTP standard does not provide any generic method to select the spanning trees and to map the VLANs to the spanning trees. MSTP achieves load balancing on a VLAN level. So if there are enough number of VLANs with traffic in the VLANs evenly distributed, the links in the network can be fairly used. But if there are multiple hosts in the network that belong to the same VLAN, traffic between them use the same links because the load balancing is on a VLAN level. This also leads to inefficient use of links in the network. Both RSTP and MVST implement a variant of distance vector routing, which suffers from the classic count to infinity problem[4] during which the ports in the network can oscillate between forwarding and blocking states that can lead to a lot of dropped data packets.

Traditionally, the bulk of the data traffic flowed in the north-south direction, which is from the clients in the outside world to the servers and back. With the evolution of clouds, social networks, and virtualization, traffic patterns have changed considerably. Traffic between servers or VMs (east-west traffic) has increased substantially. Blocking the majority of the links can lead to congestion in the links (link connecting AS-1 and DS-1 in Figure 5-2) that are in forwarding state and can potentially increase the number of hops that a frame has to traverse to reach the destination (not in Figure 5-2). This increases the server-server communication latency leading to poor throughput.

Virtual Switching System

Cisco Virtual Switching Solution (VSS),[5] which is formed by aggregating two switches, addresses the issues faced in a three-layer hierarchical network due to STP to a certain extent. The original network of Figure 5-1 now becomes as shown in Figure 5-3.

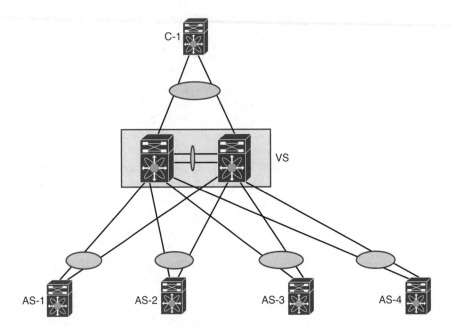

Figure 5-3   *Virtual Switching Solution*

The distribution switches are combined so that they look like a single switch running only one instance of STP. The access switches are now connected to the virtual switch (VS) through multiple links as port-channels or link-aggregation groups. The VS is connected to the core switch through multiple links as port-channels. As shown in Figure 5-3, none of the links connecting the access and the distribution switches need to be blocked. This achieves efficient load balancing of traffic that traverses the VSS topology. VSS provided a big improvement over traditional deployments and addressed a lot of the scalability concerns. But it could not address all the requirements of a Massively Scalable Data Center (MSDC) as outlined in Chapter 1, "Need for Overlays in Massive Scale Data Centers."

Giant Virtual Switch

VSS was useful in many environments, but with the growth of MSDC, even VSS fell short. Consider the case in which the number of end hosts or servers is in the range of 1000s to a few millions. To support this, there will be thousands of access switches. To serve this large number of access switches, the number of distribution switches need to be increased. This can potentially increase the number of levels in the hierarchy, as shown in Figure 5-4.

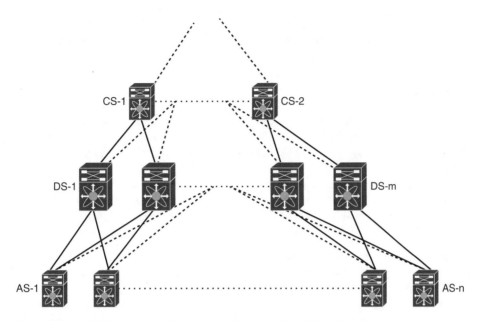

Figure 5-4   *A Hierarchical Network with More Than Three Levels*

In Figure 5-4, there are n access switches and m distribution switches. Not all the access switches are connected to all the distribution switches. To serve this demand, multiple core levels may be needed, as shown in Figure 5-4. It cannot just be the simple three-layer access-distribution-core hierarchy. Increasing the number of levels in the hierarchy means increasing the number of nodes a packet has to traverse before reaching the final destination, leading to higher latency. With more hierarchy, troubleshooting the network also gets complicated. An alternative to increasing the number of levels in the hierarchy is with a Giant Virtual Switch. With the Giant Virtual Switch solution, multiple distribution switches are combined to form a Giant Virtual Switch. This solution is an extension to the VSS that was discussed in the last section. This can be a potential solution for the networking issues faced in MSDC environments. However rosy such a solution looks on paper, it presents a big engineering challenge. Even VSS, which is a lot smaller in scale compared to the Giant Virtual Switch, had its fair share of challenging issues.

Flat Network

A possible alternative to the Giant Virtual Switch or without increasing the number of levels in the hierarchy is with a flat network. Consider the case in which the access switches are connected to many or all the distribution switches. This minimizes the amount of traffic crossing the distribution to the core level. If all the access switches are connected to all the distribution switches, no east-west traffic needs to go from the distribution to the core. With careful planning and server traffic prediction and grouping, connecting the access switches to more distribution switches, if not all, can also minimize the distribution-core traffic, and three levels should still be sufficient. But, how do you achieve this in a Layer 2 network with Spanning Tree blocking most of the access-distribution links?

Layer 3 Network

There is a school of thought that having Layer 3 (L3) at the access switches can resolve most of the requirements of MSDCs. Before you start exploring the Layer 3 network, the advantages of a Layer 2 network should be mentioned. The main advantage and the beauty of a Layer 2 network is its plug-and-play nature. You do not need to configure the interface with a MAC address and administer it. Administration of VLANs is all that is required, which is not that complicated. Moreover, Layer 2 MAC learning is automatic including the setup of the STP state. Any hosts can be moved from one location to another (extremely useful with virtual machines) wherever that VLAN exists.

Now consider the same Figure 5-1 when Layer 3 is deployed between access and distribution. Deploying Layer 3 between access and distribution switches eliminates the need for STP. Layer 3 has benefits such as computing multiple equal cost paths between any two switches. All the links can forward traffic, unlike a Layer 2 network with STP, thereby achieving better load balancing of traffic and link utilization. The hierarchical IP addressing structure enables efficient summarization and better use of the switch table resources as compared to regular MAC addresses that are inherently "flat." But Layer 3 networks do have their fair share of disadvantages. In the topology shown in Figure 5-1, an IP address needs to be assigned and administered for all the interfaces connecting the access and distribution switches. An appropriate routing protocol needs to be configured to run between the access-distribution switches—a separate one for unidestination and multidestination traffic. The main disadvantage of a Layer 3 network is that it is not plug-and-play in nature and requires more expertise to maintain, administer, and manage as compared to a Layer 2 network.

What is needed is a network that is plug-and-play without much configuration and administration, and one that uses all the resources in the network efficiently. A network with the combined advantages of a Layer 2 and Layer 3 network, thereby eliminating their disadvantages is needed to address the requirements of MSDCs.

Concepts and Terminologies

The previous section laid the foundation for the need of a technology that takes the key advantages and also addresses the issues faced in Layer 2 and Layer 3 networks. TRILL[6, 7] is an IETF standard that was developed just for this purpose. The objectives of TRILL are as follows:

- Robust loop avoidance and detection mechanisms

- Efficient utilization of links

- Achieve ECMP

- Faster network convergence and failure recovery

- Plug-and-play configuration

- Unified control protocol for unicast and multicast

- Prevent MAC address table explosion at the core

- Co-existence with existing Layer 2 or Layer 3 networks

TRILL combines the advantages of Layer 2 and Layer 3 forwarding behavior. The switches that implement TRILL are compatible with existing IEEE 802.3 bridges and routers. TRILL uses a modified IS-IS control plane to compute reachability information to the other TRILL switches. IS-IS is a link state routing protocol, which makes it possible to achieve ECMP, avoid loops, and achieve faster convergence during failure recovery. TRILL runs directly over Layer 2 and does not need configuration of IP addresses. The TRILL header has a TTL field, which makes it possible to detect and mitigate intermittent loops in the network. This section introduces some commonly used TRILL terms that are used throughout the chapter. The addressing concepts in TRILL are also discussed in this section. The subsequent sections cover these concepts in more detail.

RBridge

RBridge stands for a routing bridge and is any device that has TRILL implemented. RBridges are interconnected to form a TRILL network. An RBridge can function like a regular bridge and can also be interconnected with a regular bridge. TRILL networks can connect to a regular Layer 2/Layer 3 topology. These properties can help achieve seamless migration to TRILL. An RBridge has both a control and data plane just like a regular switch.

RBridges run a modified version of IS-IS as their control protocol. An overlay header is added to a data packet when it ingresses the TRILL network and is removed when the packet egresses out of the TRILL network. RBridges connecting a regular network (non-TRILL) to a TRILL network function as both the ingress and egress RBridges. Core RBridges connect only to other RBridges and not to any non-TRILL network. Depending on the direction of the packet flow, the RBridge that adds an overlay header or encapsulates the frame is the ingress RBridge, and the RBridge that removes the overlay header or decapsulates the frame before sending it to a non-TRILL network is the Egress RBridge. An example of a TRILL network is shown in Figure 5-5. The cloud represents a regular or non-TRILL network. RBridges RA, RB, RC, and RD are the ingress and egress RBridges. RBridges RE, RF, RG, and RH are the core RBridges. For traffic flowing from RA to RD, RA will be the Ingress RBridge and RD will be the Egress RBridge. RBridges do forwarding based on the overlay header. RBridges can be connected to each other using any link layer technology such as the Ethernet, PPP, and so on. This chapter uses Ethernet as the data link layer for illustration and described case studies.

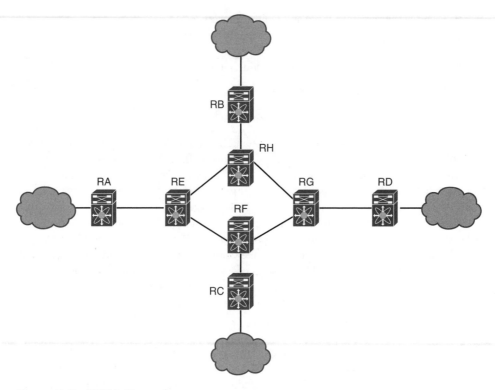

Figure 5-5   *TRILL Network*

Appointed Forwarder

The previous section showed RBridges connecting to each other as point-to-point (p2p) links. Multiple RBridges can also be connected to each other in a shared medium network (LAN). An example of such a network is shown in Figure 5-6.

Here, RBridges RA, RB, and RC are connected to a LAN. Non-TRILL nodes or hosts (H1 and H2) are also connected to this LAN. All the RBridges receive traffic sent by the end host. If the traffic is destined to go across the TRILL network, only one of the RBridges should forward that traffic. Similarly, for traffic coming from the TRILL network, only one RBridge should forward it back to the end host to avoid duplication. This is achieved as follows.

A designated RBridge is selected among the RBridges RA, RB, and RC. The designated RBridge (DR) is responsible for electing an RBridge as an appointed forwarder[8] for a set of VLANs. The DR can elect different RBridges or itself for different sets of VLANs to achieve better load balancing. The appointed forwarder acts as the Ingress and Egress RBridge for all traffic from or to the end hosts belonging to the VLAN for which it is the appointed forwarder. In other words, the appointed forwarder does the TRILL encapsulation of end host traffic before forwarding it to the TRILL network and also decapsulates the TRILL packets before forwarding it to local hosts. This is true for both unidestination as well as multidestination traffic. Needless to say, to do forwarding, the appointed forwarder is also responsible for learning the local and remote (connected to the other side of the TRILL network) hosts belonging to the VLAN for which it is the appointed forwarder.

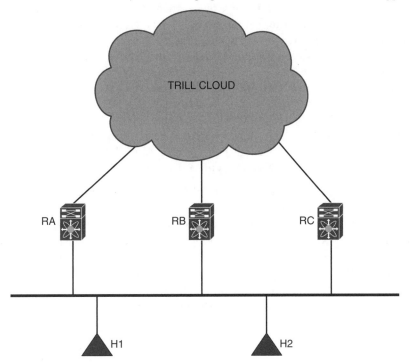

Figure 5-6   *TRILL Network Connecting to a LAN*

Addressing Concepts

An overlay header consisting of a TRILL header is added at the ingress RBridge. Forwarding of TRILL data packets is done based on the contents of the TRILL header, specifically by a field called Nickname in the TRILL header. Nickname is the addressable entity in a TRILL network. Every RBridge is identified by a Nickname, just like an Ethernet address in a Layer 2 network or an IP address in a Layer 3 network. However, unlike an IPv4 Layer 3 network, every interface does not need a Nickname. One Nickname is sufficient to identify an RBridge. However, there are some nonregular cases in which more than one Nickname may be needed. Such cases are discussed in later sections.

Nicknames are flat addresses just like Ethernet addresses, and the location of every RBridge or its Nickname is distributed by IS-IS to compute routes just like in Layer 3 routing. The Nickname is also used for representing a multicast tree. In TRILL, for multidestination traffic, multiple trees are precomputed and distributed by IS-IS (see details in Chapter 3). Each tree is identified by its Nickname. The header has a separate field that specifies whether the Nickname corresponds to a single RBridge (unicast) or a tree (multidestination). The Nickname field is not modified in the TRILL network.

Now the obvious question is how a Nickname is assigned to an RBridge. All RBridges run a protocol to assign a unique Nickname to every RBridge. When an RBridge comes up for the first time, it receives the information about all the other RBridges in the network and their assigned Nicknames. An RBridge then randomly picks a 16-bit Nickname, which is unique among all the Nicknames it has received from the network. It can use its System ID, date, and other system-related parameters such as temperature to pick a random Nickname. This Nickname is advertised to all the other RBridges. There can be collisions when two or more RBridges pick the same Nickname. This can happen when multiple RBridges are coming up at the same time or when two or more TRILL networks are combined. Because all the RBridges receive the protocol packets with the Nickname assignment of every other RBridge, collisions will be detected at a very early stage. When there is a collision, the RBridge with the highest system ID gets to keep the Nickname. Then the other RBridges randomly pick another Nickname and distribute it. When there are no more collisions, assignment of Nicknames to RBridges is complete.

A configuration option also exists wherein the administrator manually configures a Nickname for the RBridge to alleviate the collision convergence process. But, to truly make use of the plug-and-play feature of TRILL, it is best to let the protocol assign a unique Nickname to every RBridge. Similarly, the protocol takes care of sending the distribution tree information and its assigned Nickname to every RBridge. For multicast, a root node is picked among the RBridges. The root node decides the number of distribution trees that should be computed for the entire network, the root of each distribution tree, and the Nickname assigned to each tree. This information is propagated to all the RBridges. Chapter 3 goes into finer details on how this is accomplished.

TRILL Frame Format

The format of the overlay header added by the ingress RBridge is shown in Figure 5-7, when Ethernet is used as the data link layer. TRILL encapsulation is basically a MAC-in-MAC encapsulation with a TRILL header in between.

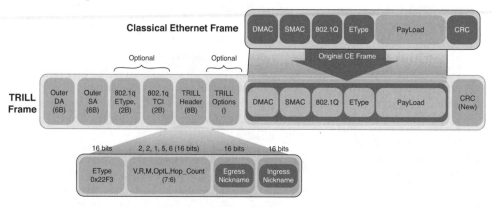

Figure 5-7   *TRILL Header Format*

The outer DA and outer SA correspond to the MAC address of the next-hop switch and the sender switch, respectively. This is similar to IP where the SA and DA are rewritten at each next-hop router. Outer DA and outer SA are of local significance and rewritten at every TRILL hop. The overlay header has an optional 802.1q tag, which is needed mainly when multiple RBridges are connected to a LAN. A TRILL header is added after the optional 802.1q tag. The 802.1q tag consists of the 802.1q EtherType and Tag Conrol Information (TCI). An EtherType of 0x22F3 indicates the presence of a TRILL header. The TRILL header fields are explained here:

Version (V): This is a 2-bit field that specifies the TRILL version. The ingress RBridge fills this field with the version it is running. If an RBridge receives a TRILL frame with a version number that is incompatible, the frame is dropped.

M bit: This bit indicates if the Egress Nickname corresponds to a single RBridge (unicast) or a distribution tree (multicast). A value of 1 in the frame indicates that it is a multidestination frame and the egress Nickname field specifies a multidestination tree.

OptL: This 5-bit field specifies the length of the optional TRILL header. A value of zero means the frame does not have any optional TRILL header. This field specifies the length of the options header in units of 4 octets for a maximum of 124 octets.

Hop Count: This 6-bit field is similar to the TTL field in the IP header. The ingress RBridge sets an initial value for this field. Every intermediate RBridge decrements the value of this field. The packet is discarded and a notification is sent to the ingress RBridge, if the value of this field becomes zero. The Count field helps to address the problems due to intermittent loops so that packets may not loop through the network forever.

Egress Nickname: This field contains the Nickname of the Egress RBridge for unicast frames and the tree identifier for multidestination frames. This field is not modified by the intermediate RBridges.

Ingress Nickname: This field contains the Nickname of the Ingress RBridge and is not modified by the intermediate RBridges.

TRILL Options: The options are present when the optL field in the TRILL header is nonzero. As of this writing, no options field has been proposed. But to ensure backward compatibility, 2 bits are defined, which have to be present at the beginning of the first octet of the options area:

CHBH bit: This stands for Critical Hop by Hop bit. If this bit is set to 1, there are some critical hop-by-hop options present. If the Transit RBridges do not support some critical options, they must drop the frame. If the bit is set to 0, the transit RBridges can forward the frame irrespective of which options they support. If a Transit RBridge does not support any options, it can transparently forward the frame bypassing the options header.

CItE bit: This stands for Critical Ingress to Egress bit. If this bit is set to 1, it means some critical ingress to egress options are present. If either this bit or the CHBH bit is nonzero, the egress RBridges that do not support some critical options must drop the frame. If either this bit or the CHBH bit is zero, the egress RBridges can process the frame irrespective of which options they support.

TRILL Control Plane

TRILL uses a modified version of Layer 2 IS-IS as its control protocol. The control protocol in TRILL has all the core functionality of regular IS-IS such as identifying neighbors, synchronizing the database with its peers, participating in the flooding process, running Shortest Path First (SPF) algorithms, and so on. The changes introduced by TRILL in IS-IS were already detailed in Chapter 3. This section discusses the core functionality of IS-IS, which is to compute the unidestination and multidestination routing tables. This provides the basis for the later sections that describe the operation of the TRILL data plane.

Unicast

As mentioned earlier, the addressable entity in a TRILL network is the Nickname assigned to every RBridge. Every RBridge is associated with a unique Nickname. SPF is run on each RBridge, which computes the shortest path route to all other RBridges (or Nicknames). In a simplified format, the forwarding table in TRILL can be thought of as consisting of Nicknames and their next hops. This is similar to an IP routing table consisting of IP addresses and their next hops. The ingress and egress Nicknames in a TRILL network can be thought of as equivalent to the source and destination IP addresses, respectively, that are carried in the IP header in Layer 3 IP networks. There can be multiple shortest paths to a destination, called ECMPs or L2MPs (Layer 2 Multiple Equal Cost Paths). Using IS-IS as the control protocol, each RBridge gets the complete topology of the network thereby making calculation of ECMPs possible. Figure 5-8 shows a sample topology with each RBridge's Nickname listed in parentheses. Interface numbers are shown near the links.

The TRILL routing tables for RBridges RC and RF are shown in Figure 5-8. The cost of each link is assumed to be 10 for illustration purposes. The routing table shows the next-hop interface and cost to reach each Nickname or destination RBridges. The actual routing table may contain more information, but these three fields are sufficient to explain the concept. The routing table of RC is straightforward. For reaching any destination, it has to go through RF, so the next hop is always 1/1. RF's routing table illustrates the concept of ECMP. There are two Equal Cost Shortest Paths between RF and RH. One path is RF – RE – RH and the other is RF – RG – RH. Because the metric of each link is assumed to be the same here, both the paths are Equal Cost Shortest Paths. So the next-hop interfaces are listed as 1/2 and 1/3, meaning both RE and RG can be next hops for destination RH.

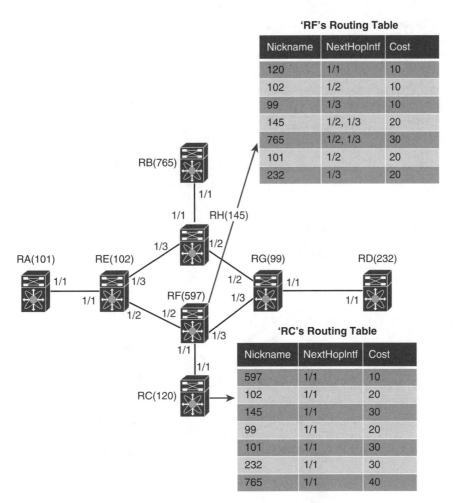

'RF's Routing Table

Nickname	NextHopIntf	Cost
120	1/1	10
102	1/2	10
99	1/3	10
145	1/2, 1/3	20
765	1/2, 1/3	30
101	1/2	20
232	1/3	20

'RC's Routing Table

Nickname	NextHopIntf	Cost
597	1/1	10
102	1/1	20
145	1/1	30
99	1/1	20
101	1/1	30
232	1/1	30
765	1/1	40

Figure 5-8   *TRILL Topology with Unicast Routing Tables*

Multicast

In addition to computing the unicast routing table, each RBridge also computes a number of distribution trees for forwarding multidestination traffic. An RBridge will be elected as the root of the TRILL network. The RBridge that has advertised the highest priority is elected as the root. Please refer to Chapter 3 for more details on the root election process as described in the detailed operation of IS-IS. The root specifies the number of distribution trees to be computed, the root RBridge for each distribution tree, and the tree number associated with each tree to be computed by every RBridge. Because the link state database is supposed to be identical in every RBridge, the trees computed by every RBridge will be the same. When there are multiple equal cost paths available, an identical tie-breaking mechanism is used to compute the distribution tree, as detailed in Chapter 3. For the same sample topology, Figure 5-9 shows two distribution trees. One tree is rooted at RBridge RD (with Nickname 232) and is shown in solid lines, and the other tree is rooted at RBridge RB (with Nickname 765) and is shown in dotted lines. Figure 5-9 shows the multidestination routing table computed in nodes RF and RH. The multidestination routing table has the list of outgoing links for each tree, represented by its Nickname.

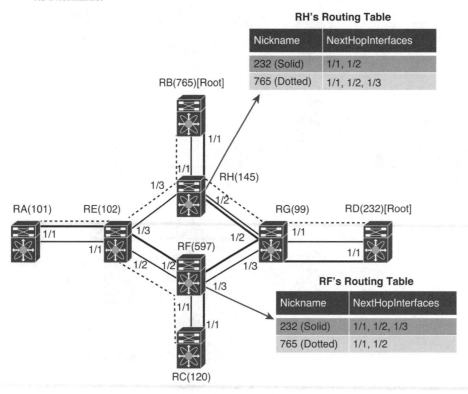

Figure 5-9   *TRILL Network with Multidestination Routing Tables*

Any distribution tree includes all the nodes in the network. The reason multiple distribution trees are computed is for traffic engineering purposes. A distribution tree is computed from a specific node or root and is the shortest path tree from that specific node. This tree may not be the shortest path tree for traffic originating from any other node other than the root. For example, a frame originating in RBridge RC and following the dotted tree takes the path RC – RF – RE (- RA) – RH (-RB) – RG – RD, as shown in Figure 5-9, even though RF and RG are directly connected nodes. The optimal case is for every node to compute a distribution tree with itself as the root so that the frame can reach every other RBridge using the shortest path. But for a large TRILL network, this may pose a heavy burden on the CPU if every node has to compute a large number of distribution trees and maintain them. Remember that every link change or node change event may trigger recomputation of all the trees.

The distribution tree chosen by a node for a multidestination frame is implementation dependent. A simple case is that of the ingress RBridge choosing the tree whose root has the least cost path from the ingress RBridge. The value for the number of distribution trees to be computed, and the root for each distribution tree is also implementation dependent. The next section on a TRILL data plane explains more about how a look up is done in the multicast routing table when forwarding a multidestination packet. Multidestination packets, as the name suggests, are the frames that need to reach more than one destination. Examples of multidestination frames are regular Layer 3 or Layer 2 multicast frames, broadcast frames such as ARP/DHCP, and unknown unicast frames that need to reach more than one RBridge in case of a destination lookup miss at the ingress RBridge, which are covered in the "Forwarding" section.

Pruning

Even though a distribution tree includes all RBridges in the network, a multidestination packet does not need to go to all the RBridges. Traffic should be sent to only the RBridges that have interested receivers downstream for the multidestination traffic. Consider the following cases of multidestination traffic.

Case A: Regular Multicast Frames

Generally, multicast frames are forwarded to routers (or switches) only when there are hosts behind the routers that are interested in receiving the multicast frames. In Layer 3 multicast, hosts communicate their interest to the network in receiving a multicast frame by sending an Internet Group Management Protocol (IGMP)[9] frame that will have the multicast group information, which is of interest to the host. This IGMP frame is propagated all the way to the multicast router. But for TRILL, the IGMP frames are terminated at the ingress RBridge. The modified version of IS-IS carries the information from IGMP in its Link State Packet (LSP) so that the other nodes in the TRILL network know which RBridges are interested in receiving frames for which multicast groups. At the same time, the IGMP message also needs to be tunneled through the TRILL cloud, if there are multicast routers on the other side of the TRILL network. The RBridges use this information to prune their trees.

The following example illustrates how pruning works with TRILL. As shown in Figure 5-10, three hosts (H1, H2, and H3) are interested in receiving the multicast traffic destined to a particular group. When the ingress RBridges RA, RD, and RG receive the IGMP interest frame from the hosts H1, H2, and H3, respectively, this information is transformed into an IS-IS LSP packet and flooded through the TRILL network. When the IS-IS frame is received, all the RBridges program their forwarding tables with the pruning information. For multicast traffic originating from a source connected to RBridge RB, the links that are pruned are shown in Figure 5-10 with an X.

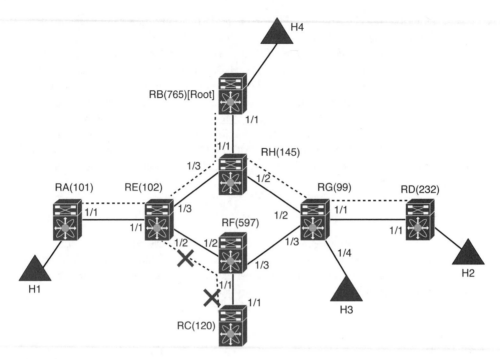

Figure 5-10 *Pruned Multicast Tree*

When the multicast frame reaches RE, it sends the frame only to RA, even though the multidestination routing table also has the link connecting to RF as another adjacency. This is because there are no active listeners attached to either RF or RC, so it's unnecessary to send the frame to RF because it would otherwise be discarded.

Case B: Unknown Unicast Frames

Generally, unknown unicast and broadcast frames are flooded to all the nodes in the network that belong to the same broadcast domain. In the other words, this frame is flooded to all the nodes configured with the same VLAN value. In a TRILL network, when an edge RBridge is configured with a VLAN on the host-facing side, that information is propagated in the TRILL network through IS-IS. The modified version of IS-IS carries the VLAN membership information of the edge RBridges, so the other RBridges in the TRILL network have the pruning information based on VLAN membership for the unknown unicast traffic. The example in Figure 5-10 is also applicable here. If the hosts H1, H2, and H3 belong to the same VLAN, the connected edge RBridges propagate the VLAN membership information through IS-IS. The RBridges prune the unknown unicast traffic based on VLAN and do not forward the traffic to RBridges that do not have any hosts belonging to the VLAN.

TRILL Data Plane

The forwarding behavior in RBridges is a combination of bridging and routing functionality. When a regular data frame arrives at the ingress RBridge from a non-TRILL network or a host, it is classified and a lookup is done in the Layer 2 table. For unicast packets (destination MAC is unicast), a lookup generally happens in the Layer 2 table based on the destination MAC address (DMAC) and VLAN. Depending on the hardware platform and the features configured, more fields can be added as part of the lookup key. Other fields can be source port, VNTAG[10] fields present in the frame, if any. Without loss of generality, this chapter always assumes the lookup key to be <DMAC, VLAN>. If the lookup in the Layer 2 table is a hit, it is classified as a unicast frame. If the lookup is a miss, it is classified as a multidestination frame for processing (unknown unicast case). Also, regular broadcast and multicast packets follow the multidestination processing logic. The subsequent sections cover unicast and multidestination processing in detail.

Unicast

This section describes the unicast packet forwarding behavior in the ingress, core, and egress RBridges.

Ingress RBridge Processing

When a native frame arrives at an ingress RBridge, a lookup happens in the Layer 2 table with the lookup key as <VLAN, DMAC>, just like a regular Layer 2 bridge. Regular SMAC learning occurs based on <SMAC, VLAN> against the incoming or source port. In a regular bridge, the lookup result would be the outgoing port along which the frame should be sent out. For TRILL, assuming a remote destination, the lookup result is the Nickname of the Egress RBridge. This essentially means the destination host is behind the RBridge identified by the Nickname, and the frame needs to go to that Egress RBridge. For packets received from the TRILL cloud, RBridges do learning of the SMAC against the ingress Nickname in the TRILL header. This section assumes that learning has already happened. The subsequent section on MAC address learning covers the different learning techniques in TRILL networks in detail. After the Egress RBridge is identified, the frame needs to be routed to that RBridge. Another lookup happens in the forwarding table with the Egress Nickname as the primary key. The lookup result will be the next-hop RBridge and the outgoing port to reach that next hop. The original frame is then encapsulated with a TRILL overlay header.

Note   The lookup result will actually be more than one port if there are multiple equal cost paths to the destination. The ECMP section covers this in more detail.

The main fields of the TRILL header will be populated as follows:

M bit: This bit will be set to 0 to indicate a unicast frame.

Hop Count: This field should be set to a predetermined value based on the maximum number of hops to reach the egress RBridge.

Egress Nickname: This field contains the Nickname of the Egress RBridge, which was the lookup result in the Layer 2 table.

Ingress Nickname: This field contains the Nickname of this Ingress RBridge.

The source and destination MAC address field in the overlay header are filled in the same way as a regular router doing Layer 3 forwarding. The Outer SMAC is the MAC address of the ingress RBridge. The Outer DMAC address is the MAC address of the next-hop RBridge. This concept is illustrated with a sample topology shown in Figure 5-11. In the figure, Host H1 generates a frame destined to Host H2 in VLAN 10. RBridge RE does a lookup for <H2,10> and the result is 99, which is the Nickname of the Egress RBridge (RG) connected to host H2. Another lookup is done in the forwarding table (not shown in the figure) with the key as 99; assuming the lookup for 99 points to RH, the original frame is encapsulated and sent out of interface 1/3. (It could be either RH or RF because both are ECMP. Assume for this flow, RH is taken as the next hop.)The outer DMAC is MAC_RH, which is the next-hop RBridge RH's MAC address. The outer SMAC address is MAC_RE. The TRILL header consists of an Egress Nickname of 99 and an Ingress Nickname of 102.

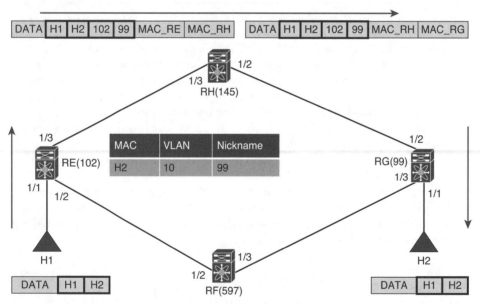

Figure 5-11   *Unicast Packet Flow*

Processing of TRILL Packets

When the encapsulated frame (TRILL frame) reaches the RBridge, the initial processing is similar to that of any Layer 2 or Layer 3 bridge/router. The RBridge checks if the DMAC address of the frame is the same as the MAC address of this RBridge. If they are different, the RBridge does regular Layer 2 switching on the frame or drops the frame depending on the configuration of the port. Otherwise, the RBridge does TRILL processing of the packet. If the EtherType of the frame is non-TRILL (for example, IP), the RBridge does regular Layer 3 switching. If the EtherType is TRILL, the RBridge does TRILL processing as follows. The RBridge checks the Egress Nickname in the TRILL header. If the egress Nickname in the TRILL header is the same as the Nickname of this RBridge processing the packet, the frame has arrived at the destination RBridge and does Egress processing. Otherwise, this RBridge is an intermediate RBridge and it does core processing.

Core Processing

The core processing is also similar to Layer 3 switching in a router. A lookup is done in the forwarding table with the key as the Egress Nickname, and the result is the next-hop RBridge and the outgoing interface. The hop count is decremented, and if the hop count is zero, the packet is discarded and the source is notified. Figure 5-11 shows the packet format when it is transmitted out of the core RBridge (RH). Just like when any intermediate router does IP forwarding, the ingress and egress Nicknames in the TRILL header are unmodified. The Outer SMAC and DMAC are modified to the MAC addresses of this RBridge and the next hop's RBridge, respectively.

Egress Processing

Egress RBridge processing of a TRILL packet is divided into three stages: (i) decapsulation of the TRILL packet; (ii) learning the inner source MAC address; and (iii) forwarding the original packet out of its local ports. The Egress RBridge removes the overlay header consisting of the Outer MAC header and the TRILL header. The Inner SMAC is learned against the ingress or source Nickname present in the TRILL header. The original Ethernet packet is then switched in a regular manner. If the destination lookup of the inner frame results in a miss, it is not flooded back to the TRILL cloud. Instead it is locally flooded out on the edge ports that are members of that VLAN. Figure 5-11 shows the packet format when the frame egresses out of RG and is sent toward destination host H2.

Multidestination

When a native frame arrives at the ingress RBridge, any of the following conditions can trigger multidestination processing. You look at all these cases in detail:

- DMAC in the frame has a unicast address, and a destination lookup in the Layer 2 table is a miss.

- DMAC in the frame has a broadcast address (all 1s).

- DMAC in the frame has a multicast address (I/G bit is 1).

The previous section on unicast assumed that the lookup in the Layer 2 table was a hit and the result of the lookup yielded the Egress RBridge Nickname. When the switch comes up for the first time, its Layer 2 table will be empty, and a lookup in the Layer 2 table for any DMAC address will be a miss. The RBridges can also age out the entries in their Layer 2 table when there's no traffic from the remote host for a certain amount of time similar to how aging is handled in conventional bridges. There may be a number of reasons that result in a destination lookup miss in the Layer 2 table. When the destination is unknown, the behavior in a regular Layer 2 network is to flood the packet to all the nodes in the network that are part of the flooding domain. Typically, the flooding domain includes nodes belonging to the same VLAN. The same mechanism is employed for TRILL, which means that on a destination lookup miss, the packet needs to go to all the RBridges in the TRILL network because the destination host can be behind any RBridge. But unlike Layer 2 networks, the frame is not flooded to all the ports, but is sent toward a distribution tree. Recall from the section "TRILL Control Plane" that every RBridge computes multiple distribution trees. These distribution trees include all the RBridges in the network. For broadcast packets or unknown unicast packets that need to be flooded via the distribution tree, pruning can be done based on the VLAN of the ingress frame. Recall that IS-IS distributes the VLAN membership information in its LSP. For unknown unicast packets that need to be flooded through the distribution tree, pruning can be done based on the VLAN of the ingress frame. When the host sends a native multicast frame, the frame is sent only to the RBridge that has hosts interested in receiving this multicast frame. As discussed in the "TRILL Control Plane" section, IS-IS distributes the information about the RBridges and the group addresses they are interested in. Pruning is done based on the VLAN and destination multicast group address of the customer frame.

Ingress Processing

When a <DMAC, VLAN> lookup in the MAC table is a miss (unknown unicast case), a distribution tree is picked for forwarding the packet so that it reaches all the RBridges in the network. Similarly, a distribution tree is also picked when the DMAC in the packet corresponds to a multicast or broadcast address. The mechanism employed to pick the distribution tree is implementation dependent. Generally, the distribution tree whose root is closest to the ingress RBridge is picked so that it follows the optimal path. Different distribution trees may be picked for different flows to achieve load balancing. Figure 5-12 depicts a sample topology for a multidestination flow in a TRILL network. Further assume that for the incoming multidestination frame under consideration, the ingress RBridge RA picks the dotted distribution tree rooted at RBridge RB.

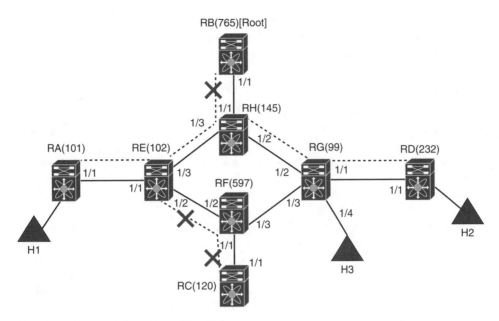

Figure 5-12 *Multicast Data Flow*

The frame follows the path of the dotted tree. The ingress RBridge after selecting the distribution tree does a lookup in its multicast forwarding table to get the list of outgoing ports. This list gives all the ports that are part of the multicast tree. Then, based on the VLAN of the ingress frame, some ports are pruned so that the frame does not go to the RBridges that do not have any hosts configured for this VLAN. In the example in Figure 5-12, the ingress RBridge RA has only one port as a part of the distribution tree and no pruning is applied. An overlay header is added to the original packet. As discussed previously, if the ingress frame is a native multicast frame, pruning is done based on the VLAN, destination multicast group address of the frame. For Layer 3 multicast, the source IP address is also optionally used for pruning apart from the VLAN destination group address of the frame. The main fields of the TRILL header are filled as follows:

> **M bit:** This bit will be set to 1 to indicate the frame is of type multidestination.
>
> **Hop count:** This field will be set to a predetermined value based on the maximum number of hops in the distribution tree.
>
> **Egress Nickname:** This field contains the Nickname specifying the distribution tree.
>
> **Ingress Nickname:** This field contains the Nickname of this ingress RBridge.

The Outer SMAC is the MAC address of the ingress RBridge, and the Outer DMAC is a special MAC address reserved for TRILL, which is in the range of 01-80-C2-00-00-40 to 01-80-C2-00-00-4F.

Then the frame is transmitted on the selected outgoing ports. The selected outgoing ports are the ports belonging to the distribution tree minus the pruned ports. In this example, the ingress RBridge RA chooses the outgoing port 1/1 for the multidestination frame.

Core and Egress Processing

For multidestination traffic, RBridges other than the ingress RBridge should perform both the core and egress functionalities. In Figure 5-12, host H3 is connected to RBridge RG. RG will be a transit or core RBridge because it's a part of the distribution tree connected to RD and an Egress RBridge because it needs to forward the original frame to the host (H3) connected to it. When the TRILL frame reaches the core, it is identified as a multidestination frame because the M bit in the frame is set. The TTL field of the frame is checked, and if it is zero, the frame is dropped. A check is also made on the outer DMAC to check if it falls within the range reserved for TRILL. The egress Nickname in the TRILL frame specifies the distribution tree through which the packets need to be sent out. A reverse path forwarding (RPF) check is done to make sure that the incoming interface is a part of the distribution tree. Otherwise, the frame is dropped. A lookup on the multicast forwarding table for the egress Nickname gives the list of outgoing ports, which are part of the distribution tree. Then, as discussed in the "Ingress Processing" section, based on the VLAN and the destination multicast group address of the inner payload, the outgoing ports are pruned. The incoming interface is also pruned from the outgoing port list. Then the frame is transmitted on the selected outgoing ports.

In the example under discussion, core RBridge RE receives the multidestination frame from ingress RBridge RA. The RPF check passes because the incoming interface 1/1 is a part of the distribution tree for the source RBridge RA. RBridge RE after doing the TTL decrement and other sanity checks determines that the distribution tree indicated by the Egress Nickname for dotted tree has interfaces 1/1, 1/2, and 1/3. Because 1/1 is the incoming interface, it is pruned from the outgoing port list. Based on VLAN and multicast group address of the inner payload, it is determined that the outgoing interface 1/2 is also pruned because the RBridges along this path of the distribution tree do not have any hosts interested in the multidestination frame. Recall the multicast state distributed via the IS-IS control plane enables each RBridge to determine the pruning information. In this example, the multidestination frame is sent out of RBridge RE only on interface 1/3 to RBridge RH. RH does similar processing and sends it only toward RBridge RG because the interface to RBridge RB is pruned. RBridge RG acts as both the core and Egress RBridge for this multidestination frame. As a part of core processing, RBridge RG sends a copy of the frame to RBridge RD. Then egress processing is done on the TRILL frame (as explained in the next section) and the frame is forwarded to host H3.

Egress Processing

If the RBridge has VLANs (or VRFs) configured for hosts that match the inner frame's VLAN (or VRF) and has hosts attached to it interested in the multicast group address present in the frame, the frame is decapsulated and sent to the hosts. The outer MAC header along with the TRILL header is removed, and the original frame is forwarded to the hosts. The inner SMAC of the original frame is learned against the source Nickname in the MAC address table. In the example under consideration, RBridges RG and RD do egress processing on the multidestination frame because they are connected to hosts interested in the multidestination frame. RBridges RG and RD after receiving the TRILL frame decapsulate it and forward it to hosts H3 and H2, respectively. Hosts H2 and H3 belong to the VLAN of the multidestination frame and are interested in the multicast group depending on whether the frame is a unicast or a multicast frame.

MAC Address Learning in TRILL-Based Networks

Learning of end host MAC addresses in a TRILL network is done through

- Dynamic or data plane learning
- Control plane learning

Dynamic Learning

In a regular Layer 2 network, learning occurs by associating the source MAC address, VLAN of the frame with the port through which the frame arrived. But in TRILL, <end host MAC addresses, VLAN> for TRILL frames are learned by associating them with the Nickname of the RBridge that served as the ingress or source RBridge for the remote end host. In other words, inner source MAC address of the frame is associated with the ingress Nickname of the TRILL header. This learning mechanism is similar to other over-lay approaches such as VPLS,[11] VXLAN (see Chapter 6, "VXLAN," for more details).

For unicast traffic, dynamic learning needs to be performed only on the Egress RBridge. The core RBridges do not need to learn all the end host MAC addresses. For multidesti-nation traffic, learning is done on all the RBridges that have interested listeners connected to them. This approach saves considerable space in the MAC address table of the core RBridges. However, this approach without any improvements results in the explosion of the MAC address table of the edge RBridges. This is because in a TRILL network the multidestination traffic reaches all the egress RBridges, which decapsulate the frame and learn the inner source MAC address if it has VLAN (or VRF) configured that matches the inner frame's VLAN (or VRF). Unicast traffic is flooded when a lookup for a destina-tion results in a miss in the ingress RBridge. Broadcast traffic such as ARP requests are also flooded throughout the TRILL network. Pruning based on VLAN does help to an extent. But, in an MSDC, this is still a serious issue. Limiting the flood traffic in a TRILL network or learning only the MAC addresses of remote hosts in active conversation are some ways to tackle this problem.

Learning Through Control Protocols

TRILL has provisions to distribute end host MAC addresses to other RBridges through the control protocol. The protocol that achieves this is called End System Address Distribution Information (ESADI).[12] The RBridges that want to participate in ESADI express their interest in its IS-IS LSP. An RBridge participating in ESADI has information about all the other ESADI RBridges. The scope of ESADI is per VLAN instance. An RBridge can be configured for the list of VLANs for which it should run ESADI. An ESADI group is a group of participating ESADI RBridges in the same VLAN. They run an ESADI instance per VLAN.

When a new RBridge joins the ESADI group, the other participating ESADI RBridges send their end host MAC addresses to it. The newly joined ESADI RBridge distributes the MAC addresses of its end hosts to the group. The ESADI protocol encodes its information in an IS-IS TLV, which are carried inside a TRILL frame. In other words, a complete ESADI frame consists of an outer Ethernet header, a TRILL header, an inner Ethernet header, followed by the IS-IS TLV containing the end host MAC address information. The ESADI PDU consists of the MAC addresses of the end hosts along with a certain confidence level associated with each MAC address. For example, MAC addresses configured statically may have a greater confidence level than the MAC addresses learned dynamically.

Choosing the MAC address to distribute and its confidence level is implementation specific. ESADI uses the underlying TRILL to transport the information. For example, if an RBridge wants to send information to the group, it can chose to multicast the frame through the distribution tree so that it can reach the RBridges of the ESADI group. An ESADI RBridge can also send the information directly to a particular ESADI RBridge (case of a new ESADI RBridge), in which case the destination address is the Nickname of the new ESADI RBridge, and TRILL takes care of routing the packet to that RBridge. When the route to an ESADI RBridge is lost or when the ESADI RBridge ceases to participate (for a VLAN or completely), all the MAC addresses learned from that ESADI RBridge is purged. For multiple RBridges connected to a shared LAN segment, the appointed forwarder for the VLAN should be the one participating in ESADI. In a TRILL network, there can be a mix of ESADI and non-ESADI RBridges. The non-ESADI RBridges should treat the ESADI frame just like a TRILL data frame and should act as a transit. Only the ESADI RBridges should decode the TRILL frame containing the ESADI PDU. Refer to Chapter 3 for more information on the ESADI control plane.

Work in Progress

This section covers the different areas of development happening within the TRILL community as of this writing. Some of the work is in progress and not standardized. The aim of this section is to educate you about the different areas of development in TRILL. For the latest information, visit the IETF TRILL charter website.[13]

Multitopology Routing

The concept of Multitopology Routing (MTR) is to construct multiple logical topologies over the same physical topology to achieve service differentiation. Some examples where this may be needed are as follows:

- Some classes of traffic that have stringent quality of service (QoS) requirements may be routed through a special topology that doesn't have interference from other flows (for service differentiation).

- Some classes of traffic may have the requirement of extra security to such an extent of having a dedicated network end to end.

To achieve this, changes to both the control plane and the data plane are required in TRILL. The control protocol (Layer 2 IS-IS) makes it possible to construct a separate forwarding table for each topology. The base TRILL specification has no provision to encode the topology information in the data packets. Some extensions are proposed to carry the topology information in the overlay header:

- Part of the existing 16-bit Nickname is used for encoding the topology information. However, this reduces the available namespace for TRILL RBridges, which is an issue in MSDC.

- The Outer VLAN field present in the overlay header, preceding the TRILL header, is used for encoding the Nickname.

- Have a special EtherType that signifies MT-ETYPE followed by the 16-bit topology information. This special EtherType and topology information are placed just before the TRILL header.

The traffic is classified into a topology at the ingress RBridge, and the topology information is carried in the TRILL overlay header. Existing core RBridges do a lookup in the forwarding table using the Nicknames present in the TRILL header. The change that is required is to first extract the topology information from the header and then do a lookup into the appropriate forwarding table for that topology using the egress Nickname to forward the packet. The challenges are to coexist with the traditional RBridges that are MT-unaware. If an RBridge supports MTR, it advertises that information using the control plane (IS-IS). Every RBridge knows the list of RBridges that are MT-aware. Non–MT-aware RBridges should be associated to a base topology. This may mean that only data traffic that belongs to the base topology traverses the non-MT-aware RBridges. Non–MT-aware RBridges should not receive a data frame that has topology information encoded in it because it may result in incorrect forwarding or dropping of the frame.

Fine-Grained Labeling

IEEE 802.1q enables the frames to be tagged with a 12-bit VLAN, which makes it possible to have 4 K entities or service instances or broadcast domains. With the rapid rise of data centers and virtual machines, 4 K different service instances may not be sufficient. Chapter 2, "Introduction to Overlay Technologies," lists overlay technologies such as IEEE 802.1ah, VXLAN, and NVGRE that enable a large number of service instances to be deployed. Similarly, TRILL facilitates more than 4 K service instances through the concept of Fine-Grained Labeling (FGL).

Intuitively, TRILL FGL is achieved by stacking two VLAN tags for a total of 24 bits of identifiers. Theoretically, this enables 2^24 (16 million) different service instances to be supported. To represent this information in the TRILL header, this can be achieved in several different ways. One way is to stack the two IEEE 802.1q tags, and the 24-bit service instance can be obtained by concatenating the outer and inner VLAN tags. Another way is to tag the frames with the existing q-in-q format. The way TRILL's FGL achieves this is with a new EtherType. The new header format is shown in Figure 5-13:

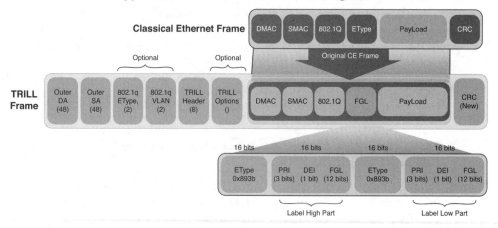

Figure 5-13   *TRILL Fine-Grained Label Data Frame*

The new EtherType allocated for this purpose is 0x893b. As can be seen, the FGL label is composed of a high part and a low part. The 2-byte tag is exactly the same as that of an 802.1q tag. The lower 12 bits of the 2-byte tag represent the FGL information; the upper 4 bits of the 2-byte tag are further classified into a 3-bit priority field and 1-bit drop eligibility indicator (DEI). The ingress RBridge is responsible for mapping the incoming port, VLAN tag in the packet, and possibly other policies in to a 24-bit tag used in the frame for FGL. Conversely, the egress RBridge is responsible for mapping the 24-bit FGL into the appropriate VLAN tag corresponding to the outgoing port. It is the responsibility of the network administrator to configure the RBridges with nonconflicting FGL values and its corresponding mapping to a local VLAN port. The RBridges that do not understand FGL are called VLAN Labeled (VL) RBridges. The RBridges that have implemented FGL are FGL-safe, meaning they don't do anything bad to the FGL TRILL data frames that they forward. VL RBridges are FGL unsafe.

Generally, traffic from VL RBridges is allowed to go through FGL RBridges, but the reverse is not true. FGL data traffic should never go through a VL RBridge because it is FGL unsafe. Depending on the implementation, the inner payload including the VLAN is used for ECMP by the transit RBridges. VL RBridges do not understand the new FGL EtherType. The behavior in such cases depends on the implementation. Some implementations may choose to drop such frames if the inner EtherType does not correspond to an IEEE 802.1q tag (0x8100). For multidestination traffic, the VLAN is also taken into account for pruning the distribution tree. When a VL RBridge receives FGL traffic, it can either result in a drop or incorrect pruning. So, it is necessary to ensure that FGL traffic does not go through VL RBridges.

The ideal scenario is to upgrade all existing VL RBridges to FGL-safe RBridges. But, this may not be practically possible, and most network administrators will migrate gradually by upgrading subsets of VL RBridges at a time. Consequently, it is imperative that a TRILL network supports a mixture of VL and FGL RBridges simultaneously. Needless to say, end hosts should communicate with each other, irrespective of whether the edge RBridges are VL or FGL. With the restriction in place that FGL traffic cannot go through a VL RBridge, you can state the following:

- There should be a path between every FGL RBridge without any other VL RBridge in between.

- There should be at least one distribution tree with the root being an FGL-safe RBridge.

This is achieved in a couple of ways. To start, an RBridge announces in its IS-IS LSP if it is FGL-safe. The edge RBridges specify the list of FGLs they are interested in and the scope of multicast traffic will be FGL (not VLAN).

- The first method is that the FGL-safe RBridge announces the cost of the link connecting to a VL RBridge to be of a high value, which is (2^{24} -2) more than the default cost of a link. This means that the link connecting an FGL RBridge to a VL RBridge is used only if there's no other path to reach the destination. An important requirement for this method to work is that the FGL RBridge should filter any FGL traffic trying to egress out of the link connecting to a VL RBridge. With a well-designed network with redundant paths, this option can provide coexistence of both FGL and VL RBridges. This option means that any VL traffic first takes the path through the FGL RBridges, even if the number of hops is more. VL traffic can still flow through the link connecting FGL and VL RBridges, if there are no other paths to reach the destination. Care must be taken by the network administrator to ensure that there's connectivity between every FGL RBridge without transiting through any VL RBridge. Otherwise, FGL data traffic will be discarded when it tries to egress out of the FGL-VL link.

- The second method is needed when the FGL RBridge cannot filter the FGL traffic when it tries to egress out of the link connecting to a VL RBridge. Here, the FGL-safe RBridge announces the cost of the link connecting to a VL RBridge to be (2^{24} -1). This means the link connecting an FGL RBridge to a VL RBridge is blocked. For this method to work, the TRILL network should not have a random mixture of FGL and VL RBridges connected together. The FGL and VL RBridges should be isolated from each other.

The main differences in the forwarding logic for RBridges that implement FGL are discussed in detail in the following sections.

Ingress RBridge

The ingress RBridge should derive the 24-bit label value as stated earlier. For multidestination frames, the root should always be the RBridge that is FGL safe. Another option is provided for multidestination frames wherein the ingress RBridge can optionally choose to unicast the frame to the selected RBridges, by setting the M bit in the TRILL header to 0 (also called headend replication). For example, if a frame is supposed to be flooded on FGL value X, the ingress RBridge would know the list of Egress RBridges interested in the FGL X through IS-IS LSPs. If there's only one RBridge interested in FGL X, it makes sense to unicast the frame to the interested Egress RBridge rather than sending it through the nonoptimal distribution tree. The choice of whether an RBridge unicasts the multidestination frame or sends it through the distribution tree is implementation dependent.

Core RBridge

The only change in core processing is that it should correctly derive the FGL value present in the inner header to do ECMP. For multidestination frames, the FGL value present in the inner header should be taken into account while making the pruning decision.

Egress RBridge

The egress RBridge should do the reverse mapping of the FGL value to the VLAN port. If a native frame is to be flooded out, it is done based on FGL membership (and not VLAN membership).

Pseudo Node

So far you have seen end hosts or switches connecting to RBridges via a point-to-point link or through a shared access link. This section focuses on changes made to the TRILL base standard to support link aggregation (LAG).

The simplest form of LAG is when two switches are connected by more than one physical link, wherein the multiple physical links (referred as bundle, LAG, port-channel, or ether-channel) appear as a single virtual port to the switches. This type of link aggregation provides load balancing of traffic across multiple flows and fault tolerance when a physical link goes down. Moreover, it provides a bigger bandwidth "pipe" that may not be possible with an individual physical link. An example of this is the Cisco ether channel or IEEE 802.3ad.

The second type of LAG is aggregating multiple switches so that they appear as one single, big virtual switch. A switch can be connected to both the member switches of the big virtual switch through multiple physical links. This will have all the benefits of the previous link aggregation plus the fault tolerance across switches and load balancing across different switches. Here, both the switches participate in forwarding of traffic. For control protocols, only one switch acts as the active and another member switch acts as the standby. Cisco VSS, described earlier, is an example of a popular virtual switch implementation.

The third type of link aggregation is similar to the second case, but the member switches behave as active-active as far as the control protocols are concerned. An example of this is Cisco virtual Port Channel (vPC)[14] implementation.

The first two forms of LAG are straightforward, and no special provision in TRILL is needed to support those. The TRILL solution is specifically for the third type of LAG, which is active-active control plane behavior. However, no assumption is made for the number of switches participating in the link aggregation, and no requirement is imposed on how the member switches of the aggregation should be connected together.

A sample LAG topology is shown in Figure 5-14. This figure shows two edge RBridges RB1 and RB2 connected to another regular switch SW through multiple physical links as link aggregates. This example shows a regular switch connected to the RBridges, but it can also be a host connecting to the two edge RBridges through a LAG. The switch can load balance the traffic between the two RBridges. In this topology, the edge RBridges are connected to each other by another link for out-of-band traffic, although TRILL doesn't mandate that. Recall that if multiple RBridges are connected to another switch through a shared media (LAN), one of the RBridge acts as the appointed forwarder for a set of VLANs. The requirement is different here because VLAN (or VLAN alone) may not be the load-balancing parameter for the connected switch, when it chooses the RBridge for carrying its traffic. Now let's walk through the behavior of native TRILL for the topology in-hand to explain the problem and the changes that are required in TRILL.

A frame from switch SW can choose any of the RBridges for carrying its traffic. Assume that for a particular unicast flow, the link connecting to RBridge RB1 is chosen as the outgoing link. RB1 encapsulates the frame in a TRILL overlay header, with the source Nickname as itself (for example, RB1) and sends it out. The remote RBridge nodes learn the MAC address of switch SW against the Nickname RB1. Now, for another flow, SW may choose RB2 as the ingress RBridge for the same source MAC address and VLAN. When RB2 encapsulates the frame, it puts its Nickname as the source Nickname. The remote RBridges when decapsulating the frame treat this as a MAC move because the same MAC address VLAN was earlier learned against RB1. If this flip-flopping occurs frequently, some switches for security reasons may stop learning this MAC address or any frames with the source Nickname as RB1 or RB2. These frequent MAC moves may also cause traffic reordering for reverse traffic. Further, RB2 also receives the unknown unicast frames sent by RB1 because it is part to the distribution tree and learns the switch SW MAC address against Nickname RB1 even though SW is directly connected to RB2.

For multidestination traffic, both the RBridges may receive the frame because they will be part of the distribution tree. Unless there's a concept similar to a designated forwarder, both the RBridges may decapsulate the TRILL traffic and send it to switch SW resulting in duplicates. TRILL addresses this set of issues as explained in the subsequent sections.

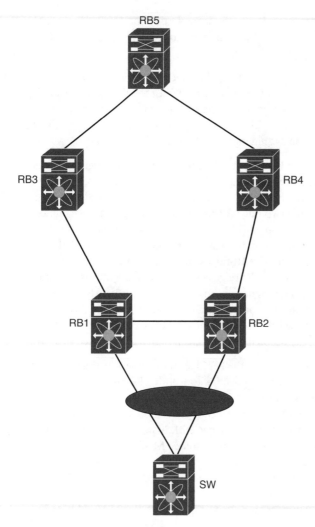

Figure 5-14   *LAG Topology*

Choosing a Pseudo Nickname

Even though switch SW is connected to two different RBridges for redundancy and load balancing, it views the two edge RBridges as a single switch. To solve the MAC move issue, traffic from any member RBridge serving the LAG should appear as if it is coming from one single RBridge. In other words, RB1 and RB2 should encapsulate the traffic with the same source Nickname. If this is done, the remote RBridges learns the end host MAC address against the common Nickname, and MAC move issue will not be seen. For this to work, even the TRILL forwarding table in the RBridges should have an entry for this common Nickname so that they can forward the frame to this common Nickname. To understand this better, look at the Figure 5-15.

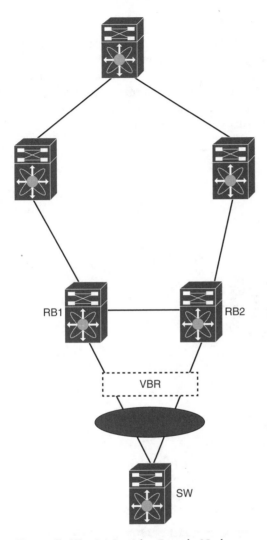

Figure 5-15 *LAG with a Pseudo-Node*

Switch SW is connected to both the RBridges RB1 and RB2 through a LAG. To the other RBridges in the TRILL network, it appears as though the member RBridges (RB1 and RB2 in this case) are connected to another Virtual RBridge (VBR) or pseudo-RBridge. All the member RBridges advertise connectivity to the virtual RBridge through IS-IS so that other RBridges can compute a path to this virtual RBridge through any of the member RBridges. For data traffic from the LAG, the member RBridges use the Nickname assigned to the Virtual RBridge as the source Nickname.

Multiple Distribution Trees per Member RBridge

Introducing the pseudo-Nickname solves the MAC move issue, but it creates an issue for multidestination frames. As discussed earlier, an RPF check is performed for multidestination frames by taking the incoming interface and the source Nickname in the frame to check if the interface is a part of the multidestination tree for the source Nickname. Because the Virtual Nickname is advertised, multidestination trees will be formed with the Virtual Nickname also as a valid node. An example of such a tree is shown in Figure 5-16.

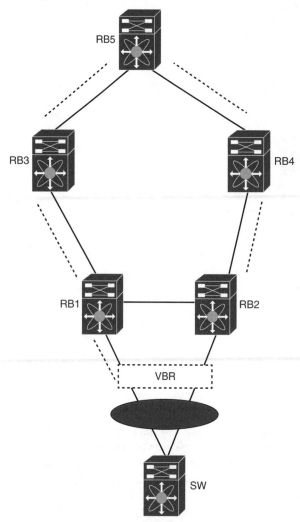

Figure 5-16   *Multicast Tree with a LAG Member*

The multicast tree shown in Figure 5-16 also includes the virtual RBridge VBR through the member RBridge RB1. For frames sent by switch SW through the LAG, it can be sent to either RB1 or RB2. If the frame is sent to RB2, and if it is a multidestination frame, it is sent on the distribution tree. RB2 encapsulates the frame with the source Nickname as the pseudo-Nickname VBR and is sent on the distribution tree, as shown in Figure 5-16. The frame traverses the links RB2-RB4-RB5. When RB5 receives the frame, its RPF check fails because the frame with source Nickname as VBR should come through the link RB3–RB5. In the example shown, even the RPF check at RB4 fails. To overcome this, RB2 needs to send the frame using the distribution tree, for which the path for traffic sourced from VBR is RB2-RB4-RB5. This is achieved as follows.

TRILL has the capability to compute a number of distribution trees. Every member RBridge should choose a tree and announce its affiliation for the tree and the pseudo-node corresponding to its connected LAG. RBridges can be associated with multiple LAGs. For every LAG, represented by its virtual Nickname, its affiliated tree must be announced. Every member RBridge needs to do this independently and arrive at an association for a tree that is conflict-free. One proposed way is to sort the RBridges and distribution trees in ascending order. Say there are four member RBridges for a LAG, RB1 to RB4, with RB1 < RB2 < RB3 < RB4, and eight distribution trees with T1 to T8 with T1 < T2 ...< T8. RB1 can pick T1 and T5, RB2 can pick T2 and T6, RB3 can pick T3 and T7, and RB4 can pick T4 and T8. The RBridges, for each of its connected LAG denoted by its pseudo-nickname, announces its affiliation for the chosen trees. Refer to Chapter 3 on the IS-IS control protocol details of how this is done. After this, when RB1 wants to encapsulate any multidestination frame with the source Nickname as the pseudo-Nickname, it uses the distribution tree T1 or T5. Because RB1's affinity with the distribution trees T1 and T5 is already announced, the RPF check will not fail when the other RBridges receive the frame.

Figure 5-17 shows two multicast trees for the sample topology, one represented by the dotted line and another represented by a solid line. Now assume for illustration of this pseudo-node concept that there are more RBridges connected above RB5. There are two distribution trees with RB1 picking the dotted line tree and RB2 picking the solid line tree. RB1 and RB2 would have announced their respective affinity toward these trees. So, when RB1 sources a multidestination frame with source Nickname as VBR, it sends it toward the distribution tree represented by the dotted line, and when RB2 sources a multidestination frame with source Nickname as VBR, it sends it toward the distribution tree represented by the solid lines. Because other RBridges know about this association, the RPF check will not fail.

Now for multidestination frames that happen to arrive at both the RBridges, only one of the member RBridges should decapsulate the frame and forward it through the LAG to the switch. The logic used by the ingress RBridge for tree selection is also used here. For a frame that arrives at a distribution tree, the member RBridge that has announced its affinity toward that tree is the one that decapsulates the frame and forwards it toward the LAG. In the previous example, if the multidestination frame arrived with the destination Nickname as T1 or T5, member RBridge RB1 decapsulates and forwards the native frame toward the LAG. For destination Nicknames T2 or T6, RB2 does the same and so on.

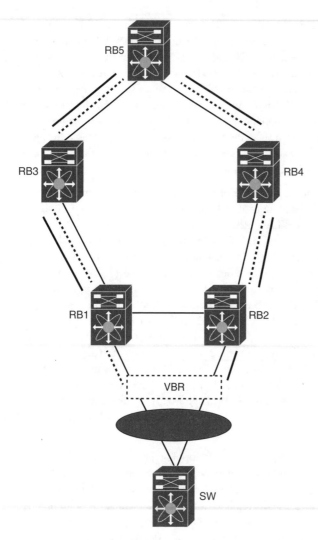

Figure 5-17 *LAG Topology with Multiple Distribution Trees*

Synchronization of MAC Addresses

Traffic for the same remote destination can ingress through any of the member RBridges, and conversely traffic destined to the switch connected through the LAG can come through any distribution tree, which means to any member RBridge. To reduce floods caused by destination lookup miss, it is essential that the MAC address originally learned by a member RBridge is synchronized to all the other member RBridges. MAC addresses can be synchronized across the other member RBridges either through ESADI or through an out-of-band mechanism if all member RBridges have a direct physical link connecting each other.

Case Studies

This section presents two case studies that demonstrate end-to-end packet flow in a TRILL network. The case studies presented here are for a regular Layer 2 forwarding over TRILL or when the source and destination hosts are in the same subnet. The RBridges can also perform Layer 3 routing in a TRILL network. However, the RBridge behavior for TRILL forwarding and learning is nothing different for Layer 3 and is covered in detail in Chapter 8.

Bidirectional Packet Flow

This section goes through a simple bidirectional packet flow using the TRILL topology shown in Figure 5-18.

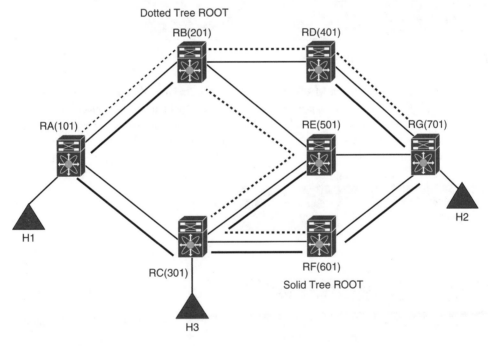

Figure 5-18   *Case Study Topology*

Three hosts in the TRILL network belong to the same broadcast domain, for example, VLAN 10. The three hosts H1, H2, and H3 are connected to RBridges RA, RG, and RC, respectively. RBridges RA, RC, and RG would have sent the VLAN association information through IS-IS so that all the RBridges can derive the pruning information. Assume that the other RBridges does not have any edge port (or host facing port) configuration for VLAN 10.

Traffic from H1 to H2

The following shows the traffic from H1 to H2:

■ Host H1 sends a frame to host H2. It's assumed that H1 already knows about H2; assume that H1 already knows the MAC address of H2. For Layer 3, assume that H1 has already resolved the ARP. An ARP broadcast request also follows the same multi-destination forwarding logic described here.

■ Ingress RBridge RA receives the frame on one of its ingress interfaces. The frame arriving at RA is shown in Figure 5-19. Assume the frame is associated with VLAN 10.

Figure 5-19   *Original Payload*

■ RBridge RA learns the MAC address of host H1. Its Layer 2 table is shown in Figure 5-20. The Layer 2 table has an entry for Interface/Nickname. The convention used in the remainder of the case studies in this chapter is interfaces are represented by the links connecting the two switches, such as RA-H1. Nicknames are represented by their numeric values.

RA's L2 Table

MAC_Address	VLAN	Interface/Nickname
MAC_H1	10	RA-H1

RA's Forwarding Table

Nickname	Multi-Dst	Interfaces	Pruned list
201	Yes	RA-RB	None
701	No	RA-RB OR RA-RC	None
201	No	RA-RB	None
301	No	RA-RC	None
.....			

Figure 5-20   *RBridge RA's Layer 2 and Forwarding Table*

- RBridge RA does a lookup in its Layer 2 table for host H2, which results in a miss. The frame will be flooded locally and over the TRILL network.

- Because there are no other host-facing interfaces that belong to VLAN 10, it is sent only across the TRILL cloud.

- RBridge RA has two distribution trees to pick from, a dotted tree and a solid tree, as shown in Figure 5-18.

- Assume that RBridge RA picks the dotted tree. Because the dotted tree is rooted at RBridge RB, the Nickname for the dotted tree will be 201. RA encapsulates the frame with a TRILL header, as shown in the Figure 5-21. The outer DMAC is a special MAC address for unknown unicast frames.

Figure 5-21   *TRILL Encapsulated Frame*

- A lookup is done in the forwarding table to determine the outgoing interfaces for the dotted tree. The forwarding table in RBridge RA is shown in Figure 5-20. The frame is sent out of the interface connecting to RBridge RB.

Note   Not all the entries in the forwarding table are shown.

- The frame arrives at RBridge RB. RBridge RB does multidestination processing on the frame because it has M=1.

- An RPF check is performed on the frame, and because the interface connecting to RBridge RA is part of the distribution tree for source Nickname RA, the RPF check passes.

- Because RBridge RB does not have any edge port configuration for VLAN 10, the frame is not decapsulated for learning.

- The frame is checked for a valid TTL field, and the TTL is decremented before the frame is forwarded out of the tree.

- A lookup is done in the forwarding table for the dotted tree to derive the list of outgoing interfaces. The forwarding table in RBridge RB is shown in Figure 5-22.

RB's Forwarding Table

Nickname	Multi-Dst	Interfaces	Pruned list
201	Yes	RB-RA RB-RD RB-RE	None
701	No	RB-RD OR RB-RE	None
101	No	RB-RA	None
501	No	RB-RE	None
.....			

Figure 5-22   *Forwarding Table in RBridge RB*

- The outgoing interfaces selected will be the links connecting to RBridges RA, RD, and RE.

- Because the interface connecting to RA is the incoming interface, it is pruned, and the frame is not forwarded along that link.

- No other interfaces are pruned here for VLAN 10 because there are RBridges along the tree that have hosts belonging to VLAN 10.

- The frame, as shown in Figure 5-23 with the modified TTL, is forwarded along the interface RB-RD and RB-RE.

Figure 5-23   *Frame Forwarded by RBridge RB*

- RBridges RD and RE do similar processing and send the frame to RBridges RG and RC, respectively, which are the next set of RBridges along the dotted distribution tree.

- The frame arriving at RBridge RG is shown in Figure 5-24.

Figure 5-24   *Frame Arriving at RBridge RG*

- RBridge RG does an RPF check on the multidestination frame, which passes and so does the TTL check.

- Subsequently, RBridge RG does a lookup in the forwarding table for the outgoing interfaces for the tree. The only outgoing interface is RG-RD, and because that happens to be the incoming interface, the frame is not forwarded any further.

- Because RBridge RG has an edge port configuration for VLAN 10, it decapsulates the frame. The inner SMAC is learned and associated with the ingress Nickname RA. The Layer 2 table post learning is shown in Figure 5-25.

RG's L2 Table

MAC_Address	VLAN	Interface/Nickname
MAC_H1	10	101

RG's Forwarding Table

Nickname	Multi-Dst	Interfaces	Pruned list
201	Yes	RG-RD	None
101	No	RG-RD OR RG-RE OR RG-RF	None
401	No	RG-RD	None
....	..		None

Figure 5-25 *RBridge RG's Layer 2 and Forwarding Table*

- The frame arriving at RBridge RC is similar to the one arriving at RBridge RG.

- RBridge RC does the RPF check on the multdestination frame, which passes and so does the TTL check.

- RBridge RC does a lookup in the forwarding table for the outgoing interfaces for the dotted tree with Nickname 201.

- The forwarding table at RBridge RC is shown in Figure 5-26.

- The outgoing interfaces for the tree are RC-RE and RC-RF. Because RC-RE is the incoming interface, the frame is not forwarded along that link.

- Because RBridge RF does not have any edge port configuration for this VLAN, the RC-RF link is pruned and the frame is not transmitted any further. Recall, RBridge RF would have already communicated this pruning information through IS-IS to all the other RBridges.

- Because RBridge RC has an edge port configuration for VLAN 10, it decapsulates the frame. The inner SMAC is learned and associated with the ingress Nickname 101 of RBridge RA. The Layer 2 table after learning is shown in Figure 5-26.

RC's L2 Table

MAC_Address	VLAN	Interface/Nickname
MAC_H1	10	101

RC's Forwarding Table

Nickname	Multi-Dst	Interfaces	Pruned list
201	Yes	RC-RE RC-RF	RC-RF
701	No	RC-RE OR RC-RF	None
101	No	RC-RA	None
.....	..		

Figure 5-26   *Layer 2 Table and Forwarding table at RBridge RC*

- Both RBridges RC and RG decapsulate the TRILL frame and forward the original frame. Because the Layer 2 table does not have an entry for address H2, both the RBridges RC and RG flood the frame on its host facing ports that are members of VLAN 10.

- The original frame looks the same, as shown in Figure 5-19. Based on the host facing port configuration, the inner 802.1q tag may or may not be present. In this way, the frame from host H1 is delivered to host H2.

Traffic from H2 to H1

Now let's go through the flow for the reverse traffic from host H2 to host H1:

- Ingress RBridge RG receives the response frame on one of its ingress interfaces. The frame arriving at RBridge RG is shown in Figure 5-27. Assume the frame is associated with VLAN 10.

Figure 5-27   *Ingress Frame Arriving at RBridge RG*

- RBridge RG learns the MAC address of host H2. Its Layer 2 table is shown in Figure 5-28.

RG's L2 Table

MAC_Address	VLAN	Interface/Nickname
MAC_H1	10	101
MAC_H2	10	RG-H2

RG's Forwarding Table

Nickname	Multi-Dst	Interfaces	Pruned list
201	Yes	RG-RD	None
101	No	RG-RD OR RG-RE OR RG-RF	None
401	No	RG-RD	None
....	..		None

Figure 5-28 *Layer 2 and Forwarding Table at RBridge RG*

- RBridge RG does a lookup in its Layer 2 table for host H1, which results in a hit.

- The Layer 2 table shows the address MAC_H1 is located behind remote RBridge whose Nickname is 101 (RBridge RA).

- A lookup is done in the forwarding table for Nickname 101. The forwarding table is shown in Figure 5-28.

- From the topology, you can observe four equal cost paths:

  RG-RD-RB-RA for which the next-hop interface is the link toward RBridge RD

  RG-RE-RB-RA for which the next-hop interface is the link toward RBridge RE

  RG-RE-RC-RA for which the next-hop interface is the link toward RBridge RE

  RG-RF-RC-RA for which the next-hop interface is the link toward RBridge RF

- The lookup result yields three next-hop interfaces. The next-hop interface for the second and third equal cost path are the same, which is RG–RE.

- Assume the path RG–RF-RC–RA is taken and the frame is sent on the interface RG–RF. RBridge RG encapsulates the frame with a TRILL header, as shown in Figure 5-29. The path taken by the frame is shown as a solid line in Figure 5-30.

| DMAC =MAC_RF | SMAC =MAC_RG | EType= 22F3 | V=0, R=0, M=0 OptL=0, hopcnt=36 | Egr_Nick =101 | Ing_Nick =701 | DMAC =MAC_H1 | SMAC =MAC_H2 | EType= 8100 | VLAN= 10 | PayLoad | CRC |

Figure 5-29 *TRILL Frame Encapsulated from RBridge RG*

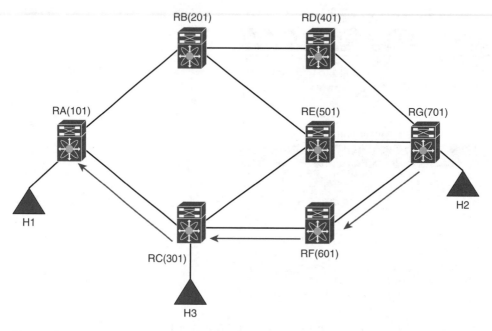

Figure 5-30 *TRILL Frame Encapsulated from RBridge RG*

- The frame arrives at RBridge RF, which does unicast processing on the frame because the TRILL header has M bit as 0.

- The Egress Nickname is checked, and because it is not equal to RBridge RF's Nickname, it does core or transit RBridge processing on the frame.

- A lookup for Egress Nickname 101 is done in the forwarding table. The forwarding table at RBridge RF is shown in Figure 5-31.

RF's Forwarding Table

Nickname	Multi-Dst	Interfaces	Pruned list
201	Yes	RF-RC	None (Depends on VLAN)
101	No	RF-RC	None
701	No	RF-RG	None
.....			

Figure 5-31 *Forwarding Table at RBridge RF*

- The outgoing interface selected is the link connecting to RBridge RC.

- The frame is checked for a valid TTL field, and the TTL is decremented before the frame is forwarded out of the interface.

- The outer DMAC is modified to the MAC address of RBridge RC, and the outer SMAC is modified to RBridge RF's MAC address.

- RBridge RC also does similar processing and forwards the frame to RBridge RA.

- The frame received by RBridge RA is shown in Figure 5-32.

Figure 5-32 *TRILL Frame Received by RBridge RA*

- RBridge RA compares the Nickname in the TRILL header with its own and decides that it is the Egress RBridge for the frame because it matches its own Nickname.

- RBridge RA decapsulates the TRILL frame and forwards the original frame.

- The inner SMAC is learned and associated with the ingress Nickname of RBridge RG (that is, 701). The Layer 2 table after learning is shown in Figure 5-33.

RA's L2 Table

MAC_Address	VLAN	Interface/Nickname
MAC_H1	10	RA-H1
MAC_H2	10	701

Figure 5-33 *Layer 2 Table at RBridge RA*

- A lookup is done in the Layer 2 table for the inner DMAC, namely <MAC_H1, 10>. Because it's a hit in the Layer 2 table, the decapsulated frame is forwarded out of the interface connecting to host H1.

- The original frame that is forwarded to host H1 is the same as shown in Figure 5-27. Recall that depending on the host-facing port configuration, an inner 802.1q tag may or may not be present in the frame.

Packet Flow for Pseudo Node

This case study goes through the packet flow for a host connected to a pseudo-node, that is, two RBridges through a LAG.

A host H1 is attached to RBridges RB1 and RB2 via a LAG, as shown in Figure 5-34.

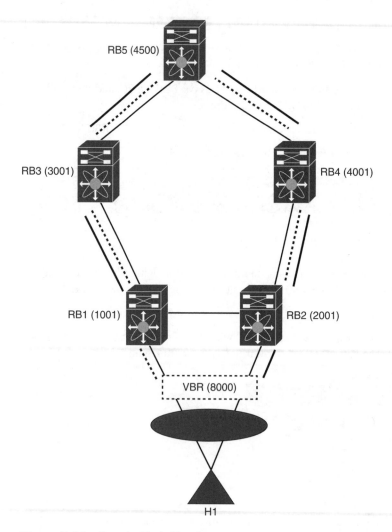

Figure 5-34   *Pseudo-Node Topology*

Initially, the Layer 2 table in both the RBridges is empty. Now assume that there are two distribution trees in the network, represented as dotted and solid line trees with Nicknames assigned as 5001 and 5002, respectively. Also assume that the roots for the distribution trees are connected above RBridge RB5, which are not shown in Figure 5-34. RBridges RB1 and RB2 have been assigned Nicknames 1001 and 2001, respectively. The pseudo-node is assigned Nickname 8000. To associate the member RBridge with the distribution tree, in a distributed manner, the following general procedure is followed:

■ Member RBridge Nicknames are arranged in an ascending order. All distribution tree Nicknames are also sorted in a similar manner.

■ A modulo operation is performed with each tree number and the total number of available member RBridges that constitute the pseudo-node, that is, are members of the LAG.

■ If the resulting value is equal to its position in the ordered Nickname list, the corresponding member RBridge picks that tree for sending multidestination traffic. In other words, that member RBridge develops an "affinity" for those sets of trees.

To illustrate the concept better, assume there are six distribution trees and three member RBridges. Table 5-1 has the sorted Nickname along with its position. The third member RBridge with the Nickname value of 2500 is not a part of the topology shown in Figure 5-34. It is just shown for describing the concept.

Table 5-1   *Sorted RBridge Nicknames Along with Their Respective Position*

Position	Member RBridge Nickname
0	1001
1	2001
2	2500

Table 5-2 shows the sorted distribution tree number and the corresponding Nickname.

Table 5-2   *Sorted Distribution Tree Nicknames Along with the Associated Tree Number*

Tree Number	Tree Nickname
0	5001
1	5002
2	5005
3	5010
4	5020
5	5025

Because the total number of available member RBridges is three, after doing the calculation:

■ 0 MOD 3 = 0 => Tree Number 0 belongs to RBridge with Nickname 1001 because it's in Position 0.

■ 1 MOD 3 = 1 => Tree Number 1 belongs to RBridge with Nickname 2001 because it's in Position 1.

- 2 MOD 3 = 2 => Tree Number 2 belongs to RBridge with Nickname 2500 because it's in Position 2.

- 3 MOD 3 = 0 => Tree Number 3 belongs to RBridge with Nickname 1001 because it's in Position 0.

- 4 MOD 3 = 1 => Tree Number 4 belongs to RBridge with Nickname 2001 because it's in Position 1.

- 5 MOD 3 = 2 => Tree Number 5 belongs to RBridge with Nickname 2500 because it's in Position 2.

Table 5-3 shows the member RBridge and the tree with which it is affiliated.

Table 5-3 *Affiliation of Tree Nicknames for Member RBridges*

Member RBridge Nickname	Tree Nickname
1001	5001, 5010
2001	5002, 5020
2500	5005, 5025

In the example in Figure 5-34, there are two member RBridges: RBridge RB1 and RB2. Because there are two distribution trees with Nicknames 5001 and 5002, respectively, after performing this procedure, RBridge RB1 with Nickname 1001 will be associated with the dotted tree having Nickname 5001, and RBridge RB2 with Nickname 2001 will be associated with the solid tree having Nickname 5002. The LAG is assigned a virtual Nickname of 8000, and both member RBridges RB1 and RB2 would have sent their affinities toward their respective trees for this particular LAG to all the other RBridges using the TRILL IS-IS control plane.

Packet Originating from Host H1

Host H1 sends a frame to host H2 with the outgoing interface as the LAG connecting to both the RBridges RB1 and RB2. Assume host H2 (not shown in Figure 5-34) is reachable via the TRILL cloud via RBridge RB5. Based on the hash calculation, one physical link is selected. Now assume the frame goes to RBridge RB1. The frame arriving at RBridge RB1 is shown in Figure 5-35. Assume that the frame is associated with VLAN 10.

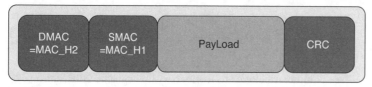

Figure 5-35 *Frame from Host H1 via Switch S*

RBridge RB1 learns the MAC address of host H1. The Layer 2 table now looks like that shown in Figure 5-36.

RB1's L2 Table

MAC_Address	VLAN	Interface/Nickname
MAC_H1	10	LAG1

RB1's Forwarding Table

Nickname	Multi-Dst	Interfaces	Pruned list
5001	Yes	RB1-RB3	None
5002	Yes	RB1-RB3	None
....	..		

Figure 5-36 *RBridge RB1's Layer 2 and Forwarding Table*

Because the frame arrived at a LAG interface, the MAC address learned will be distributed to other member RBridges. In this topology, RB2 is the other member RBridge. RBridge RB2 learns the address MAC_H1 learned by RBridge RB1 via an out-of-band channel and installs it in its Layer 2 table.

RBridge RB1 does a DMAC lookup in its Layer 2 table for host H2. Because the lookup results in a miss, it needs to flood the frame. The frame will be flooded in VLAN 10 locally and over the TRILL network. Because there are no other host facing interfaces in VLAN 10, the frame is sent only across the TRILL cloud. In general, for multidestination traffic, RBridge RB1 has two distribution trees to pick from, that is, the dotted tree with Nickname 5001 and solid tree with Nickname 5002, as shown in Figure 5-34. However, because the frame was received on the LAG interface, it should pick only one of the distribution trees it is affiliated with based on the calculations described previously. In this example, tree 0 with Nickname 5001 is associated with RBridge RB1. Therefore, RBridge RB1 picks the dotted tree; it encapsulates the frame with a TRILL header, as shown in Figure 5-37.

Figure 5-37 *TRILL Encapsulated Frame from RBridge RB1*

The source Nickname in the TRILL header is 8000, which is the Nickname associated with the pseudo-node and advertised by both the member RBridges. A lookup is done in the forwarding table to determine the list of outgoing interfaces for the dotted tree. The forwarding table in RBridge RB1 is shown in Figure 5-36. The frame is sent out of the interface connected to RBridge RB3. RBridge RB3 on receiving the frame does multidestination processing on the same because the TRILL header has M bit equal to 1. An RPF check is performed on the frame, and because the interface connected to RBridge RB1 is a part of the dotted-line distribution tree affiliated with the pseudo-node 8000, the RPF check passes. Because RBridge RB3 does not have any edge port configuration on VLAN 10, the frame is not decapsulated for learning. The frame is checked for a valid TTL field, and after that check passes, the TTL is decremented before the frame is forwarded out along the tree. A lookup is done in the forwarding table for the dotted tree to derive the list of outgoing interfaces. The frame is sent out of the interface connected to RBridge RB5. Similar sets of steps are followed at RBridge RB5 as was done at RBridge RB3. The frame is checked for a valid TTL field, and if there are hosts behind RBridge RB5 belonging to VLAN 10, the frame is decapsulated and the native frame is forwarded to those hosts. RBridge RB5 learns the inner SMAC address and its Layer 2 table is shown in Figure 5-38.

If the frame from RBridge RB1 had arrived on the interface connected to RBridge RB3 with the TRILL header signifying the solid-line tree, the RPF check would have failed, and the frame would have been dropped. This is because for the solid-line tree with Nickname 5002, the frame should have been received on the interface connected to RBridge RB4, if the source Nickname is that of the pseudo-node, that is, 8000.

RB5's L2 Table

MAC_Address	VLAN	Interface/Nickname
MAC_H1	10	8000

Figure 5-38 *RBridge RB5's Layer 2 Table*

Reverse Traffic from Host H2 to H1

Now assume host H2 connected to an RBridge (not shown in Figure 5-34) sends the reverse traffic destined to host H1. For reverse traffic arriving at RBridge RB5 for destination H1, consider two cases.

Destination Lookup Miss

If the entry in the Layer 2 table has aged out or if the entries are purged for some reason, a lookup for destination, namely <MAC_H1, 10>, results in a miss. In that case, the source RBridge can choose either tree with Nickname 5001 or 5002 to forward the multidestination frame (unknown unicast case). Assuming it chooses the tree with Nickname 5002 (solid-line tree), the frame arrives at both RBridges RB1 and RB2 because they are part of both the trees. The processing of the multidestination frame at RBridges RB3 and RB4 is the same and follows the logic explained in previous sections. RBridges RB3 and RB4 would have reduced the TTL by one. The incoming frame at RBridge RB1 is shown in the Figure 5-39. The frame arriving at RBridge RB2 is the same except for the outer SMAC, which will be MAC_RB4.

Figure 5-39   *TRILL Frame Received at RBridges RB1 and RB2*

When RBridges RB1 and RB2 receive the frame, they decapsulate the frame because they have hosts connected to them in VLAN 10. Both member RBridges learn the inner SMAC, as shown in Figure 5-40.

RB1 and RB2's L2 Table

MAC_Address	VLAN	Interface/Nickname
MAC_H1	10	LAG1
MAC_H2	10	4800

Figure 5-40   *Layer 2 Table at RBridges RB1 and RB2*

Because the frame is destined to a LAG, RBridge RB1 forwards the frame on the LAG only if it arrived on the tree affiliated with itself, which is the dotted tree with Nickname 5001. Because this frame came on the solid tree with Nickname 5002, it will not be forwarded by RBridge RB1. RBridge RB2 forwards the frame on the LAG because it is affiliated with the tree with Nickname 5002.

Destination Lookup Hit

If the lookup for destination H1 is a hit, the destination Nickname will be that of the pseudo-node, that is, 8000. The forwarding table in RBridge RB5 is shown in Figure 5-41.

RB5's Forwarding Table

Nickname	Multi-Dst	Interfaces	Pruned list	Pruned list for incoming traffic
5001	Yes	RB5-RB3, RB5-RB4	None	RB5-RB4 (for VLAN=10, pseudo node = 8000)
5002	Yes	RB5-RB3, RB5-RB4	None	RB5-RB3 (for VLAN=10, pseudo node = 8000)
8000	No	RB5-RB3 OR RB5-RB4	None	None

Figure 5-41   *Forwarding Table at RBridge RB5*

For reaching the pseudo-node represented by Nickname 8000, RBridge RB5 has two available ECMP paths. One is through RB5-RB3-RB1 and another is through RB5–RB4–RB2. If the path RB5–RB4–RB2 is chosen, RBridge RB5 encapsulates the frame with a TRILL header, as shown in Figure 5-42.

Figure 5-42   *TRILL Frame Encapsulated by RB5*

The processing of the TRILL frame in the transit RBridge RB4 is similar to what was described in the previous case study. When RBridge RB2 receives the frame, it does unicast egress processing on the frame because the TRILL header has M bit as zero and the egress Nickname corresponds to a LAG that this RBridge is a member of. The inner SMAC is learned and associated with the Nickname 4500. The new MAC address learned is synchronized with the member RBridge RB1. The Layer 2 table now appears, as shown in Figure 5-40. The inner frame is forwarded toward host H1 based on the Layer 2 table lookup hit result. The lookup will be a hit in the Layer 2 table because the member RBridge RB1 had already synchronized the MAC address when it received the frame from host H1.

Summary

This chapter covered the architecture and data plane aspects of TRILL in detail. An overview of the control plane was presented, which gives you a good understanding of the functionality of the control plane and where it fits in the overall TRILL architecture. You are encouraged to review Chapter 3 to get an in-depth working knowledge of the TRILL control plane. This chapter also briefly described the work that is currently in progress in the TRILL community as of this writing. Various case studies and examples have been presented that give you a solid foundation and working knowledge of TRILL.

References

1. Understanding Rapid Spanning Tree Protocol: http://www.cisco.com/en/US/tech/tk389/tk621/technologies_white_paper09186a0080094cfa.shtml.

2. http://blog.ine.com/wp-content/uploads/2010/04/understanding-stp-rstp-convergence.pdf.

3. IEEE802.1s, "Virtual Bridged Local Area Networks, Amendment 3: Multiple Spanning Trees," 2006.

4. "Understanding and Mitigating the Effects of Count to Infinity in Ethernet Networks" - Elmeleegy, K.; Cox, A.L.; Ng, T.S.E. IEEE/ACM Transactions on Networking, Volume: 17, Issue: 1

5. http://www.cisco.com/en/US/prod/collateral/switches/ps5718/ps9336/white_paper_c11_429338.pdf.

6. R. Perlman, "RBridges: Transparent Routing," INFOCOM, 2004.

7. "Routing Bridges (RBridges): Base Protocol Specification" – RFC 6325.

8. "Routing Bridges (RBridges): Appointed Forwarders" - RFC 6349.

9. Internet Group Management Protocol, Version 3 – RFC 3376.

10. http://www.ieee802.org/1/files/public/docs2009/new-pelissier-vntag-seminar-0508.pdf.

11. http://en.wikipedia.org/wiki/Virtual_Private_LAN_Service.

12. TRILL (Transparent Interconnection of Lots of Links): ESADI (End Station Address Distribution Information) Protocol - draft-ietf-trill-esadi-02.

13. http://datatracker.ietf.org/wg/trill/charter/.

14. http://www.cisco.com/en/US/prod/collateral/switches/ps9441/ps9670/C07-572831-00_Dsgn_Nexus_vPC_DG.pdf.

Additional Resources

■ Brad Hedlund's blog on "setting the stage for TRILL."

■ 802.1D IEEE Standard for Local and Metropolitan Area Networks. Media Access Control (MAC) Bridges: IEEE. 2004. p. 154. Retrieved 19 April 2012.

■ Transparent Interconnection of Lots of Links (TRILL) Use of IS-IS – RFC 6326.

■ Routing Bridges (RBridges): Adjacency – RFC 6327.

■ RBridge: Pseudo-Nickname - draft-hu-trill-pseudonode-Nickname-04.

■ TRILL (Transparent Interconnection of Lots of Links): Fine-Grained Labeling - draft-ietf-trill-fine-labeling-05.

■ TRILL: Header Extension - draft-ietf-trill-rbridge-extension-05.

Chapter 6

VXLAN

This chapter has the following objectives:

- **VXLAN overview:** This section provides a brief overview of VXLAN with a focus on what led to its invention.

- **VXLAN architecture:** This section starts with a description of the VXLAN architecture along with the details of the VXLAN header format.

- **Packet forwarding in VXLAN:** This section forms the core of the chapter with detailed packet flows related to VXLAN unicast, multicast, and broadcast packet flows. VXLAN deployments with and without multicast support are discussed along with interoperability with barebone legacy workloads.

- **VXLAN basic configuration:** This section outlines the steps required to enable VXLAN functionality on the Cisco Nexus switches, specifically the Cisco Nexus 1000v distributed virtual switch.

Today, VXLAN is perhaps the most popular overlay technology especially for realizing an IP-based data center fabric. The initial part of this chapter provides an overview of VXLAN along with its primary benefits highlighting the popularity of VXLAN for multitenant cloud deployments. The subsequent sections provide details of the VXLAN architecture along with a comprehensive set of packet flows covering basic to more advanced use cases. This chapter describes how VXLAN is deployed in data center networks. Sample configuration examples are also provided toward the end of the chapter.

VXLAN Overview

VXLAN stands for Virtual eXtensible Local Area Network. Because it extends the traditional VLAN boundary beyond 4 K, it is no coincidence that the inventors chose the name VXLAN. VXLAN employs a MAC over IP/UDP overlay scheme. It increases the number of supported Layer 2 networks from 4 K to 16 million. Primarily designed to address the growing scalability requirements of multitenant virtualized data centers, VXLAN allows Layer 2 segments to be extended all over the data center and even across data centers. It achieves this by proposing a framework for overlaying virtual Layer 2 networks on top of Layer 3 networks. Today, VXLAN is the most widely deployed host-based overlay. (See Chapter 1, "Need for Overlays in Massive Scale Data Centers," for more details on host-based overlays versus network-based overlays.)

VXLAN is built on data plane constructs and doesn't have an explicit control plane, so it relies on multicast running in the underlying IP core for forwarding traffic and host discovery. Some network admins consider this undesirable especially from the point of view of network manageability and debugability. These issues could be overcome by deploying VXLAN without multicast by employing a data dictionary-based approach. In this chapter, both forms of deployment are described at length.

Advent of VXLAN

Server virtualization led to a radical paradigm shift in bringing virtualization to large-scale data centers. The number of end hosts, that is, virtual machines (VMs) increased dramatically, and so did the requirement to support a large number of networks. The following were the major motivation factors that led to the invention of VXLAN:

- **STP issues:** Layer 2 networks employ the well-known Spanning Tree Protocol (STP) for loop prevention. This comes with the side effect that a large number of links are put to "blocked" state thereby making the links unusable for forwarding data traffic, leading to underutilization of links. Data center operators were wary of a large amount of wasted resources and wanted a solution that used the available link capacities. With Layer 3 networks, utilization of redundant paths has already been solved by using Equal Cost Multipathing (ECMP); Layer 2 networks also merited a similar solution.

- **Multitenancy:** Layer 2 networks are scoped by a VLAN; a 12-bit VLAN value can accommodate a maximum of 4 K broadcast domains. With large, highly multitenant data centers, 4 K VLANs were never going to be enough because a single tenant may require multiple VLANs. Going the Layer 3 route was not the solution either because multiple tenants may have networks with overlapping IP addresses that need to be isolated. The need was to achieve Layer 2 isolation at a tenant network level while still retaining the vanilla Layer 2 bridging semantics. The option of employing two 802.1q tags that was popularly employed in the metro-Ethernet space was also not sufficient because that allowed addressing the needs of 4 K tenants each having 4 K VLANs. For multitenancy, the typical use case consisted of having a large number of tenants (>> 4 K) with each requiring a few VLANs.

- **IP core:** IP has become the de facto standard for communication, especially within data centers. All vendor switches support IP, and data center administrators prefer an IP core because it's easier to maintain and debug. Although overlays may be necessary to achieve high scalability, it would be desirable if the overlays operate over an IP core so that no new expertise needs to be developed.

■ **ToR table scalability:** As identified with TRILL and FabricPath (as covered in Chapter 4, "FabricPath," and Chapter 5, "TRILL," respectively, in great detail), Layer 2 table scalability is a big concern in virtualized data centers. Ordinarily, a Top-of-Rack (ToR) switch with, say, 48 ports had to learn one MAC address per local host and then some more depending on the number of active Layer 2 conversations. With virtualization, the number of MAC addresses per port can be quite large (say, 50 to a 100 VMs per server). This coupled with the learning of addresses for remote in-conversation hosts puts a huge burden on the ToR Layer 2 hardware tables. The numbers become worse with Fabric Extender (FEX[17]) and blade chassis deployments. After the ToR tables become full, more and more Layer 2 traffic will be treated as unknown unicast, resulting in a large amount of floods in the network.

Because overlays are a natural solution that address these issues, VXLAN uses a MAC over IP/UDP overlay solution. This enables the underlying core to be IP, thereby eliminating the need for STP. Consequently, VXLAN naturally inherits the Layer 3 ECMP feature. The entropy that enables load balancing across multiple paths is typically embedded into the UDP source port number of the overlay header. Each VXLAN segment has a unique 24-bit Virtual Network Identifier (VNI). This serves as an identifier for a given virtual Layer 2 network, much like a VLAN except that there can be 16 million unique VXLAN segments. All Layer 2 bridging semantics are retained with VXLAN.

Perhaps the most distinguishing factor for the VXLAN overlay is that it was one of the first host-based overlays. What this means is that the VXLAN encapsulation or decapsulation can begin from the physical server or, more precisely, the virtual switch sitting on the physical server to which virtual machines are connected. This enables VXLAN tunnels to be end to end all the way from the server that hosts the source VM to the server that hosts the destination VM. Consequently, the ToRs that the servers are attached to need to operate only on the outer IP header to deliver the packet to the server where the destination VM resides. The ToRs do not need to learn the individual VM MAC address in the inner payload that is stamped with a VXLAN overlay header. This has a massive impact on the ToR table scalability because now they need to only scale in the order of the number of servers (in the order of 100s to 1000s) and not in the order of the number of end hosts or VMs (in the order of millions). Also, like the other overlays such as TRILL, FabricPath, and so on, VXLAN can be used as a network-based overlay. Just like other network-based overlays, VXLAN provides the scalability advantages to switches at the core of the network because they operate only on the outer overlay header. In this scenario, the access layer switches (ToRs) do need to keep track of the individual end hosts. More details on both these deployment models are presented in the subsequent sections. The next section provides a detailed description of the VXLAN architecture.

VXLAN Architecture

This section delves into the details of the VXLAN architecture followed by sample packet flows for unicast, broadcast, and multicast packets. Given that VXLAN is more commonly deployed as a host-based overlay, the initial part of the chapter concentrates on these deployments. Subsequently, the usage of VXLAN as a network-based overlay is described in detail. The architecture, packet flow, and general VXLAN operational semantics remain the same irrespective of the type of overlay mode. As identified earlier, a VXLAN network represents an isolated virtual Layer 2 network where VMs in that network can communicate using regular Layer 2 semantics. VMs in different VXLAN segments are naturally isolated from one another. VXLAN is completely transparent to the end host-VM operation. The VXLAN encapsulation and decapsulation is completely handled by an entity called the Virtual Tunnel End-Point (VTEP). The VTEP can be implemented either as a software module in the virtual switch (aka vswitch) on a server or as a hardware module on a ToR ASIC. Each VTEP is associated with a unique IP address. The VTEP interface can be considered equivalent to a loopback interface on a switch that is commonly employed as a tunnel endpoint. The terms *VTEP* and *VTEP interface* are used interchangeably in the literature.

At a high level, when a VM in a given VXLAN segment wants to communicate with a remote VM in the same segment, the VTEP associated with the source VM performs the appropriate VXLAN encapsulation. Specifically, it inserts a VXLAN overlay header over the original packet sourced by the VM with a Source IP address (SIP) in the outer IP header to be the VTEP's IP address. The Destination IP address (DIP) corresponds to the address of the VTEP behind which the destination VM resides. The VNI identifies the particular VXLAN segment under consideration. Typically, when a tenant network is created, it is assigned a unique VNI (24-bit identifier) from a preconfigured pool. The appropriate related configuration for this tenant network is pushed to a vswitch (more generally to a set of vswitches managed by a distributed virtual switch [DVS]) so that appropriate port groups may be created to which the VMs on this tenant network may attach (see Figure 6-1). This DVS configuration may be automatically pushed via a trigger from a higher-level orchestrator that is aware of the available compute resources assigned to the tenant. Examples of popular cloud orchestrators that support this high-level workflow include Openstack,[12] UCS Director,[13] Cloudstack,[11] and Vmware Cloud Director (vCD[14]). The underlying IP core network is responsible for transporting the VXLAN encapsulated packet from the source VTEP to the destination VTEP. When the packet reaches the destination VTEP, the VXLAN header is decapsulated, and the inner packet is sent out to the destination VM.

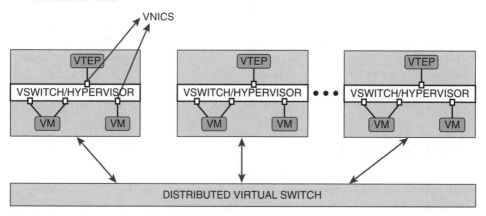

Figure 6-1   *Logical View of a Virtualized Server*

In the Layer 2 table, all remote MAC addresses behind a given remote VTEP are learned against this VTEP IP address. The association of the MACs (more specifically <MAC, VNI>) to the VTEP behind which they reside may be communicated to other VTEPs in a number of ways. There may be a control protocol that may disseminate this information. Or there may be a central controller such as a software defined network (SDN) controller or data dictionary[1] that may be employed from whom unknown (<MAC, VNI>) information is queried. Example deployments include integrating VXLAN with the Location ID Separation Protocol (LISP[16]) map server where the latter can be used to keep track of the VM-to-VTEP mappings. The most popular approach for VTEP-to-MAC association is based on data plane learning facilitated by IP multicast. The remainder of this chapter concentrates on this approach and provides more details on the alternative approaches toward the end of the chapter.

VXLAN Header Format

Figure 6-2 depicts the VXLAN overlay header format. Note the different pieces of the header where the original packet sourced from an end host is encapsulated with a VXLAN header, an outer UDP header, an outer IP header, and finally the outer MAC header with an optional 802.1q tag. Following are the different fields in the VXLAN header, whose size is 8 bytes.

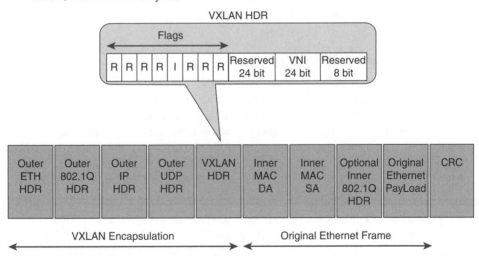

Figure 6-2 *VXLAN Header Format*

- **Flags (8 bits):** The 1-bit I flag must be set to 1 to indicate that the VNI is valid. The remaining 7 bits are reserved and must be set to 0.

- **VXLAN Network Identifier (24 bits):** Also called the VNI, this is the unique identifier for a VXLAN segment that VMs within that segment use to communicate with each other.

■ **Reserved fields (24 bits and 8 bits):** As the name suggests, these represent the reserved bits for future use.

The important fields of the outer UDP header are the source port and destination ports that are set by the source VTEP that stamps the VXLAN overlay header. The recommendation is to set the destination port to the well-known value from IANA, which is 4789;[10] however, some implementations enable the flexibility to have this field set to a customized value. The source port is the field that can provide the entropy, thereby enabling a way to exploit the diversity of paths that may exist between the source and destination VTEPs (ECMP). Typically, the source port is derived based on the fields of the original packet sourced by the VM. The UDP checksum should be set to 0, but if the source VTEP sets it to a nonzero value, the destination VTEP may either ignore it or, if it chooses to validate the checksum, the packet must be dropped in case of a mismatch.

The source IP address field of the outer IP header is always set to that of the source VTEP IP address. The outer destination IP address field may be set to a unicast or multicast address. For example, when the destination VM to VTEP binding is known, this is set to the IP address of the destination VTEP. If it is unknown, this is set to the multicast IP address associated with the VXLAN segment on which all VTEPs are interested receivers. The outer Ethernet header fields are filled based on regular bridging or routing semantics depending on whether the destination VTEP is in the same or a different subnet as compared to the source VTEP.

VXLAN Packet Forwarding

The lookup key with VXLAN is always based on (VNI and DMAC) where VNI is the 24-bit VXLAN segment identifier and DMAC is the MAC address of the destination VM. By default, just like VMs in the same VLAN can communicate via bridging and across VLAN communication is facilitated by a router, the same applies to VXLAN where the VXLAN gateway functions as the router-like device facilitating inter-VXLAN communication. Hence, for VMs in the same VXLAN segment, a Layer 2 lookup is sufficient for packet forwarding. As mentioned earlier, IP multicast is used for data plane learning of VXLAN packets, specifically, the remote MAC-to-VTEP binding.

The prerequisites for a VXLAN setup involve provisioning the appropriate VTEP, enabling IP multicast on the upstream switches that transport the VXLAN packets, and configuring the VXLAN segments so that the VM virtual network interface cards (vNICs) can bind to them. For example, consider the VXLANs used as host-based overlays. As shown in Figure 6-3, three virtualized servers S1, S2, and S3 have VTEPs provisioned on them. As mentioned earlier, a VTEP is a logical interface that sits on the virtual switch such as Nexus 1000V, Open Virtual Switch (OVS) and so on, of the physical server (aka host) and is provisioned with a certain IP address. The VTEP interfaces with the IP core via the upstream switch. S1, S2, and S3 have been provisioned with VTEP1, VTEP2, and VTEP3 with IP addresses 1.1.1.1, 2.2.2.2, and 3.3.3.3, respectively.

For every VXLAN segment, a VNI along with a multicast group address needs to be configured. An appropriate port group corresponding to the VNI is created to which the VM vNICs are attached. A distributed virtual switch enables this to be done dynamically across multiple hosts at one time. In Figure 6-3, a VXLAN segment with a VNI 11000 and corresponding multicast address 235.1.1.1 is provisioned on all the hosts. Three VMs (namely, A, B, and C) in servers S1, S2, and S3, respectively, are placed in this VXLAN segment. They are provisioned with IP addresses 192.168.1.1, 192.168.1.2, and 192.168.1.3, respectively. When a VM below a certain VTEP joins a particular segment for the first time, the VTEP sends an Internet Group Management Protocol (IGMP) join for the multicast group corresponding to that segment toward the upstream switch. Similarly, when the last VM in a given segment below a VTEP goes away, an IGMP leave message is sent by the VTEP for the corresponding multicast group. Accordingly, VTEPs in all the three servers S1, S2, and S3 become part of the multicast group 235.1.1.1.

The following sections describe sample VXLAN packet flows.

Broadcast: ARP Request

Figure 6-3 shows the packet path for an ARP packet through a VXLAN network from VM-A to VM-B.

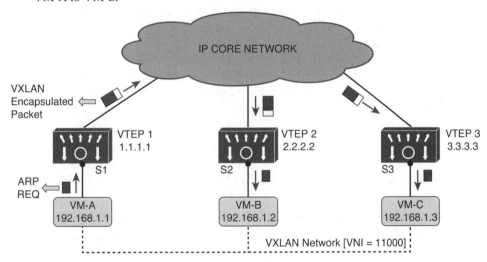

Figure 6-3 *Broadcast ARP Request*

Following are the steps for the ARP request:

1. VM-A wants to start a communication with VM-B. Because VM-B is in the same subnet as VM-A, it sends out an ARP request for VM-B with DMAC set to the broadcast address (ff:ff:ff:ff:ff:ff) and source 00:00:00:00:00:0a of VM-A.

2. The vswitch associates the frame from VM-A with a VNI of 11000. The vswitch on S1 gets this packet and performs a layer lookup based on (VNI=11000, DMAC=ff:ff:ff:ff:ff:ff). Typically, the VNI is mapped to an internal broadcast domain

(BD) value that is used in the lookup pipeline and for storage in the MAC table. For ease of understanding, use the actual VNI value in the MAC table in all the case studies. Because this is a lookup miss in the Layer 2 table, the packet is handed off to the VTEP. The VTEP on S1 encapsulates the packet with an appropriate VXLAN header with SIP set to 1.1.1.1, DIP set to 235.1.1.1, and the VNI in the VXLAN header set to 11000. The UDP source port field is generated and filled based on the hash of the original packet received from VM-A. The UDP destination port is set to the well-known VXLAN port. This encapsulated multicast IP packet is now forwarded toward the upstream switch.

3. The upstream switch forwards the packet based on the outer IP header. In other words, based on the DIP being a multicast address (235.1.1.1), the packet is Layer 3 multicast forwarded.

4. Regular multicast forwarding results in a packet being forwarded to the VTEPs on S2 and S3, respectively. Recall that these VTEPs are interested receivers for the multicast group 235.1.1.1 because they sent an IGMP join when VM-B and VM-C were powered on.

5. The VTEPs in servers S2 and S3 receive the VXLAN packet and appropriately decapsulate the packet. The well-known UDP destination port serves as the identification of the VXLAN packet. Post-decapsulation, the VTEPs are aware that this is a packet in VNI 11000 (from the VXLAN header) and first perform Layer 2 MAC learning, that is, (11000, 00:00:00:00:00:0a) -> 1.1.1.1 (the SIP in the outer VXLAN header). Subsequently, the vswitch performs a regular Layer 2 lookup on the inner packet, namely based on the key (11000, ff:ff:ff:ff:ff:ff), and the packet is forwarded to VMs B and C, respectively. This is because a packet with a broadcast MAC is typically sent to all end hosts within that segment.

6. In this way, both VMs B and C receive the broadcast ARP request from VM-A. Because the ARP request is for 192.168.1.2, which is the IP address of VM-B, only VM-B responds to the same. VM-C does not respond to this ARP request but can create an appropriate IP-MAC binding for VM-A in its ARP cache.

7. In this way, VTEPs on servers S2 and S3 learn about remote 00:00:00:00:00:0a aided by IP multicast forwarding. The upstream switches that form the IP core network are completely unaware of the end host MAC addresses and forward only the packet based on the overlay header. In the next section, the packet flow for the unicast ARP response packet is described.

Unicast: ARP Reply

In response to the ARP request from VM-A, VM-B sends out a unicast ARP reply. Figure 6-4 shows the packet flow for an ARP response packet through the VXLAN network from VM-B to VM-A.

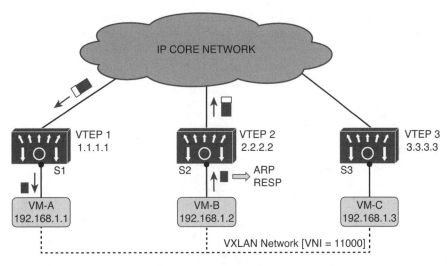

Figure 6-4 *Unicast ARP Reply*

Following are the steps for the ARP response:

1. The ARP response from VM-B is a unicast packet with SMAC=00:00:00:00:00:0b and DMAC=00:00:00:00:00:0a.

2. The vswitch on S2 gets this packet and performs a Layer 2 lookup based on (VNI=11000, DMAC=00:00:00:00:00:0a). Because this entry was learned on the vswitch based on the earlier incoming ARP request, the lookup results in a hit. However, compared to a conventional Layer 2 lookup hit that directly yields the port over which the packet needs to be forwarded, this lookup result yields an IP address toward which the packet must be forwarded. Consequently, the VTEP on S2 takes care of encapsulating the packet with an appropriate VXLAN header. The important fields set by the VTEP are as follows: DIP is set to 1.1.1.1, the SIP is set to 2.2.2.2, and the VNI to 11000. Because the 00:00:00:00:00:0a to VTEP binding is known, the encapsulated packet is a unicast IP packet.

3. This encapsulated unicast IP packet is now forwarded toward the upstream switch. Again, the upstream switch looks at only the outer IP header and forwards the packet toward the VTEP on S1.

4. The VXLAN packet received with the DIP corresponding to the VTEP address on S1 will be appropriately decapsulated. Post-decapsulation, the VTEP performs MAC learning as usual based on the inner packet SMAC and outer overlay header SIP, namely (11000, 00:00:00:00:00:0b) -> 2.2.2.2. Subsequently, the vswitch performs a regular Layer 2 lookup on the inner packet, namely based on the key (11000, 00:00:00:00:00:0a), and the packet is forwarded to VM-A.

5. VM-A and VM-B now have the IP-MAC binding for each other and can subsequently start sending data traffic to each other. The corresponding VTEPs on servers S1 and S2, respectively, are also aware of the MAC-to-VTEP binding and therefore packets between VM-A and VM-B can be forwarded via regular unicast IP forwarding.

Unicast: Data

Figure 6-5 shows the packet path for a unicast packet through the VXLAN network from VM-A to VM-B post-ARP resolution.

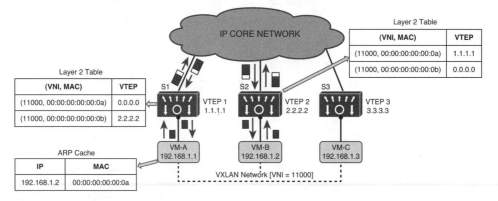

Figure 6-5   *Unicast Data Flow*

Following are the steps for a unicast data packet flow from VM-A to VM-B:

1. Host A now transmits an IP packet with SIP=192.168.1.1 and DIP=192.168.1.2 in a standard Ethernet frame with SMAC=00:00:00:00:00:0a and DMAC=00:00:00:00:00:0b.

2. The vswitch on S1 gets this packet and performs a Layer 2 lookup based on (VNI=11000, DMAC=00:00:00:00:00:0b). Because this entry was learned on the vswitch based on the earlier incoming ARP response, the lookup results in a hit with the result pointing toward VTEP 2.2.2.2. Consequently, the VTEP on S1 takes care of encapsulating the packet with an appropriate VXLAN header. The important fields set by the VTEP are as follows: DIP is set to 2.2.2.2, the SIP is set to 1.1.1.1, and the VNI is set to 11000. Because the 00:00:00:00:00:0b-to-VTEP binding is known, the encapsulated packet is a unicast IP packet.

3. The VXLAN encapsulated frame is sent to the upstream switch toward S2 where VTEP=2.2.2.2 resides. If there are multiple paths to reach from 1.1.1.1 to 2.2.2.2, the standard ECMP-based logic would kick in to select one of these paths. The vswitch may choose to select a path based on the inner frame fields such as SMAC. This applies to all unicast-forwarding cases including the ARP reply case listed in the previous section.

4. The VXLAN packet received with the DIP=2.2.2.2 corresponding to the VTEP address on S2 will be appropriately decapsulated. Post-decapsulation, the VTEP reinforces the Layer 2 table entry corresponding to (11000, 00:00:00:00:00:0a) -> 1.1.1.1 and subsequently based on the inner payload lookup (11000, 00:00:00:00:00:0b) sends the packet toward VM-B.

5. Reverse traffic from VM-B to VM-A will be similarly unicast forwarded.

Unknown Unicast

The (VNI, MAC)->VTEP-IP entry in the Layer 2 table is subjected to the same Layer 2 learning semantics as any other Layer 2 table entry. In other words, if a given entry is not refreshed within a certain time interval, it is automatically aged out. Subsequently, if a new flow to the aged-out destination MAC is initiated, it is treated as an unknown unicast case. Figure 6-6 shows how unknown unicast cases are handled in a VXLAN network. The packet flows for multidestination packets including broadcast, multicast, and unknown unicast cases are fairly identical.

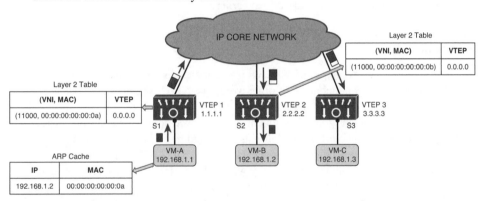

Figure 6-6 *Unknown Unicast Case*

Following are the steps for handling an unknown unicast packet:

1. Assume that the ARP cache for VM-A and VM-B has a larger aging timer as compared to the Layer 2 aging timer on the vswitches on the servers S1, S2, and S3, respectively. Assume VM-A-to-VM-B communication has stalled for a certain time interval such that the vswitch on server S1 purges the entry for 00:00:00:00:00:0b. However, the ARP cache in VM-A still has the IP-MAC binding for VM-B. Now VM-A sends a data packet out to VM-B. This packet has SMAC=00:00:00:00:00:0a and DMAC=00:00:00:00:00:0b.

2. The vswitch on S1 gets this packet and performs a layer lookup based on (VNI=11000, DMAC=00:00:00:00:00:0b). Because this is a miss in the Layer 2 table, the packet is treated as an unknown unicast case. In other words, it will be bridged to all local VMs within this VXLAN segment and handed off to the VTEP so that it can be sent over to the remote VMs. The VTEP on S1 encapsulates the packet with

an appropriate VXLAN header with SIP set to 1.1.1.1, DIP set to 235.1.1.1, and the VNI in the VXLAN header set to 11000. This encapsulated multicast IP packet is now forwarded toward the upstream switch.

3. Regular IP multicast forwarding results in a packet being forwarded to the VTEPs on S2 and S3, respectively, and subsequently to all VMs below those VTEPs within that VXLAN segment.

4. The VTEPs in servers S2 and S3 receive the VXLAN packet and perform Layer 2 MAC learning or reset the aging timer if the entry already exists, that is, (11000, 00:00:00:00:00:0a) -> 1.1.1.1 (the SIP in the outer VXLAN header). Subsequently, the vswitch on S2 performs a regular Layer 2 lookup on the inner packet, namely based on the key (11000, 00:00:00:00:00:0b) and packet is forwarded to VM-B. The vswitch on S3 suffers a lookup miss and the packet will be forwarded to VM-C because this is treated as an unknown unicast and VM-C drops the packet.

5. The reverse traffic from VM-B to VM-A ensures that 00:00:00:00:00:0b is learned on the vswitch on S1, and subsequent traffic will be unicast forwarded as described in the unicast forwarding case described earlier.

VM Mobility Case

One of the primary advantages of VXLAN is that it enables the Layer 2 domain to be stretched over Layer 3 boundaries. In other words, a VXLAN segment can span across multiple racks within a data center and across multiple data centers. This also means that virtual machines in a VXLAN segment can be moved across Layer 3 boundaries. This provides a huge amount of flexibility as compared to traditional VLANs, where the Layer 2 domain was constrained to those racks where the VLAN is instantiated and the VMs within a VLAN could be moved only within those racks. When a VM moves from one server to another, it retains all its properties such as the MAC address, IP address, its vNICs, and so on. The presence of the hypervisor layer in between the VM and the physical hardware is what enables the VM to be easily dismounted from the physical server that it currently resides on to another server.

When it is stated that VMs within a VXLAN can migrate across Layer 3 boundaries, this does not mean that, for example, the VM-A in a VXLAN segment corresponding to subnet 192.168.1.0/24 and having 00:00:00:00:00:0a and IP 192.168.1.1 can be moved to a different subnet. This is because post-VM mobility the VM retains its IP/MAC address; the VM is not even aware that it has moved. With live migration, the move-time requirements are extremely stringent because the application stack on the VM, including its current state, and existing network connections, and so on, should transparently continue without requiring any connection breakdown during and post-migration.

To illustrate the network handling post a VM mobility event, VM-A is moved from server S1 to server S3, as shown in Figure 6-7. Assume that prior to the VM migration event, all the VMs were in active conversation with each other.

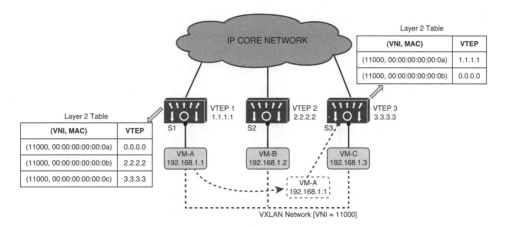

Figure 6-7 *VM Mobility Case (Initial)*

Following are the steps in the handling of a VM mobility event:

1. Because VM-A was in active communication with VM-B and VM-C, its ARP cache is populated with the IP-MAC binding for these VMs. Similarly, the vswitches on S1, S2, and S3 have learned about the MAC-VTEP binding for all the remote VMs. For example, servers S2 and S3 have learned the binding (11000, 00:00:00:00:00:0a) ->1.1.1.1 in their Layer 2 table.

2. When VM-A is migrated from server S1 to server S3, the vswitches on both S1 and S3 are aware of the VM migration event. Some vswitches such as the Cisco Nexus 1000V or the VMware vsphere Distributed Switches broadcast out a RARP message on behalf of the moved VM. Other vswitches such as Microsoft's Hyper-V instead send out a gratuitous ARP (GARP) message on the VM's behalf. This enables the rest of the network to update their forwarding tables' entries to point to the new location of the VM. In this way, all traffic to the VM can be rapidly redirected to its new location with minimal disruption.

3. For this example, assume that the vswitch on S3 sends out a reverse ARP (RARP) message with DMAC=ff:ff:ff:ff:ff:ff and SMAC=00:00:00:00:00:0a. This RARP message undergoes a Layer 2 lookup on the vswitch just like any other Layer 2 packet. The lookup based on the key (11000, ff:ff:ff:ff:ff:ff) results in the packet being flooded locally within that segment and also a packet being sent toward the upstream switch with a VXLAN encapsulation with SIP=3.3.3.3, DIP=235.1.1.1, VNI=11000. In other words, this is handled in a similar manner as any other broadcast packet.

4. The RARP notification encapsulated in the IP multicast packet reaches both servers S1 and S2. They decapsulate the packet and update their Layer 2 tables with the updated entry for VM-A namely (11000, VM-A)->3.3.3.3. In this way, traffic from VM-B and VM-C to VM-A is now unicasted to the VTEP on S3. Figure 6-8 shows the state of the Layer 2 tables post VM-A migration.

5. There is no change in the ARP cache of any of the VMs including VM-A. They retain the MAC-IP binding because nothing has changed. How fast the network migrates the VM from server S1 to S3 and subsequently processes the notification about the VM move determines how much traffic disruption is suffered by active flows to and from VM-A.

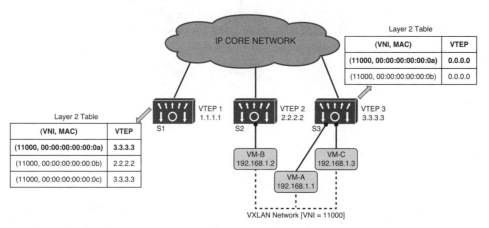

Figure 6-8   *VM Mobility Case (Final)*

IPv6 Data Forwarding

With the IP address space exhaustion with IPv4 becoming a reality, the popularity of IPv6 and its adoption has increased in the past few years. Data center environments represent a popular choice where IPv6 can be readily deployed. Much like IPv4 employs ARP to resolve the IP-to-MAC binding for the destination IP address, IPv6 employs the Neighbor Discovery (ND) protocol for the destination IPv6 address to MAC resolution. IPv6 is becoming increasingly popular in enterprise environments;[7] here a sample packet flow is illustrated where IPv6 hosts communicate with each other over a VXLAN cluster.

With VXLAN, the forwarding mechanism with IPv6 is almost identical to IPv4. The reason for this is that VXLAN is an MAC over IP/UDP overlay. Consequently, the forwarding is based on (VNI and MAC) lookups that are essentially independent of the Layer 3 protocol employed by the end hosts. The original IPv6 packet from the end host will be encapsulated with a VXLAN header; the outer header may be IPv4 or IPv6 depending on whether the overlay IP core is an IPv4 or IPv6 cloud.

Figure 6-9 shows a sample topology with servers S1, S2, and S3 forming a VXLAN cluster with IPv4 servicing as the core network that transports VXLAN packets. S1, S2, and S3 have been provisioned with VTEP1, VTEP2, VTEP3, and IPv4 addresses 1.1.1.1, 2.2.2.2, and 3.3.3.3, respectively. A VXLAN segment with a VNI 21000 and corresponding multicast address 235.1.1.1 is provisioned on all the hosts. Virtual machines A, B, and C are provisioned in servers S1, S2, and S3. They are all placed in this VXLAN segment and assigned IPv6 addresses 2001:A:A::1, 2001:A:A::2, and 2001:A:A::3, respectively.

Accordingly, VTEPs in all the three servers S1, S2, and S3 become part of the multicast group 234.1.1.1.

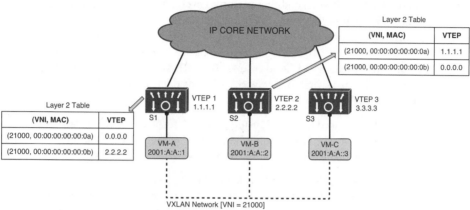

Figure 6-9 *IPv6 VM-to-VM Flow*

NS Request and NA Response

The next steps involved in the transit of an IPv6 packet through a VXLAN network from VM-A to VM-B are highlighted. Although IPv6 involves exchange of router solicitation (RS), router advertisement (RA), and NS messages for duplicate address detection (DAD) for both link-local and global addresses, here the concentration is on the flow involving communication of VM-A to VM-B employing global IPv6 addresses. The steps involved are as follows:

1. VM-A wants to start a communication with VM-B. Because VM-B is in the same subnet as VM-A, it sends out an NS request for VM-B with DMAC set to the solicited node multicast address (3333.0000.0002) and source 00:00:00:00:00:0a of VM-A. The NS packet employs an ICMPv6 payload of type 135 with the target address as 2001:A:A::2.

2. The vswitch on S1 gets this packet and performs a layer lookup based on (VNI=21000, DMAC=3333.0000.0002). Because this is a lookup miss in the Layer 2 table, the packet is handed off to the VTEP. The VTEP on S1 encapsulates the packet with an appropriate VXLAN header with SIP set to 1.1.1.1, DIP set to 235.1.1.1, and the VNI in the VXLAN header set to 21000. The UDP source port field is generated and filled based on the hash of the original packet received from VM-A. The UDP destination port is set to the well-known VXLAN port. Consequently, this represents an IPv6 in IPv4 tunneled packet that is forwarded toward the upstream switch.

3. The upstream switch forwards the packet based on the outer IP header. In other words, based on the DIP being a multicast address (235.1.1.1), the packet is Layer 3 multicast forwarded. The packet is forwarded to the vswitches on both servers S2 and S3.

4. The VTEPs in servers S2 and S3 receive the VXLAN packet and appropriately decapsulate it. Post-decapsulation, the VTEPs are aware that this is a packet in VNI 21000 (from the VXLAN header) and first perform Layer 2 MAC learning, that is (21000, 00:00:00:00:00:0a) -> 1.1.1.1 (the SIP in the outer VXLAN header). Subsequently, the vswitches perform a regular Layer 2 lookup on the inner packet, namely based on the key (21000, 3333.0000.0002), and the packet is forwarded to VMs B and C, respectively (treated as a flood case). If IPv6 ND snooping were enabled on the vswitches, only the vswitch on server S2 forwards the packet to VM-B, but the vswitch on server S3 drops it.

5. The NS packet received by VM-B results in an NA response being unicasted to the requestor. The NA response with DMAC=00:00:00:00:00:0a and SMAC=00:00:00:00:00:0b are sent out by VM-B.

6. The vswitch in S2 receives the NA packet and performs a Layer 2 lookup based on (VNI=21000, DMAC=00:00:00:00:00:0a). The lookup result indicates that the destination is behind VTEP with IP=1.1.1.1. Consequently, the IPv6 packet is encapsulated with a VXLAN header with VNI=21000, SIP=2.2.2.2, and DIP=1.1.1.1.

7. The encapsulated packet is forwarded toward the IP core, which in turn delivers it to the vswitch on server S1 where VTEP with IP=1.1.1.1 resides. The packet is decapsulated, and MAC learning results in the entry (21000, 00:00:00:00:00:0b) ->2.2.2.2 being added to the Layer 2 table. The destination lookup based on (21000, 00:00:00:00:00:0b) results in the decapsulated NA response being sent to VM-A.

8. After the IPv6 address of VM-B is resolved, subsequently data traffic from VM-A to VM-B will be unicast forwarded.

VXLAN Gateway

VTEPs handle the VXLAN encapsulation and decapsulation at the sending and receiving ends, respectively, which enables VMs to transparently communicate with other VMs in the same VXLAN segment. This enables the end hosts to be completely independent of VXLAN and its inner workings. Although this is ideal for virtual workloads, today data centers are not completely virtualized. Given the legacy workloads and the demand for different types of applications, there is generally going to be a healthy mix of physical and virtual workloads. Legacy non-virtualized, barebones servers may either host services or require services that are hosted in a virtual form factor. In other words, physical and virtual machines may need to frequently communicate with each other. With VXLAN, this mandates that physical machines have a VTEP-like functionality, which would have severely impaired the adoption of VXLAN. Backward compatibility and interoperability are extremely important with newer technologies especially in data center environments. Even virtual workloads that have still not migrated to VXLAN suffer from the interoperability issue because they are using vanilla VLANs.

At the outset, the inventors of VXLAN anticipated these scenarios and proposed an elegant solution for migration and interoperability with non-VXLAN endpoints. The interoperation is made possible via an intermediate device called a VXLAN gateway. Simply put, this device does the stitching of traffic between VXLAN and vanilla VLAN environments. The VTEP functionality is embedded in the VXLAN gateway device so that the appropriate encapsulation and decapsulation of VXLAN headers can be handled at this gateway device. In a VXLAN cloud, each VXLAN segment represents a virtual Layer 2 domain, whereas in a traditional Layer 2 cloud, this is represented by a VLAN. The gateway device is the one where the mapping of the VXLAN segment to VLAN is configured so that it can perform the appropriate translation. (See Figure 6-10 for a logical representation of a VXLAN gateway.) For packets going from the VLAN cloud (legacy environments) to the VXLAN cloud, the gateway device removes the 802.1q VLAN tag and stamps the mapped VXLAN header, and for reverse traffic it does the opposite. The subsequent sections go through some sample packet flows involving a VXLAN gateway.

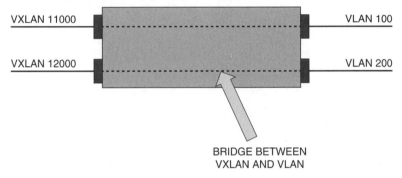

Figure 6-10   *Logical View of a VXLAN Gateway*

Figure 6-11 shows a scenario in which a VXLAN gateway enables communication between the physical server P (non-VXLAN) and virtual machines VM-A and VM-B that are part of the VXLAN segment 11000. All hosts, virtual machines, and the physical server are part of the same subnet 192.168.1.0/24. Although Figure 6-10 shows the legacy physical server directly attached to the VXLAN gateway, this is not required. The VXLAN gateway just serves as the entry and exit point into and out of the VXLAN cloud. The physical server may be connected to the VXLAN gateway device via a legacy Layer 2 or Layer 3 network. End hosts VM-A, VM-B, and P are assigned (MAC, IP) addresses (00:00:00:00:00:0a, 192.168.1.1), (00:00:00:00:00:0b, 192.168.1.2), and (00:00:00:00:00:10, 192.168.1.10), respectively. A sample packet flow is initiated from a virtual machine directed toward the physical server.

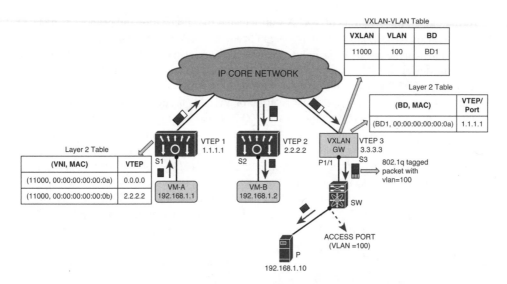

Figure 6-11   *Virtual Machine to Physical Machine via VXLAN Gateway (Initial)*

Following are the steps in the handling these events:

1.   VM-A wants to start a communication with physical host P, so it sends out an ARP request with DMAC=ff:ff:ff:ff:ff:ff, SMAC=00:00:00:00:00:0a, and the target IP address for which it needs to know IP-to-MAC binding as 192.168.1.10.

2.   The vswitch on S1 gets this packet and performs a layer lookup based on (VNI=11000, DMAC=ff:ff:ff:ff:ff:ff). Because this is a miss in the Layer 2 table, the packet is handed off to the VTEP. The VTEP on S1 encapsulates the packet with an appropriate VXLAN header with SIP=1.1.1.1, DIP=235.1.1.1, and VNI=11000. As before, this encapsulated multicast IP packet is forwarded toward the upstream switch.

3.   The VTEP (3.3.3.3) on the VXLAN gateway is also an interested receiver for the multicast group associated with VNI 11000. Typically, the VXLAN 11000 to VLAN 100 configuration on the VXLAN gateway triggers this interest, that is, an appropriate IGMP join would be sent upstream. For the rest of the discussion, assume that both VNI=11000 and VLAN=100 map to the same common bridge-domain BD1, which are employed as the key for Layer 2 lookup.

4.   Regular multicast forwarding results in a packet being forwarded to the VTEPs on both S2 and the VXLAN gateway.

5.   The VTEP on server S2 performs appropriate VXLAN header decapsulation; performs Layer 2 MAC learning, that is, (BD1, 00:00:00:00:00:0a) -> 1.1.1.1; and forwards the inner ARP request packet to VM-B. Because the ARP request is not for VM-B, it does not send out any ARP response.

6. The VTEP on the VXLAN gateway also performs a similar decapsulation operation and MAC learning operation as the VTEP on server S2. In addition, because the inner packet is an ARP broadcast, it needs to be flooded out toward the non-VXLAN domain. The configured mapping of VXLAN-11000->VLAN-100 on the VXLAN gateway provides information about the dot1q tag that needs to be stamped on the packet before it is sent out. Refer to the "VXLAN Basic Configuration" section at the end of the chapter for sample configuration commands related to enabling the VXLAN gateway feature. This packet is composed of the original ARP payload sent out by VM-B with DMAC=ff:ff:ff:ff:ff:ff, SMAC=00:00:00:00:00:0a, and 802.1q tag with VLAN=100.

7. When this packet reaches the intermediate switch SW, it performs regular Layer 2 learning on the packet based on the incoming interface, that is (VLAN=100, SMAC=00:00:00:00:00:0a)->P1/1. Subsequently, Layer 2 lookup on SW results in the packet being flooded out on all ports of VLAN 100 including the one toward the physical server P.

8. Given that the ARP request is for 192.168.1.10, which is the IP address of P, an appropriate ARP response will be sent out with DMAC=00:00:00:00:00:0a, SMAC=00:00:00:00:00:10. The Layer 2 lookup on SW results in the packet being sent toward the VXLAN gateway with an 802.1q tag with VLAN=100.

9. The incoming ARP response packet at the VXLAN gateway triggers Layer 2 learning, that is (BD1, 00:00:00:00:00:10)->P1/1. The subsequent DMAC lookup results in a hit of the previously learned entry (BD1, 00:00:00:00:00:0a) -> 1.1.1.1. Consequently, VXLAN gateway functionality kicks in where the original 802.1q tag with VLAN=100 is stripped and an appropriate VXLAN header is stamped on the packet with SIP=3.3.3.3, DIP=1.1.1.1, and VNI=11000. This encapsulated packet is sent out toward the IP core.

10. Regular IP forwarding ensures that the packet reaches the VTEP on server S1 where the packet will be first decapsulated and appropriate Layer 2 learning will be performed, that is (11000, 00:00:00:00:00:10) ->3.3.3.3. In other words, to the rest of the VXLAN cloud, it appears that 00:00:00:00:00:10 is behind the VXLAN gateway. Layer 2 lookup on the inner payload ensures that the ARP response is sent to VM-A and the ARP cache is updated with the IP-to-MAC binding of the physical server P.

11. Subsequent traffic from VM-A to physical server P is unicast forwarded via the VXLAN gateway. Similarly, flows initiated from the physical server P are handled via the VXLAN gateway. Figure 6-12 depicts the state of the tables on the VXLAN gateway after the nonvirtualized server P has responded to VM-B's ARP request.

12. In this way, VXLAN and non-VXLAN end hosts can communicate with each other without any changes required to either endpoint. This enables a rather attractive option for incremental deployment of VXLAN.

In general multiple VXLAN gateways may provide the gateway functionality in terms of transporting packets to and from legacy networks toward the VXLAN-enabled endpoints. To avoid duplication for a given VNI, one VXLAN gateway needs to be the designated the "forwarder" (likely assigned via configuration) that is responsible for forwarding multidestination frames from and to the VXLAN domain. In this way, the load for different VNIs can be spread across multiple VXLAN gateways.

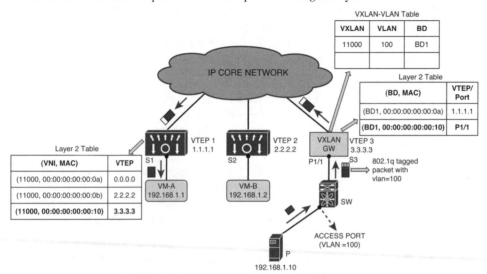

Figure 6-12   *Virtual Machine to Physical Machine via VXLAN Gateway (Final)*

Inter-VXLAN Communication

Up to 16 million unique virtual network segments can be obtained with VXLAN. As mentioned earlier, this is one of the primary benefits of VXLAN over VLAN, which suffered from the 4 K limitation and couldn't support the growing demands of multitenant cloud deployments. Typically, in public cloud deployments, a tenant may lease a few VXLAN segments. Each VXLAN segment usually corresponds to a network subnet, and a tenant may want the end hosts in these segments to communicate with each other. However, by default, only hosts in a given VXLAN segment may communicate with each other, and hosts in different VXLANs are automatically shielded from one another. Initially, VLANs also had the same limitation where only hosts within a VLAN could communicate with one another via Layer 2 switching. Subsequently, the need for inter-VLAN communication became apparent, and this was facilitated via routing using a Switch Virtual Interface (SVI) or more commonly known as an Integrated Routing and Bridging Interface (IRB).

Similarly with VXLAN, it is desirable to support inter-VXLAN communication especially for scenarios in which a tenant may lease multiple virtual networks and require communication between end hosts in these networks. However, it is still mandatory for the end hosts of the tenant to be shielded from other tenant end hosts to provide the necessary isolation and security. This can be achieved via tenant-specific virtual routing and forwarding instances (VRFs). Just like a router enables inter-VLAN communication, a similar VXLAN router device is required to facilitate inter-VXLAN communication. Sometimes to distinguish the functionality explicitly, a VXLAN gateway is called a Layer 2 VXLAN gateway (described in the previous section) and a VXLAN router is called a Layer 3 VXLAN gateway.

Such a device would need to perform the following; recall that SIP and DIP refer to source and destination IP addresses, respectively:

1. Decapsulate an incoming VXLAN packet, and extract the source_VNI and the inner payload.

2. Perform Layer 2 learning based on (source_VNI, Inner_SMAC) ->Outer_SIP in the VXLAN header.

3. Perform a (source_VNI, Inner_DMAC) lookup on the inner payload that in turn can drive a Layer 3 lookup based on a router MAC (RMAC) match.

4. The source_VNI would yield the VRF-ID corresponding to the tenant that in turn would be used in the Layer 3 Forwarding Information Base (FIB) lookup based on (VRF-ID, Inner_DIP) where Inner_DIP is derived from the payload.

5. The FIB lookup hit results in providing the (destination_VNI, DMAC) corresponding to the destination end host that in turn would go through another Layer 2 lookup to determine where that end host resides.

6. This Layer 2 lookup in turn yields the VTEP behind which the destination end host resides.

7. The DMAC, SMAC of the inner payload is appropriately rewritten to the destination end host MAC and RMAC, respectively, along with a TTL decrement indicating that the packet was routed.

8. Subsequently, the packet is VXLAN encapsulated with VNI set to destination_VNI, DIP corresponding to the destination VTEP, SIP corresponding to that of the VXLAN router device VTEP, and then dispatched toward the VTEP behind which the destination resides.

Again, such a device can be implemented in both a software or hardware form factor, although given the extensive functionality and high throughput that it needs to support, the latter seems like a more suitable choice. Figure 6-13 shows a scenario in which a given tenant has leased two VXLAN segments: 11000 corresponding to tenant subnet 192.168.1.0/24 and 12000 corresponding to tenant subnet 192.168.2.0/24. End hosts VM-A and VM-B are deployed in segment 11000 and end hosts VM-D and VM-E are deployed in segment 12000.

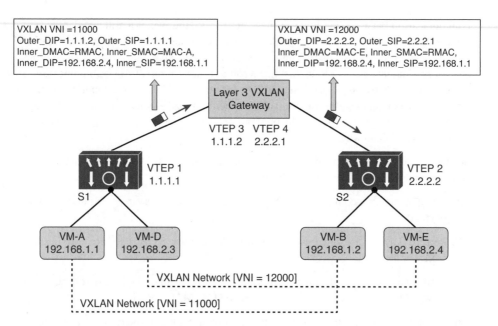

Figure 6-13 *Inter-VXLAN Communication*

VMs in different VXLAN segments can communicate via the Layer 3 VXLAN gateway shown in the figure. Specifically, the figure depicts the salient fields in the VXLAN encapsulated packet going to and from the Layer 3 VXLAN gateway for a sample packet flow from VM-A to VM-E.

Layer 3 Multicast

Recall that the Layer 2 VXLAN gateway makes it possible to communicate between legacy (non-VXLAN) and VXLAN workloads within the same VXLAN segment. Similarly, the Layer 3 VXLAN gateway makes inter-VXLAN communication possible. The previous section provided an end-to-end unicast packet flow between two hosts that belong to different VXLANs. In this section, for completeness, a sample Layer 3 multicast flow is described where the interested receivers may be either legacy hosts or hosts sitting behind a VTEP. Figure 6-14 shows a sample topology of some legacy hosts H0, H6, H7, and H8, and VTEPs on servers S1 and S2 are directly attached to a Layer 3 VXLAN gateway. The gateway in turn is connected via the IP core to a remote VTEP on S3 that has VMs H9 and H10 behind it. The VNIs and VLANs shown next to the hosts indicate the subnet or tenant network to which they belong. Assume that VNI 10000 and VLAN 10 correspond to the same tenant subnet 10.10.10.0/24. Similarly, VLAN 20 and VNI 20000 belong to a different subnet belonging to the same tenant, namely 20.20.20.0/24. VNI 30000 and vlan 30 correspond to the tenant subnet 30.30.30.0/24. P0 to P7 correspond to the labels for the various links shown in the figure.

Assume that Protocol Independent Multicast Sparse Mode (PIM-SP) is employed as the multicast routing protocol with the Rendezvous Point (RP) sitting somewhere within the Layer 3 IP core. In addition, some hosts in the tenant are interested receivers in multicast group G1; this includes H1, H2, H4, H5, H6, H7, H9, and H10. These hosts send IGMP joins for that interested group toward their respective subnet router. The IGMP joins in turn will be terminated at the first-hop router and translated into appropriate PIM-joins toward the RP. Assume that H0 is the source of a multicast stream that is sent to group G1.

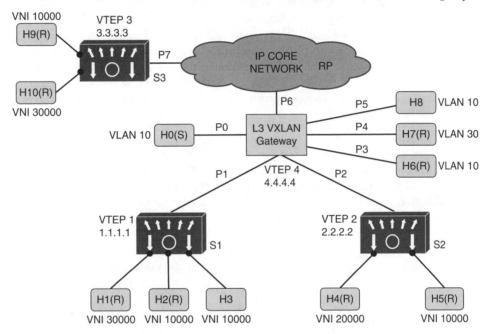

Figure 6-14 *Layer 3 Multicast Case*

Following are the steps for handling the multicast packets sourced from H0 toward group G1. The exact semantics of how the packets flow through the forwarding pipeline are highly implementation-dependent and a function of the forwarding engine employed for implementing VXLAN functionality in the Layer 3 VXLAN gateway device. What is presented here are the steps listed in a logical manner to satisfy the requirements of such a packet flow with an emphasis on the expected forwarding behavior. Assume that all VTEPs are part of the multicast distribution group DG1.

1. When the multicast packet is received at the Layer 3 VXLAN gateway via link P0, the gateway needs to perform the steps of a conventional multicast router to cater to the legacy hosts and generate appropriate VXLAN encapsulated packets so as to cater to the hosts that reside behind the VTEPs that are reachable via the VXLAN tunnels.

2. Assuming IGMP snooping is enabled on the gateway; optimal Layer 2 multicast lookup based on (VLAN=10, Multilcast_MAC(G1)) results in the multicast packet being bridged to host H6. Host H8 is not an interested receiver for G1, so no packets are sent to it.

3. The Layer 3 multicast lookup based on a (S, G) or (*, G) lookup within the tenant vrf results in the generation of the Layer 3 outgoing interface list as SVI 30 after going through the RPF checks. This results in the packet being routed to SVI 30 and a post routed lookup resulting in the rewritten multicast packet to be sent toward host H7 via link P4. So far only legacy interested receivers have been covered.

4. For interested receivers sitting behind VTEPs, the multicast lookup should also result in the generation of appropriate VXLAN encapsulated packets toward the VTEPs that have interested receivers behind them. For receivers in each VNI, the multicast packet is encapsulated in a VXLAN header and tunneled toward the distribution group DG1. Specifically, for VLAN 10 (aka VNI 10000), the original multicast packet will be encapsulated in a VXLAN header with VNI=10000, SIP=4.4.4.4, and DIP=DG1. For receivers in VNI 20000, the multicast packet post-routing will be encapsulated in a VXLAN header with VNI=20000, SIP=4.4.4.4, and DIP=DG1. This is similar for VNI 30000.

5. Because the VTEPs are part of the distribution group DG1, the VXLAN encapsulated multicast packets are received by them. This includes VTEP3 to which the packets are multicast forwarded via the RP in the IP core. The VTEPs decapsulate the VXLAN encapsulated packets and employ the inner (VNI, DMAC=Multicast_ MAC(G1)) and the IGMP snooping database to deliver the multicast packets only to the interested receivers. For example, VTEP1 residing on S1 receives three VXLAN encapsulated packets with VNI 10000, 20000, and 30000. For VNI 20000, post-decapsulation it discards the packet because there are no interested receivers in that VNI. For VNI 10000, the decapsulated multicast packet is sent only to the interested receiver H1 and not to H3. Similarly, for VNI 30000, the decapsulated packet is sent only toward the interested receiver H2.

6. Instead of using distribution group DG1, the gateway can potentially send the VXLAN encapsulated packets for each VNI to the DIP corresponding to that VNI. In that case, VTEP1 receives only two VXLAN encapsulated packets, one for VNI 10000 and another for VNI 30000 because it has no VMs in VNI 20000. However, this assumes that every VNI has a unique multicast address associated with it (which may not be practical because there are 16 million possible VNIs and not that many multicast addresses). This also requires more sophisticated processing on the gateway device and completely depends on the capability of the forwarding engine.

Multicast-Less VXLAN

All the discussion so far has assumed that IP multicast is employed for data plane learning of VXLAN packets. By associating a segment with a multicast group and employing IP multicast to carry broadcast, multicast, and unknown unicast traffic in a VXLAN segment, the mapping of MAC to VTEP for remote end hosts is communicated to the interested parties in a VXLAN cluster. Consequently, this avoids the need for a separate contro channel to communicate this binding among the VTEPs. However, using IP multicast with VXLAN has the following main drawbacks:

- The number of IP multicast groups especially with IPv4 is limited (Class D ranging from 224.x.x.x to 239.x.x.x). Given that it's possible to have 16 million unique VXLAN segments, clearly each segment cannot have a 1:1 mapping to a unique IP multicast address. This may result in VTEPs receiving unnecessary multicast traffic for segments for which they may not have any local end hosts.

- Although multiple VXLAN segments may share a multicast group, the problem is that this eats into the shared IP multicast group space that may be employed for other applications such as live video streaming, and so on.

- The network administrators are required to enable multicast routing in the IP transport core, which is something that they are wary of doing mainly due to the complexity associated with setting up and troubleshooting multicast traffic.

- Multicast across data centers, especially in a hybrid cloud deployment, may not be practically feasible due to the complexity of coordination among the involved administrative entities and the related deployment challenges.

These drawbacks are addressed via a *data dictionary*-based approach. The data dictionary in its simplest form can be considered as a database that stores information at various granularities. At the least, it must maintain the set of all VTEPs in a given VXLAN cluster. If this information is available at all VTEPs, for any unknown unicast, multicast, or broadcast traffic, *head-end* replication at the source VTEP ensures that the packet is sent to all the remote VTEPs. Appropriate filtering at the remote VTEPs ensures that packets are forwarded further only if there are local members behind that VTEP in the VNI in question. Remote VTEPs perform (VNI and SMAC) learning against the source VTEP so that the reverse traffic can be unicasted. This can be termed as a *flood-and-learn* approach. Clearly, with N VTEPs in a VXLAN cluster, this approach creates an N-by-N virtual topology so that every VTEP logically connects to every other VTEP in a full-mesh topology.

Instead, a more efficient implementation would require the data dictionary to maintain a list of VNIs to interested VTEP mappings. In other words, it tracks for each VXLAN VNI the set of VTEPs that have end hosts behind them in that VNI. For unknown unicast or broadcast traffic, head-end replication at the VTEP servicing a source end host ensures that traffic is replicated to only the interested VTEPs which in turn forward the packet to the end hosts behind them in that VNI. In this way, the filtering is done at the source VTEP. As before, remote VTEPs perform (VNI and SMAC) learning against the source VTEP so that the reverse traffic need not be flooded.

The data dictionary can be maintained at a central well-known location. For example, it can be hosted on an Openflow controller in an VXLAN implementation with open virtual switch (OVS). Or for a distributed virtual switch such as the Cisco Nexus 1000V, it can be maintained at the Virtual Supervisor Module (VSM), which is the manager of that distributed virtual switch. VTEPs can communicate their interest for a given VNI based on the active end hosts below them in that VNI so that the data dictionary has the mapping of the list of VNIs to interested VTEPs. A VTEP can in turn query this interest list for a VNI as needed when it has to send out unknown unicast, broadcast, or multicast traffic sourced by an end host in that VNI. The data dictionary response can be locally cached at this VTEP for efficiency purposes. In addition, if there are any changes in the VNI-VTEP interest membership, that information needs to be pushed to the interested VTEPs so that they always have the updated information. In that sense, this is a hybrid push-pull data dictionary-based approach. Learning along the data plane ensures that (VNI and MAC) mappings are maintained for active flows, thereby reducing the amount of traffic that needs to be flooded.

Head-end replication at a virtual switch may be a cause of concern, especially if the VMs in a VXLAN are spread across more and more servers. Ideally, replication should be performed at the physical switch (aka ToR) whose ASIC capabilities are typically streamlined to perform such replication efficiently. However, in a typical cloud provider scenario with multitenancy, a VXLAN may not stretch across thousands of servers making soft switch performance concerns less critical.

Figure 6-15 shows the proposed data dictionary-based scheme where four physical servers (S1, S2, S3, and S4) host some VMs in VXLAN segments 11000 and 12000. End hosts VM-A, VM-B, and VM-C are assigned (MAC and IP) addresses (00:00:00:00:00:0a, 192.168.1.1), (00:00:00:00:00:0b, 192.168.1.2), and (00:00:00:00:00:0c, 192.168.1.3) as part of VXLAN segment 11000 that corresponds to subnet 192.168.1.0/24. Similarly, end hosts VM-D and VM-E are part of segment 12000 that corresponds to subnet 192.168.2.0/24 and are assigned addresses (00:00:00:00:00:0d, 192.168.2.3) and (00:00:00:00:00:0e, 192.168.2.4), respectively.

Based on this topology, the data dictionary has been populated appropriately with the (VNI, VTEP) membership information, as shown in Figure 6-15. VTEPs (1.1.1.1, 2.2.2.2, 3.3.3.3) are in the interest list for VNI 11000, and VTEPs (3.3.3.3, 4.4.4.4) are in the interest list for VNI 12000. As mentioned earlier, this data dictionary could be maintained at a central location or replicated at the vswitches on servers S1, S2, S3, and S4.

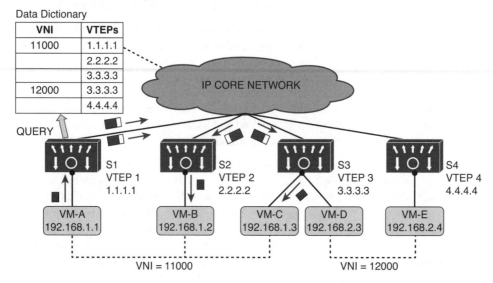

Figure 6-15 *Deploying Multicast-Less VXLAN*

Following are the steps in handling a sample multicast-less VXLAN flow:

1. Assume that VM-A wants to communicate with VM-C. Therefore, it sends out an ARP request with DMAC=ff:ff:ff:ff:ff:ff, SMAC=00:00:00:00:00:0a, and target IP address for which it needs to know IP-to-MAC binding as 192.168.1.3.

2. The vswitch on S1 gets this packet and performs a layer lookup based on (VNI=11000, DMAC=ff:ff:ff:ff:ff:ff). Because this is a miss in the Layer 2 table, the packet is handed off to the VTEP. The VTEP on S1 refers to the (VNI, VTEP) membership table and determines it needs to make two copies of this packet, one for VTEP 2.2.2.2 and another one for VTEP 3.3.3.3. Consequently, it prepares two VXLAN encapsulated unicast packets, first one with SIP=1.1.1.1, DIP=2.2.2.2, and VNI=11000 and the second one with SIP=1.1.1.1, DIP=3.3.3.3, and VNI=11000. These packets are forwarded toward the IP core network.

3. The respective unicast packets destined to VTEPs 2.2.2.2 and 3.3.3.3 will be received by the vswitches on servers S2 and S3, respectively.

4. The VTEP on server S2 performs appropriate VXLAN header decapsulation; performs Layer 2 MAC learning, that is (11000, 00:00:00:00:00:0a) -> 1.1.1.1; and forwards the inner ARP request packet to VM-B. Because the ARP request is not for VM-B, it does not send out any ARP response. Similar operation on server S3 can result in VM-C receiving the ARP request from VM-A. Because the ARP request is for VM-C, it sends out a unicast ARP response to VM-A.

5. The incoming ARP response packet at S3 results in a Layer 2 lookup on the vswitch on S3. DMAC lookup results in a hit of the previously learned entry (11000, 00:00:00:00:00:0a) -> 1.1.1.1. Consequently, the VTEP on S3 encapsulates the packet with an appropriate VXLAN header with SIP=3.3.3.3, DIP=1.1.1.1, and VNI=11000. This encapsulated packet is sent out toward the IP core network.

6. Regular IP forwarding results in the packet being delivered to VM-A via the vswitch on S1 after appropriate VXLAN decapsulation. Layer 2 learning is performed on S1 resulting in (11000, VM-C) -> 3.3.3.3 being learned. In this way, subsequent traffic between VM-A and VM-C will be unicast forwarded via the IP core network.

Although the example illustrated the packet flow for a broadcast packet, the same procedure is employed for unknown unicast packets as well. The same semantics apply for multicast packets if there is no additional pruning information about the interested receivers for a given multicast group.

Floodless VXLAN Forwarding

Forwarding in VXLAN clouds can be made efficient by reducing the amount of flood traffic due to unknown unicast packets. Specifically, the data dictionary introduced in the previous section can maintain more granular information in the form of the end host database. In other words, it can maintain an up-to-date mapping of (VNI, MAC) ->VTEP of all the end hosts in the VXLAN cluster. An end host coming up (either first time or post VM move) will be known to the vswitch running on the physical host, which in turn can communicate this information to the data dictionary via an appropriate control protocol such as Openflow, LISP, and so on. This information will be queried from the data dictionary on demand by the vswitch VTEP when it doesn't know how to forward a packet.

When an unknown unicast packet is received by the virtual switch, the data dictionary can be queried for resolution of the destination MAC by obtaining the (VNI, MAC) ->VTEP mapping. The corresponding Layer 2 entry can be installed and traffic can be appropriately VXLAN encapsulated with the DIP corresponding to the VTEP behind which the destination MAC resides. In this way, the flood traffic due to unknown unicast packets can be considerably reduced and potentially eliminated.

In case the resolved mapping is unavailable at the data dictionary for the unknown unicast query, various options are available:

1. The packet can be dropped on the premise that because the mapping is not available at the data dictionary, the destination may be unavailable or down. This provides security from malicious VMs sending a continuous stream of unknown unicast traffic.

2. The packet may be replicated only to a limited set of VTEPs in the VXLAN segment that are called *forwarding-incapable* VTEPs. These represent VTEPs residing on a VXLAN gateway or potentially other physical hosts, which are incapable of reporting their local (VNI, MAC) mappings to the data dictionary.

Figure 6-16 shows how such a scheme operates. The topology is the same as in Figure 6-15 where four physical hosts with five VMs have been deployed in VXLAN segments 11000 and 12000. End-hosts VM-A, VM-B, VM-C, VM-D, and VM-E are assigned (MAC, IP) addresses (00:00:00:00:00:0a, 192.168.1.1), (00:00:00:00:00:0b, 192.168.1.2), (00:00:00:00:00:0c, 192.168.1.3), (00:00:00:00:00:0d, 192.168.2.3), and (00:00:00:00:00:0e, 192.168.2.4), respectively. When the VMs come up, the virtual switches sitting on the respective physical hosts are aware of their corresponding (VNI, MAC) binding. These bindings are reported and stored at the data dictionary, as shown in Figure 6-16.

Following are the steps in floodless VXLAN forwarding:

1. Assume that VM-A wants to communicate with some end-host in segment 11000 with 00:00:00:00:00:0f, so it sends out a data packet with DMAC=00:00:00:00:00:0f, SMAC=00:00:00:00:00:0a.

2. The vswitch on S1 gets this packet and performs a layer lookup based on (VNI=11000, DMAC=00:00:00:00:00:0f). Because the lookup is a miss, the virtual switch queries the data dictionary for the corresponding (VNI=11000, MAC=00:00:00:00:00:0f) binding. Because this is not known in the data dictionary as well, the packet will be dropped (option 1 mentioned earlier).

3. Assume VM-A wants to communicate with VM-C and is aware of its IP-MAC binding. So it sends out a packet with DMAC=00:00:00:00:00:0c, SMAC=00:00:00:00:00:0a.

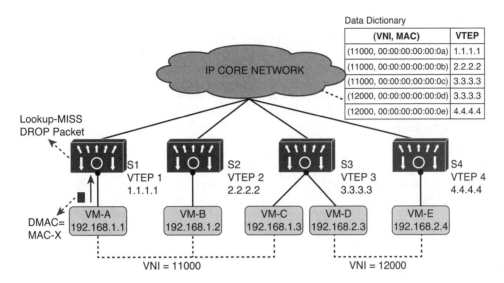

Figure 6-16 *Flood-Less VXLAN Forwarding*

4. Again, the lookup on the vswitch on S1 results in a miss but the subsequent query to the data dictionary for the same, results in a hit and the entry (11000, 00:00:00:00:00:0c) ->3.3.3.3 is returned in response. The vswitch on S1 caches this entry, and the packet will be VXLAN encapsulated with SIP=1.1.1.1, DIP=3.3.3.3, and VNI=11000 and forwarded toward the IP core.

5. Regular IP forwarding results in the packet being delivered to VM-C via the vswitch on S3 after appropriate VXLAN decapsulation.

In this way, flooding because of unknown unicast traffic can be completely avoided in a VXLAN cluster.

VXLAN as a Network Overlay

So far the discussion has revolved around VXLAN tunnels being originated from the virtual switch on the physical hosts. These constitute host-based overlays where the VTEP is implemented in a software form factor. However, as mentioned at the outset, VTEPs can be implemented in a hardware form factor on a physical switch (typically a ToR switch). In such environments, the VXLAN tunnels originate and terminate at the ToR thereby employing VXLAN as a network-based overlay. It should be reiterated that all the packet flows mentioned so far are applicable for both types of VTEP implementations.

Although host-based overlays do have the advantage of a quick deployment of virtual overlay networks with the minimal requirement of a backbone IP core network for transport, they do have some disadvantages:

- Every packet originated from the end host that is sent toward the IP core will be stamped with a VXLAN header. Consequently, there is an overhead of approximately 50 bytes added on a per-packet basis from the source server all the way to the destination server.

- The encapsulation and decapsulation of the VXLAN header on the virtual switch takes some computing cycles, which otherwise could be employed by the application workloads. With the shift to 10 G already happening on the server and the computing capacity of the servers going further up, the VM density on a single server and the ingress and egress network traffic are going to go further up thereby increasing the load on the virtual switch.

- In multicast-less VXLAN deployments, where head-end replication for unknown unicast and broadcast traffic is performed on the soft switch, the performance of the virtual switch may be a bottleneck especially in scenarios in which VXLAN virtual segments span across thousands of physical servers.

- With host-based overlays, special devices such as VXLAN gateways are required for communication between virtual and physical barebones legacy workloads. This also results in all traffic between virtual and physical machines being hair-pinned via the VXLAN gateway.

- Network-based overlays constitute VXLAN overlay inception and termination on the ToR to which the virtualized servers are attached. The ToRs in turn are interconnected via a set of spine switches that form an IP-based Data Center Fabric (see Figure 6-17). This enables any-to-any communication within the data center. With network-based overlays, both legacy and virtualized workloads including service nodes can be attached to the ToRs, and traffic can be optimally forwarded between virtual and physical workloads without any hair-pinning.

We provide a brief description of a flow when VXLAN is employed as a network-based overlay in Figure 6-17. Traffic to and from the ToR to the virtualized servers is native 802.1q tagged where the tag identifies the virtual network segment. Orchestration engines continue to deploy VMs in appropriate virtual network segments (> 4 K) while the ToR and the directly attached virtual switch coordinate on the mapping of the segment to a local 802.1q tag. The mapping may be dynamically exchanged via a handshake-based reliable protocol such as Virtual Station Interface Discovery Protocol (VDP)[8] that is part of IEEE 802.1Qbg Edge Virtual Bridging standard. Or the mapping may be allocated by a central controller and communicated to the ToR and the virtual switch via some standard transport protocol such as Extensible Messaging and Presence Protocol (XMPP).[9]

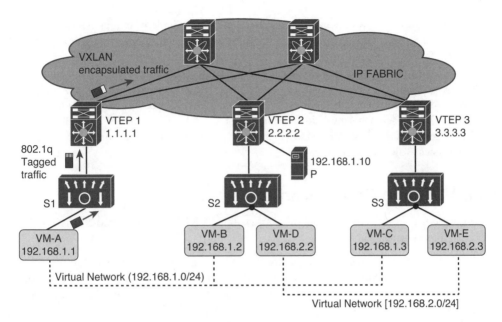

Figure 6-17 *Using VXLAN as a Network Overlay*

The IP fabric may employ multicast for data path learning of (VNI, MAC)->VTEP mappings or may opt for the more efficient multicast-less option. The powerful ToR ASICs can efficiently perform head-end replication for unknown unicast, broadcast, and multicast traffic. An appropriate control protocol may be required for exchange of VNI to VTEP interest membership between the ToRs. Again, the packet flows and the data path with network-based overlays are identical to what have been discussed so far in the previous sections with host-based overlays.

Other VXLAN Considerations

This section highlights some VXLAN considerations. Post-VXLAN decapsulation at a VTEP (implemented in either software or hardware form factor) if the inner payload has a 802.1q tag, the packet must be dropped by the VTEP unless otherwise configured. Similarly, on the encapsulation side, a VTEP must not include an inner 802.1q tag (that is, unless otherwise configured the tag must be stripped off if present) for a packet that needs to be VXLAN encapsulated.

With VXLAN, the Layer 2 virtual segment can be extended across Layer 3 boundaries. Consequently, the attack zone in terms of intrusion becomes much larger as compared to VLANs where the Layer 2 broadcast domain was much smaller. Because the VXLAN standard does not have any inbuilt security, its Layer 2 over IP/UDP overlay format enables it to leverage existing security mechanisms that have been widely deployed with IP traffic. On a physical switch, typically Access Control Lists (ACLs) enable classification of traffic based on common IP/UDP header fields that can be used for allowing

VXLAN traffic to flow only via authenticated endpoints. Similarly, rate-limiters and Quality-of-Service classifiers for IP traffic can be used to limit, shape, or potentially drop non-conformant VXLAN traffic. The VXLAN payload may be encrypted using IPsec or similar crypto schemes. Schemes such as 802.1x can be augmented for admission control of individual VTEPs so that rogue endpoints may not inject traffic into the VXLAN cloud. Also, it is expected that the orchestration engines that deploy the VMs in the different VXLAN segments must do so securely, and the information about the deployed VM in terms of the (VNI, VM-MAC) mapping is communicated to the virtual switch or the physical ToR via a secure channel.

VXLAN Basic Configuration

Example 6-1 provides the minimal steps for enabling VXLAN on the Cisco Nexus 1000V distributed virtual switch.[15]

From the prerequisite perspective, before VXLAN is configured, the Nexus 1000V Virtual Supervisor Module (VSM) and Virtual Ethernet Module (VEM) should be appropriately installed and set up. Connectivity to an upstream switch has already been established with appropriate port profiles to carry system and data VLANs.

Example 6-1   *Nexus 1000V VXLAN Configuration Example*

```
/* 1. Enable VXLAN  */
N1000v# conf t
N1000v(config)# feature segmentation

/* 2. Create vxlan transport VLAN */
N1000v(config)# VLAN 28

/* 3. Create a port-profile for the VTEP */
N1000v(config)# port-profile type vethernet vxlanencap
N1000v(config-port-prof)# switchport mode access
N1000v(config-port-prof)# switchport access VLAN 28
N1000v(config-port-prof)# capability vxlan
N1000v(config-port-prof)# no shutdown
N1000v(config-port-prof)# state enabled

/* 4. Create a uplink port-profile that carries VXLAN traffic */
N1000v(config)# port-profile type ethernet uplink
N1000v(config-port-prof)# switchport mode trunk
N1000v(config-port-prof)# switchport trunk allowed VLAN 28
N1000v(config-port-prof)# no shutdown
N1000v(config-port-prof)# state enabled
N1000v(config-port-prof)# mtu 1550
```

```
/* 5. Create a VXLAN virtual network segment */
N1000v(config)# bridge-domain vxlan-11112
N1000v(config-bd)# segment id 11112
N1000v(config-bd)# group 224.1.1.1

/* 6. Create a port-profile for a vnic with this VXLAN segment */
N1000v(config)# port-profile type vethernet vxlan-11112
N1000v(config-port-prof)# switchport
N1000v(config-port-prof)# switchport access bridge-domain vxlan-11112
N1000v(config-port-prof)# state enabled
N1000v(config-port-prof)# no shutdown

/* 7. Finally save the config */
N1000v(config)# copy running-config startup-config
N1000v(config)#
```

After the port profiles have been configured on the VSM, on each of the hosts where
the VEM resides, a loopback interface must be created to serve as a VTEP. This interface
is assigned a unique IP address in the subnet corresponding to the VXLAN transport
VLAN, and attached to the VTEP port-profile. An example illustration of how this is
done for VMware environments is shown in Figure 6-18.

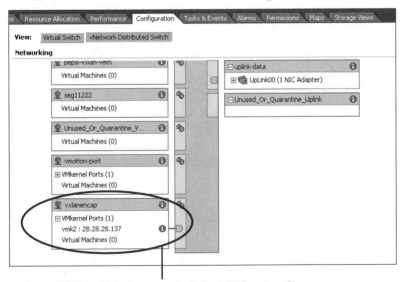

Create VMKernel Interface and attach it to VTEP port-profile

Figure 6-18   *VTEP in VMware ESXi Environments*

Finally, on the upstream switch to which the N1KV VEMs are connected, IGMP snooping (enabled by default on Cisco switches) and proxy ARP must be enabled. If the VTEPs on the VEMs reside in different subnets, then IP multicast routing must be enabled on the upstream switches.

VXLAN Gateway Configuration

Example 6-2 provides an overview of the configuration required for enabling VXLAN gateway functionality on the Cisco Nexus 1000V Distributed Virtual switch.[15]

Example 6-2   *Nexus 1000V VXLAN Gateway Configuration Example*

```
/* 1. Enable VXLAN Gateway Functionality */
N1000v# conf t
N1000v(config)# feature segmentation
N1000v(config)# feature vxlan-gateway


/* 2. Create port-profile for the VXLAN gateway uplink */
N1000v(config)# port-profile type ethernet gw-uplink
N1000v(config-port-prof)# switchport mode trunk
N1000v(config-port-prof)# switchport trunk allowed VLAN 500-600
N1000v(config-port-prof)# mtu 1550
N1000v(config-port-prof)# no shutdown
N1000v(config-port-prof)# state enabled


/* 3. Create VXLAN termination VTEP on VXLAN gateway */
N1000v(config)# port-profile type vethernet gw-vtep
N1000v(config-port-prof)# switchport mode access
N1000v(config-port-prof)# switchport access VLAN 500
N1000v(config-port-prof)# capability vxlan
N1000v(config-port-prof)# transport ip address 192.168.1.253 255.255.255.0 gateway
192.168.1.1
N1000v(config-port-prof)# state enabled
N1000v(config-port-prof)# no shutdown


/* 4. Create the VXLAN to VLAN mappings on the VXLAN gateway */
N1000v(config)# port profile type Ethernet gw-uplink
N1000v(config-port-prof)# service instance 4
N1000v(config-port-prof-srv)# encapsulation dot1q 502 bridge-domain vxlan5002
N1000v(config-port-prof-srv)# encapsulation dot1q 503 bridge-domain vxlan5003
N1000v(config-port-prof-srv)# encapsulation dot1q 504 bridge-domain vxlan5004
N1000v(config-port-prof-srv)# encapsulation dot1q 505 bridge-domain vxlan5005


/* 5. Finally save the config */
N1000v(config)# copy running-config startup-config
```

VXLAN is native supported on the VMware distributed vswitch called the vsphere Distributed Switch (vDS). The security edge gateway that is part of the VMware vCloud Networking suite supports VXLAN gateway functionality. The VMware VXLAN deployment guide[6] provides detailed instructions on how VXLAN functionality can be enabled in native VMware environments.

Summary

This chapter covered VXLAN in detail. It covered various aspects including the origin of VXLAN, VXLAN basics, the overall VXLAN architecture, and VXLAN forwarding including details of encapsulation and decapsulation for a number of packet flow cases. VXLAN is perhaps the most popular overlay protocol in use today. With support from a number of networking vendors and the fact that it runs over an IP core, VXLAN is likely going to be a popular choice for deployment in massive scale data centers. Although today the primary mode of deployment with VXLAN is with IP multicast, the related manageability issues have resulted in exploring multicast-less options, which are gaining popularity. Head-end replication-based VXLAN schemes along with data dictionary–based approaches are going to gain ground especially with the natural integration of SDN controller-related implementations. Moreover, VXLAN is probably one of the few overlay protocols that can be and has been deployed both as a host-based overlay and a network-based overlay. With various virtual switches supporting VXLAN encapsulation and decapsulation natively, customers have already rapidly brought up virtual applications with integrated services by employing VXLAN as a host-based overlay. The support for VXLAN in networking switches came a bit later, which has increased interest toward deploying VXLAN as a network-based overlay. By employing VXLAN gateways, VXLAN can be incrementally deployed, thereby enabling communication with legacy (non-VXLAN) workloads.

There has been an incredible rise in the popularity of VXLAN as an overlay of choice in data center environments especially in the past couple of years. The MAC over IP/ UDP overlay format along with the potential to support up to 16 million virtual network segments makes VXLAN a prime choice for massive scale multitenant data center cloud deployments.

References

1. Mahalingam, Dutt et al., A Framework for Overlaying Virtualized Layer 2 Networks over Layer 3 Networks draft-mahalingam-dutt-dcops-vxlan-02.txt, work in progress, August, 2012.

2. http://www.cisco.com/en/US/prod/collateral/switches/ps9441/ps9902/white_paper_c11-685115.pdf.

3. http://www.cisco.com/en/US/docs/switches/datacenter/nexus1000/sw/vxlan_wo_vcd/video/Deploying_Cisco_Nexus_1000V_without_vCD_Part_3_of_3.html.

4. http://www.vmware.com/solutions/datacenter/vxlan.html.

5. https://communities.cisco.com/servlet/JiveServlet/
    downloadBody/33499-102-1-61197/Nexus%201000V%20v2.2%20for%20
    vSphere%20v1.pdf.

6. http://www.vmware.com/files/pdf/techpaper/VMware-VXLAN-Deployment-
    Guide.pdf.

7. http://www.ciscopress.com/store/ipv6-for-enterprise-networks-9781587142277.

8. http://www.ieee802.org/1/pages/802.1bg.html.

9. http://xmpp.org/xmpp-protocols/rfcs/.

10. http://www.iana.org/assignments/service-names-port-numbers/service-names-port-
    numbers.txt.

11. http://cloudstack.apache.org/.

12. http://www.openstack.org/.

13. http://www.cisco.com/en/US/products/ps13050/index.html.

14. http://www.vmware.com/products/vcloud-director/.

15. http://www.cisco.com/en/US/docs/switches/datacenter/nexus1000/
    sw/4_2_1_s_v_2_2_1/VXLAN/b_VXLAN_Configuration_4_2_1SV_2_2_1.pdf.

16. RFC 6830: The Locator/ID Separation Protocol (LISP).

17. http://www.cisco.com/en/US/netsol/ns1134/index.html.

Chapter 7

FabricPath Deployment, Migration, and Troubleshooting

This chapter has the following objectives:

- **Virtual Port Channel (vPC):** This section provides an overview of the feature and benefits of vPC.

- **Virtual Port Channel (vPC+):** This section gives detailed information about the basics and improvement in the vPC+ feature as compared to vPC.

- **Migrating to FabricPath Network:** This section covers two case studies, including

  FabricPath Migration case study (Classical Layer 2 to FabricPath): This section gives a detailed overview on how to migrate from classical Ethernet (CE) environments to FabricPath environments

  FabricPath Migration case study (vPC to vPC+): This section gives a detailed overview on how to migrate from classical Ethernet VLAN vPC environments to FabricPath vPC+ environments.

- **Monitoring and Troubleshooting in FabricPath networks:** This section gives information about how to monitor and troubleshoot a FabricPath network.

This chapter gives an overview of vPC deployment and how the feature is implemented in data center environments. Cisco developed vPC on the Nexus line of switches to extend link aggregation across two physical switches. Other technologies that have provided similar benefits include the multichassis link aggregation (MLAG) and Etherchannels with Virtual Switching System (VSS) on catalyst 6500.[1] The first section provides an overview of the vPC feature and briefly highlights its benefits. The subsequent sections give an introduction to design, operations, configuration, and verification of vPC+, which is a significant enhancement over vPC that is briefly explained in this chapter. Finally, you should go through the migration case study while moving from vPC to vPC+. This can help you understand the feature properly.

Chapter 4, "FabricPath," started with the basics of FabricPath and touched on vPC/vPC+. This chapter starts with the discussion and implementation of these technologies in detail. The description and implementation of these technologies give the required information to enable you to deploy FabricPath networks. Finally, this chapter covers migration scenarios and troubleshooting FabricPath networks. In migration to FabricPath you see two migrations: Layer 2 network to FabricPath and vPC to vPC+ conversion.

vPC

The following sections go through various aspects of vPC starting from the overview, terminology, deployment, configuration, traffic flow, and verification.

vPC Overview

Generally, access switches use Spanning Tree Protocol (STP) to connect redundant switches in distribution layers. The STP blocks all the redundant links to prevent loops. It unblocks the blocked link when the primary link fails. However, this leads to wastage of available bandwidth on redundant links, longer convergence times, and transient loops. VSS and vPC,[2] support a fully redundant architecture that uses all the available bandwidth on redundant links thereby addressing many of the drawbacks of STP. VSS and vPC can converge faster in case of failures.

In data center environments, typical deployments employ either an end-of-row (EoR) or top-of-rack (ToR) model (see Chapter 1, "Need for Overlays in Massive Scale Data Centers," for more details). The idea is that servers are arranged in racks, multiple racks form a row, and multiple sets of rows form the crux of the data center. With the ToR model, the server connectivity is typically facilitated via a ToR switch. However, if the ToR switch goes down, the entire rack of servers becomes unreachable until the ToR comes back up. This may result in significant downtime that is unwanted. Therefore, typically the servers are dual-homed and attached to a pair of ToR switches. From the server point of view, they are attached to one single upstream switch via a Link Aggregation Group (LAG) or port channel. The pair of ToR switches per rack operates by allowing data forwarding simultaneously, but the control plane may either be shared (VSS) or segregated (vPC) depending on the implementation. This enables an active-active model for the data plane. The pair of ToR switches, in turn, are connected upstream to the distribution layer that enables interconnectivity to the rest of the data center.

A vPC enables physical links on different switches to form a single port channel to a third device. vPC is supported on Cisco Nexus 5000/6000/7000 series switches, and the third device can be an access switch, a server, a Cisco Nexus 2000 Fabric extender (FEX), or any other third-party networking device that supports port channels.

After the feature vPC is enabled on both switches, the switches can monitor their statuses by exchanging heartbeat messages using a peer-keepalive link. In general, a vPC domain includes a vPC peer link, a vPC peer-keepalive link, two vPC devices, and all the port channel links connected to a downstream device. Each of these terms is explained in the following section.

vPC Terminology

Figure 7-1 shows a sample vPC topology. The common terminology associated with vPC is shown in the following list:

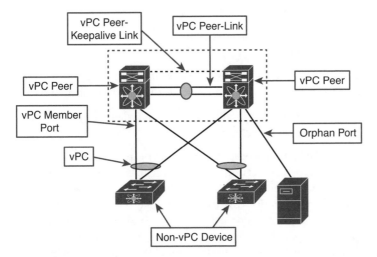

Figure 7-1 *vPC Terminology*

- **vPC peer:** The switches that comprise the vPC pair are referred to as vPC peers. The pair of vPC peers appear as a single switch when connected using a port channel to the downstream device. The peers are connected using a special port channel link called the vPC peer-link and also have a vPC peer-keepalive link to exchange heartbeat messages.

- **vPC member port:** The ports used for forming a vPC are referred to as vPC member ports. In general, only Layer 2 ports can be part of the vPC port channel.

- **vPC peer link:** The vPC peer link is used for synchronizing the states between two vPC peer switches. This link is used for carrying control traffic between both vPC peer switches and also for carrying data traffic. As per best practices, it is recommended that at least two 10 G links be used for vPC peer link.

- **vPC peer-keepalive link:** The keepalive link is used to monitor the health status of the vPC peer switch. The peer switch sends the heartbeat messages after every 2 seconds. Messages are 96 bytes long consisting of information such as vPC domain, device system ID, source, and destination information. The heartbeat messages are generally sent over a Layer 3 (L3) interface configured in a different virtual routing and forwarding (VRF) context. The common recommendation for Cisco switches deployed with vPC is to use a 1 G peer-keepalive link via the management interface that is part of the management context. The keepalive link does not carry any control, data, or synchronization information.

- **vPC domain:** The vPC domain consists of vPC peer switches, a vPC peer link, a vPC keepalive link, and all port channels in vPCs connecting to the downstream device. This also includes the global vPC parameters that need to be applied to switches. The same vPC domain must be configured on both the vPC peers.

- **Non-vPC device:** It can be any networking device that supports link aggregation protocol (LACP) or port channels.

- **Orphan ports:** If a device connects to only one of the switches of the vPC pair of switches, the switch port on which this device connects is called the orphan port.

- **vPC VLANs:** The VLANs carried over the vPC peer link are called the vPC VLANs. These VLANs are used by the vPC member ports.

- **vPC role (primary/secondary):** Each of the switches in a vPC pair has a role assigned to it. The role is negotiated between the vPC peers based on their system MAC addresses (generically system-ID) and priorities. Priority can be configured by the administrator using the role priority *<priority>* command. The switch with the lower priority and lower system MAC address in case of a tie in priority becomes the primary switch, and the second switch takes the role of the secondary switch in a vPC pair. The primary switch responds to bridge protocol data units (BPDUs) and address resolution protocol (ARP) requests. When the peer link fails, a switch detects if its peer is alive using the vPC peer-keepalive link. When the peer link fails and if the vPC secondary switch finds that the vPC primary is alive, it suspends its vPC member ports. This behavior prevents any potential looping issues.

vPC Benefits

The following are the benefits of vPC feature:

- It enables a single device to form a logical port channel bundle connecting to two upstream devices.

- It fully uses the redundant uplinks thereby eliminating the blocked links caused by the STP. Therefore, it provides an active-active configuration for the data plane leading to doubling of the bandwidth.

- It provides a loop-free topology.

- It provides faster convergence of traffic in case of a link failure.

- It ensures high availability and also provides link-level resiliency.

- Because the control plane runs independently on each of the vPC peers, failure of one peer does not adversely affect the virtual switch (as compared to VSS where the active peer going down brings down the entire system because there is only one active with respect to the control plane). Traffic will be rapidly diverted to the "live" peer causing minimal disruption.

vPC Deployment Scenarios

vPC allows the user to create a port channel from a switch or a server. Any server that supports dual-homing can be connected to a Cisco Nexus 5000 series switch after configuring vPC on the Nexus switches. Moreover, vPC can be deployed using Nexus 2000 series Fabric Extenders[3] or any Catalyst switches that support PortChannel (LACP). Figure 7-2 uses two ports on each of the Nexus 2000 series Fabric Extenders to form a vPC.

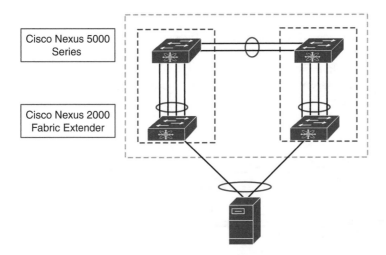

Figure 7-2 *vPC Deployment Scenario Using Two Ports on Each of Nexus 2000 Series Fabric Extender to Form a vPC*

vPC can also be deployed, as shown in Figure 7-3, where two Nexus 2000 series Fabric Extenders connect to each Nexus 5000 Series switch and all the links are active.

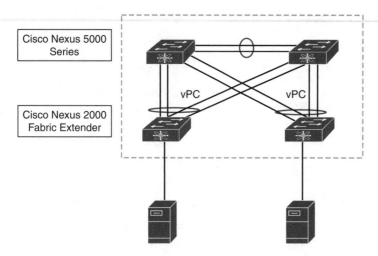

Figure 7-3   *Nexus 2000 Series Fabric Extenders Interfaces, Each Connected to Cisco Nexus 5000 Series*

Double-Sided vPC

Figure 7-4 shows a vPC topology that superposes two layers of the vPC domain. In this topology the bundle between the two vPC domains that is vPC domain 1 and vPC domain 2 is by itself a vPC. In this topology the bottom vPC domain is used for active-active connectivity from the servers. The top vPC domain is used for active-active connectivity from the access layer.

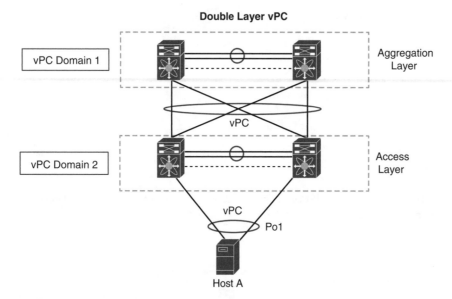

Figure 7-4   *Double-Sided vPC Topology*

This model provides additional benefits including (a) larger Layer 2 domains, (b) higher network resiliency as the two access switches connect to two aggregation switches, and (c) doubling of the bandwidth between access distribution as the number of links is doubled.

vPC Operations

Before designing a vPC-based data center, it is crucial to understand the working of the vPC technology. While designing the network with vPC, you should keep in mind how the topology would be if the STP were to be implemented. If any uplink failure in vPC occurs, the STP kicks in and chooses the best available path.

A port channel is formed when two or more physically connected links are bundled together to form a single logical link, thus increasing an overall bandwidth of the entire logical link. However, vPC is formed by bundling physically connected links from two different switches to form a single logical link. This allows the downstream device to be connected to one logical switch.

Cisco recommends using the LACP for link aggregation. The reasons for this recommendation are that the LACP is standard, and the debugging becomes a lot easier as compared to the **channel-group <*number*> mode on**, as there are extensive commands to debug in case the link aggregation is not working. For better understanding of the vPC feature, consider the vPC topology shown in Figure 7-5.

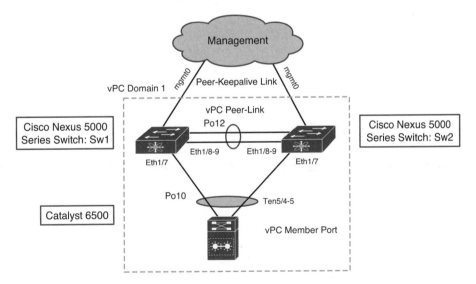

Figure 7-5   *Typical vPC Topology*

Following are the configuration steps on Cisco Nexus 5000 series switches to enable the vPC feature.[4] The same set of steps can be employed for enabling the vPC feature on Nexus 6000/70000 series switches.

1. **Enabling vPC and LACP feature:** The vPC feature should be configured on both the Cisco Nexus 5000 series switches that are going to form the vPC pair. The feature can be enabled by executing the commands shown in Example 7-1.

Example 7-1   *Enabling vPC and LACP Feature*

```
Nexus5k-Sw1# config t
Nexus5k-Sw1(config)# feature vpc
Nexus5k-Sw1(config)# feature lacp


On Switch Nexus5k-SW2:
Nexus5k-Sw2# config t
Nexus5k-Sw2 (config)# feature vpc
   Nexus5k-Sw2 (config)# feature lacp
```

2. **Creating VLANs:** The VLANs for which traffic will be forwarded across the vPC peer link are referred to as vPC VLANs. These are the set of VLANs for which the vPC functionality will be realized. The VLANs can be enabled by executing the command shown in Example 7-2.

Example 7-2   *Configuring VLAN*

```
Nexus5k-Sw1# config t
Nexus5k-Sw1(config)# VLAN 101-105


On Switch Nexus5k-SW2:
Nexus5k-Sw2# config t
   Nexus5k-Sw2(config)# VLAN 101-105
```

3. **Define a vPC domain:** The vPC domain should be configured with the same value on both peer switches. The vPC domain can be enabled by executing the command shown in Example 7-3.

Example 7-3   *Defining vPC Domain*

```
Nexus5k-Sw1# config t
Nexus5k-Sw1(config)# vpc domain 12


On Switch Nexus5k-SW2:
Nexus5k-Sw2# config t
   Nexus5k-Sw2(config)# vpc domain 12
```

4. **Configuring the vPC role priority (optional):** When a vPC pair is formed between two switches, it needs to negotiate the roles for each switch. The switch role is elected as primary or secondary upon comparison of the system MAC address (more generally system-ID) and priority values of both the switches. A switch with a lower system MAC address becomes the primary switch when both switches have the same priority. A switch configured with a lower priority can take up the role of the primary switch. The priority can be configured from 1 to 65635, and the default value is 32667. The vPC role priority is configured by executing the command shown in Example 7-4.

Example 7-4 *Configuring vPC Role Priority*

```
Nexus5k-Sw1# config t
   Nexus5k-Sw1(config-vpc-domain)# role priority 1000
```

5. **Assigning the management interface with an IP address and installing a default route:** Although any L3 interface can be used for configuring the keepalive link, this example uses the management interface for the keepalive link. So configure the management (mgmt0) interface on each peer switch with an appropriate unique IP address. This interface is used for exchanging heartbeat messages thereby serving as the vPC peer-keepalive link. This configuration is achieved by executing the command shown in Example 7-5.

Example 7-5 *Assigning the Management Interface with an IP Address*

```
Nexus5k-Sw1(config)# int mgmt 0
Nexus5k-Sw1(config-if)# ip address 192.169.1.1/24
Nexus5k-Sw1(config-if)# vrf context management
Nexus5k-Sw1(config-vrf)# ip route 0.0.0.0/0 192.169.1.51


On Switch Nexu5k-Sw2:

Nexus5k-Sw2(config)# int mgmt 0
Nexus5k-Sw2(config-if)# ip address 192.169.1.2/24
Nexus5k-Sw2(config-if)# vrf context management
   Nexus5k-Sw2(config-vrf)# ip route 0.0.0.0/0 192.169.1.51
```

6. **Configuring peer-keepalive link:** The peer-keepalive configuration is performed under the vPC domain and lists the destination peer's IP address to which keepalives are periodically sent. This can be enabled using the commands shown in Example 7-6.

Example 7-6 *Configuring the vPC peer-keepalive Link*

```
Nexus5k-Sw1 (config-vpc-domain)# peer-keepalive destination 192.169.1.2

On Nexu5k-Sw2:
   Nexus5k-Sw2 (config-vpc-domain)# peer-keepalive destination 192.169.1.1
```

7. **Configuring the vPC peer link:** The vPC peer link should be configured as a regular inter-switch Layer 2 trunk. The trunk should allow the VLANs that are configured as part of vPC member ports. The vPC peer link can be enabled by executing the commands shown in Example 7-7.

Example 7-7 *Configuring the vPC Peer Link*

```
Nexus5k-Sw1(config)# int po12
Nexus5k-Sw1(config-if)# vpc peer-link
Nexus5k-Sw1(config-if)# switchport mode trunk
Nexus5k-Sw1(config-if)# switchport trunk allowed VLAN 101-105

Nexus5k-Sw1(config)# int ethernet 1/8-9
Nexus5k-Sw1(config-if-range)# channel-group 12 mode active

On Switch Nexus-Sw2:

Nexus5k-Sw2(config)# int po12
Nexus5k-Sw2(config-if)# vpc peer-link
Nexus5k-Sw2(config-if)# switchport mode trunk
Nexus5k-Sw2(config-if)# switchport trunk allowed VLAN 101-105

Nexus5k-Sw2(config)# int ethernet 1/8-9
   Nexus5k-Sw2(config-if-range)# channel-group 12 mode active
```

8. **Configuring the downstream switch:** The CE VLAN interfaces connecting the Catalyst 6500 and two Cisco Nexus 5000 switches should be configured as Layer 2 trunk port channel interfaces with appropriate VLANs enabled. The commands shown in Example 7-8 need to be executed on a downstream device (Catalyst 6500 series switch).

Note the Port-Channel operation mode should be configured as an LACP.

Example 7-8 *Configuring the Catalyst 6500 Interface as Layer 2*

```
Catalyst6500(config)# int r t5/4-5
Catalyst6500 (config-if-range)# switchport
Catalyst6500 (config-if-range)# switchport trunk allowed VLAN 101-105
Catalyst6500 (config-if-range)# switchport mode trunk
Catalyst6500 (config-if-range)# channel-group 10 mode active
Catalyst6500 (config-if-range)# no shutdown


Configuring the Port-channel as Layer-2 interface


Catalyst6500 (config)# int Port-channel10
Catalyst6500 (config-if)# switchport
Catalyst6500 (config-if)# switchport trunk allowed VLAN 101-105
Catalyst6500 (config-if)# switchport mode trunk
   Catalyst6500 (config-if)# no shutdown
```

9. **Adding the CE VLAN interface as part of the vPC:** CE interfaces on both the vPC peers should be added as part of a Layer 2 port channel. After all the interfaces on both sides of the switches are bundled successfully, the port channel should be configured as part of the vPC. The PortChannel number on the vPC peers can be different, but the vPC number under those port channels should be the same on both the peers for a correct bundling with the downstream device. Example 7-9 provides the set of commands required to enable the vPC bundle.

Example 7-9 *Adding the Port Channel as Part of vPC*

```
Nexus5k-Sw1(config-if)# int po10
Nexus5k-Sw1(config-if)# switchport mode trunk
Nexus5k-Sw1(config-if)# switchport trunk allowed VLAN 101-105
Nexus5k-Sw1(config-if)# vpc 10

Nexus5k-Sw1(config-if)# int ethernet 1/7
Nexus5k-Sw1(config-if)# channel-group 10 mode active


On Switch Nexus5k-Sw2:


Nexus5k-Sw2(config-if)# int po20
Nexus5k-Sw2(config-if)# switchport mode trunk
Nexus5k-Sw2(config-if)# switchport trunk allowed VLAN 101-105
Nexus5k-Sw2(config-if)# vpc 10

Nexus5k-Sw2(config-if)# int ethernet 1/7
   Nexus5k-Sw2(config-if)# channel-group 20 mode active
```

vPC Traffic Flow

Traffic through a vPC system is symmetric and optimized with local preference when exiting the switch. This should be clear with an example of access, aggregation, and core layer, as shown in Figure 7-6. The traffic from Host A to the Internet reaches the access switch, which uses a hash to send the traffic toward aggregation switch Ag1. After the traffic reaches the aggregation switch, the aggregation switch consults the routing table to send the traffic toward the core switches. For cost paths, Equal Cost Multi-Pathing (ECMP) will be used to send traffic toward the core switches. Some of the flows from Host A to the Internet go through the access switch-aggregation switch (Ag1)-core1 path, whereas the other flows go through the access switch-aggregation switch (Ag1)-core2 path. Similarly, traffic from Host B can flow through either of the aggregation switches (Ag1 or Ag2) to the core switches. Figure 7-6 shows traffic from Host B selecting the Ag2-core1 path for reaching the Internet. Similar traffic flows are seen for the traffic from Host B except that the access switch uses a hash function while selecting the link toward the aggregation switch (Ag2) leading to path selection of the access switch-aggregation switch(Ag2)-core1 and the access switch-aggregation switch(Ag2)-core2. The important point to note here is that the traffic does not get forwarded through the vPC peer link of the aggregation switches unless absolutely necessary. Some scenarios during which traffic may need to go through the vPC peerlink are when there are orphan ports connected to the peer switches or if link failures occur.

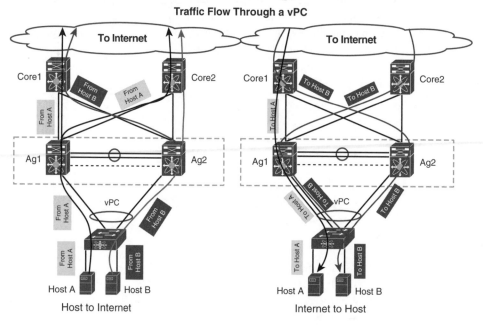

Figure 7-6   *vPC Traffic Flow*

Similarly, you can see that the Internet-to-host traffic also uses the local preference to send the traffic back to the hosts. In case one of the vPC links between the access switch and aggregation switch fails, the traffic is forwarded over the peer link. In Figure 7-6, if the link between the access switch and aggregation switch Ag1 fails, any traffic coming from the Internet to the aggregation switch Ag1 for Host A or Host B is forwarded over the peer link to aggregation switch Ag2, which, in turn, forwards it to the hosts.

In essence the peer link is used for data traffic only when necessary and not in normal working scenarios. This design allows unnecessary traffic passing over the peer links.

Cisco Fabric Services over Ethernet

The Cisco Fabric Services over Ethernet (CFSoE) protocol is a reliable state transport mechanism used in vPC to provide various infrastructural services including ARP synchronization, MAC synchronization, STP state synchronization, Internet Group Management Protocol (IGMP) synchronization, verification of mismatched configuration, and locking the configuration while upgrading the vPC peer.

CFSoE is enabled automatically when the vPC feature is enabled on the device. The user does not have to configure anything for CFSoE to work properly for vPCs. The subsequent sections cover some of the services provided by CFSoE.

vPC ARP Sync

ARP synchronization between Layer 3 vPC peers is enabled by default. ARP synchronization speeds up the reconvergence between the two switches. The ARP synchronization helps with faster convergence time when a vPC switch is reloaded. When the vPC switch comes up after reload, it uses the Cisco Fabric Services Protocol to perform the synchronization of the ARP table. ARP sync works basically in two scenarios:

- ARP synchronization listens to peer link-up messages. On receiving these messages, the ARP entries are synchronized on all vPC VLANs to the other switch using CFSoE.

- ARP synchronization module also looks for Switched Virtual Interface (SVI) up messages of vPC VLANs, and on seeing an SVI up message, it sends a pull request to the peer switch to get the peer's ARP entries using CFSoE.

vPC Peer Gateway

The concept of vPC peer gateway[6] is to enable the Layer 3 forwarding of packets destined to the gateway MAC address. In essence, if a packet is forwarded to the Layer 3 gateway of a vPC pair of switches and if the packet's destination MAC address points to the HSRP MAC address, the packet forwarding works as expected in vPC. But if the destination MAC address in the packet is the burned-in MAC address of a vPC member switch instead of the HSRP MAC address, based on the PortChannel hash the frame may be forwarded to the wrong vPC peer. In this case the frame is bridged over to the vPC peer. This scenario can cause problems when the vPC peer switch owning the burned-in MAC address has to route the frame to a member vPC port. In this situation the packet is dropped because of the vPC duplicate prevention rule. According to the vPC duplicate prevention rule, a packet is not allowed to egress out of the vPC member port if it ingresses from the vPC peer link.

Figure 7-7 shows the source (Host A) and destination (Host B) are in different subnets with the aggregation switch (vPC pair) acting as the default gateway. Host A sends traffic destined to a gateway MAC of 0000.0000.00AA, which is the burned-in MAC address of Ag1. Based on hash resulting from the flow, the access switch can send the traffic to either Ag1 or Ag2. If the traffic is forwarded to the second aggregation switch Ag2, the aggregation switch Ag2 bridges the traffic over to the Aggregation switch Ag1. As the final destination of this frame is Host B, the frame is dropped at Ag1 because of the duplicate prevention rule.

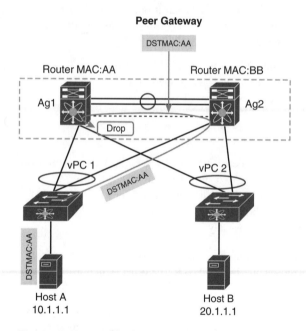

Figure 7-7   *Problem Without vPC Gateway Feature*

To make this scenario work under this situation, the **peer-gateway** command should be configured under the vPC domain. Execution of this command under the vPC domain enables the vPC peers to exchange their burned-in MAC addresses. This allows the peers to forward the traffic locally instead of forwarding over the peer-link, when the traffic is destined to the burned-in MAC address of a vPC pair.

vPC Verification

This section provides details on the verification steps involved in validating the vPC configuration.

First, you need to take a look at LACP system identifiers. As shown in Example 7-10, the LACP system ID consists of two fields: the LACP system priority value and the MAC address of the switch.

Example 7-10   *LACP System Identifiers*

```
Nexus5k-Sw1# show lacp system-IDentifier
32768,54-7f-ee-a5-d-41


Nexus5k-Sw2# show lacp system-IDentifier
32768,54-7f-ee-9e-99-c1


  Catlayst6500#show lacp sys-id
  32768,001d.7064.59c0
```

The LACP neighbor information of the vPC should show the same system-ID information on both the Cisco Nexus 5000 series switches. This information can be verified by executing the command shown in Example 7-11 on both of the Nexus switches.

Example 7-11   *LACP Neighbor Information (vPC)*

```
Nexus5k-Sw1# show lacp neighbor interface port channel 10
Flags:  S - Device is sending Slow LACPDUs F - Device is sending Fast LACPDUs
        A - Device is in Active mode      P - Device is in Passive mode
port channel1 neighbors
Partner's information
          Partner              Partner                 Partner
Port      System ID            Port Number     Age     Flags
Eth1/7    32768,0-1d-70-64-59-c00x505         2616     SA
          LACP Partner         Partner                 Partner
          Port Priority        Oper Key                Port State
          32768                0xa                     0x3d


/* Similarly on Switch Sw2 */

Nexus5k-Sw2# show lacp neighbor interface port channel 10
Flags:  S - Device is sending Slow LACPDUs F - Device is sending Fast LACPDUs
        A - Device is in Active mode      P - Device is in Passive mode
port channel1 neighbors
```

```
Partner's information
        Partner              Partner                    Partner
Port    System ID            Port Number     Age        Flags
Eth1/7  32768,0-1d-70-64-59-c00x505         2529        SA
        LACP Partner         Partner                    Partner
        Port Priority        Oper Key                   Port State
        32768                0xa                        0x3d
```

As shown in the Example 7-11 output, the LACP system-ID matches on both the switches. Similarly, the vPC peer link port channel should also have the same system-ID information, as shown in Example 7-12.

Example 7-12 *LACP Neighbor Information (vPC)*

```
Nexus5k-Sw1# show lacp neighbor interface port channel 12
Flags:  S - Device is sending Slow LACPDUs F - Device is sending Fast LACPDUs
        A - Device is in Active mode       P - Device is in Passive mode
port channel1 neighbors
Partner's information
        Partner              Partner                    Partner
Port    System ID            Port Number     Age        Flags
Eth1/8  32768,54-7f-ee-9e-99-c10x108        3808        SA
        LACP Partner         Partner                    Partner
        Port Priority        Oper Key                   Port State
        32768                0xb                        0x3d
Partner's information
        Partner              Partner                    Partner
Port    System ID            Port Number     Age        Flags
Eth1/9  32768, 54-7f-ee-9e-99-c100x109      3808        SA
        LACP Partner         Partner                    Partner
        Port Priority        Oper Key                   Port State
        32768                0xb                        0x3d


On Switch Nexus5k-Sw2:

Nexus5k-Sw2# show lacp neighbor interface port channel 10
Flags:  S - Device is sending Slow LACPDUs F - Device is sending Fast LACPDUs
        A - Device is in Active mode       P - Device is in Passive mode
port channel1 neighbors
```

```
Partner's information
            Partner              Partner                      Partner
Port        System ID            Port Number      Age         Flags
Eth1/8      32768,54-7f-ee-a5-d-410x108           3811        SA
            LACP Partner         Partner                      Partner
            Port Priority        Oper Key                     Port State
            32768                0xb                          0x3d
Partner's information
            Partner              Partner                      Partner
Port        System ID            Port Number      Age         Flags
Eth1/9      32768,54-7f-ee-a5-d-410x109           3811        SA
            LACP Partner         Partner                      Partner
            Port Priority        Oper Key                     Port State
            32768                0xb                          0x3d
```

As shown in the Example 7-12 output, the LACP system-ID of each interface matches in the case of both switches. Therefore, the PortChannel is successfully formed and all ports are in an operational state. As shown in Example 7-13, this can be verified by executing the **show port channel summary** command on the switch.

Example 7-13 *show port channel Summary*

```
Nexus5k-Sw1# show port channel summary
Flags:  D - Down        P - Up in port channel (members)
        I - Individual  H - Hot-standby (LACP only)
        s - Suspended   r - Module-removed
        S - Switched    R - Routed
        U - Up (port channel)
--------------------------------------------------------------------
Group Port-       Type    Protocol  Member Ports
      Channel
--------------------------------------------------------------------
10    Po10(SU)    Eth     LACP      Eth1/7(P)
12    Po12(RU)    Eth     LACP      Eth1/8(P) Eth1/9(P)
```

The vPC is formed using two different switches; each has different control and data planes, respectively. It is important that the control planes' consistency is maintained between the two vPC peers for configuration element types. These types are classified as Type 1 and Type 2.

In Type 1, configuration elements of the local switch and the peer switches are compared while forming a vPC. A mismatch in any of the configuration elements may prevent the switches from forming a vPC. The Type 1 configuration elements follow:

- STP configurations

- Speed

- Port-channel mode (passive, active, or ON)

- Duplex

- MTU

- Native VLAN

- Locally suspended VLANs

- Port mode (trunk or access)

- VLAN mapping

- Allowed VLANs (on trunks)

- HSRP configuration consistency

- Quality of service (QoS) configurations

In this example both switches have consistent parameters, allowing the vPC to be established. These elements can be verified using the **show vpc consistency-parameters global** command. Moreover, the consistency for PortChannel can also be verified, as shown in Example 7-14.

Example 7-14   *show vpc consistency-parameters*

```
Nexus5k-Sw1# show vpc consistency-parameters global
Legend:
        Type 1 : vPC will be suspended in case of mismatch


Name                    Type  Local Value             Peer Value
-------------           ----  ---------------------   ---------------------
QoS                     2     ([], [3], [], [], [],   ([], [3], [6], [], [],
                              [])                     [])
Network QoS (MTU)       2     (9216, 0, 0, 0, 0,0)    (1538, 2196, 1538, 0, 0,
                                                      0, 0)
Network Qos (Pause)     2     (F, F, F, F, F, F)      (F, T, T, F, F, F)
Input Queuing (Bandwidth)  2  (50, 50, 0, 0, 0, 0)    (50, 50, 0, 0, 0, 0)
Input Queuing (Absolute  2    (F, F, F, F, F, F)      (F, F, F, F, F, F)
Priority)
Output Queuing (Bandwidth) 2  (50, 50, 0, 0, 0, 0)    (50, 50, 0, 0, 0, 0)
Output Queuing (Absolute  2   (F, F, F, F, F, F)      (F, F, F, F, F, F)
```

```
Priority)
STP Mode                    1      Rapid-PVST              Rapid-PVST
/* Output removed for brevity */
Allowed VLANs               -      101-105                 101-105
   Local suspended VLANs    -      -                       -
```

vPC+

A vPC+ domain allows a CE vPC domain and a FabricPath cloud to inter-operate. vPC+ is an extension to vPC. The rest of the section goes through the various aspects of vPC+.

vPC+ Overview

Even for a FabricPath network, it is required to support a configuration where a device (host or other switch) is connected to two physical FabricPath edge switches using a PortChannel. The FabricPath edge switches can be vPC peers. In general, for traffic destined to go over the FabricPath cloud, the edge switches encapsulate the traffic from the host with a FabricPath header with the source switch-ID in the header as itself. As discussed in Chapter 4, the remote edge switches learn the source MAC and associate it with the source switch-ID in the packet. Different flows originating from the same host can be sent to either of the FabricPath edge switches. Because the source switch-ID in the FabricPath header will be different for packets coming from different edge switches for the same host, there will be MAC address flaps or MAC moves in the remote edge switches. To solve this issue of MAC flaps, FabricPath has implemented a concept of an emulated switch or virtual switch in vPC+.

vPC+ requires a virtual (or emulated) switch-ID configuration in each of the peer switches. Each peer switch, apart from its unique switch-ID, will also be identified using the emulated switch-ID. All dual-attached devices downstream from the vPC+ peers will be identified in the FabricPath cloud as being associated with the emulated switch-ID. Orphan or singly attached hosts will continue to be associated with the individual switch-ID of the peer that they are connected to. In addition, the peer link will now become FabricPath-enabled so that it can carry traffic for FabricPath VLANs. So vPC+ with the help of FabricPath adds significant benefits over conventional vPC. Any network device (a router, firewall, or switch) that supports ether channels (port channels) can use the capabilities of vPC+. Dynamic (LACP) and static modes of ether channel are supported by vPC+ over links from a lone classical Ethernet device to a pair of FabricPath switches. For dual-homed hosts, vPC+ offers active-to-active uplink capability similar to that of regular vPC.

vPC+ Basics

Configuring vPC+ is similar to conventional vPC, except for a few differences. The FabricPath peer switch in vPC+ is a FabricPath-enabled switch. Each vPC+ peer in addition to its unique switch-ID is configured with an emulated or virtual switch-ID. The emulated switch-ID is also distributed via Intermediate Systems – Intermediate Systems (IS-IS) to all the switches in the FabricPath network. Following is the summary of the differences for vPC+ compared to vPC:

1. Within the Virtual PortChannel domain, the switch ID for FabricPath should be configured (**fabricpath switch-id <>**) such that the switch ID acts as a virtual switch and the FabricPath cloud sees the downstream dual-attached hosts as being connected to one single device.

2. The vPC+ peer link should be configured as a FabricPath core port. It can be configured by executing the command **switchport mode fabricpath**.

Before going into the details of vPC+, look at the physical and logical topologies with vPC+. Figure 7-8 and Figure 7-9 show the vPC+ physical and logical topologies, respectively.

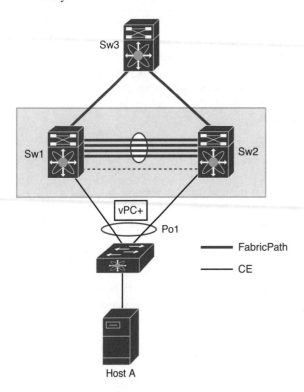

Figure 7-8 *vPC+ Physical Topology*

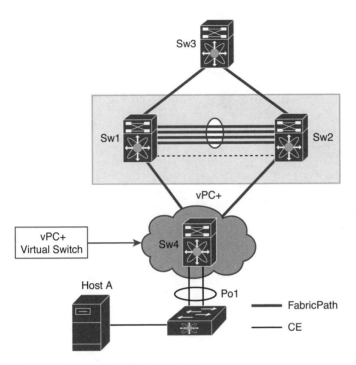

Figure 7-9 *vPC+ Logical Topology*

In the vPC+ topology shown in Figure 7-8, vPC+ peer switches are defined as Sw1 and Sw2. Similar to traditional vPC, keepalive and peer links are needed between the two switches.

Inside the vPC domain, the virtual switch-ID (SID) should be unique; there should not be any other devices using the same SID under the same FabricPath domain. Packets received via vPC+ PortChannel will be sent toward the FabricPath cloud with the source switch-ID in the outer header equal to the virtual SID. Optionally, if a subswitch-ID is employed, for packets received from a given vPC+ member ports, both peers will employ the same subswitch-ID for a PortChannel. A subswitch-ID is negotiated via the control plane (CFSoE) that runs between the peers over the vPC+ peer link.

Before going into packet forwarding details, look at a few of the important vPC+ commands for the FabricPath network, as shown in Figure 7-10.

The output of the commands listed here are based on the topology shown in Figure 7-10.

Example 7-15 shows the details of the switches that are part of the FabricPath network. Note that "200" is the emulated switch-ID that is configured on the vPC+ peers.

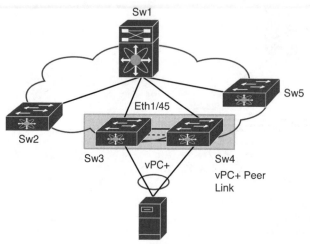

Figure 7-10 *Sample FabricPath Topology with vPC+*

Example 7-15 *show fabricpath switch-id*

```
Sw2# show fabricpath switch-id
                    FABRICPATH SWITCH-ID TABLE
Legend: '*' - this system
=====================================================================
SWITCH-ID      SYSTEM-ID        FLAGS         STATE      STATIC   EMULATED
----------+----------------+------------+-----------+-------------------
  200       002a.6a19.91bc   Primary      Confirmed   No       Yes
  200       002a.6a22.0e01   Primary      Confirmed   No       Yes
  254       0000.0411.0538   Primary      Confirmed   Yes      No
 1009       002a.6a45.75c1   Primary      Confirmed   No       No
*1535       002a.6a19.91bc   Primary      Confirmed   No       No
 2321       0026.9821.8042   Primary      Confirmed   No       No
 2527       002a.6a22.0e01   Primary      Confirmed   No       No
Total Switch-ids: 7
```

Example 7-16 lists some additional details for the switches as distributed via IS-IS.

Example 7-16 *show fabricpath isis switch-id*

```
Sw2# show fabricpath isis switch-id
FabricPath ISIS domain: default
Fabricpath IS-IS Switch-ID Database
Legend: C - Confirmed, T - tentative, W - swap
        S - sticky, E - Emulated Switch
      A - Anycast Switch
```

```
      '*' - this system
  System-ID          Primary  Secondary  Reachable  Bcast-Priority  Ftag-Root  Capable
MT-0
0000.0411.0538     254 [C]      0[C]     Yes            64            [S]        Y
0026.9821.8042     2321[C]      0[C]     Yes            64                       Y
002a.6a19.91bc*    1535[C]      0[C]     Yes            64                       Y
002a.6a19.91bc*    200 [C]      0[C]     Yes            0[E]                     Y
002a.6a22.0e01     2527[C]      0[C]     Yes            64                       Y
002a.6a22.0e01     200 [C]      0[C]     Yes            0[E]                     Y
002a.6a45.75c1     1009[C]      0[C]     Yes            64                       Y
```

Example 7-17 shows the IS-IS calculated routes from the perspective of Switch Sw2. The IS-IS route table indicates the reachability information about the different switches in the FabricPath network.

Example 7-17 *show fabricpath switch-id*

```
Sw2# show fabricpath route
FabirPath Unicast Route Table
'a/b/c' denotes ftag/switch-id/subswitch-id
'[x/y]' denotes [admin distance/metric]
Ftag 0 is local ftag
Subswitch-id 0 is default subswitch-id


Fabricpath unicast Route Table for Topology-Default

0/1535/0, number of next-hops: 0
        via ---- , [60/0], 0 day/s 15:12:02, local
1/200/0, number of next-hops: 0
        via ---- , [60/0], 0 day/s 11:11:18, local
1/254/0, number of next-hops: 1
        via Eth1/45, [115/440], 0 day/s 15:11:05, isis_fabricpath-default
1/1009/0, number of next-hops: 1
        via Eth1/45, [115/80], 0 day/s 11:11:18, isis_fabricpath-default
1/2321/0, number of next-hops: 1
        via Eth1/45, [115/40], 0 day/s 15:11:05, isis_fabricpath-default
1/2527/0, number of next-hops: 1
        via Eth1/45, [115/80], 0 day/s 00:54:33, isis_fabricpath-default
2/200/0, number of next-hops: 0
        via ...,[60/0, 0 day/s 11:11:18, local
```

vPC+ Basic Packet Flow

Before starting the packet flow through a vPC+ system, you must understand the concept of an emulated switch and affinity trees. For multidestination frames sent by one of the vPC+ peers using the emulated switch-ID, the RPF check will fail in some of the FabricPath switches. This is because the multidestination tree to the emulated switch can be through only one of the vPC+ member switches. To solve this issue, the concept of affinity trees was introduced. As can be recalled from Chapter 3, "IS-IS," and Chapter 4, FabricPath has the capability to compute a number of distribution trees for a given FabricPath topology. Distribution trees are used for forwarding multidestination traffic. For vPC+, every vPC+ peer switch (FabricPath switch) should choose a tree and announce its affiliation for the tree and the emulated switch corresponding to its connected vPC+ PortChannel. Switches can be associated with multiple vPC+ PortChannels. For every vPC+ PortChannel, represented by its emulated switch, its affiliated tree must be announced. The two peer switches that form the vPC+ pair should do this and arrive at an association for a tree that is conflict-free. Now for multidestination frames that happen to arrive at both the vPC+ peer switches via a distribution tree, only one of the peers should decapsulate the frame and forward it downstream to the dual-attached device (host or switch). The vPC+ peer that has announced its affinity toward that tree is the one that will decapsulate the frame and forward it downstream. For a multidestination frame that arrives at vPC+ peer switch from a dual-homed host, that switch will encapsulate the frame with a FabricPath header using the FabricPath tag (FTAG) corresponding to the tree for which it has announced its affinity.

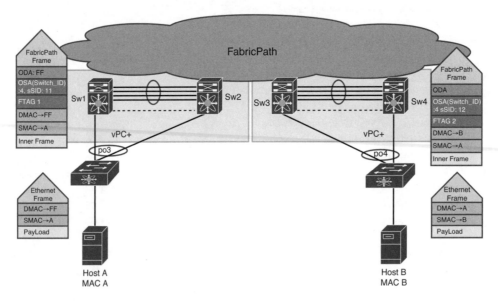

Figure 7-11 *Packet Flow and Outer-SA Fields in vPC+*

In Figure 7-11, assume that there are two trees in the FabricPath cloud. Switch Sw1 has announced its affinity to FTAG1 and Switch Sw2 to FTAG2. Similarly, Switch Sw3 has announced its affinity to FTAG1 and switch Sw4 to FTAG2. For multidestination frames that arrive at Switch Sw1 or Switch Sw3 from the host, the switches use the tree corresponding to FTAG1 to forward the traffic. Similarly, for the multidestination frames that arrive at Switch Sw2 and Switch Sw4 from the hosts, it uses FTAG2. For multidestination traffic arriving at both the vPC+ peer switches using the tree corresponding to FTAG1, only Sw1 and Sw3 decapsulate the traffic and send it toward the vPC+ member port. Similarly, Sw2 and Sw4 act on the multidestination frame arriving on the tree corresponding to FTAG2.

The following steps cover the packet flow assuming that the MAC address of Host A is 0000.0000.0000A and that of Host B is 0000.0000.000B. Further, assume that both Host A and Host B are in the same subnet (and belong to VLAN 10):

1. Host A wants to start a communication with Host B. Assuming the ARP table in Host A does not have the IP-MAC binding of Host B, it sends an ARP request frame with the broadcast destination MAC (ffff.ffff.fff) and source MAC 0000.0000.000A of Host A.

2. The ARP request frame goes to the access switch, which, in turn, can send the frame to any of the vPC+ peer switches based on the computed hash for the port channel. Assume that the ARP request frame goes to Sw1. Switch Sw1 receives the frame from Host A on the vPC+ (po3) link in VLAN 10. A Layer 2 forwarding lookup is performed on the frame. First, the source lookup ends up in a miss for {VLAN=10, MAC=0000.0000.000a} and hence the forwarding engine learns the Host A MAC address on the ingress interface. As Switch Sw1 is the vPC+ peer of Switch Sw2, the MAC address of Host A is synchronized with the peer Switch Sw2 over CFSoE.

3. The destination MAC address {VLAN=10, MAC=ffff.ffff.ffff} is a broadcast frame, so it needs to be sent on a distribution tree. Because Switch Sw1 has announced it affinity to FTAG1, it encapsulates the ARP request frame in a FabricPath header and sends the frame over Tree 1 (multicast tree corresponding to FTAG1). The source switch-ID used in the FabricPath header is the virtual switch-ID (emulated switch-ID) of 1000 based on the vPC+ configuration between Switch Sw1 and Sw2. The FTAG field in the FabricPath header will have the value of 1. The vPC+ peer Switches Sw3 and Sw4 receive the frame, and as Switch Sw3 has announced its affinity to FTAG1, it decapsulates the frame and sends it on the vPC+ port channel (po4). Because the frame is a multidestination frame that arrived over the FabricPath network, source MAC address learning is not performed. (Recall that by default conversational learning is enabled for FabricPath VLANs.) The access switch receives the ARP request frame and floods it over the VLAN 10. Host B receives the frame and sends an ARP reply frame with its own source MAC (MAC=0000.0000.000b) and destination MAC of Host A (MAC=0000.0000.000a).

4. The frame reaches the access switch connected to Host B. Assume that the access switch forwards the ARP response frame to Switch Sw4 based on its hash computation. Switch Sw4 receives the unicast frame and does a source MAC address lookup

(VLAN=10, MAC=0000.0000.0000b), which results in a miss. So Sw4 learns the MAC address of Host B on its local/edge port (po4). The MAC address of Host B is synced to its corresponding vPC+ peer Switch Sw3 using CFSoE.

5. Switch Sw4 uses the virtual switch-ID 2000 in the source switch-ID field when it encapsulates the ARP response frame with a FabricPath header. Because the inner destination MAC address (VLAN=10, MAC =0000.0000.000a) was a miss and because the Switch Sw4 has announced its affinity for FTAG2, the multidestination frame is sent on the distribution tree corresponding to FTAG2. The FTAG field in the FabricPath header will have the value of 2.

6. The vPC+ peer switches Sw1 and Sw2 receive the frame. The switches decapsulate the frame and because the destination MAC of inner frame (VLAN=10, MAC=0000.0000.000a) is known, they learn the inner source MAC (VLAN=10, MAC=0000.0000.000b) against the virtual switch-ID of 2000. Switch Sw1 will not forward the frame on the vPC+ member link for po3 because the frame arrived with an FTAG value of 2 and Sw1 does not have affinity to FTAG2. Instead, Sw2 forwards the frame to Host A via the vPC+ port channel.

7. Host A receives the ARP response frame. Further traffic from Host A to Host B follows the unicast processing logic. The switch (Sw1 or Sw2) encapsulates the frame and sends it toward virtual switch-ID 2000. Because this is a unicast frame, it arrives at either Sw3 or Sw4 from the FabricPath cloud. When this unicast frame reaches the Switch Sw3 or Sw4 after traversing the FabricPath network, the frame is decapsulated and the inner source MAC address (VLAN=10, MAC=0000.0000.000a) is learned against the virtual switch-ID 1000 as the inner destination MAC (VLAN=10, MAC=0000.0000.000b) is known. The MAC address of Host A will be synced to the vPC+ peer switch using CFSoE. Either Switch Sw3 or Sw4, depending on where it arrived from the FabricPath cloud, then forwards the frame to Host B.

This completes the packet flow and the conversational learning in a vPC+ environment, when the two hosts are on the same Layer 2 network.

Active/Active HSRP Forwarding

The basic Layer 2 flow with vPC+ presented in the previous section now is extended to describe a sample Layer 3 flow. Perhaps the most commonly deployed vPC+ deployment is with HSRP. HSRP active/active[5] forwarding can be achieved using vPC+ after HSRP active/standby relationship has been established. Figure 7-12 shows the physical topology for an active/active HSRP deployment. The active/active refers to the data plane in that either HSRP-enabled vPC+ peer can forward traffic destined to the HSRP virtual MAC (VMAC). In Figure 7-12, FabricPath runs between the access and aggregation switches. The host is dual-attached to the FabricPath access switches, which are configured as vPC+ peer switches. HSRP is configured at the aggregation switches, which are also vPC+ peers. Note that any Layer 3 frames destined to the VMAC will be forwarded by any of the peer switches.

HSRP hello packets are sent out by the vPC+ peer that runs the active HSRP control plane instance. These are sent over the FabricPath core ports; the hellos are directed to all the HSRP router addresses and sourced with the HSRP VMAC. The HSRP VMAC is learned by the FabricPath access switches against the vPC+ emulated switch-ID contained in the outer SA (source address) field.

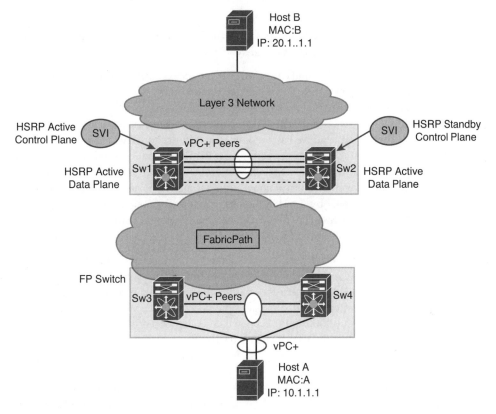

Figure 7-12   *Active/Active HSRP Topology*

This technology enables all the devices to be connected through a vPC+ port channel or through native FabricPath ports, and it helps to take advantage of the active/active HSRP forwarding functionality of vPC+. Moreover, it helps the end host to forward packets to the default gateway via multiple paths. When a frame is sent to HSRP's VMAC from the FabricPath edge switch, the MAC address lookup table returns the vPC+ virtual switch-ID (SID) as the destination switch. When a frame is sent to HSRP VMAC from a host device connecting to a vPC+ port channel, the traffic can take any of the physical links in port channel and can arrive on either of the vPC+ peer switches.

In Figure 7-12, assume that Switch Sw1 has announced its affinity to FTAG1 and Switch Sw2 to FTAG2. Similarly, Switch Sw3 has announced its affinity to FTAG1 and Switch Sw4 to FTAG2. Switches Sw1 and Sw3 use FTAG1 for multidestination frames, and Sw2 and Sw4 use FTAG2 for multidestination frames.

The traffic flow from the Host A to Host B is as follows:

1. Host A wants to start a communication with Host B. As Host B is in a different subnet than Host A, the frame is sent to the default gateway. Because Host A doesn't know the MAC address of the gateway, it sends an ARP request frame with the broadcast destination MAC (ffff.ffff.fff) and source MAC (0000.0000.000A) of Host A.

2. Assuming the ARP request frame, based on the PortChannel hash arriving at Sw3, it learns the MAC address of Host A and synchronizes it to Sw4 over CFSoE.

3. Switch Sw3 based on its affinity forwards the broadcast ARP frame over the multi-destination tree with FTAG1. While forwarding the frame, the source switch-ID used in the FabricPath header is the virtual switch-ID (emulated switch-ID) of 2000. Both Switches Sw1 and Sw2 receive the ARP request frame. Because Switch Sw1 running the HSRP control plane active has announced its affinity to FTAG1, it processes the frame and sends an ARP response with the HSRP VMAC address and source switch-ID as virtual switch-ID of 1000. Switch Sw2 drops the frame as it is received over the FTAG1, and Switch Sw2 has announced its affinity to FTAG2. Note that the ARP frames are handled only by the HSRP control plane active switch, which is Switch Sw1. Assume that the Switches Sw1 and Sw2 have previously learned the MAC address of Host A against the virtual switch-ID.

4. The ARP reply from Switch Sw1 has the source switch-ID of the virtual switch-ID 1000. The reply is sent back by Switch Sw1 with the destination switch-ID in the outer header as the virtual switch-ID of 2000. Assume that this packet arrives at Switch Sw4. The Switch Sw4 decapsulates the packet and because the destination MAC of Host A (0000.0000.000A) is known, Switch Sw4 learns the source MAC (HSRP VMAC) against the virtual switch-ID 1000.

5. The frame after decapsulation is forwarded to Host A.

6. Now Host A sends a unicast frame to Host B with source MAC of Host A and destination MAC as HSRP VMAC. Based on the Portchannel hash, assume that the frame arrived at Switch Sw4. Sw4 encapsulates the packet with a destination switch-ID as the virtual switch-ID of 1000. Assume that the frame arrived at Switch Sw2 after the ECMP computation in the FabricPath network.

7. As the HSRP data plane is active/active, Switch Sw2 decapsulates the packet, and after doing a Layer 3 routing lookup, the frame is forwarded over the Layer 3 network toward Host B.

8. The frame follows the normal routing rules and reaches Host B. The reverse traffic from Host B to Host A will be forwarded through the FabricPath network in a similar manner.

This completes the packet walkthrough of a vPC+ system with the HSRP active/active forwarding plane. The concepts are the same as a regular FabricPath network except for the concept of the emulated switch-ID and the ARP responses are sent only by the HSRP control plane active switch.

FabricPath Topologies

Before discussing case studies, look at some of the topologies that FabricPath enables.[6] Figure 7-13 shows some of these topologies.

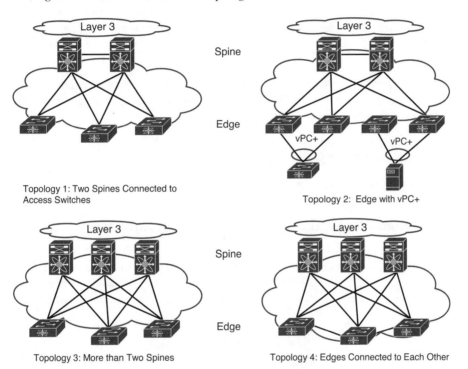

Figure 7-13 *FabricPath Topologies*

The topologies enabled by FabricPath are motivated by data center requirements and are optimized for server-to-server communication.[7] The Layer 3 in each of the topologies is connected at the Aggregation/Spine layer. FabricPath allows you to horizontally scale the network as the traffic needs increase.

Topology 1 in Figure 7-13 shows a topology similar to an aggregation-access STP design, where a set of edge switches connects to two spines. Because this topology is based on the FabricPath technology, all the links are in a forwarding state, and any hosts connected to the edge switches can use all the available paths through both of the spines.

Topology 2 in Figure 7-13 shows a topology similar to an aggregation-access STP design, where a set of edge switches connects to two spines except that in this topology the servers are connected to the edge devices in the vPC+ mode.

Topology 3 in Figure 7-13 shows a topology where FabricPath capabilities are used; that is, the edge switches connect to more than two spines. This topology allows the administrator to increase bandwidth between the spine and edge layers by adding more spines as the need arises.

Topology 4 in Figure 7-13 shows a topology where a set of edge switches in addition to being connected to the spine are also connected directly to each other. This could be useful when a direct connection between edge switches is needed. In general the usage of this topology makes sense only when a direct connectivity from one of the spines is not possible, for example, access switches in a ring topology connected to the aggregation switches. In such a scenario FabricPath provides enhanced bandwidth because all the links are forwarding.

Each of the topologies in Figure 7-13 also shows a Layer 3 network connected to the spines. In this case the spine keeps forwarding the Layer 2 traffic based on the switch-IDs but also acts as the edge switch for the routed traffic.

Migration to FabricPath Network

The following section describes the various migration scenarios.

Conversion from Classical Layer 2 to FabricPath Network

This section recaps the three-tier data center network topology, its limitations, and how FabricPath addresses these limitations. In the first chapter as well as in Chapter 4, you already saw the need for a large Layer 2 network in a data center. The traditional three-layer hierarchical network shown in Figure 7-14 could not meet the demands of new data centers.

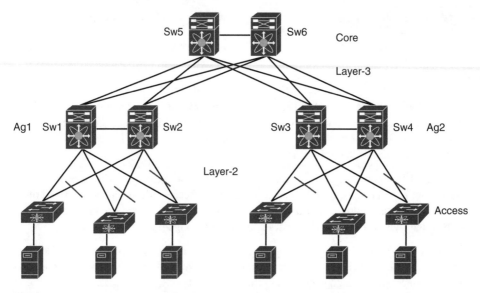

Figure 7-14   *Three-tier Topology*

In the classical three-tier model shown in Figure 7-14, all hosts are connected to access switches. The access switches are regular Layer 2 switches. It's preferable for all the hosts connected to the access switch to be in the same subnet so that host-host communication within the same subnet is Layer 2 switched by the directly attached access switch. All the access switches connect to distribution switches. For redundancy purposes, an access switch is connected to two distribution switches. The distribution switch serves as the Layer 2/Layer 3 boundary. It does Layer 2 switching when hosts of the same subnet, which are connected to different access switches, want to communicate with each other. It does Layer 3 switching when hosts that belong to different subnets want to communicate with each other. This hierarchical deployment model is suitable when

- The Layer 2 domain is not large (that is, the Layer 2 domain is contained within a distribution switch).

- Traffic is mostly north-south (host-to-Internet).

- There is no immediate need for a large Layer 2 domain or plans for expanding the network.

Now use this example and convert one aggregation layer at a time to a FabricPath network. Figure 7-14 shows two aggregation layers: Ag1 and Ag2. In these aggregation layers before the conversion of access–aggregation layer to FabricPath, the links to switch Sw2 and Sw4 are blocked due to STP.

To start the conversion process, follow the following steps on aggregation Ag1 (Chapter 4 gives exact commands to be configured on the switches):

1. Install the feature FabricPath on all the switches under Ag1 (aggregation and access switches).

2. Configure the FabricPath mode for the VLANs under the switches.

3. Configured the spanning tree domain on both the aggregation switches (optional).

4. Configure the links between the aggregation switches to be in FabricPath mode.

5. Configure the links between the aggregation switch and one of the access switches in FabricPath mode.

6. Repeat step 5 for each of the links connecting between the access switches under aggregation switches under aggregation layer Ag1.

7. Repeat step 1 through step 6 for the aggregation layer Ag2.

After these steps are executed, the network of Figure 7-14 transforms to two independent FabricPath networks with all the links forwarding between the access-aggregation layer, as shown in Figure 7-15.

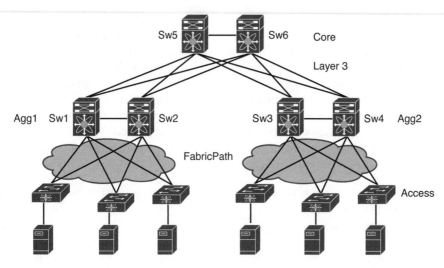

Figure 7-15   *FabricPath Network After Conversion*

Conversion of vPC to vPC+ (Classical Ethernet to FabricPath)

This case study focuses on the migration of vPC classical Ethernet VLAN to FabricPath. However, this type of migration may not be implemented in a real-world scenario, but it gives a general understanding of how FabricPath vPC+ works. When converting from vPC to vPC+, the network allows interaction with both FabricPath and CE. The upgrade process leads to some amount of traffic drop.

This migration case study considers switches in the access and distribution layers. The distribution switches are acting as root switches for the STP and also as the Layer 2 and Layer 3 boundary in the network. The migration strategy is explained next with different scenarios, and the expected downtime is highlighted with dashed lines.

Before discussing the migration strategy, start with a sample topology, as shown in Figure 7-16. Figure 7-16 depicts a standard vPC setup consisting of two access and distribution switches. The HSRP feature is enabled on different VLANs connecting to the primary and secondary vPC peer switches.

Following are the vPC configurations enabled on primary (Sw1) and secondary (Sw2) switches:

1. **Enabling vPC and LACP feature:** The vPC feature should be configured on both the Cisco Nexus 5000 series switches. The feature can be enabled by executing the following commands. Refer to Example 7-1 to enable the vPC feature on the switches.

2. **Creating a VLAN/SVI:** For enabling Layer 3 forwarding to and from a VLAN, a switched virtual interface (SVI) needs to be created for that VLAN. After the SVI is created, the HSRP feature needs to be enabled on that SVI interface. This can be achieved by executing the following commands in the distribution switches, as shown in Example 7-18.

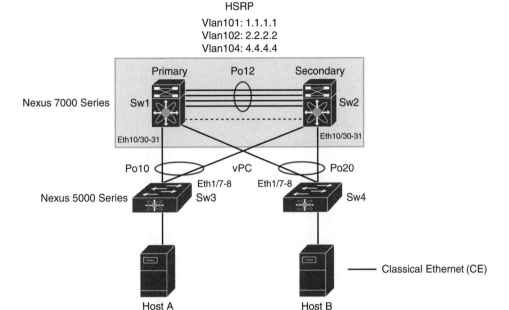

Figure 7-16   *Initial Topology (Standard vPC Setup)*

Example 7-18   *Creation of SVI and Enabling HSRP*

```
/* 1. Configuration on switch Nexus7k-Sw1 */
Nexus7k-Sw1# config t
Nexus7k-Sw1(config)# interface VLAN101
Nexus7k-Sw1(config-if)# ip address 2.1.0.3/24
Nexus7k-Sw1(config-if)# hsrp 0
Nexus7k-Sw1(config-if)# ip 2.1.0.1                    /* Virtual IP address (VIP) */


Nexus7k-Sw1# config t
Nexus7k-Sw1(config-if)# int VLAN102
Nexus7k-Sw1(config-if)# ip address 2.2.0.3/24
Nexus7k-Sw1(config-if)# hsrp 0
Nexus7k-Sw1(config-if)# preempt
Nexus7k-Sw1(config-if)# priority 140
Nexus7k-Sw1(config-if)# ip 2.2.0.1                    /* Virtual IP address (VIP) */

Nexus7k-Sw1# config t
Nexus7k-Sw1(config)# interface VLAN104
Nexus7k-Sw1(config-if)# ip address 4.0.0.3/24
Nexus7k-Sw1(config-if)# hsrp 0
```

```
Nexus7k-Sw1(config-if)# preempt
Nexus7k-Sw1(config-if)# priority 140
Nexus7k-Sw1(config-if)# ip 4.0.0.1                    /* Virtual IP address (VIP) */


/* For brevity reasons we will show configuration only on VLAN 101 on switch SW2 */
/* 2. Configuration on Switch Nexus7k-SW2 */
Nexus7k-Sw2# config t
Nexus7k-Sw2(config)# int VLAN 101
Nexus7k-Sw2(config-if)# ip address 2.1.0.4/24
Nexus7k-Sw2(config-if)# hsrp 0
Nexus7k-Sw2(config-if)# ip 2.1.0.1                    /* Virtual IP address (VIP) */
   Nexus7k-Sw2(config)#
```

The rest of the configuration related to vPC remains the same as explained in detail in the earlier section, "vPC Operations."

Now you need to migrate to vPC+. The step-wise migration strategy from vPC to vPC+ involves

- Configuring vPC+ on secondary Switch (Sw2)

- Configuring vPC+ on primary Switch (Sw1)

- Configuring FabricPath on the access Switch (Sw3)

Configuring vPC+ on Secondary Switch

Figure 7-17 shows that the FabricPath feature needs to be enabled on the secondary vPC Switch (Sw2) and the links highlighted as dashed lines are shut down. After enabling FabricPath, Switch Sw2 is assigned an appropriate switch-ID via configuration or it can pick one automatically. Example 7-19 shows the configuration commands involved in this process.

Example 7-19   *Enabling FabricPath Feature*

```
Nexus7k-Sw2# config t
Nexus7k-Sw2(config)# install feature-set fabricpath
Nexus7k-Sw2(config)# feature-set fabricpath

Nexus7k-Sw2(config)# fabricpath switch-id 36
   Nexus7k-Sw2(config)#
```

For migration, after the FabricPath feature is enabled, the vPCs and vPC peer-link on the secondary Switch Sw2 need to be shut down (see Example 7-20).

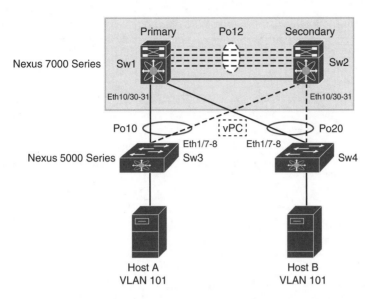

Figure 7-17   *Configuring FabricPath on Secondary Switch*

Example 7-20   *Shutting Down vPC and vPC Peer*

```
Nexus7k-Sw2# config t
Nexus7k-Sw2(config)# int po range 12-20
Nexus7k-Sw2(config-if-range)# shutdown
   Nexus7k-Sw2(config-if-range)#
```

The previously configured vPC peer-link has to be changed to FabricPath mode, and similarly the VLAN mode needs to be changed to FabricPath. Example 7-21 shows the commands that need to be executed on the secondary switch.

Example 7-21   *Change vPC peer-link and VLAN Mode*

```
Nexus7k-Sw2# config t
Nexus7k-Sw2(config)# int po12
Nexus7k-Sw2(config-if)# switchport mode fabricpath

/* VLAN mode change to fabricpath*/
Nexus7k-Sw2(config-if)# VLAN 101-105
Nexus7k-Sw2(config-VLAN)# mode fabricpath
   Nexus7k-Sw2(config-VLAN)#
```

The FabricPath switch-ID needs to be configured under the vPC domain. Example 7-22 shows the commands that need to be executed on the switch.

Example 7-22   *Configuring Virtual switch-id and vPC Domain*

```
/* 1. Configure vpc domain and switch-id */
Nexus7k-Sw2# config t
Nexus7k-Sw2(config-VLAN)# vpc domain 12
Nexus7k-Sw2(config-vpc-domain)# fabricpath switch-id 36
Configuring fabricpath switch id will flap vPCs. Continue (yes/no)? [yes]
---------:: Re-init of peer-link and vPCs started  ::--------


/* 2.The vPC peer-link and vPC PortChannel interfaces should be brought up by exe-
cuting "no shutdown" command. */

Nexus7k-Sw2(config)# int range po 12-20
Nexus7k-Sw2(config-if-range)# no shut
   Nexus7k-Sw2(config-if-range)#
```

After this point, the traffic starts flowing through the aggregation switches, but the vPC
peer link state on the secondary switch (Sw2) is in down state. The FabricPath VLANs
such as VLAN 101–105 will be in an err-disabled state, and the vPC peer link will be in a
down state. Example 7-23 depicts the status of the FabricPath VLANs 101–105.

Example 7-23   *Status of FabricPath-Enabled VLANs*

```
Nexus7k-Sw2#show interface po 12 trunk


--------------------------------------------------------------------------------
Port          Native  Status        Port
              Vlan                  Channel
--------------------------------------------------------------------------------
Po1           1       fabricpath    --


--------------------------------------------------------------------------------
Port          Vlans Allowed on Trunk
--------------------------------------------------------------------------------
Po1           1-4094


--------------------------------------------------------------------------------
Port          Vlans Err-disabled on Trunk
--------------------------------------------------------------------------------
Po1           101-105

Nexus7k-Sw2# show vpc brief
vPC domain id               : 12
vPC+ switch id              : 36
Peer status                 : peer link is down
```

```
vPC keep-alive status              : peer is alive
vPC fabricpath status              : peer is not reachable through fabricpath
   Nexus7k-Sw2#
```

Configuring vPC+ on Primary Switch

After the vPC secondary switch has been FabricPath-enabled and vPC+-enabled, now the same procedure needs to be followed for the primary vPC switch. Figure 7-18 shows the state of the network after the FabricPath and vPC+ features are enabled on the primary vPC switch (Sw1). The links are now operational. A similar set of steps (Examples 7-19 to 7-22) need to be followed on the primary vPC Switch Sw1.

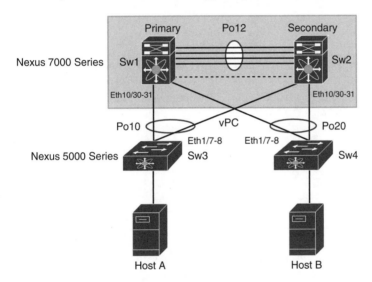

Figure 7-18   *Configuring FabricPath on Primary Switch*

After the vPC+ peer link is operational, using the **show vpc brief** command can verify the peer and vPC keep-alive status. The peer status in the output shown in Example 7-24 indicates that the peer adjacency is formed and the peer is reachable through FabricPath.

Example 7-24   *show vpc brief*

```
Nexus7k-Sw1#
Nexus7k-Sw1# show vpc brief
vPC domain id                      : 12
vPC+ switch id                     : 36
Peer status                        : peer adjacency formed ok
vPC keep-alive status              : peer is alive
vPC fabricpath status              : peer is reachable through fabricpath
   Nexus7k-Sw1#
```

At this stage you can look at the spanning-tree summary and see the operational VLAN on the primary switch. Example 7-25 depicts the output of the **show spanning-tree summary** command on the primary switch.

Example 7-25   *show spanning-tree summary on Primary Switch*

```
Nexus7k-Sw1#
Nexus7k-Sw1# show spanning-tree summary
Switch is in rapid-pvst mode
Root bridge for: VLAN0101-VLAN0105
L2 Gateway STP bridge for: VLAN0101-VLAN0105 <<<
L2 Gateway Domain ID: 1  <<<
Bridge Assurance                  is enabled
vPC peer-switch                   is enabled (non-operational) <<
STP-Lite                          is enabled


Name             Blocking Listening Learning Forwarding STP Active
---------------- -------- --------- -------- ---------- ----------
VLAN0101               0         0        0          2          2
VLAN0102               0         0        0          2          2
VLAN0103               0         0        0          2          2
VLAN0104               0         0        0          2          2
VLAN0105               0         0        0          2          2

---------------- -------- --------- -------- ---------- ----------
5 VLANs                0         0        0         10         10
   Nexus7k-Sw1#
```

At this stage of conversion, the vPC peer-link is part of FabricPath network and therefore can be removed from the peer switch, as shown in Example 7-26.

Example 7-26   *Unconfiguring vPC Peer Switch*

```
/* 1. On Switch Nexus7k-Sw1 */
Nexus7k-Sw1# conf t
Nexus7k-Sw1(config)# vpc domain 12
Nexus7k-Sw1(config-vpc-domain)# no peer-switch


/* On Switch Nexus7k-Sw2*/
Nexus7k-Sw2#conf t

Nexus7k-Sw2(config)# vpc domain 12
Nexus7k-Sw2(config-vpc-domain)# no peer-switch
   Nexus7k-Sw2(config-vpc-domain)#
```

Conversion of Access Switch (Sw3) Connecting to Secondary (Sw2) to FabricPath

As shown in Figure 7-19, the FabricPath feature needs to be configured on access switch (Sw3) ports connecting to the secondary vPC+ (Sw2). The following are the commands that need to be executed on uplinks connecting to Switch Sw2. Example 7-27 depicts the steps required to change the mode to FabricPath on the access switch ports connecting to the secondary Switch (Sw2).

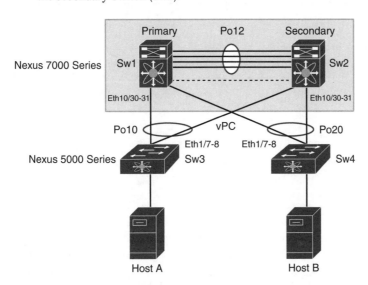

Figure 7-19   *Configuring Access Switch (Sw3) Connecting to Secondary (Sw2) to FabricPath*

Example 7-27   *Change the Mode to FabricPath on Access Switch*

```
Nexus5k-Sw3# conf t

Nexus5k-Sw3(config)# int ethernet 1/8
Nexus5k-Sw3(config-if)# shut
Nexus5k-Sw3(config-if)# no channel-group 10
Nexus5k-Sw3(config-if)# switchport mode fabricpath
Nexus5k-Sw3(config-if)# no shut

Nexus7k-Sw2(config)# int ethernet 10/30
Nexus7k-Sw2(config-if)# shut
Nexus7k-Sw2(config-if)# no channel-group 10
Nexus7k-Sw2(config-if)# switchport mode fabricpath
Nexus7k-Sw2(config-if)# no shut
   Nexus7k-Sw2(config-if)#
```

After the FabricPath uplink is up, IS-IS adjacency is established between the switches. At this moment IS-IS can be verified using the **show** command **sh fabric isis adjacency** on Sw1. Example 7-28 shows the output of this command.

There are no FabricPath VLANs configured, and it can be enabled by executing the commands shown in Example 7-28.

Example 7-28   *show fabric isis adjacency*

```
Nexus7k-Sw1#


Nexus7k-Sw1# show fabric isis adjacency
Fabricpath IS-IS domain: default Fabricpath IS-IS adjacency database:
System ID       SNPA        Level  State  Hold Time  Interface
0026.9826.7fc4  N/A          1      UP     00:00:24   Ethernet10/30


Nexus7k-Sw1# conf t
Nexus7k-Sw1(config)# VLAN 101-105
Nexus7k-Sw1(config)# mode fabric
Nexus7k-Sw1(config)# end
   Nexus7k-Sw1#end
```

After changing the VLANs to FabricPath, the syslog message shown in Example 7-29 is displayed on all FabricPath VLANs. This syslog is an expected behavior because Sw1 is a Layer 2 gateway and it is not acting as a root. This behavior can be verified by executing **show spanning-tree VLAN <VLANid>** for that particular VLAN.

Example 7-29   *Syslog msg and show fabric isis adjacency*

```
Sw1 %STP-2-L2GW_BACKBONE_BLOCK: L2 Gateway Backbone port inconsistency blocking port
port channel10 on VLAN0904.


Nexus7k-Sw1# show spanning-tree VLAN 101


Interface       Role Sts Cost      Prio.Nbr Type
--------------- ---- --- --------- -------- -----------------------------
Po10            Desg BKN*2         128.4105 P2p *L2GW_Inc <<< Po10 indicates L2GW
inconsistency
Eth10/29        Desg FWD 2         128.1309 Edge P2p


/* In order to find the root cause for the problem we need to check on primary
switch (Sw1). Firstly, we need to check spanning-tree protocol on primary switch
(Sw1).*/
```

```
Nexus7k-Sw1# show spanning-tree VLAN 101

Interface        Role Sts Cost        Prio.Nbr Type

---------------- ---- --- ---------- -------- ------------------------------

Po10             Desg FWD 1           128.4105 (vPC) P2p

Po12             Desg FWD 1           128.4106 (vPC) P2p  <<

   Nexus7k-Sw1#
```

Then you need to check where the source MAC address of the host corresponding to the bridged flow is learnt. It can be verified by executing the commands in Example 7-30.

Example 7-30   *Source MAC Address Check*

```
Nexus7k-Sw1# sh mac add address 0018.74c0.2400 VLAN 101ed

   VLAN     MAC Address      Type      age     Secure NTFY Ports

---------+-----------------+--------+---------+------+----+----------------

* 101      0018.74c0.2400   dynamic   570       F    F   Po10


/*As shown in the output, the mac-address is still learnt from PortChannel 10
instead of

the FabricPath peer-link. This issue can be fixed by issuing shutdown command on

PortChannel 10 either on Sw1 or Sw3. After toggling the Port-Channel 10 the mac
address

is learned through FabricPath. */


Nexus7k-Sw1# sh mac add address 0018.74c0.2400 vl 101

   VLAN     MAC Address      Type      age     Secure NTFY SWID.SSID.LID

---------+-----------------+--------+---------+------+----+-------------- 101

0018.74c0.2400   dynamic   0         F    F   1.0.64 <<< learned through FabricPath

   Nexus7k-Sw1#
```

The migration process that you went through can be further improved by converting the VLANs to FabricPath and shutting down the port channel on Sw1. By migrating using the improved methodology, the convergence time for both the routed and bridged flows is lower. Figure 7-20 shows this improved migration process.

Example 7-31 shows the configuration steps required to achieve improved convergence time.

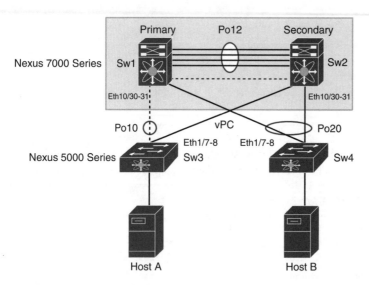

Figure 7-20   *Converting VLANs on Sw1 to FabricPath and Shutting Port Channels*

Example 7-31   *Step to Improve Convergence Time*

```
Nexus7k-Sw1# conf t
Nexus7k-Sw1(config)# VLAN 101-105
Nexus7k-Sw1(config-VLAN)# mode fabricpath
Nexus7k-Sw1(config-VLAN)# int po 10
Nexus7k-Sw1(config-if)# shut
   Nexus7k-Sw1(config-if)#
```

Converting Access Switch Sw3 Uplink Connecting to Sw1 to FabricPath

The final migration step involves converting the uplink connecting Sw3 and Sw1 to FabricPath. This conversion process is shown in Figure 7-21.

The running configuration of the interface on Sw1 and Sw3 is shown in Example 7-32.

Example 7-32   *Running Configuration from Primary Switch and Access Switch*

```
Nexus7k-Sw1#
Nexus7k-Sw1# show run int Ethernet 10/30

interface Ethernet10/30
  switchport mode trunk
  switchport trunk allowed VLAN 101-105
  channel-group 10 mode active
```

```
  no shutdown
 !


/* From Access switch */
Nexus5k-Sw3# show run int Ethernet 1/7

interface Ethernet1/7
  switchport mode trunk
  switchport trunk allowed VLAN 101-105
  channel-group 10 mode active
  no shutdown
   Nexus5k-Sw3#
```

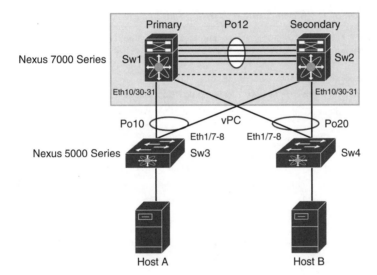

Figure 7-21   *Converting Sw3 Connecting to Sw1 Uplink to FabricPath*

The channel modes on both the interfaces of the PortChannel need to be changed to
FabricPath. The following are the commands that need to be executed on both the
Switches Sw1 and Sw3. Example 7-33 depicts the changing of the channel mode.

Example 7-33   *Changing the Mode to FabricPath*

```
Nexus7k-Sw1# conf t
Nexus7k-Sw1(config)# int ethernet 10/30
Nexus7k-Sw1(config-if)# shut
Nexus7k-Sw1(config-if)# no channel-group 10
Nexus7k-Sw1(config-if)# switchport mode fabricpath
Nexus7k-Sw1(config-if)# no shut
```

```
On Sw3:

Nexus5k-Sw3(config)# int ethernet 1/7

Nexus5k-Sw3(config-if)# shut

Nexus5k-Sw3(config-if)# no channel-group 10

Nexus5k-Sw3(config-if)# switchport mode fabricpath

Nexus5k-Sw3(config-if)# no shut
    Nexus5k-Sw3#
```

Now that you have completed the migration process, **show isis adjacency** on the core switch shows the downstream and peer vPC switch interfaces are FabricPath-capable. As shown in Example 7-34, you can see that the virtual switch[36] has two ECMP paths.

Example 7-34   *Verification of IS-IS and Route to Virtual Switch*

```
/* Core switch :The "show fabric isis adjacency" shows whether the uplinks are
FabricPath capable. As shown in the following output interface eth 10/31 is
FabricPath capable.*/

Nexus7k-Sw1# show fabric isis adjacency

System ID       SNPA         Level  State  Hold Time  Interface
0026.9826.7fc4  N/A            1     UP     00:00:23   Ethernet10/30 << FabricPath
capable


/* The access switch Sw3 has two interfaces connecting to the virtual switch, as
shown in the following command it can reach virtual switch 36 via Ethernet 1/7 and
Ethernet 1/8. */


Nexus5k-Sw3# show fabricpath route


FabricPath Unicast Route Table for Topology-Default


0/1/0, number of next-hops: 0
        via ---- , [60/0], 2 day/s 21:50:47, local
1/3/0, number of next-hops: 1
        via Eth1/8, [115/40], 0 day/s 00:00:12, isis_fabricpath-default
1/6/0, number of next-hops: 1
        via Eth1/7, [115/40], 0 day/s 00:13:18, isis_fabricpath-default
1/36/0, number of next-hops: 2
        via Eth1/7, [115/40], 0 day/s 00:13:18, isis_fabricpath-default
        via Eth1/8, [115/40], 0 day/s 00:00:12, isis_fabricpath-default
 Nexus5k-Sw3#
```

Monitoring and Troubleshooting in FabricPath Networks

FabricPath allows deployment of an extremely flexible, scalable, highly available, and resilient network. Among other features, the built-in Layer 2 multipath feature, topology/tree-based forwarding for both unidestination and multidestination traffic as well as a single control protocol (IS-IS) for all types of traffic are highly desirable. The plug-and-play deployment model, after the FabricPath feature is enabled, certainly eases the burden of lots of manual configuration on the network administrator. However, like any technology, sufficient tools need to be provided to allow the network administrator to easily debug and troubleshoot problems in a FabricPath network.

FabricPath, much like TRILL (see Chapter 5, "TRILL," for more details), relies on the Operations, Administration, and Maintenance (OAM) framework[8, 9] for this purpose. Although there are subtle differences in the operation of TRILL and FabricPath, at the end of the day, both are Layer 2 overlay technologies that rely on a MAC-in-MAC encapsulation and use similar concepts for both the control and data plane. The specifics of OAM in terms of the message formats, extensions to IS-IS to carry these messages, and related functionality in terms of advertisement of OAM capabilities are covered in detail in Chapter 8, "TRILL Deployment, Migration, and Troubleshooting." To avoid redundancy, we will skip re-describing the TLVs, but it's important to understand that there will be some combination of standard OAM TLVs and vendor-specific TLVs (aka extension to organization-specific TLVs) that have been used to realize the FabricPath OAM tools. Here, some specific tools are presented that allow easier troubleshooting of FabricPath networks.

FabricPath OAM tools allow diagnosing, monitoring, and reporting of problems in FabricPath networks. Similar to utilities such as ping and traceroute/tracepath that allow quick determination of problems in IP networks, equivalent troubleshooting tools have also been introduced to diagnose problems in FabricPath networks. The FabricPath OAM tools can be categorized as shown in Table 7-1. In general, FabricPath OAM messages may be identified via the reserved OAM ethertype or by using a well-known reserved source MAC address in the OAM packets depending on the implementation on different platforms. This constitutes a signature for recognition of FabricPath OAM packets.

Table 7-1 *FabricPath OAM Tools*

Category	Tools
Fault Verification	Loopback Message
Fault Isolation	Path Trace Message, Multicast Trace Message
Performance	Delay Measurement, Loss Measurement
Auxiliary	MAC Discovery, Address Binding Verification, IP End Station Locator, Error Notification, OAM Command Messages, and Diagnostic Payload Discovery for ECMP Coverage

Although all the FabricPath OAM tools in the various categories listed in Table 7-1 have not been fully developed, the support for them will gradually come in subsequent software releases of Nexus OS for various switching platforms such Nexus 7k, Nexus 5k, Nexus 6k, and so on that support FabricPath. This section concentrates on describing some of the most commonly used tools.

Loopback Message

The loopback message is the simplest to understand of all the FabricPath OAM tools, but at the same time it is perhaps the most useful. This is analogous to how the ping utility works for IP packets. It is primarily used for fault verification. Consider the topology shown in Figure 7-22 where there are three core (aka spine) switches labeled S1, S2, S3 and five ToR switches connected in the form of a CLoS topology. The path of an example loopback message initiated from ToR T1 for T5 is shown when it traverses via spine S3 (see dotted line). When the loopback message initiated by ToR T1 reaches spine S3, it forwards it as any other FabricPath encapsulated data packet based on the outer header. The packet is not sent to software on Spine S3. On ToR T3, based on the appropriate loopback message signature (more generally a FabricPath OAM message signature), the packet will be sent to software FabricPath OAM module, which, in turn, will generate a loopback response that will be sent back to the originator ToR T1. The loopback message utility is useful in detecting various errors such as cross connection (for example, mismatch of VLANs) and path failure, and also has the ability to respond to loopback messages either in-band or via an out-of-band channel.

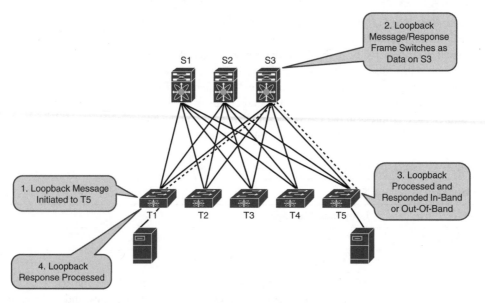

Figure 7-22   *FabricPath OAM Loopback Message Illustration*

Path Trace Message

The primary goal of the path trace message is fault isolation. It is analogous to how the utility **traceroute** or **tracepath** works in the IP world. In a FabricPath network, it may be desirable to find the list of switches that are traversed by a frame to reach the destination. When the loopback test from a source switch to a destination switch fails, the next step is to find out the offending switch in the path. The operation of the Path Trace message begins with the source switch transmitting a FabricPath OAM frame with a TTL value of 1. The next-hop switch receives this frame; decrements the TTL; and on finding that TTL is 0, transmits a TTL expiry message to the sender switch. The sender switch records this message as an indication of success from the first-hop switch. Then the source switch increases the TTL value by one in the next path trace message to find the second hop. At each new transmission, the sequence number in the message will be incremented. Each intermediate switch along the path decrements the TTL value by 1 as is the case with regular FabricPath forwarding. This process continues until a response is received from the destination switch, or path trace process timeout occurs, or the hop count reaches a maximum configured value. The payload in the OAM FabricPath frames is referred to as the flow entropy. The flow entropy can be populated so as to choose a particular path among multiple ECMP paths between a source and destination switch. Just like the loopback message, it is possible to request a response to the path trace message via an in-band or out-of-band channel. The TTL expiry message may also be generated by intermediate switches for actual data frames. The same payload of the original path trace request is preserved for the payload of the response. If there are intermediate switches along the path that do not understand FabricPath OAM, this feature will not work.

Multicast Trace Message

For forwarding multidestination traffic, FabricPath employs multicast trees formed using IS-IS that are each identified by a unique FTAG. The ingress switch decides the FTAG, aka the multicast tree, along which the multidestination frame must be forwarded in the FabricPath network. To trouble-shoot multidestination forwarding in the FabricPath network, the multicast trace or multicast tree verification (MTV) OAM messages have been introduced. The primary goal of the MTV messages is to allow verification of the multicast tree integrity and the multicast address pruning. These messages are designed to detect multicast connectivity defects. In addition, they can be used for plotting a given multicast tree in a FabricPath network.

Multicast Trees

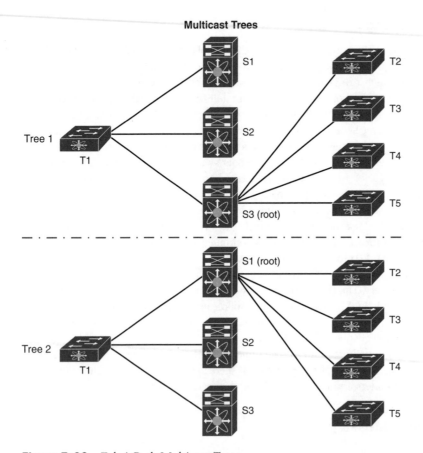

Figure 7-23   *FabricPath Multicast Trees*

The MTV messages are copied to software at the intermediate switches that are part of the multicast tree under verification. By default, every switch that is part of the tree responds to the originator of the MTV request with an appropriate MTV response message. However, typical use cases of multicast tree verification or group verification involve verifying multicast connectivity for a selected set of switches as opposed to the entire network. This can be achieved by the sender switch specifying the scope of switches in the MTV request message from whom a response is wanted. Only the switches in the scope field respond to the original MTV request. Figure 7-23 shows two multicast trees for the sample topology shown in Figure 7-22. Multicast tree 1 is rooted at Switch Sw1, and multicast tree 2 is rooted as Switch Sw2. Figure 7-24 depicts the path taken by the MTV request and subsequent response messages for an MTV trace triggered from Switch Sw1 for tree 1. There are three categories of multicast tree verifications:

■ **Overall tree verification:** The goal here is to verify a particular tree without any pruning information. The user must specify a multicast tree number (aka FTAG) of interest for this purpose. By default, an OAM VLAN will be automatically brought up on all OAM-capable switches. The tree will be verified on the OAM.

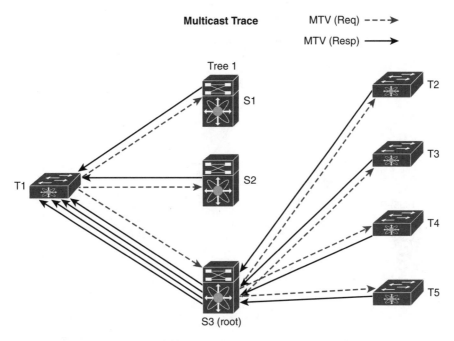

Figure 7-24 *FabricPath Multicast Tree Verification*

- **L2 multicast verification:** The user specifies a VLAN and destination multicast MAC address. As before, a well-known source MAC address may be employed for identifying OAM MTV frames.

- **IP multicast verification:** The user specifies a VLAN, destination multicast IP address, and optionally a source IP address in case (S, G) pruning is wanted instead of the default (*, G). The destination MAC address is derived from the destination multicast IP address as is the case for regular multicast packets.

As with the other OAM messages, if there are intermediate switches along the path that do not understand FabricPath OAM, this feature will not work. Also, OAM messages are not allowed to egress out of any non-FabricPath interfaces.

FabricPath OAM Configuration Model

This section shows some sample CLI outputs for the FabricPath OAM feature as seen on a Cisco Nexus 6 k box that has the FabricPath feature enabled. The goal of this section is not to provide a comprehensive configuration and show a CLI guide related to FabricPath[10] OAM, but instead to provide a flavor of some common FabricPath OAM debugging commands that were introduced in the earlier sections. For illustration, consider a simple topology with three FabricPath switches connected, as shown in Figure 7-25.

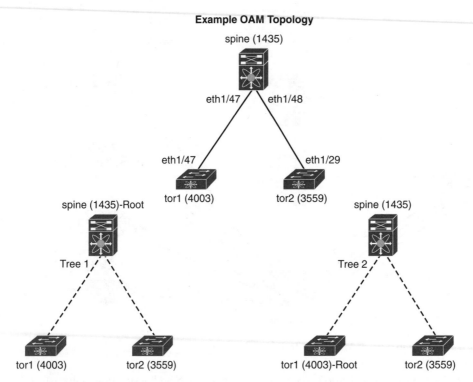

Example OAM Topology

Figure 7-25 *Sample Topology for FabricPath OAM Illustration*

Example 7-35 shows sample outputs with the FabricPath loopback test. Example 7-36 shows sample outputs with the FabricPath traceroute utility. Example 7-37 shows sample outputs with the FabricPath mtrace utility for multicast tree verification. All the outputs are gathered from a switch labeled tor1.

Example 7-35 *FabricPath OAM Ping*

```
tor1# show fabricpath switch-id
                    FABRICPATH SWITCH-ID TABLE
Legend: '*' - this system

=====================================================================
SWITCH-ID       SYSTEM-ID       FLAGS        STATE       STATIC  EMULATED
----------+----------------+------------+-----------+--------------------
 1435          a44c.11e8.528c   Primary      Confirmed   No      No
 3559          a44c.11e8.2c4c   Primary      Confirmed   No      No
*4003          a44c.11e8.2ccc   Primary      Confirmed   No      No
Total Switch-ids: 3


tor1# show fabricpath isis adjacency
Fabricpath IS-IS domain: default Fabricpath IS-IS adjacency database:
```

```
System ID       SNPA            Level  State  Hold Time  Interface
spine           N/A             1      UP     00:00:26   Ethernet1/47

tor1# ping ?
  <CR>
  A.B.C.D or Hostname  IP address of remote system
  WORD                 Enter Hostname
  fabricpath           Fabricpath oam ping
  multicast            Multicast ping

tor1# ping fabricpath ?
  <CR>
  switch-id  Fabricpath oam ping target switch id

tor1# ping fabricpath switch-id ?
  <1-65535>  Fabricpath oam ping target switch id

tor1# ping fabricpath switch-id 3559 ?
  <CR>
  asynchronous   Run Fabricpath oam ping asynchronously (dont wait for output)
  forward        Fabricpath oam ping forward flow
  hop            Fabricpath oam ping hop count to use
  ingress        Ingress interface for fabricpath oam ping
  interface      Egress interface for fabricpath oam ping
  interval       Specify fabricpath oam ping interval in milliseconds
  payload        Configure fabricpath oam ping payload
  profile        Fabricpath oam profile to use
  repeat         Fabricpath oam ping repeat count to use
  reply          Fabricpath oam ping reply details
  size           Fabricpath oam ping data tlv size to use
  sweep          Fabricpath oam ping to sweep packet sizes
  tag            Fabricpath oam ping tag to use
  timeout        Specify fabricpath oam ping timeout duration in seconds
  topology       Fabricpath oam ping topology to use
  use-host-VLAN  Fabricpath oam ping to use host VLAN (will not translate VLAN
                 in any scenario)
  validate       Validate fabricpath oam ping response
  verbose        Display verbose output
  VLAN           Fabricpath oam ping VLAN to use

tor1# ping fabricpath switch-id 3559

Codes: '!' - success, 'Q' - request not sent, '.' - timeout,
```

```
'D' - Destination Unreachable, 'X' - unknown return code,
'V' - VLAN nonexistent, 'v' - VLAN in suspended state,
'm' - malformed request, 'C' - Cross Connect Error,
'U' - Unknown RBridge nickname, 'n' - Not AF,
'*' - Success, Optional Tlv incomplete,
'I' - Interface not in forwarding state,
'S' - Service Tag nonexistent, 's' - Service Tag in suspended state,
'c' - Corrupted Data/Test


Sender handle: 3
!!!!!

Success rate is 100 percent (5/5), round-trip min/avg/max = 1/1/1 ms
Total time elapsed 47 ms
```

Example 7-36 *FabricPath OAM Traceroute*

```
tor1# show fabricpath isis switch-id

Fabricpath IS-IS domain: default
Fabricpath IS-IS Switch-ID Database
Legend: C - Confirmed, T - tentative, W - swap
        S - sticky, E - Emulated Switch
        A - Anycast Switch
        '*' - this system
System-ID        Primary  Secondary  Reachable  Bcast-Priority Ftag-Root Capable
MT-0


a44c.11e8.2c4c   3559[C]     0[C]    Yes           64               Y


a44c.11e8.2ccc*  4003[C]     0[C]    Yes           64               Y


a44c.11e8.528c   1435[C]     0[C]    Yes           64               Y

tor1# traceroute ?
  A.B.C.D or Hostname  IP address of remote system
  WORD                 Enter Hostname
  fabricpath           Fabricpath oam traceroute

tor1# traceroute fabricpath ?
  <CR>
```

```
   switch-id  Fabricpath oam traceroute target switch id

tor1# traceroute fabricpath switch-id ?
  <1-65535>  Fabricpath oam traceroute target switch id

tor1# traceroute fabricpath switch-id 1435

Codes: '!' - success, 'Q' - request not sent, '.' - timeout,
'D' - Destination Unreachable, 'X' - unknown return code,
'V' - VLAN nonexistent, 'v' - VLAN in suspended state,
'm' - malformed request, 'C' - Cross Connect Error,
'U' - Unknown RBridge nickname, 'n' - Not AF,
'*' - Success, Optional Tlv incomplete,
'I' - Interface not in forwarding state,
'S' - Service Tag nonexistent, 's' - Service Tag in suspended state,
'c' - Corrupted Data/Test


Sender handle: 1
Hop Code SwitchId Interface      State TotalTime PathId
=========================================================
  1 !    1435     Rcvd on Eth1/47  fwd        2ms


tor1# traceroute fabricpath switch-id 3559

Codes: '!' - success, 'Q' - request not sent, '.' - timeout,
'D' - Destination Unreachable, 'X' - unknown return code,
'V' - VLAN nonexistent, 'v' - VLAN in suspended state,
'm' - malformed request, 'C' - Cross Connect Error,
'U' - Unknown RBridge nickname, 'n' - Not AF,
'*' - Success, Optional Tlv incomplete,
'I' - Interface not in forwarding state,
'S' - Service Tag nonexistent, 's' - Service Tag in suspended state,
'c' - Corrupted Data/Test


Sender handle: 2
Hop Code SwitchId Interface      State TotalTime PathId
=========================================================
  1 !    1435     Rcvd on Eth1/47  fwd        3ms   3559
  2 !    3559     Rcvd on Eth1/29  fwd        3ms
```

Example 7-37 *FabricPath OAM Mtrace*

```
tor1# show fabricpath isis trees
Fabricpath IS-IS domain: default
Note: The metric mentioned for multidestination tree is from the root of that tr
ee to that switch-id
*:directly connected neighbor or link
P:Physical switch-id, E:Emulated, A:Anycast


MT-0
Topology 0, Tree 1, Swid routing table
1435, L1
 via Ethernet1/47, metric 0
3559, L1
 via Ethernet1/47, metric 40


Topology 0, Tree 2, Swid routing table
1435, L1
 via Ethernet1/47, metric 40
3559, L1
 via Ethernet1/47, metric 80


tor1# mtrace ?
  WORD       IP address or hostname of source
  fabricpath  Fabricpath oam multicast trace


tor1# mtrace fabricpath ?
  <CR>
  data       Fabricpath oam mtrace data
  forward    Fabricpath oam mtrace forward flow
  ftag       Ftag
  hop        Fabricpath mtrace hop count
  ingress    Ingress interface for fabricpath oam mtrace
  interval   Specify fabricpath oam mtrace interval in milliseconds
  ip         Fabricpath oam multicast ip
  mac        Fabricpath oam multicast MAC
  profile    Fabricpath oam multicast profile
  repeat     Fabricpath repeat count to use
  reply      Configure fabricpath oam service reply
  size       Fabricpath oam mtrace data size
  switch-id  List of switch-ids to test
  tag        Fabricpath oam mtrace tag to use
  timeout    Specify fabricpath oam mtrace timeout duration in seconds
  topology   Fabricpath oam mtrace topology to use
  tree       Multicast tree
```

```
            use-host-VLAN  Fabricpath oam mtrace to use host VLAN (will not translate
                           VLAN in any scenario)
      validate             Fabricpath oam multicast validate reply
      verbose              Fabricpath oam multicast verbose
      VLAN                 Fabricpath oam multicast VLAN

tor1# mtrace fabricpath f
forward    ftag
tor1# mtrace fabricpath ftag ?
  <1-1023>  Multicast Ftag Id

tor1# mtrace fabricpath ftag 1 ?
   <CR>
   data           Fabricpath oam mtrace data
   forward        Fabricpath oam mtrace forward flow
   hop            Fabricpath mtrace hop count
   ingress        Ingress interface for fabricpath oam mtrace
   interval       Specify fabricpath oam mtrace interval in milliseconds
   ip             Fabricpath oam multicast ip
   mac            Fabricpath oam multicast MAC
   profile        Fabricpath oam multicast profile
   repeat         Fabricpath repeat count to use
   reply          Configure fabricpath oam service reply
   size           Fabricpath oam mtrace data size
   switch-id      List of switch-ids to test
   tag            Fabricpath oam mtrace tag to use
   timeout        Specify fabricpath oam mtrace timeout duration in seconds
   topology       Fabricpath oam mtrace topology to use
   use-host-VLAN  Fabricpath oam mtrace to use host VLAN (will not translate
                  VLAN in any scenario)
   validate       Fabricpath oam multicast validate reply
   verbose        Fabricpath oam multicast verbose
   VLAN           Fabricpath oam multicast VLAN

tor1# mtrace fabricpath ftag 1

Codes: '!' - success, 'Q' - request not sent, '.' - timeout,
'D' - Destination Unreachable, 'X' - unknown return code,
'V' - VLAN nonexistent, 'v' - VLAN in suspended state,
'm' - malformed request, 'C' - Cross Connect Error,
'U' - Unknown RBridge nickname, 'n' - Not AF,
'*' - Success, Optional Tlv incomplete,
'I' - Interface not in forwarding state,
'S' - Service Tag nonexistent, 's' - Service Tag in suspended state,
```

```
'c' - Corrupted Data/Test

Sender handle: 1

Fabricpath mtrace for multicast ftag 1, VLAN 1

Code SwitchId Interface      State TotalTime
===========================================
!    1435      Rcvd on Eth1/47  fwd         15ms
!    3559      Rcvd on Eth1/29  fwd         25ms


Fabricpath mtrace for multicast ftag 1, VLAN 1

Code SwitchId Interface      State TotalTime
===========================================
!    3559      Rcvd on Eth1/29  fwd         1ms
!    1435      Rcvd on Eth1/47  fwd         1ms


Fabricpath mtrace for multicast ftag 1, VLAN 1

Code SwitchId Interface      State TotalTime
===========================================
!    1435      Rcvd on Eth1/47  fwd         1ms
!    3559      Rcvd on Eth1/29  fwd         1ms


Fabricpath mtrace for multicast ftag 1, VLAN 1

Code SwitchId Interface      State TotalTime
===========================================
!    1435      Rcvd on Eth1/47  fwd         1ms
!    3559      Rcvd on Eth1/29  fwd         2ms


Fabricpath mtrace for multicast ftag 1, VLAN 1

Code SwitchId Interface      State TotalTime
===========================================
!    1435      Rcvd on Eth1/47  fwd         1ms
!    3559      Rcvd on Eth1/29  fwd         1ms


tor1# mtrace fabricpath ftag 2

Codes: '!' - success, 'Q' - request not sent, '.' - timeout,
'D' - Destination Unreachable, 'X' - unknown return code,
'V' - VLAN nonexistent, 'v' - VLAN in suspended state,
```

```
'm' - malformed request, 'C' - Cross Connect Error,
'U' - Unknown RBridge nickname, 'n' - Not AF,
'*' - Success, Optional Tlv incomplete,
'I' - Interface not in forwarding state,
'S' - Service Tag nonexistent, 's' - Service Tag in suspended state,
'c' - Corrupted Data/Test


Sender handle: 2


Fabricpath mtrace for multicast ftag 2, VLAN 1


Code SwitchId Interface      State TotalTime
================================================
!    1435     Rcvd on Eth1/47  fwd          1ms
!    3559     Rcvd on Eth1/29  fwd          1ms


Fabricpath mtrace for multicast ftag 2, VLAN 1


Code SwitchId Interface      State TotalTime
================================================
!    1435     Rcvd on Eth1/47  fwd          1ms
!    3559     Rcvd on Eth1/29  fwd          1ms


Fabricpath mtrace for multicast ftag 2, VLAN 1


Code SwitchId Interface      State TotalTime
================================================
!    1435     Rcvd on Eth1/47  fwd          1ms
!    3559     Rcvd on Eth1/29  fwd          3ms


Fabricpath mtrace for multicast ftag 2, VLAN 1


Code SwitchId Interface      State TotalTime
================================================
!    1435     Rcvd on Eth1/47  fwd          1ms
!    3559     Rcvd on Eth1/29  fwd          1ms


Fabricpath mtrace for multicast ftag 2, VLAN 1


Code SwitchId Interface      State TotalTime
================================================
!    1435     Rcvd on Eth1/47  fwd          1ms
!    3559     Rcvd on Eth1/29  fwd          1ms
```

Summary

This chapter covered the different deployment possibilities with FabricPath along with representative examples. Migration strategies to FabricPath including classical Layer 2 to FabricPath and vPC to vPC+ were also discussed. In addition, some common FabricPath deployment topologies were presented. The chapter concluded with a high-level description of troubleshooting and monitoring tools for FabricPath networks.

References

1. "Virtual Port Channel Quick Configuration Guide," http://www.cisco.com/en/US/prod/collateral/switches/ps9441/ps9670/configuration_guide_c07-543563.html.

2. http://www.cisco.com/en/US/prod/collateral/switches/ps5718/ps708/white_paper_c11_589890.html.

3. http://www.cisco.com/en/US/docs/switches/datacenter/nexus2000/sw/configuration/guide/rel_4_1/Cisco_Nexus_2000_Series_Fabric_Extender_Software_Configuration_Guide_chapter2.html.

4. http://www.cisco.com/en/US/docs/switches/datacenter/sw/4_2/nx-os/interfaces/configuration/guide/if_vPC.html.

5. http://www.cisco.com/en/US/prod/collateral/switches/ps9441/ps9670/guide_c07-690079.html.

6. http://www.cisco.com/en/US/prod/collateral/switches/ps9441/ps9670/design_guide_c07-625857.pdf.

7. http://www.cisco.com/en/US/prod/collateral/switches/ps9441/ps9402/white_paper_c11-709336.html#wp9002611.

8. "Requirements for Operations, Administration, and Maintenance (OAM) in Transparent Interconnection of Lots of Links (TRILL)"—RFC 6905.

9. Internet Draft - TRILL Fault Management draft-ietf-trill-oam-fm-00.

10. http://www.cisco.com/en/US/netsol/ns1151/index.html.

Chapter 8

TRILL Deployment, Migration, and Troubleshooting

Introduction

This chapter covers the migration strategies, deployment, and troubleshooting for TRILL networks.[1, 2] This chapter discusses in detail the current network designs, practices, and migration strategies for TRILL networks. Some of the existing network architectures and the advantages of deploying TRILL in such scenarios are discussed. The pros and cons of the migration are also discussed for each case. Finally, the most important aspect of any new protocol or technology, apart from reliability, scalability, and fault-tolerance aspects, is the hooks it provides for network troubleshooting and monitoring. Applications can always be developed over the underlying technology that enables you to troubleshoot the network. But, if the underlying technology has provisions in place for troubleshooting and monitoring, developing applications can be more efficient and a lot easier. This chapter covers the troubleshooting requirements and work in progress for TRILL.

It's highly recommended to read Chapter 5, "TRILL," before this chapter because a lot of material in this chapter can be better appreciated after understanding the nitty-gritty details of TRILL. This chapter has the following sections.

- **TRILL deployment:** This section discusses the different network architectures and how they can be converted to using TRILL.

- **Migration strategies:** This section discusses some of the migration strategies that can be employed to convert a regular network to a TRILL network.

- **Troubleshooting and monitoring:** This section goes over the TRILL network troubleshooting and monitoring techniques.

TRILL Deployment

This section discusses the various existing data center network topologies, the limitations, and how TRILL addresses them.

In Chapter 1, "Need for Overlays in Massive Scale Data Centers," and in Chapter 5, you saw the need for a large Layer 2 networks in a data center. The traditional three-layer hierarchical network, as shown in Figure 8-1, and its improved Virtual Switching Layer (VSL)[3] architecture, as shown in Figure 8-2, could not meet the demands of new data centers and even enterprise networks in some cases.

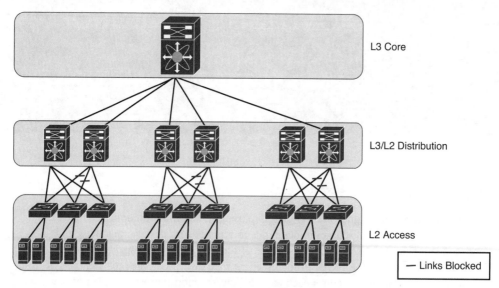

Figure 8-1   *Three-Layer Simple Data Center Network*

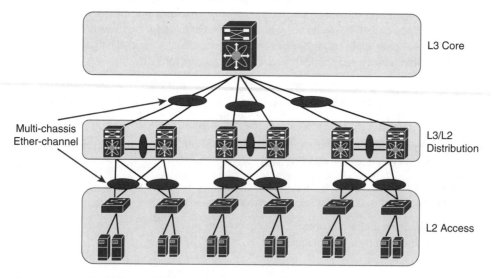

Figure 8-2   *Three-Layer Data Center Network with VSL*

Referring to Figures 8-1 and 8-2, all hosts connect to access switches. The access switches are regular Layer 2 switches and do not perform routing or Layer 3 (L3) switching. It's preferable for all the hosts connected to the access switch to be in the same subnet so that host-host communication within the same subnet is Layer 2 switched by the directly attached access switch. All the access switches connect to distribution switches. For redundancy and load balancing purpose, an access switch is connected to two distribution switches. The distribution switch serves as the Layer 2 or Layer 3 boundary. It does Layer 2 switching when hosts of the same subnet that are connected to different access switches want to communicate with each other. It does Layer 3 switching when hosts that belong to different subnets want to communicate with each other. Many deployments follow this classic hierarchical model (refer to Figure 8-1). This deployment is suitable when

- The Layer 2 domain is not large. (That is, the Layer 2 domain is contained within a distribution switch.)

- Traffic is mostly north-south (host-to-Internet).

- There is no immediate need for a large Layer 2 domain or plans for expanding the network.

TRILL may not be a classic use case for such scenarios. However, there are scenarios such as Remote Switch Port Analyzers (RSPANs)[4] that require a large Layer 2 domain that cannot be contained within a distribution switch but that still follow the models shown in Figures 8-1 and 8-2. The Layer 2 domain is extended by creating tunnels such as VPLS,[5, 6] GRE,[7] and so on across the distribution switches, as shown in Figure 8-3. The subnet spanning across distribution switches is important for some customers who have devices spanning across multiple sites that need Layer 2 connectivity between them to communicate with each other. From a data center perspective, the extended Layer 2 connectivity is used for Layer 2 data center interconnect (DCI) and for virtual machine (VM) mobility. The number of tunnels created is proportional to the number of peers or the number of distribution switches. If the number of distribution switches in a network is N, the number of tunnels that need to be administered is roughly N^2. Here, the traffic still needs to go through the extra core switch even though there is room for increasing the number of distribution switches in a site or a Points of Delivery (POD). Needless to say, this is configuration-intensive. Whenever a new distribution switch is introduced into the topology, the tunnel configuration needs to be set up in all the other distribution switches, assuming that all the distribution switches want to be peers with each other.

TRILL can be a classic use case for requirements in which the number of hosts in a site increases, and as a result, the number of distribution switches must also be increased; the Layer 2 segments has to span across distribution switches. Now let's consider the different deployment cases.

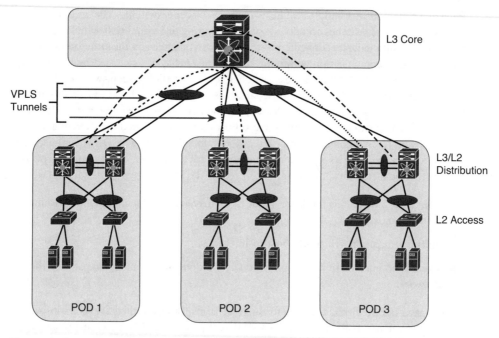

Figure 8-3 *Layer 3 Interconnect Using VPLS Tunnels*

TRILL Between Access and Distribution

As shown in Figure 8-4, the classic hierarchical architecture is transformed into a TRILL network. Here, TRILL runs between the access and distribution switches. As can be seen, no links are blocked due to Spanning Tree Protocol (STP) unlike a regular Layer 2 network (refer to Figure 8-1). This is a simple yet common TRILL deployment. This still runs Layer 3 between the distribution and core switches. The benefits achieved are the regular TRILL benefits such as the ease of configuration, better utilization of links, better load balancing of traffic, and so on. If a subnet spans across distribution switches, you still need tunnels such as VPLS, GRE, and so on.

TRILL Core

Now, consider an alternative TRILL design, as shown in Figure 8-5. Here, TRILL runs between the distribution and core switches. This deployment can be considered when the situation is such that

■ The number of hosts in a Layer 2 domain increases.

■ The number of distribution switches within a POD cannot be increased.

■ The number of PODs can be increased,

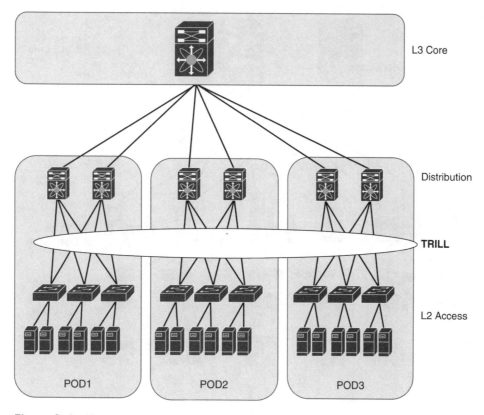

Figure 8-4   *TRILL Between Access and Distribution*

■ Because of these factors, the number of core switches has to be increased to serve the large number of distribution switches.

■ Layer 2 is extended across the distribution switches (that is, subnet spans across PODs).

The distribution switches still serve as the Layer 2 or Layer 3 boundary, but pairs of distribution switches are connected using VSL. Spanning Tree Protocol (STP) still runs between access and distribution switches, but the presence of VSL minimizes some of the STP issues such as blocking redundant links. The distribution and core switches run integrated Layer 2 or Layer 3 TRILL. A subnet or Layer 2 domain can be extended across the distribution switches using TRILL, which provides a smoother interconnection or stitching of Layer 2 domains. Unlike VPLS, TRILL does not have the N^2 scalability problem and is not configuration-intensive. New core or distribution switches can be added to the network without a lot of configuration changes at the TRILL core. In this topology, Layer 2 is extended across the distribution switches in different PODs. This is because for traffic within the same subnet or Layer 2 domain, Layer 2 termination does not need to occur at the distribution, which is the case with VPLS. There's also no Virtual Routing and Forwarding (VRF)[8] specific configuration needed at each distribution for extending a Layer 2 domain. To clarify this concept, consider the packet flow for the following cases:

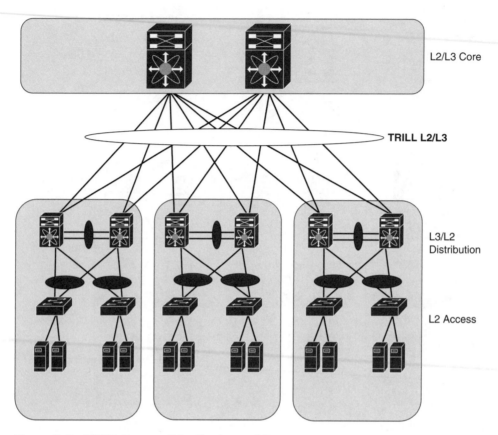

Figure 8-5   *TRILL Between Distribution and Core*

Layer 2 Bridging Case

The following summarizes the packet flow when the source and destination are within the same subnet:

- If the source and destination are within the same POD, it is pure vanilla Layer 2 switching in both the access and distribution switches. Traffic does not leave the POD.

- If the source and destination are located in different PODs, the traffic has to flow through the TRILL core.

- The number of subnets is not restricted to 4 K, which is the limitation in a vanilla Layer 2 network, imposed by the size of the VLAN field. Every distribution TRILL switch can be configured with Fine-Grained Labeling (FGL) where the service instance is represented by a 24-bit value, which enables a huge number of Layer 2 domains in the network. The concept behind FGL was discussed in detail in Chapter 5. Now we'll go over a simple packet flow to illustrate how forwarding within the same subnet (but across PODs) occurs in this topology.

- Traffic from a server is Layer 2 switched by the access switches. The distribution switches receive the Layer 2 frame, which is tagged with a 12-bit VLAN field.

- The distribution switch (DS) associates the frame with a service instance. The incoming port, VLAN, and possibly other fields can be used to associate the frame with a service instance.

- The DS maps the service instance to a FGL value. The service instance to the FGL mapping configuration needs to be uniformly done in all the distribution switches.

- The DS encapsulates the Layer 2 frame with a TRILL header. Depending on whether the destination is a hit or a miss, unicast or multidestination TRILL forwarding occurs. Further, TRILL supports Multi Topology Routing (MTR) for better traffic engineering, security, and troubleshooting. The frame is associated to a topology, and the appropriate TRILL routing table is used to forward the frame. Refer to Chapter 5 for the detailed forwarding concepts.

- The core TRILL switches act as the transit for the TRILL frames and forward it to the appropriate destination DS.

- The destination DS decapsulates the TRILL header and remaps the FGL field in the TRILL header to the correct service instance. Depending on the local configuration, the DS tags the Layer 2 frame with the VLAN corresponding to the service instance. Then it forwards the frame locally within the POD using regular Layer 2 switching. With TRILL, the VLANs can be totally localized to a POD and are reusable across PODs. This is because across PODs a global FGL value corresponding to a service-instance enables seamless communication within the same subnet.

Layer 3 Routing Cases

Layer 3 routing with TRILL is a little involved because it has quite a number of cases to be considered. This section discusses the different Layer 3 scenarios so that the reader is aware of the issues. The intention is to offer the best solution for Layer 3 with TRILL. When hosts want to communicate across subnets (Layer 3 forwarding aka routing), Layer 2 is terminated at the distribution and Layer 3 routing happens across the TRILL core. This section starts with a packet flow study of Layer 3 in TRILL networks, which is when source and destination are in different subnets and the RBridge acts as the integrated router bridge. This sets the foundation for the remainder of this chapter, which discusses Layer 3 in TRILL for different topologies. Then, a packet flow analysis is done when subnets are contained in a single POD and when subnets span across PODs.

Basic Layer 3 Case with TRILL

Figure 8-6 shows a sample topology where two edge RBridges connect to hosts in different subnets.

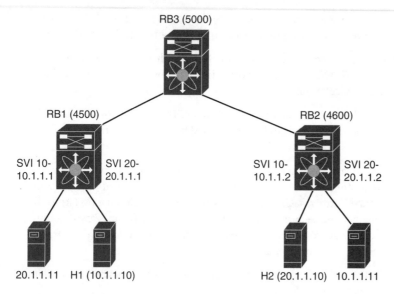

Figure 8-6 *Layer 3 Case with TRILL*

Both the RBridges (RB1 and RB2 with Nicknames 4500 and 4600, respectively) are configured with switched virtual interfaces (SVIs) in 10.1.1.0 and 20.1.1.0 subnets. The 10.1.1.0 subnet is configured under SVI corresponding to VLAN 10, and 20.1.1.0 subnet is configured under SVI corresponding to VLAN 20. Both the RBridges connect through a core RBridge, RB3 (Nickname 5000). Now consider the case in which a host (H1) with IP address 10.1.1.10 wants to communicate with another host (H2) with IP address 20.1.1.10. (Refer to Figure 8-6 to see both the hosts.) The default gateway for H1 is configured as 10.1.1.1, and H2 is configured as 20.1.1.2. Now also assume that ARP for the default gateway is resolved at both H1 and H2:

- The frame originated by H1 with a source IP address (SIP) of 10.1.1.10, and the destination IP address (DIP) of 20.1.1.10 is received at RB1.

- RB1 decides to route the frame because the destination MAC address of the frame received from H1 will be its gateway MAC address.

- Because the destination subnet of 20.1.1.0 is configured as SVI and assuming no other host route in the subnet is configured, the next hop is the SVI in VLAN 20. The ARP table is checked for the corresponding MAC address for 20.1.1.10.

- Assuming the ARP cache is empty, an ARP request is sent by RBridge RB1. Depending on the implementation, the original data frame from H1 is either buffered until the ARP for the destination is resolved or it is dropped. The broadcast frame is flooded locally and over the TRILL network. Figure 8-7 shows the TRILL encapsulated ARP request frame. Only the fields of interest are shown in the ARP header. The TRILL frame is sent over a distribution tree assumed to be rooted at RB3, which has the Nickname 5000.

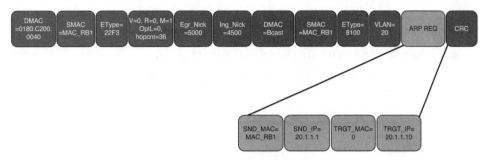

Figure 8-7   *TRILL Encapsulated ARP Request Frame*

■ RB3 acts as a core RBridge and forwards the frame to RB2.

■ RB2 decapsulates the TRILL frame and floods the inner ARP Request frame locally
on VLAN 20. RB2 also learns the MAC address of RB1 (MAC_RB1, VLAN 20) and
associates it with the Nickname RB1.

■ The ARP request is received by H2, and an appropriate ARP response is sent to
RBridge RB1.

■ RB2 on receiving this ARP reply in VLAN 20 does a lookup for <MAC_RB1, VLAN
20>. Because the MAC address of RB1 was already learned from the ARP request
frame, the lookup results in a hit.

■ Because the lookup result points to a remote RBridge RB1, RB2 encapsulates the
ARP response in a TRILL header, as shown in Figure 8-8. The unicast TRILL frame is
sent toward RB1.

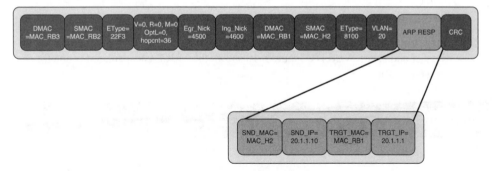

Figure 8-8   *TRILL-Encapsulated ARP Response Frame*

■ RB3 acts as a transit/core RBridge and forwards the frame to RB1.

■ RB1 decapsulates the TRILL frame and processes the ARP response packet because
the DMAC points to its router MAC. RB1 also learns the MAC address of H2
(MAC_H2, VLAN 20) and associates it with the Nickname RB2. The ARP cache has
the IP MAC binding of 20.1.1.10, MAC_H2.

■ RB1 receives the next frame from H1 with the SIP of 10.1.1.10 and DIP of 20.1.1.10.

- As mentioned earlier, RB1 routes the frame because the destination MAC address points to its gateway MAC.

- An ARP lookup for 20.1.1.10 gives the result as MAC_H2.

- A lookup for MAC_H2 in the Layer 2 table results in a hit pointing to remote RBridge RB2.

- RB1 encapsulates the IP frame in a TRILL header, as shown in Figure 8-9. Only the SIP and DIP in the IP payload is shown. The TRILL-encapsulated frame is sent toward RB2.

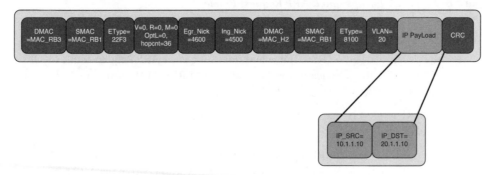

Figure 8-9   *TRILL-Encapsulated IP Data Frame from RB1*

- RB2, after receiving the TRILL frame, decapsulates the frame because the destination switch-ID points to itself. The inner IP frame is sent toward H2 based on the DMAC lookup corresponding to <20, MAC_H2>.

- For the reverse traffic from H2 to H1, a similar procedure is followed by RB2.

- After the ARP for H1 is resolved, data packets from H2 are encapsulated in a TRILL header and sent toward H1. Figure 8-10 shows the TRILL-encapsulated frame for the reverse traffic.

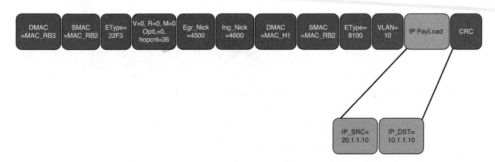

Figure 8-10   *TRILL-Encapsulated IP Data Frame from RB2*

Layer 3 Routing Case; Subnets Do Not Span Across PODs

The previous section enlisted a sample Layer 3 flow in a TRILL network. With that background, start with a simple case when hosts belonging to one subnet wants to communicate with hosts belonging to another subnet, where the subnets are restricted to just one POD. In other words, subnets do not span across PODs, as shown in Figure 8-11. Two hosts with IP addresses of 10.1.1.2 and 20.1.1.2, respectively, connect to access switches in their respective PODs. The default gateway for the hosts will be configured at the DS in their respective PODs, which are 10.1.1.1 and 20.1.1.1, also as shown in Figure 8-11. For traffic that traverses across PODs, the next hop for the DS will be 100.1.1.1, which is configured at the core switch. This is not a classic use case for TRILL and is just mentioned here for completeness.

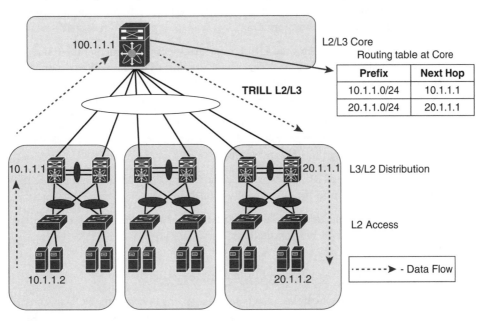

Figure 8-11 *Subnets Not Spanning Across PODs*

For traffic flowing across subnets aka PODs:

- If the source and destination are within the same POD, the Layer 2 termination occurs at the distribution. The frame has to be Layer 3-routed by the DS. If the destination subnet doesn't span across DSes, the traffic does not cross the DS.

- If the source and destination are located in different PODs, the traffic has to flow through the TRILL core.

The concept of FGL that was mentioned earlier for traffic within the same subnet is also applicable here. Now we'll go over a simple packet flow to illustrate how Layer 3 routing happens across the TRILL core.

1. Traffic from a server is Layer 2-switched by the access switches. The DS receives the Layer 2 frame, which is tagged with a 12-bit VLAN field.

2. Usually the distribution switches are the default gateways for traffic across subnets.

3. Because the frame is destined to the gateway MAC address, the DS routes the frame. The next hop is determined by consulting the Layer 3 routing (or FIB) table, which happens to be the core router. The core router has the routes to reach the destination subnet. The next hop in this example is 100.1.1.1.

4. The DS modifies the inner frame's destination MAC address to the next hop's (core's) MAC address. Then, regular TRILL forwarding happens by doing a lookup on the next-hop MAC address. Depending on whether the lookup is a hit or a miss, unicast or multidestination TRILL forwarding happens. The Layer 2 frame encapsulated with a TRILL header will be sent by the DS.

5. The core switch decapsulates the TRILL frame irrespective of whether the frame is a unicast or multidestination frame. This is because unicast frames will be destined to this core switch, and multidestination frames will be decapsulated for local switching because the core switch will have the VLAN of the inner frame configured.

6. The core switch performs all the functionalities for Layer 3 forwarding of the inner frame such as determining the next Layer 3 hop, modifying the destination MAC address, decrementing the TTL, and so on.

7. The resulting frame is TRILL encapsulated and forwarded to the destination DS. In this example, it is sent to the DS where SVI 20.1.1.1 resides.

8. The destination DS decodes the TRILL header and forwards the frame locally within the POD using regular Layer 2 switching.

Layer 3 Routing Case; Subnets Span Across PODs

Now consider the case in which the subnets span across the PODs. If the POD has hosts belonging to both the source and destination subnets and if the destination subnet also spans across the PODs, the DS will have both the source and destination subnets configured. This is shown in Figure 8-12, where the 30.1.1.0 and 40.1.1.0 subnets span across the PODs. Both the DS pair act as the default gateway for the access switches in their respective PODs for both the 30.1.1.0 and 40.1.1.0 subnets. In Figure 8-12, DS-1 and DS-2 acts as the default gateways in POD1 for the respective access switches. Similarly DS-5 and DS-6 act as the default gateways in POD3 for the respective access switches. This is similar to the Layer 3 routing in the TRILL case study described in the previous section.

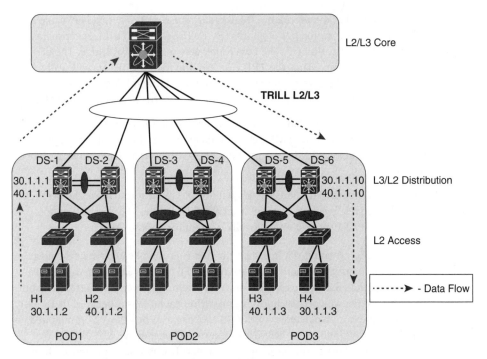

Figure 8-12   *Subnets Spanning Across PODs*

A sample packet flow follows:

- Traffic from a server is Layer 2 switched by the access switches. The DS receives the Layer 2 frame, which is tagged with a 12-bit VLAN field.

- Usually the distribution switches are the default gateways for traffic across subnets.

- Because the frame is destined to the gateway MAC address, the DS routes the frame.

- Because the destination subnet is also configured in the DS, it checks if the ARP is resolved for the destination host.

- If the ARP is already resolved and the destination MAC address is learned in the Layer 2 table, it's a hit case. The DS modifies the inner frame's destination MAC address to the MAC address present in the ARP table. The source MAC address is modified to the MAC address of the DS.

- For the hit case, if the destination is within the same POD, the frame is Layer 2 switched and not sent over the TRILL cloud. In Figure 8-12, this is the case for frames between hosts H1 and H2 or between hosts H3 and H4.

- If the MAC table has the destination MAC address associated with a Nickname of another DS, the destination lies in another POD. The frame is TRILL encapsulated and sent to the destination DS. The core router acts as a transit RBridge. The destination RBridge decapsulates the TRILL header and forwards the frame locally. In Figure 8-12, this is the case for frames between hosts H1 and H3 or between hosts H2 and H4. Figure 8-12 shows the direction of packet flow between H1 and H3.

- If the MAC table does not have an entry for the destination host, the frame is flooded locally and over the TRILL cloud (unknown unicast case). It can be pruned at the core to send the TRILL frame to only the DSs that have the destination subnet configured.

- If the ARP is not resolved, the DS sends out an ARP request to resolve the destination. This request is sent locally and over the TRILL core. The destination host responds to the ARP request either locally or from the remote DS.

This method works in general if the hosts are static. It gets complicated when the hosts are virtual that can be migrated across servers connected to different DSes; that is, Live Migration or VMotion. Such cases are not discussed here. However, the traffic within the same subnet (Layer 2) also works well for live migration cases. This is because in TRILL the host MAC address is associated with the DS Nickname. When the VM is migrated, the association changes, and all the RBridges modify their respective MAC tables by associating the moved host to the Nickname of the new DS, as long as the moved host continues to send traffic. Typically, on a VM move, the hypervisor/virtual switch running in the host/server sends out a broadcast RARP or GARP with the moved VM's MAC address, which serves to update the Layer 2 tables of all the switches (including RBridges) where the VLAN/subnet exists.

Now consider the case when the subnet does not span across all the PODS, as shown in Figure 8-13. Take the case when a host in POD P belonging to subnet 50.1.1.0 wants to communicate with another host belonging to subnet 60.1.1.0. In addition, there are no hosts in POD P that belong to subnet 60.1.1.0, but POD Q and POD R have hosts in subnet 60.1.1.0. The previous solution also works here, provided 60.1.1.0 subnet is also configured in POD P, even though there are no hosts belonging to subnet 60.1.1.0 in POD P. This leads to a waste of HW resources. Another solution is to send it to the next-hop core router, and the core router should have host routes so that it knows to which DS to send the frame for a specific host.

As shown, for a regular Layer 2 case, the TRILL deployment is easy and it works well. For Layer 3, a lot of cases need to be considered.

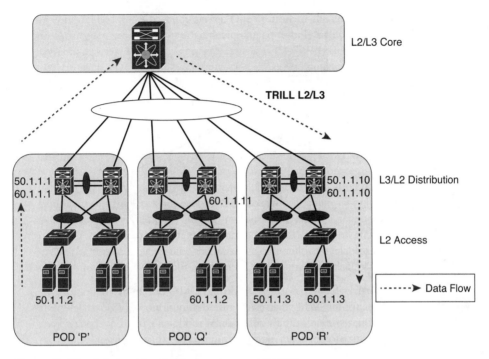

Figure 8-13   *Subnets Not Spanning Across All PODs*

Expanding the POD

This section discusses the case in which there's scope for adding more access and distribution switches in a POD to serve the increasing demands of a large Layer 2 domain. A POD can support more hosts in a domain by increasing the number of distribution and access switches. TRILL runs between the access and distribution switches, which is shown in Figure 8-14. Without TRILL, a network of this type suffers from the classic spanning tree drawbacks and scalability issues that were previously described. Even in the presence of VSL, which can bundle two distribution switches, the issues still persist. Here, the VSL is removed and there's no STP running between the access and distribution switches. In this scenario, all the benefits of TRILL such as plug-and-play, ECMP, and so on can still be achieved. The distribution and core switches still run Layer 3 between them. It should be mentioned that for traffic flowing in a north-south direction and for traffic across subnets within the same distribution, there's a penalty of an extra TRILL encapsulation or decapsulation. But the benefits of TRILL and the reduced OPEX outweigh the penalty, which is minimized with the newer generation of ASICs that support TRILL forwarding in hardware.

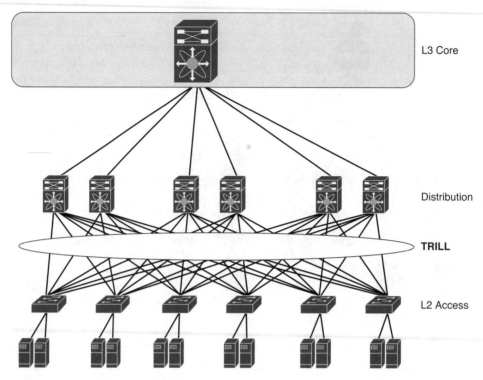

Figure 8-14 *Expanding the POD*

TRILL Everywhere

Now, consider the case of a large Layer 2 domain. Here, TRILL runs between the access and distribution as well as the distribution and core switches, as shown in Figure 8-15. Figure 8-15 shows a single POD with an increased number of distribution switches. The Layer 3 is extended all the way to the core, which means the default gateway for the hosts is configured at the core switches. This is a good use case when the majority of traffic does not cross the Layer 2 boundary and the Layer 2 domain is large enough so that it extends to the other POD even though the number of distribution switches are increased in a POD. This scenario is not uncommon especially in a multitenant cloud deployment. Non-IP Layer 2 communication between hosts is common. With a large number of tenants, typically FGL is used as discussed previously. As shown in Figure 8-15, there is 'n' way ECMP for communication within the same POD, where 'n' is the number of distribution switches, and 'm' way ECMP for communication across PODs, where 'm' is the number of core switches.

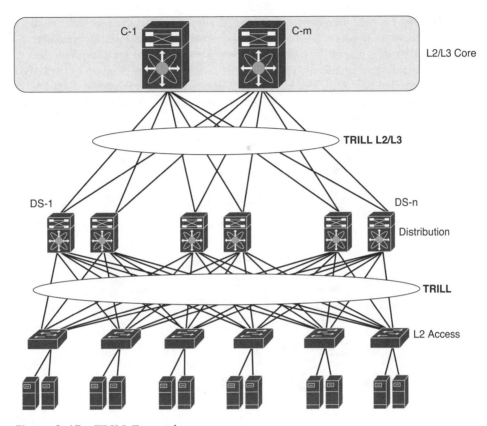

Figure 8-15   *TRILL Everywhere*

Meshed Distribution with No Core

This is the same as the previous case, but all the distribution switches are fully meshed resulting in a collapsed core. TRILL can still run between the distribution switches. One of the distribution switches (or a pair of them) acts as the border entry or exit points for north-south traffic.

Link Aggregation or Pseudo-Node Deployments

The previous sections did not consider link aggregation (LAG) cases, which is when a host is connected to multiple access switches for load balancing and fault tolerance purposes. LAGs are commonly deployed in today's networks. Figure 8-16 shows a host connected to two access switches through a LAG. Here, TRILL runs between the access and distribution switches. Either vanilla Layer 3 or TRILL can be deployed between the core and the distribution layer; this doesn't change the TRILL LAG behavior. TRILL has built-in support for LAG, through the concept of pseudo-nodes. The concept of TRILL pseudo-nodes has been described in detail in Chapter 5. The TRILL access switches allocate a unique nickname for the pseudo-node corresponding to this LAG. Each member access switch that is part of the LAG independently picks a unique set of distribution trees for multidestination frames. The number of switches that are members of the LAG is not restricted to two. Also, a switch can be associated with more than one LAG. For example, consider the alternative deployment shown in Figure 8-17, where there are two LAGs, one with three members and another with two members.

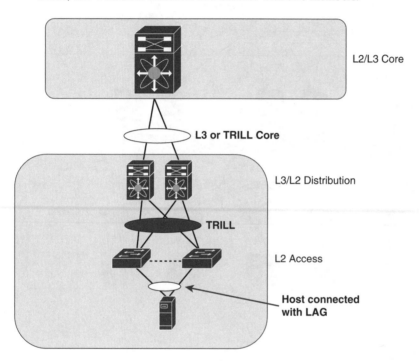

Figure 8-16   *TRILL Pseudo-Node Deployment*

Host H1 is connected to two access switches AS1 and AS2 through LAG1. Host H2 is connected to three access switches AS1, AS2, and AS3 through LAG2. Each LAG is associated with a unique pseudo-nickname. Each access switch picks a unique set of distribution trees for multidestination traffic. For example, if there are six distribution trees, namely t1 through t6, the tree allocation can be as follows:

- Access switch 1 can use trees t1, t3, and t5 for traffic belonging to LAG1. It can use trees t1 and t4 for traffic belonging to LAG2.

- Access switch 2 can use trees t2, t4, and t6 for traffic belonging to LAG1. It can use trees t2 and t5 for traffic belonging to LAG2.

- Access switch 3 can use trees t3 and t6 for traffic belonging to LAG2.

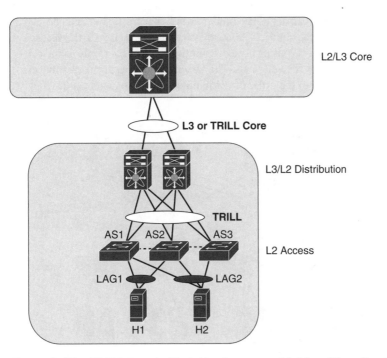

Figure 8-17 *TRILL Pseudo-Node Deployment with More Than One LAG*

In these examples, the access switches are connected through an in-band channel for state sync-up, although TRILL doesn't specify this as a requirement. Again, refer to Chapter 5 for more details.

CLOS Network Model

This is a two-level hierarchy that follows a CLOS topology, as shown in Figure 8-18. This can be a good deployment for

- A lot of east-west traffic

- Traffic between hosts in the same subnet or if they don't use IP for east-west traffic

All the access switches are connected to all the distribution switches providing N way ECMP, where N is the number of distribution switches. Using TRILL's FGL, the number of Layer 2 domains that can be supported is large. TRILL runs between the access and distribution switches. Traffic from the host is encapsulated into TRILL packets by the access switch. The destination should be one of the other access switches in case of nonlocal traffic. The TRILL frame can be load balanced into any of the connected distribution switches. The destination access switch decapsulates the TRILL frame and sends it to the destination host. For multidestination traffic, the TRILL frame is sent through the distribution tree, which preferably is rooted at one of the DSes. In case of north-south traffic, one of the DS switches can act as the border switch. For traffic between hosts in different subnets and when the subnets spans across the access switches, the access switches have to perform Layer 3 routing. The distribution switches act only as the transit RBridges and are unaware of the end-hosts. The forwarding tables in the distribution switches need to increase only in the order of the number of access switches that they connect to.

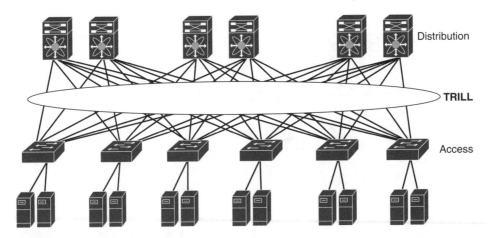

Figure 8-18   *TRILL CLOS Topology*

Migration Toward TRILL

The ideal scenario for TRILL is a green field deployment wherein every switching node starting from the access layer switch is converted to a TRILL RBridge. However, a more practical scenario is to migrate an existing network to a TRILL network. The existing network may be composed of access-level nodes such as Catalyst 3K, Nexus 3K,[9] Nexus 5K,[10] Nexus 6K,[11] and so on to higher-end distribution and core switches such as Catalyst 4K, Catalyst 6K, Nexus 7K, and so on. One aspect of migration is to convert the existing switches to TRILL-aware RBridges. This may mean a hardware and software upgrade or just a software upgrade. The other aspect of migration is the interworking aspect of the TRILL RBridges with the existing switches and bridges. The network administrator may choose to gradually migrate a subset of the network to a TRILL network. The subset may be a subnetwork if there is a clear separation or some individual network nodes. This section discusses how an existing network interworks with a TRILL network. Then, it discusses the specifics of the migration strategy for some of the deployments that you saw in the earlier sections. Top-down and bottom-up migration strategies are explained in a three-layer hierarchical network. As mentioned Chapter 5, the outer Ethernet header in a TRILL-encapsulated frame is an IEEE standard Ethernet header and can be treated like a regular Layer 2 frame by non-TRILL–aware bridges or switches. Strictly speaking, the outer header is an Ethernet header if the link layer protocol is Ethernet. If the link layer protocol is PPP, the outer header in a TRILL-encapsulated frame is a PPP header. The TRILL-encapsulated frame format should look like the one in Figure 8-19.

Figure 8-19   *Generic TRILL-Encapsulated Frame*

A TRILL cloud can act as a transit Layer 2 network or can provide TRILL service for end-hosts, as shown in Figure 8-20. A TRILL cloud can also interwork with other transit networks such as Ethernet and PPP, as shown in Figure 8-21.

Figure 8-20   *TRILL Transit Network*

Figure 8-21   *TRILL Clouds Connected Through Another Transit Network*

TRILL and Spanning Tree

Existing Layer 2 network topologies run STP to avoid loops. If a TRILL network has to interwork with regular Layer 2 networks, TRILL and STP should interoperate with each other. TRILL is designed to interwork with STP from the beginning. Chapter 5 briefly touches upon this concept. The TRILL network does not run STP. The STP terminates at the ingress RBridge. Figure 8-22 shows two edge RBridges connected to a Layer 2 network as well as with other RBridges. This means that an RBridge also may need to run the STP toward the Layer 2 network in some cases. It is important to remember that STP does not run through the RBridges; it always terminates at RBridge ports. There are multiple ways RBridges can connect to a Layer 2 network. If a network's entry point to a TRILL cloud is through a single RBridge, it's an ideal scenario. However, a network could have multiple entry points to a TRILL cloud. This means multiple nodes in a network can be connected to multiple RBridges, which makes the TRILL and STP interaction more interesting. Now consider some cases.

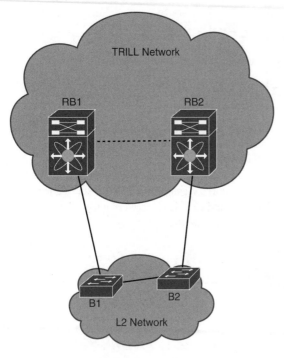

Figure 8-22   *Multiple RBridges Connected to a Layer 2 Network – Appointed Forwarder Solution*

Appointed Forwarder Solution

Refer to the network shown in Figure 8-22, where it is essential to have connectivity between the bridges B1 and B2 and at the same time have different RBridges connecting it to the TRILL cloud. Regular bridges B1 and B2 of the Layer 2 network are connected to two different RBridges, RB1 and BR2, which in turn could be connected directly or through the TRILL cloud. As discussed in Chapter 5, RB1 and RB2 would receive each other's TRILL HELLOs. Either RB1 or RB2 would become the designated RBridge (DBR) in the network and would elect itself or the other RBridge as the appointed forwarder for a group of VLANs. The appointed forwarder, as the name suggests, acts as the ingress or egress RBridge for the group of VLANs for which it is designated as the appointed forwarder. This includes encapsulating the data from the Layer 2 network to TRILL packets before forwarding it to the TRILL cloud, decapsulating the TRILL traffic to native packets before sending it to the Layer 2 network, learning of remote end station addresses, and so on. If RB1and RB2 are evenly distributed as appointed forwarders for the VLANs in the Layer 2 network such that the traffic is also evenly balanced across both the RBridges, this is a simple way to provision the network. Now consider the following cases:

1. There's only one VLAN in the Layer 2 network that spans across the TRILL cloud.

2. Traffic in certain VLANs is high and it's not possible to predict the traffic pattern.

3. The link between RB1 and B1 or RB2 and B2 goes down.

Now take the first case in which there's only one VLAN in the Layer 2 network when either RB1 or RB2 will be the Appointed Forwarder for that VLAN. For example, if RB1 is the Appointed Forwarder, the traffic from B2 also follows the B2-B1-RB1 link, leading to inefficient utilization of links and the B2-RB2 link not being used. The situation is not a lot different for the second case. If the traffic for the VLANs for which RB1 is the Appointed Forwarder is high compared to the VLANs for which RB2 is the Appointed Forwarder, the B1-RB1 link will be heavily used as compared to B2-RB2 link. In both these cases, the B1-RB1 link and the RBridge RB1 becomes the choke point. The third case is also not a lot different, in which one RBridge and its link connecting to the Layer 2 cloud become the choke point.

Spanning Tree Solution

As discussed in the previous section, the Appointed Forwarder solution does not work efficiently for all cases. Referring to the topology shown in Figure 8-22, if you need a clear way to split the network so that any traffic from B2 takes the RB2-B2 link and any traffic from B1 takes the B1-RB2 link, STP needs to be run so that it includes the links to both the RBridges. Then, the link B1-B2 shown in Figure 8-22 will be put in blocking state, thereby achieving the wanted functionality. Now expand the Figure 8-22 to include more bridges to illustrate the concept better, as shown in Figure 8-23. The Layer 2 network runs regular STP, which blocks the B2-B3 link. Here, both the RBridges RB1 and RB2 are configured to emit spanning tree BPDUs on their edge ports with the highest root priority. In other words, both the RBridges are configured in such a way that both emit the same root bridge and their respective cost to the root bridge as zero. According to STP, the link that has the least cost to reach the root becomes the forwarding port. Consequently, in this example, B1-RB1 and B2-RB2 are in forwarding state. The link B1-B2 will be put in blocked state. So, the network itself gets partitioned in such a way that RB1-RB2 will not see each other's control traffic through the Layer 2 cloud. Then, both RB1 and RB2 become the DRB because they assume that they are the only RBridges serving the Layer 2 cloud. Now, any traffic from hosts connected to bridges B1, B3, and B4 go through the RBridge RB1, and any traffic from hosts connected to B2 go through the RBridge RB2.

When any of the links connected to the RBridges, say B1-RB1 or B2-RB2, fails, the STP unblocks the B1-B2 link so that all the bridges still remain connected to one of the RBridges providing TRILL functionality. This solves the problem when there's only a single VLAN in the Layer 2 network. The links may get evenly used. However, for uneven traffic patterns in certain VLANs, even this solution is inadequate in the sense that certain links or RBridges become more heavily used. This is a generic Layer 2 issue with STP. Because this solution splits the network logically, the RBridge may be seen as a transit node. Consider the case in which a host connected to B2 wants to communicate with another host connected to B4. The traffic may have to go through the TRILL cloud, which involves not only extra encapsulation or decapsulation, but may also incur additional hops. This may even mean additional cost in some cases because the TRILL service is used. This is unwanted because the two hosts are located in the same Layer 2 network.

Consider another problem, wherein the link connecting B1-B3 fails. The B2-B3 link will be unblocked, as shown in Figure 8-24. Rapid Spanning Tree Protocol (RSTP) sends a topology change notification (TCN) as soon as the link failure is detected. In RSTP,[12] only nonedge ports that move to the forwarding state cause a topology change notification to be generated. In Figure 8-24, the TCN will be sent by B3 to B2 because this port transitioned from a blocked state to a forwarding state. B2 also sends the TCN to the connected RBRidge RB2. Because the STP terminates at the RBridge, the other bridges, namely B1, B4, connected to the partitioned network will not receive the TCN. This presents the following issues in this example:

- The bridge B4 does not know about the topology change and may not purge the MAC addresses for the hosts connected through B3.

- The remote RBridges may also not purge the MAC addresses leading to connectivity issues. In Figure 8-24, RB3 is a remote RBridge.

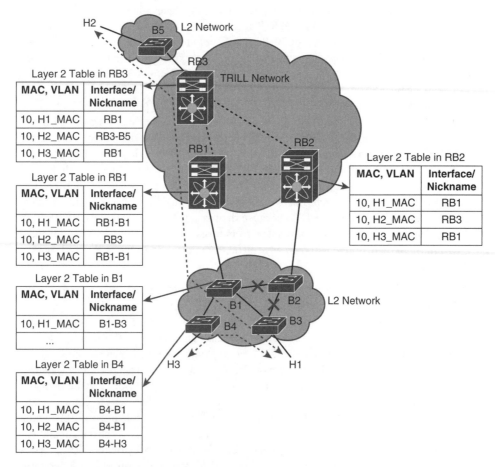

Figure 8-23 *Spanning Tree Solution*

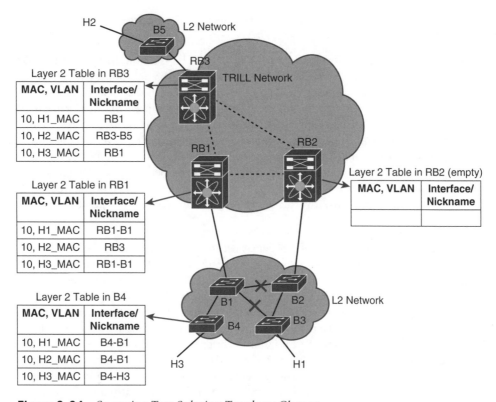

Layer 2 Table in RB3

MAC, VLAN	Interface/Nickname
10, H1_MAC	RB1
10, H2_MAC	RB3-B5
10, H3_MAC	RB1

Layer 2 Table in RB1

MAC, VLAN	Interface/Nickname
10, H1_MAC	RB1-B1
10, H2_MAC	RB3
10, H3_MAC	RB1-B1

Layer 2 Table in B4

MAC, VLAN	Interface/Nickname
10, H1_MAC	B4-B1
10, H2_MAC	B4-B1
10, H3_MAC	B4-H3

Layer 2 Table in RB2 (empty)

MAC, VLAN	Interface/Nickname

Figure 8-24 *Spanning Tree Solution Topology Change*

To further elaborate, say a host H1 connected to B3 is having a bidirectional communication with a local host H3 connected to B4 and with a remote host H2 across the TRILL cloud. Assume that all hosts belong to VLAN 10. The traffic between H1 and H2 would have gone through the path B3-B1-RB1—RB3-B5 before the link failure had occurred, as shown in Figure 8-23. Similarly, traffic between H1 and H3 would have taken the path B3-B1-B4. Figure 8-23 also shows the Layer 2 table in all the RBridges. As discussed in Chapter 5, the remote RBridge RB3 would have associated the end-host H1 with the RBridge RB1. Any traffic from the remote host H2 destined to host H1 will get encapsulated by the remote RBridge RB3 with the destination RBridge as RB1. Figure 8-24 shows the same topology after the B1-B3 link has failed and B3-B2 link is unblocked by RSTP. After getting the TCN, RB2 flushes its Layer 2 table. Because the TCN is not received by RB1, RB3, B1, and B4, their Layer 2 tables are not flushed, as shown in Figure 8-24. The traffic flow will be as follows:

- Traffic from the remote host H2 destined to H1 is sent to RB1 because RB3's Layer 2 table is not flushed, as shown in Figure 8-24. RB1 sends the frame to B1. Because there's no path from B1 to H1, the traffic is not sent to H1. This black-holing of traffic from H2 to H1 exists until the Layer 2 table in RB3 is flushed or updated with the correct Nickname. The Layer 2 table is updated when the reverse traffic from H1 arrives at RB3 from RB2. RB3 then updates its Layer 2 table entry of H1 to point to RB2's Nickname.

■ Similarly, traffic from the local host H3 destined to H1 is sent to B1 by B4. B1 would have purged the MAC addresses it learned from the B1-B3 link. So, any frames destined to H1 result in a lookup miss in B1, which then floods the frame on all interfaces belonging to VLAN 10. RB1 receives the frame. Because RB1's MAC table is not flushed, as shown in Figure 8-24, the lookup result for H1's MAC address points to the RB1-B1 link. The frame is dropped because the incoming Layer 2 frame also arrived through the RB1-B1 link (same interface check). This black-holing of traffic from H3 to H1 exists until the MAC table in RB1 is flushed or updated with the correct Nickname. The MAC table in RB1 is updated when the reverse traffic from H1 arrives at RB1 from RB2. RB1 then updates its MAC entry of H1 to point to RB2's Nickname.

Because of the reasons discussed, it becomes necessary to communicate the TCN messages to the rest of the network. As of this writing, there are IETF drafts that propose tunneling of the BPDUs across the TRILL cloud. The TCN messages are tunneled across the TRILL cloud to the RBridges that serve the same network. The RBridges that serve the same network are assigned the same root bridge group. In this example, the RBridges RB1 and RB2 belong to the same root bridge group. RB2 tunnels the TCN frames to RB1. After receiving the TCN frame, RB1 informs the bridges B1 and B4 connected to it regarding the topology change. RB2 also sends a special MAC withdraw message to inform the remote RBridges (RB3 as shown in Figure 8-24) to purge the MAC addresses associated with RBridge RB1. If possible, the VLAN information is also included so that not all entries are purged. The remote RBridge, as soon as it receives the MAC withdraw message, purges the MAC entries associated with RBridge RB1, and therefore traffic will not be black-holed. Refer the IETF TRILL charter[13] for the latest information on this.

Bottom-up Migration Toward TRILL

In bottom-up migration strategy, each POD is gradually migrated to a TRILL network. The POD that is TRILL capable has its access and distribution switches running TRILL. The distribution to core still runs Layer 3. When all the PODs are migrated to be TRILL compatible, the core can also be migrated to TRILL. The previous sections discussed the deployment scenario in which TRILL runs between the access to distribution and the core runs Layer 3. As discussed, TRILL is a classic use case in which the Layer 2 domain in a POD becomes large thereby increasing the number of distribution switches to support it. Not all the PODs in a data center may have this large Layer 2 domain requirement. So the entire network does not need to be converted to a TRILL network. A sample topology is shown in Figure 8-25.

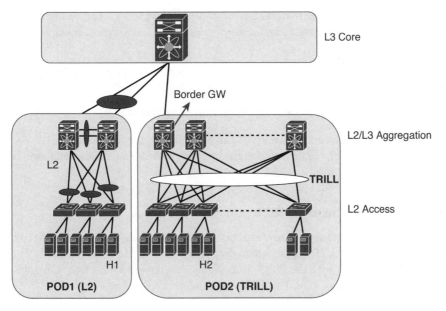

Figure 8-25 *Bottom-up Migration Toward TRILL*

Figure 8-25 shows two PODs. POD1 is untouched and runs classic Layer 2 with STP to eliminate loops. POD2 supports a large Layer 2 domain and has more access and distribution switches. It runs TRILL between the access and distribution switches. STP and TRILL's IS-IS are contained within the PODs providing clean separation and less interworking scenarios to worry about. The subnet (aka VLAN) is contained within a POD. When two hosts, say H1 and H2 in Figure 8-25, belonging to different subnets want to communicate with each other, the communication goes through the core switch. Now consider a step-by-step packet flow:

■ Host H1 sends the frame to the default gateway, which is the distribution switch in POD1.

■ The distribution switch does a Layer 3 lookup and based on the result sends the frame to the core switch.

■ The core switch knows that the destination subnet is contained within the TRILL POD and sends the frame to the default border gateway (aka router) of the TRILL POD.

■ The default border router in the TRILL POD routes the frame internally. It first resolves the ARP for the destination IP address. Then, it encapsulates the frame in a TRILL header and sends it to the access switch to which the destination host is connected. It sends the frame on a TRILL distribution tree if it does not know the access switch (egress RBridge) that has the destination host behind it (unknown unicast or broadcast ARP request case).

- Similarly, the reverse traffic from H2 is sent to the border gateway. The border gateway removes the TRILL header and sends the frame to the core switch, which is the next hop.

- The core switch knows that the destination subnet is contained within the Layer 2 POD and sends the frame to the distribution switch of the Layer 2 POD.

- The distribution switch then routes the frame internally within POD1.

Depending on the requirements, all the PODs can be gradually migrated to a TRILL network without modifying the distribution to core. This provides a seamless migration towards TRILL.

Top-down Migration Toward TRILL

In top-down migration strategy, all the distribution and core switches are first converted to TRILL RBridges. Then the PODs are gradually migrated to TRILL. The non-TRILL PODS should interoperate with the TRILL core and the remaining TRILL PODs. Consider the example shown in Figure 8-26. The distribution switches serve as the ingress RBridges in POD1, POD2, and POD3.

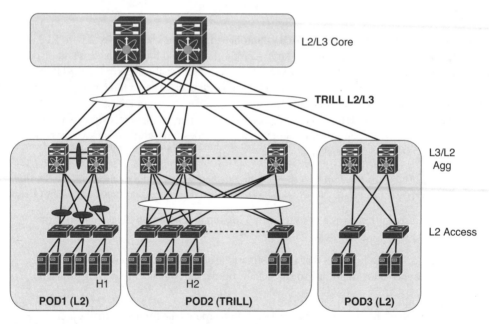

Figure 8-26   *Top-down Migration Toward TRILL*

The left POD (POD1) has the access switches connected to the distribution switches through a LAG. POD1 runs vanilla Layer 2, and there is no TRILL between access and distribution switches. Now consider two LAG scenarios.

In the first case, the LAG can be something similar to the Cisco VPC+ solution,[14] where both the RBridges (distribution switches here) run the TRILL control protocol independently. Chapter 5 discusses this concept in greater detail. The access switches load balance the traffic among the distribution switches. This is regular Layer 2 port-channel–based selection. There is no Appointed Forwarder and the RBridge that gets the native frame from the access switch does the TRILL encapsulation for the frames going to the core. Due to the LAG configuration, the access switches forward the frame to only one of the RBridges. If both the RBridges receive a TRILL frame from the core, it uses the tree identifier in the frame (Nickname) to decide the RBridge that decapsulate the frame to send it on the LAG. (Refer to Chapter 5 for more details.) STP may still need to run between the access and distribution switches to prevent accidental loops.

In the second case, the LAG can be something similar to the Cisco Cat6500 VSL where both the distribution switches resemble a big virtual switch and run one single instance of the TRILL control protocol. The virtual switch is represented using one single Nickname. As of this writing, there are no Cisco products that support TRILL/FabricPath in a VSL environment.

The middle POD (POD2) is already migrated to a TRILL network. In Figure 8-26, POD2 has more distribution switches to cater to a large Layer 2 domain. The access switches acts as ingress or egress RBridges. Traffic between hosts in POD2 follow the regular TRILL forwarding semantics. Traffic between hosts belonging to a TRILL POD and a non-TRILL POD follow similar forwarding behavior as detailed in the previous bottom-up migration strategy section.

The right POD (POD3) has the access switches connected to the distribution switches without using LAGs. POD3 runs vanilla Layer 2, and there is no TRILL between access and distribution switches. The Appointed Forwarder (AF) and the STP solution have been discussed. Here, the access switches are connected to both the distribution switches, and the distribution switches also act as regular bridges between the access switches. This necessitates the need for the TRILL distribution switches to participate in STP. With the AF solution, both the distribution switches see each other as TRILL neighbors. One of the RBridges becomes the DBR, and an AF is elected as discussed previously. With the STP solution, where both the RBridges send a highest root priority BPDU, the access switches are connected to only one distribution switch; the link to the other distribution switch will be blocked. Forwarding concepts for a TRILL core and Layer 2 access distribution were discussed in the deployment section; they apply here as well.

Monitoring and Troubleshooting in TRILL Networks

By now, it is clear that TRILL is not just an overlay technology providing just encapsulation and decapsulation. TRILL has its own forwarding model that includes the forwarding elements (RBridges) that run both the control and data planes. TRILL brings in many benefits such as plug-and-play, automatic assignment of Nicknames to RBridges, single control protocol for both unicast, and multicast routes. However good the technology is, there will always be issues related to both software and hardware due to which any

RBridge can misbehave. Providing a plug-and-play feature is good for the network administrator because it eases the burden of manual configuration. But at the same time, TRILL should also provide enough visibility and provisions that enable the network administrator to troubleshoot and monitor the network.

TRILL has introduced the operations, administration, and maintenance (OAM) framework,[15, 16] for this purpose. TRILL OAM is in addition to link-level OAM, which is specific to link-level protocols such as Ethernet. The operations aspect refers to troubleshooting problems and the monitoring of the network that enables to find problems in advance. Administration refers to keeping track of network resources. Maintenance activities focus on facilitating repairs and upgrades as well as corrective and preventive measures. OAM is a huge topic. This section gives enough information about the requirements for OAM in TRILL networks and discusses, at a high level, the support that TRILL provides for OAM. This is an evolving topic. Interested readers can refer to IETF for more information on TRILL OAM. TRILL OAM interworks with other related technologies such as Ethernet Connectivity Fault Management (CFM), Bidirectional Forwarding Detection (BFD), and link-level OAM. CFM provides end-to-end fault management capabilities for the user and can operate over the TRILL network. BFD, in general, provides rapid detection of link and node failures. It can run between regular adjacent bridges. TRILL BFD runs between adjacent RBridges providing the same link and node failure detection capabilities. TRILL OAM must have support for continuity check, path tracing, packet loss, packet delay, and so on. Before going into the details of OAM, let's define the following:

- Maintenance end points (MEPs) are the RBridges that source the TRILL OAM messages. MEPs ensure that TRILL OAM messages do not leak outside a TRILL network.

- Maintenance intermediate points (MIPs) are the RBridges responsible for forwarding TRILL OAM messages and selectively responding to some messages.

OAM Packet Format

The general packet format for the TRILL OAM messages is shown in Figure 8-27.

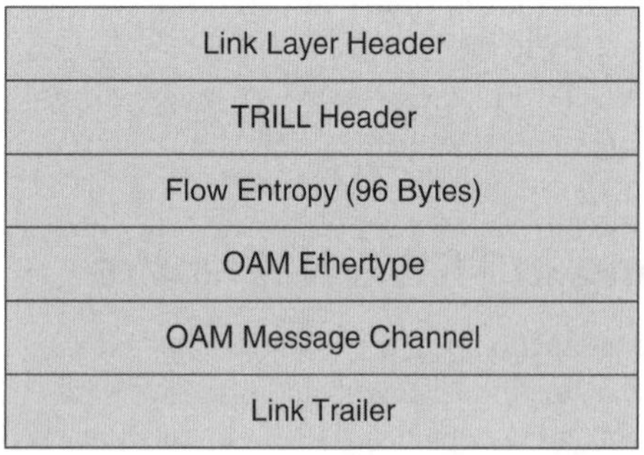

| Link Layer Header |
| TRILL Header |
| Flow Entropy (96 Bytes) |
| OAM Ethertype |
| OAM Message Channel |
| Link Trailer |

Figure 8-27 *TRILL OAM Frame Format*

The link header refers to the outer Ethernet header for Ethernet networks. The TRILL header was already discussed in Chapter 5. To specifically identify the TRILL OAM frames, there's a proposal to use a reserved bit in the TRILL header for this purpose. The new TRILL header is shown in Figure 8-28.

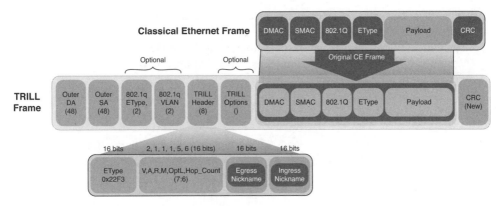

Figure 8-28   *Modified TRILL Header for OAM*

The Reserved bit after the version field is made the A bit, called the Alert bit. The sender of the OAM messages sets this bit. The OAM fields are explained here:

■ The idea behind the "flow entropy" in the packet format is to mimic the actual packet flow. It contains the complete inner payload. For example, it can have the inner Ethernet header followed by the FGL fields, the IP header, and some portions of the payload. The length of flow entropy is 96 bytes. The OAM frames are originated by the MEPs and traverse the core RBridges until arriving at the destination MEP. For the core RBridges, the OAM packets should appear as regular payload so that they can forward the traffic in the normal way. The OAM TRILL header is the same as the regular TRILL header except for the Alert bit, and that bit is ignored by the regular RBridges. Forwarding happens using the Nickname field in the TRILL header like before. The TRILL RBridges look at the inner payload to prune multidestination traffic and the FGL, as detailed in Chapter 5. This is the reason for the presence of flow entropy in the OAM frame. For regular Ethernet non-IP traffic, the flow entropy must specify the Ethernet header with an optional VLAN tag or FGL. For Ethernet IP traffic, the flow entropy must specify the Ethernet header, VLAN or FGL tag, IP header, and the TCP or UDP header. The purpose of the flow entropy becomes clear in the subsequent sections when discussing the use cases.

■ The OAM EtherType is present after the flow entropy field, which is of a fixed size. The EtherType is a 2-byte field that identifies the OAM message channel.

■ The OAM Message channel field carries OAM-specific information and is understood by the MEPs. The message channel should have the OAM message header that identifies the type of OAM message and one or more TLVs to carry the message contents.

Before sending any OAM message to a receiver, the sender must ensure that the receiving RBridge is OAM-capable. This is achieved by all OAM-capable RBridges announcing their OAM capability using the IS-IS Router Capability TLV, specifically the TRILL Version Sub-TLV. TRILL OAM frames *must* remain within a TRILL campus and must not be sent out of a TRILL network as native frames.

Connectivity Verification

Connectivity verification is commonly used for troubleshooting. In the IP world, ping is generally used to verify connectivity between two routers. A similar mechanism is needed in the TRILL network to verify connectivity between two RBridges. The administrator should specify the following:

■ The destination RBridge for which connectivity has to be tested.

■ The appropriate TTL value in the TRILL header.

■ As discussed earlier, there can be multiple equal cost paths to reach the destination RBridge. It is likely that there can be an issue in one of the equal cost paths—say an intermediate RBridge in one of the paths is dropping the message. The frame may go through the faulty intermediate RBridge for only certain flows. So the administrator should specify different flow entropy values so that all possible paths can be verified for connectivity.

After the parameters are specified, the originating RBridge constructs the OAM message header by specifying the appropriate opcode for connectivity verification, sequence number, and other fields in the TLV. The TRILL OAM packet sent by the originating RBridge traverses the TRILL network until it reaches the destination RBridge identified by the Nickname field in the TRILL header. The destination RBridge identifies the frame as an OAM frame using the Alert bit in the TRILL header and the OAM EtherType, which is present after the flow entropy field. The OAM module in the destination RBridge constructs the response for the request. The opcode in the OAM header is set to response. The sequence number and the flow entropy of the received message are copied in the OAM payload for the sender to easily associate the response frame with the original request. The OAM response is transmitted by the destination RBridge.

Similarly, connectivity verification must also be performed for multidestination trees. Recall that a TRILL network has a number of multidestination trees rooted at different RBridges that are uniquely identified by a Nickname. Similar to unicast, it is important to have OAM connectivity verification for every multidestination tree. Multidestination trees are pruned based on some combination of the following fields: VLAN or FGL, multicast group address (*, G), source, and multicast group address (S, G). Connectivity verification needs to be performed for both pruned and unpruned trees. So, the adminis-trator performing the connectivity verification for multidestination trees should specify the following:

- The multicast tree for which connectivity has to be tested.

- VLAN/FGL for verifying all the RBridges in the tree belonging to the VLAN/FGL.

- (*, G) or (S, G) along with the VLAN/FGL for verifying the connectivity in the pruned tree.

- So based on these pruning parameters, the flow entropy should be constructed.

The sender performing the connectivity verification for multicast should receive the OAM response from all the members of the multidestination tree. Only the RBridges that are OAM aware send the response. Optionally, the sender can specify a scope parameter in the OAM message channel that lists the RBridges that need to send the response. This limits the number of responses received if the sender is troubleshooting connectivity issues for only some specific RBridges in a multidestination tree. FabricPath has a similar tool for OAM. Refer to Chapter 7, "FabricPath Migration, Deployment, and Troubleshooting," for some sample CLI outputs.

Path Tracing

It may be preferable to find the list of RBridges that are traversed by a frame to reach the destination. When the continuity check verification fails, the next step would be to figure out the offending RBridge in the path. This is similar to the traceroute or tracepath feature used in IP networks. The concept behind path tracing in TRILL is also the same. The source RBridge constructs the OAM TRILL packet using similar mechanisms as that of connectivity verification. The destination RBridge, flow entropy fields are specified appropriately. However, the source RBridge transmits the first path-tracing message with a TTL value of 1. The next-hop RBridge sends a Timer expiry message, the nickname of which is recorded by the sender. Then the source RBridge increases the TTL value by one in the next path trace OAM message to find the second hop. This process continues until the source RBridge finds the complete list of RBridges in its selected path to the destination. The source RBridge constructs the message with the appropriate opcode cor-responding to a path tracing request. As soon as the intermediate RBridge finds that the TTL has expired, it does some OAM verification. The intermediate RBridge identifies the frame as an OAM frame using the Alert bit in the TRILL header and the OAM EtherType, which is present after the flow entropy field. The OAM module in the intermediate RBridge that detected the TTL has expired constructs the response for the request. The opcode in the OAM header is set to Path Trace Reply, and the return code is set to TTL expired. The flow entropy of the received message is copied in the OAM payload for the sender to easily associate the message. The intermediate RBridge transmits the OAM response. The source RBridge does OAM verification of the response and stores the Nickname. Finally, the destination RBridge after receiving the path trace request message does similar processing and sends the response back with the opcode in the OAM header set to Path Trace Reply. If there are intermediate RBridges that do not understand OAM, this feature does not work. FabricPath has a similar tool for OAM. Refer to Chapter 7 for some sample CLI outputs.

TRILL Configuration Model

This is vendor-specific. Refer to the chapters on FabricPath for the Cisco configuration and debugging commands. Cisco TRILL should also have similar CLIs. There should be CLIs for at least the following:

- Displaying the Nickname of the local RBridge. This carries more significance in TRILL networks because it is dynamically assigned in the TRILL network.

- Configuring the Nickname of the local RBridge. This deviates from the plug-and-play nature of TRILL. However, a CLI may still be required for troubleshooting and debugging purposes.

- Displaying the Nickname of all the RBridges in the TRILL network.

- Displaying the shortest paths to reach every other RBridge. This should also include the ECMPs.

- Displaying the multicast distribution tree IDs and their associated Nicknames.

- Displaying the paths of every multicast distribution tree.

- Displaying all the pseudo-node Nicknames that an RBridge is a part of. This should also include the affiliation of the RBridge with the multicast trees for this pseudo-node.

- Displaying the dynamically learned end-host MAC addresses and ESADI learned MAC addresses with the associated Egress Nickname.

- Displaying the routing table for every topology (in case of MTR).

- Configuring a static MAC address with its associated Egress Nickname.

- FGL and related configurations.

Apart from this, OAM should also have mechanisms to measure packet loss, packet delays, utilization of all links, and so on.

Summary

This chapter covered the different deployments possible with TRILL along with examples. Migration strategies to TRILL networks were also discussed. This chapter concluded with some high-level requirements needed in TRILL for troubleshooting and monitoring. TRILL's support for OAM was also discussed. There's no one-fit-deployment-solution-for-all. Various examples gave you a good understanding of the pros and cons of the various TRILL deployment and migration scenarios.

References

1. "TRILL – RBridges Base Protocol Specification," RFC 6325.

2. "Extensions to IS-IS for Layer 2 Systems," RFC 6165.

3. Virtual Switching Solution, http://www.cisco.com/en/US/prod/collateral/switches/ ps5718/ps9336/white_paper_c11_429338.pdf.

4. RSPAN, https://supportforums.cisco.com/docs/DOC-32763.

5. VPLS - http://www.cisco.com/en/US/docs/switches/lan/catalyst6500/ios/12.2SY/ configuration/guide/vpls.pdf.

6. "Virtual Private LAN Service (VPLS) Using Label Distribution Protocol (LDP) Signaling," RFC 4762.

7. "Generic Routing Encapsulation over IPv4 Networks," RFC 1702.

8. VRF, http://www.cisco.com/en/US/docs/net_mgmt/active_network_ abstraction/3.7/reference/guide/vrf.html.

9. Nexus 3K Switches, http://www.cisco.com/en/US/products/ps11541/.

10. Nexus 5K Switches, http://www.cisco.com/en/US/products/ps9670/.

11. Nexus 6K Switches, http://www.cisco.com/en/US/products/ps12806/index.html.

12. RSTP, http://www.cisco.com/en/US/tech/tk389/tk621/technologies_white_ paper09186a0080094cfa.shtml.

13. TRILL IETF Charter, http://datatracker.ietf.org/wg/trill/charter/.

14. vPC+, http://www.cisco.com/en/US/docs/switches/datacenter/sw/5_x/nx-os/ fabricpath/configuration/guide/fp_interfaces.html#wp1674221.

15. "Requirements for Operations, Administration, and Maintenance (OAM) in Transparent Interconnection of Lots of Links (TRILL)," RFC 6905.

16. Internet Draft - TRILL Fault Management, draft-ietf-trill-oam-fm-00.

Chapter 9

Multi-Overlay Deployments

This chapter has the following objectives.

- **Multi-overlay deployment scenarios:** This chapter describes some specific deployments where multiple overlay technologies may be employed to realize an end-to-end solution in data center (DC) environments. The mechanisms for intra-DC and inter-DC interconnection scenarios discussed in this chapter include

- **TRILL or FabricPath network with VXLAN to virtualized servers:** This is an intra-DC case study. It focuses on how a VXLAN overlay from a virtualized server to the Top-of-Rack (ToR) switch and FabricPath or TRILL overlay in the core of the network can be made to work in conjunction. This case study describes how the VXLAN segment identifier is carried when the packet traverses the TRILL or FabricPath network.

- **Traditional Layer 2 data centers connected using OTV:** This is an inter-DC case study, which discusses how an OTV overlay is used to connect multiple data center sites thereby providing Layer 2 extension.

- **FabricPath or TRILL data centers connected using OTV:** This is an inter-DC case study, which discusses how an OTV overlay is used to connect data center sites running FabricPath or TRILL.

Overview

With so many options available for overlay technologies, the challenge lies in determining which overlay or combination of overlays should be employed and how they should be stitched together to build a massive scale data center that would satisfy not only current application needs, but also exhibits flexibility to tackle future requirements. After all, the goal for most service provider and large enterprises is to deploy a large, secure, multi-tenant cloud that enables rapid provisioning of applications with great agility, high availability, and extreme flexibility.

Although MPLS and VPLS are technologies that are heavily used to interconnect data centers, this chapter doesn't include MPLS- and VPLS-related deployments to interconnect data centers. These scenarios have been specifically omitted because this book doesn't delve into MPLS/VPLS and is specifically targeted toward Layer 2 overlay technologies such as FabricPath, TRILL, and VXLAN. The use of VPLS for intra-DC deployments is discussed in Chapter 8, "TRILL Deployment." For inter-DC deployments, VPLS[9] provides an architecture for multipoint Ethernet LAN services across geographically dispersed locations using MPLS as a transport. It enables flexible and highly available deployment of Layer 2 and Layer 3 virtual private network (VPN) services.

The introduction of various overlays, including TRILL, FabricPath, and VXLAN discussed in previous chapters, have led to new network architectures. As the new architectures evolve, there arises a need to interconnect and interoperate between new and existing network architectures. For a new architecture or technology to become successful, it is important that it interoperates with existing and legacy deployments and has a viable migration strategy that enables incremental deployment. Any new technology that requires a rip-and-replace of the existing network infrastructure is likely not going to be a feasible option for most practical cases. Most if not all the initial deployments of TRILL, FabricPath and VXLAN are taking place in the DC environments. This chapter goes over the different interconnection scenarios including both intra-DC and inter-DC deployments.

The case studies covered in this chapter give a brief overview on how the different technologies can be used with each other. These case studies are not meant to be exhaustive, but the main idea is to educate you on interoperability scenarios, some of which may not have been practically deployed as of today. The mechanisms for intra-DC and inter-DC interconnection scenarios discussed in this chapter are shown in Table 9-1.

Table 9-1   *High-Level Outlines of Each Case Studies*

Number	Case Study	Description	Comment
1	TRILL or FabricPath network with VXLAN to virtualized servers	This is an intra-DC case study, that provides L2 extension with VXLAN across PODs that runs over a ToR using FabricPath or TRILL as a fabric overlay.	24-bit VNI translation to Double 802.q tag conversion.
2	Traditional Layer 2 DC interconnected with OTV	This is an inter-DC case study, that provides L2 extension between multiple data center sites.	Interconnection technology used is OTV.
3	FabricPath or TRILL DCs connected with OTV	This is an inter-DC case study, that interconnects FabricPath or TRILL running data center sites.	Interconnection technology used is OTV.

Case Study 1: TRILL or FabricPath Network with VXLAN to Virtualized Servers

This case study describes the deployment scenario in which VXLAN (see Chapter 6, "VXLAN," for more details on VXLAN) is employed as a host-based overlay that terminates at the ToR from where TRILL or FabricPath (see Chapter 4, "FabricPath," and Chapter 5, "TRILL," for more details on FabricPath and TRILL, respectively) is employed as a network or fabric overlay. Typically, the VXLAN[1, 2, 3] overlay originates from the vswitch sitting on a virtualized server where any packets originating from the virtual machine (VM) toward the upstream ToR switch are stamped with a VXLAN header. The VM belongs to a given VXLAN virtual segment identified by the corresponding unique Virtual Network Identifier (VNI) in the VXLAN header. The main idea is that the 24-bit VNI needs to be mapped to an equivalent network-based identifier, which uniquely identifies that network segment in the network fabric. For packets received from the vswitch, the termination and mapping to the network identifier are performed at the ToR switch, which is typically connected to the virtualized server. Both legacy and virtualized workloads are serviced by the same network fabric, so at the egress or destination ToR switch, the network overlay must be terminated and the packet must be sent out to the destination with the appropriate host-overlay header (native 802.1q tag or VXLAN). Following is a list of the various options for network-based (TRILL and FabricPath) and host-based overlays (VXLAN and native 802.1q):

- **VXLAN-TRILL-VXLAN:** In this case study, the core of the network employs a TRILL overlay. As shown in Figure 9-1, the vswitch encapsulates the packets from the VMs with a VXLAN header. At the ToR switch, the VXLAN encapsulation is terminated and translated into the TRILL header with the preservation of appropriate fields, especially VNI. The reverse operation happens at the egress ToR where the TRILL header is terminated and a VXLAN header is generated by the ToR and sent toward the destination vswitch.

- **VXLAN-TRILL-Native Layer 2:** In this deployment model, the network fabric still employs a TRILL overlay, but the fabric caters to a mix of virtual and physical (legacy nonvirtualized) workloads. The main difference from the previous case is that the ToR switch needs to perform appropriate ingress and egress translation from or to either a VXLAN header or a native 802.1q header depending on the source or destination being VXLAN capable.

- **VXLAN-FabricPath-VXLAN:** In this deployment model, the network fabric employs a FabricPath overlay. This is similar to the TRILL case except that the VXLAN VNI (24 bits) is translated to two 802.1q headers stamped back to back so that they can serve as an appropriate identifier for the network segment in the fabric.

- **VXLAN-FabricPath-Native Layer 2:** Again, this is similar to the equivalent TRILL case study except that FabricPath is used as the fabric overlay for a network fabric that caters to both legacy and VXLAN virtualized workloads.

Figure 9-1 shows an example deployment where VMs residing in virtualized servers that may or may not be VXLAN-capable, are interconnected by the same TRILL or FabricPath network fabric.

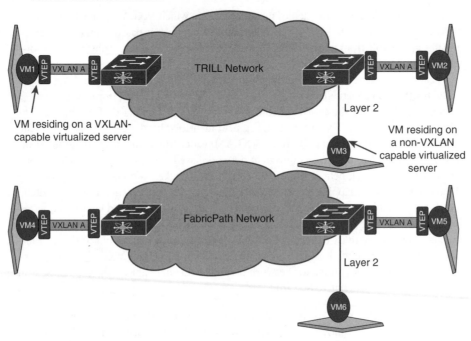

Figure 9-1 *Inter-Operation of VXLAN with TRILL or FabricPath*

Out of the four intra-DC case studies (VXLAN-TRILL-VXLAN, VXLAN-TRILL-Native Layer 2, VXLAN-FabricPath-VXLAN, and VXLAN-FabricPath-Native Layer 2) previously discussed, you can use the VXLAN-TRILL-VXLAN case study to see how the VNI is translated back and forth when the packet traverses from VXLAN to TRILL network and vice-versa. For this scenario to work, the main requirement is that the TRILL RBridges need to support fine-grained labeling (FGL). The support of FGL enables the TRILL RBridges to support a 24-bit network identifier in the TRILL network. The availability of FGL enables the 24 bits of VXLAN VNI to be inserted as DoubleQ (or 2Q) in the inner TRILL frame. FGL is described in detail in Chapter 5. For ease of perusal, Figure 9-2 presents a refresher by depicting the TRILL frame format with FGL support.

Figure 9-3 shows the packet flow between two VMs in the same segment with the MAC addresses MAC1 and MAC2, respectively. The vswitch is only aware of the VXLAN connectivity, and the intermediate TRILL network is transparent to the vswitches on these hosts. All the translation logic happens on the edge ToR switches. Next, you go through a sample packet flow for a packet as it traverses this network.

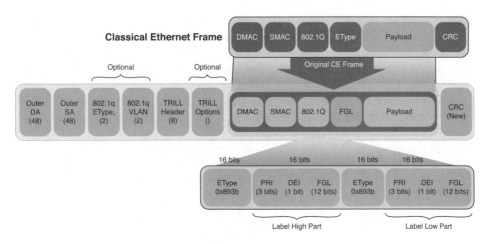

Figure 9-2   *TRILL Frame Format with FGL Support*

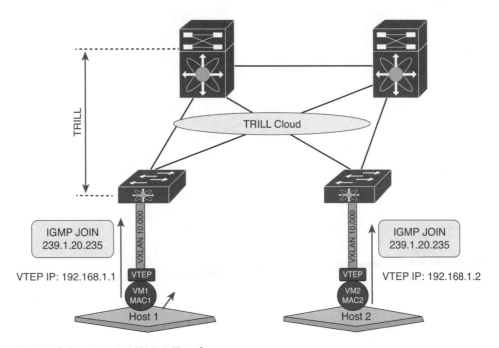

Figure 9-3   *VXLAN TRILL Topology*

As shown in Figure 9-3 there are two servers: Host1 and Host2. Each of these servers has a VXLAN Tunnel Endpoint (VTEP) configured with IP addresses 192.168.1.1 and 192.168.2.2, respectively. Recall that a VTEP interface is like a loopback interface that resides on the vswitch and is responsible for appropriate encapsulation and decapsulation of VXLAN packets so that the VMs are completely unaware of the presence of VXLAN. Each of these servers has one VM connected to a VXLAN segment with VNI 10,000. Consequently, the VTEP on each of these servers sends an Internet Group Management Protocol (IGMP) join to the corresponding multicast address of VNI 10,000. In this example, the corresponding configured multicast group for this VNI 10000 is 239.1.20.235. VTEPs with IP addresses 192.168.1.111 and 192.168.2.112, respectively, are configured on ToR1 and ToR2, respectively. The ToRs are equipped with appropriate Layer 2 VXLAN gateway functionality (see Chapter 6 for additional details on the VXLAN gateways). Initially, the Layer 2 forwarding table at the vswitch residing on the hosts will be aware of only its directly attached VM MACs, that is, vswitch on Host1 will be aware of (10000, MAC1) and vswitch on Host2 will be aware of (10000, MAC2). When VM1 tries to communicate to VM2, VM1 sends out an ARP request to determine the IP-MAC binding associated with VM2. Figure 9-4 depicts this frame as it traverses through the network.

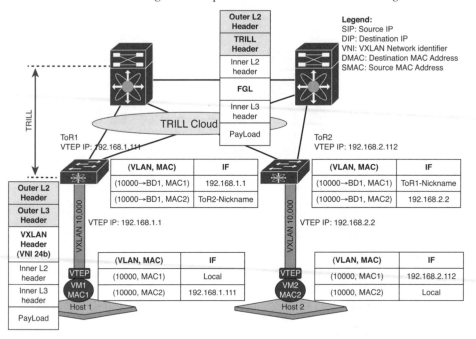

Figure 9-4 *ARP Frame and Response Transversal*

Following are the steps involved in the traversal of the ARP frames through the VXLAN-TRILL-VXLAN network:

1. VM1 sends an ARP request frame with DMAC of FF:FF:FF:FF:FF:FF, SMAC=MAC1, and target IP address of VM2.

2. ARP, being a broadcast frame, the vswitch locally floods this frame to all local VMs that are part of the same VNI. It also encapsulates the ARP request into a VXLAN frame and sends it toward the ToR1 switch. The outer destination IP address (DIP) that is used in the VXLAN header in this example is 239.1.20.235— that is, multicast address associated with VNI 10000. The outer source IP address (SIP) will be set to the VTEP IP address of Host1, namely 192.168.1.1.

3. When the VXLAN-encapsulated packet arrives at the ToR1 switch, it is first appropriately decapsulated. The SMAC of VM1 is learned against the VTEP's IP address, as shown in Figure 9-4. As the incoming frame is a multidestination frame and the core of the network is TRILL, the frame needs to be sent over an appropriate distribution tree. The VXLAN header is removed, and the VNI is mapped to the FGL field in the TRILL payload. The TRILL-encapsulated frame is then sent over the distribution tree.

4. The TRILL-encapsulated frame arrives at the ToR2 switch because it is part of the distribution tree. The TRILL header is decapsulated, and inner SMAC MAC1 will be learned against the ToR1-Nickname. Because DMAC is a broadcast MAC, the FGL field is converted back to VNI 10000, and because DMAC is a broadcast MAC, packets are sent out with a VXLAN header toward Host2. The DIP is set to 239.1.20.235 because the frame is sent over IP multicast with SIP set to local VTEP at ToR2, namely 192.168.2.112.

5. The VXLAN frame received at the vswitch on Host2 is decapsulated, and appropriate Layer 2 learning is performed based on the inner frame, namely (10000, MAC1) ->192.168.2.112. Because DMAC is a broadcast MAC, the DMAC lookup based on (10000, FF:FF:FF:FF:FF:FF) results in the packet being flooded locally to all VMs in that VNI. Consequently, the ARP request from VM1 is received at VM2.

6. VM2 responds to the ARP request with an appropriate ARP response providing its own IP-MAC binding as requested by VM1. The ARP response is unicasted back to VM1—that is, the DMAC in the packet is MAC1 and SMAC is MAC2.

7. The vswitch on Host2 performs a regular Layer 2 lookup based on (10000, MAC1). The lookup indicates that the packet needs to be VXLAN encapsulated with DIP set to 192.168.2.112 and SIP set to 192.168.2.2 (that is, its local VTEP's address) with VNI as 10000.

8. The VXLAN-encapsulated ARP response is sent to the ToR2 switch where the VTEP with destination IP 192.168.2.112 resides. The VXLAN header is stripped off after appropriate Layer 2 learning of MAC2 against source VTEP, namely 192.168.2.2. A Layer 2 lookup based on the inner payload indicates that the packet must be TRILL encapsulated and sent toward ToR1 based on the previously learned entry in the Layer 2 table. VNI 10000 is mapped to the FGL field in the TRILL payload and the source Nickname set to ToR2-Nickname. The destination Nickname will be set to ToR1-Nickname based on the Layer 2 lookup hit result.

9. The ToR1 switch receives the TRILL-encapsulated unicast ARP response. The TRILL header is stripped off with MAC2 learned against the ToR2-Nickname. Layer 2 lookup based on the inner payload results in a hit. The packet will be appropriately stamped with a VXLAN header with VNI mapped from FGL in the TRILL frame to 10000, DIP set to 192.168.1.1, and SIP to 192.168.1.111.

10. The vswitch on Host1 receives the VXLAN-encapsulated packet destined to its hosted VTEP. The VXLAN header is stripped off; appropriate Layer 2 learning is performed; and lookup based on (10000, MAC1) results in the ARP response being forwarded to VM1. Subsequent data traffic from VM1 to VM2 will be unicast forwarded along the VXLAN-TRILL-VXLAN path.

Although the ARP broadcast request case has been discussed, all unknown destination packets including broadcast and multicast will be treated the same way. That is, they will be encapsulated as multicast packets and forwarded by the vswitch VTEP. Also, all these frames go through a similar translation at the ToR switch connected to the hosts before they are sent over the TRILL distribution tree. This conversion at the ToR switch is transparent to the VXLAN overlay, and all the benefits such as support for any type of protocol, even non-IP protocols, over VXLAN overlay are retained. The end-host VMs are completely unaware of the different types of encapsulations required for the packet to traverse through the hybrid-overlay network.

Finally we note that in this case study, described an example packet flow between two virtual machines running on a distributed virtual switch attached to a TRILL cluster. However, the scenario is equally valid for both physical and virtual workloads. Moreover, this flow is applicable for other combinations of hybrid-overlay deployments, namely VXLAN-VXLAN-VXLAN where VXLAN is used both as network and host overlay and VXLAN-FabricPath-VXLAN where VXLAN is employed as a host overlay and FabricPath as a network overlay.

In this case study, the VXLAN frames were terminated at the ToR switch. Another approach is to tunnel the VXLAN frame inside a TRILL or FabricPath payload without terminating the VXLAN frame at the ToR switch. With this approach, the ToR switch does not learn the end-host's (VM's) MAC address because the VXLAN frame is not decapsulated. The VXLAN frame is treated as a regular Layer 2 frame at the ToR, and forwarding is done based on the outer MAC, IP header of the VXLAN frame. The main advantage of this approach over the earlier approach is the gains in ToR table scalability. Specifically, because the inner VM MACs are never seen by the ToR switch, the ToR forwarding tables don't need to scale in the order of end-hosts, but only in terms of the number of unique end points (aka VTEPs). The main disadvantage of this approach over the earlier approach is that every packet that flows through the TRILL network has an overhead of a double overlay header—that is, a VXLAN header plus a TRILL header.

Case Study 2: Data Center Interconnect Using OTV

The overlay technologies discussed in-depth so far are mostly applicable for intra-data center deployments. For completeness, a brief description is provided of the most popular multisite data center deployment.[4] Having an efficient mechanism that enables extension of a Layer 2 segment across multiple data center sites has become extremely critical especially with the popularity of virtualization. Virtual machine mobility across public, private, and hybrid clouds is an extremely desirable if not mandatory feature for data center deployments. *Overlay Transport Virtualization* (OTV) is perhaps the most popular and complete data center interconnect (DCI) choice for Layer 2 extension across data centers. It is a MAC-routing scheme that operates over any core that can carry IP traffic. OTV does not have the inherent complexity that other DCI schemes such as EoMPLS,[11] MPLS,[10] VPLS, [12, 13] and so on require. It employs dynamic encapsulation without the need for any pseudo-wire or tunnel state management. Current OTV implementations support up to 10 remote data center sites to be interconnected. OTV is supported by the Cisco Nexus 7K, ASR 1K,[7] and Cloud Services Router (CSR[8]) platforms. OTV was introduced in Chapter 2, "Introduction to Overlay Technologies"; check out the section on OTV for more details. It has numerous desirable features as listed here, including operational simplicity. All the listed features are automatically enabled after OTV is configured:

- **Fault-domain isolation:** OTV does not transport spanning tree bridge protocol data units (BPDUs) across data centers, thereby allowing faults within a data center to be contained and not affect remote data center operations (for example, spanning tree loops, and so on). This preserves the Layer 2 domain failure boundaries and fosters site independence and isolation while providing seamless multisite connectivity.

- **No unknown unicast flooding:** OTV-enabled edge devices at a site advertise the learned MAC address, VLAN via the control plane. There is no data plane learning for traffic ingressing from remote data center sites via the wide area network (WAN) core. Consequently, any unknown unicast traffic directed toward the WAN core is dropped at the OTV edge device, thereby avoiding the ill effects of unknown unicast floods.

- **Multihoming support:** If multiple OTV edge devices are enabled at a site, the devices go through an election process that results in the nomination of per-VLAN designed forwarders, called authoritative edge devices (AEDs) to be evenly spread among these devices. Only the elected designed forwarder for a VLAN advertises MAC reachability to the remote sites for that VLAN and is responsible for forwarding multidestination traffic for that VLAN to and from the WAN core. This process is fully automated and does not require any additional protocols and configuration.

- **Broadcast reduction:** By snooping and caching ARP reply packets from the core, OTV edge devices learn these entries. Consequently, the edge device can proxy for inter-site ARP requests for hosts in remote sites, thereby preventing ARP request packet floods across the core.

■ **Extremely simple configuration:** The OTV functionality needs to be enabled only at the edge devices and essentially involves the following simple configuration with five CLI commands:

Example 9-1 *OTV Configuration Example*

```
Nexus7k-Sw#config t
/* Go to overlay interface submode */
Nexus7k-Sw(config)# otv site-VLAN 100
Nexus7k-Sw(config)# interface overlay0
Nexus7k-Sw(config-if)# otv join interface ethernet1/10
Nexus7k-Sw(config-if)# otv control-group 235.1.1.1
Nexus7k-Sw(config-if)# otv data-group 232.1.1.1
Nexus7k-Sw(config-if)# otv extend-VLAN 101-1000
Nexus7k-Sw(config-if)# no shutdown
```

■ The **join interface** command specifies the interface that connects to the core, and its IP address will be employed as the source IP for OTV encapsulation and also in OTV control plane MAC advertisements. The **control-group** is the any-source multicast (ASM) or Bidir group that is used for the OTV control plane and the **data-group** is the source-specific multicast (SSM) group that is used for carrying the site's multicast data traffic. The **extend-VLAN** command indicates the list of VLANs that should be extended across sites by OTV. Finally, the **site-VLAN** is the one that is used within the site for communication between edge devices at the same site. This enables multiple OTV edge devices hosted within a site to discover each other via OTV hello messages. The OTV edge device has an internal interface toward the DC site that operates a regular interface where vanilla Layer 2 learning is performed and an external interface toward the core network where the previous configuration is applied.

With this OTV configuration, the OTV edge devices join the ASM via the join interface and simultaneously play the role of a sender and a receiver. An IGMP join report is sent out toward the ASM group. To establish peer adjacencies with the OTV edge devices in other sites, an edge device sends OTV hellos that are encapsulated in an outer IP header with the destination IP set to the ASM group address and source IP address set to that of its own join interface. The underlying transport core then delivers these control packets to other edge devices thereby allowing establishment of appropriate peering. After neighborship is established, all OTV control plane messages from one edge device are delivered to other edge devices using the same mechanism as previously listed.

Although the configuration listed earlier assumes a core transport that can support multicast, OTV can also be deployed over a unicast-only transport infrastructure with some additional configuration. The OTV control plane over a unicast-only transport works exactly the same way as OTV with multicast mode. The only difference is that for each control plane packet, each of the OTV edge devices performs head-end replication—that is, it creates multiple copies of each packet and unicasts them to each OTV edge device that is part of the same logical overlay. The list of the OTV edge devices is obtained from an entity called the Adjacency server. One or more of the edge devices are configured as the Adjacency server. Other edge devices need to only be configured with the Adjacency server addresses. This allows easier extension of OTV service to the newer DC sites without requiring any additional configuration on existing edge devices.

Initially, an OTV edge device registers with the Adjacency server via OTV Hello messages. Subsequently, it discovers the OTV neighbor addresses dynamically via the Adjacency server called the unicast replication list. This list is periodically refreshed by the Adjacency server to each OTV edge device so that the latter has up-to-date information about all the other OTV edge devices. Similarly for Layer 2 multicast data traffic,[5] head-end replication is required at the OTV edge devices to deliver the packet to interested receivers sitting behind other OTV edge devices. In general, head-end replication does put additional burden on the edge devices but enables OTV to run over a unicast-only transport that is desirable for customers that don't support multicast in their core network. The OTV configuration guide[6] provides detailed configuration information on how this can be achieved. For the rest of this section, assume the presence of a multicast-enabled transport core that does not require head-end replication for both OTV control and data plane traffic.

As mentioned earlier, the OTV control plane proactively advertises MAC address reachability after OTV is configured. Before advertising MAC information, the OTV edge device needs to build a neighbor relationship that is done by sending an IGMP join for the control group toward the core. In this way, a new remote site can be seamlessly added to the inter-DC OTV cluster without any configuration required on existing edge devices. IS-IS (see Chapter 3, "IS-IS," for additional details) is the control plane of choice for OTV. A single OTV control plane update may contain multiple MACs belonging to different VLANs, and with a multicast-enabled transport, a single update reaches all the neighbors (see Figure 9-5).

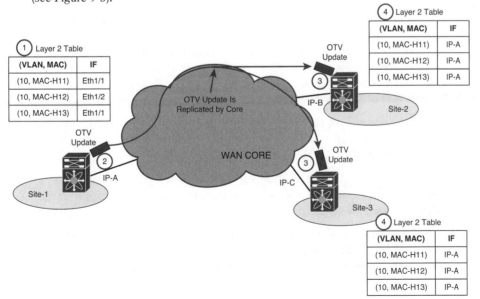

Figure 9-5 *OTV Control Plane*

As shown in Figure 9-6, OTV adds a 42-byte IP encapsulation. The OTV shim header contains the following main fields: a VLAN ID, Class of Service (CoS), and an overlay number field. OTV provides QoS hooks that enable the 802.1q header CoS and IP header DSCP fields to be picked up from the original packet. OTV edge devices do not perform any fragmentation and reassembly, so packets failing the MTU check are dropped. Consequently, appropriate DCI MTU configuration should be applied taking the 42-byte overhead into account.

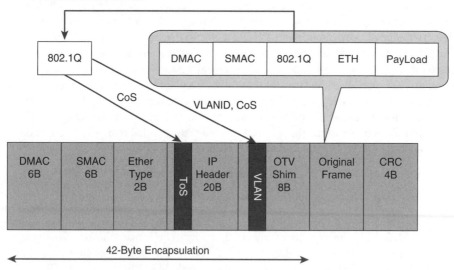

Figure 9-6   *OTV Encapsulation*

Figure 9-7 depicts a sample intersite packet flow with OTV. Following are the steps involved in the traversal of a data frame from Site-1 to Site-2 using OTV:

1. Assume that a host H1 in Site-1 with MAC-H1 in VLAN 10 wants to communicate with a remote host with MAC-H2 at Site-2. Based on the control plane advertisement, OTV edge devices (aka AEDs) on Site-1 and Site-2 would have learned the remote host MACs.

2. When the packet from H1 to H2 reaches the OTV edge device (AED) in Site-1, a Layer 2 lookup yields that MAC-H2 is located behind IP-B, which corresponds to the AED at Site-2.

3. Consequently, the AED on Site-1 appropriately encapsulates the packet with the OTV header with DIP in the outer IP header set to IP-B, and SIP set to IP-A and sends it toward the WAN core.

4. The WAN core delivers the packet to AED at Site-2 based on the DIP in the packet using regular IP-based forwarding. The AED at Site-2 decapsulates the packet, strips off the OTV header, and then performs a Layer 2 lookup based on the inner payload.

5. The lookup based on (10, MAC-H2) yields the internal interface along which the packet should be forwarded.

6. Similarly, if host H1 wants to communicate with host H3 with MAC-H3, which is not known in the control plane at AED of Site-1, this packet will be dropped and not sent toward the WAN core thereby mitigating the floods due to unknown unicast traffic.

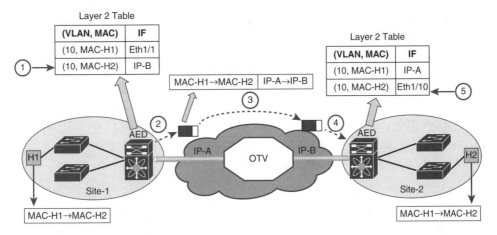

Figure 9-7   *OTV Data Plane*

Live migration of VMs from one data center site to another is supported over OTV. This presents a significant advantage for virtualized environments by simplifying and accelerating long-distance workload migrations. Figure 9-8 shows a sample VM migration scenario in which a host VM with MAC-H1 is moved from Site-1 to Site-2. Initially, MAC-H1 is located in Site-1 so that the AED at Site-1 advertises the reachability of MAC-H1 via the OTV control plane to all sites, including Site-2. Post-VM migration, the following steps ensure that the traffic to the new location of the VM is rapidly redirected:

1. After the VM shows up on Site-2, the host VM or virtualized server in Site-2 sends a GARP or RARP packet.

2. The AED in Site-2 receives this packet with SMAC as MAC-H1 via its internal interface.

3. AED in Site-2 updates it local MAC table entry for MAC-H1.

4. AED in Site-2 now sends out an OTV control plane update advertising MAC-H1 reachability with a better metric to all remote sites. Site-1 also receives this advertisement and changes MAC-H1 into a remotely learned entry.

5. Now the traffic to the VM is redirected to the new location.

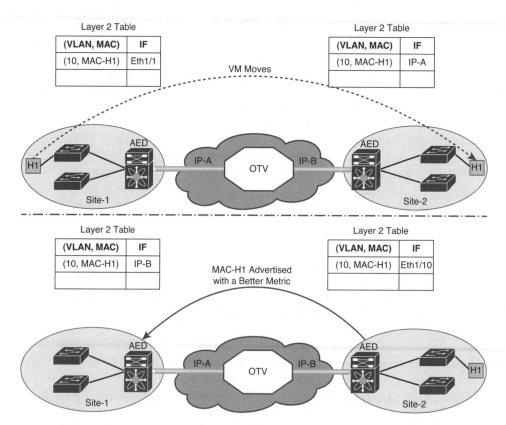

Figure 9-8 *Virtual Machine Move Handling with OTV*

It should also be noted that Layer 2 extension across data center sites brings in some challenges for optimal routing. The challenge lies in the placement of the gateway and consequently the advertisement of the routing prefix corresponding to that subnet. With HSRP-like configurations where the hosts resolve the default gateway to the advertised virtual IP address (VIP), the HSRP active may reside in a different data center site due to which routed traffic between hosts in the same site may trombone across the WAN core link resulting in suboptimal routing. Moreover, with VM mobility, the actual location of the VM may change due to which traffic may be temporarily sent to a location where the application is not available. OTV with features such as First Hop Resolution Protocol (FHRP – HSRP, VRRP) Localization, /32 Route Injection, and LISP overcomes most of these challenges. This allows for the same default gateway to exist at different sites, thus allowing the optimization for outgoing traffic from the site.[6]

Case Study 3: Interconnecting TRILL or FabricPath Data Centers Using OTV

The previous chapters saw the need to run TRILL or FabricPath inside a data center. This section discusses interconnecting data centers running TRILL or FabricPath using OTV. There are three possible scenarios in which data centers with TRILL or FabricPath could be interconnected using OTV:

- **TRILL-OTV-TRILL:** In this case study, the core of the data center network employs a TRILL overlay. The two data centers are interconnected using OTV.

- **FabricPath-OTV-FabricPath:** In this case study, the core of the data center network employs a FabricPath network. The two data centers are interconnected using OTV.

- **FabricPath-OTV-TRILL:** In this case study, the first data center uses FabricPath in its core, whereas the second data center is implemented with TRILL in its core. The two data centers are interconnected using OTV.

Because FabricPath and TRILL share a lot of common characteristics, the issues and challenges in interconnecting a TRILL or a FabricPath data centers are similar. There are a couple ways in which two TRILL or FabricPath networks are interconnected.

Merging TRILL or FabricPath Networks

This method can be visualized as merging the data center networks running TRILL or FabricPath. The connected data centers form a single topology that share the same Nickname or Switch-ID domain. The Nickname or Switch-ID has to be unique in all the connected data centers. This implies that the intermediate system-to intermediate system (IS-IS) protocol frames need to be tunneled across the data centers. The provider network connecting the edge switches of the data center is seen as one single link, and the metric for that link has to be chosen in such a way that the inter data center, aka WAN link, is used only for traffic that has to traverse across data centers. Multicast introduces more complexity in this model because the multicast tree spans across the data centers. This method suffers from the IS-IS information exchange explosion wherein the size of the IS-IS database and the number of protocol data units (PDUs) exchanged could increase exponentially. This method of connecting the data center can be used if the data center sites are not large. In case of large data centers, if a link or the root goes down, it takes more time for the tree to be reconstructed, and consequently more time for the network to become stable. Figure 9-9 shows a sample topology when two data centers running FabricPath are merged.

Both FabricPath control and data plane packets that need to be sent between sites are tunneled over OTV. As discussed in Chapter 3 events such as metric change, link flaps, switches going down, and so on can trigger a Link State Packet (LSP) that is flooded throughout the IS-IS network. In this method of merging the two data centers, effectively there is only one control plane that extends across sites. Consequently, the LSP has to be flooded to the remote sites as well. When the number of connected FabricPath sites increases, the IS-IS control traffic carried over the provider network also increases. Although the example employed FabricPath between two sites, similar concerns are applicable when multiple sites running TRILL are merged.

When two data centers running TRILL or FabricPath are merged using OTV, the following interesting cases arise.

Routing Table in SW1

Switch	Next Hop	Metric
SW2 (950)	AED1	700
SW3 (951)	AED1	200
SW4 (952)	AED1	700
AED1 (953)	AED1	100
AED2 (954)	AED1	600

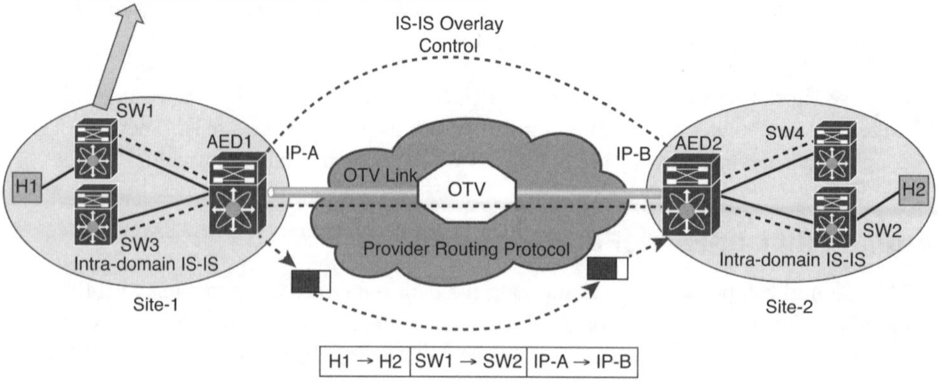

Figure 9-9 *Merged FabricPath Data Center Networks*

- The AED in each site needs to run three different instances of routing protocols:

  - IS-IS for intra-data center TRILL or FabricPath routing

  - IS-IS for OTV control protocol using each AED's peer with each other and exchange end-host MAC addresses

  - Another routing protocol for routing in the provider network

As shown in Figure 9-9, Site-1 and Site-2 each run their intradomain IS-IS routing protocol for FabricPath. Because the IS-IS frames are tunneled, both the sites are seen as one single virtual network. The routing table for SW1 is shown in Figure 9-9. The Switch-ID of each node is given in parentheses, and it can be seen that the Switch-ID across both the sites are unique. It is assumed that the cost of each link inside a site is 100 and the cost of the OTV virtual link connecting AED1 and AED2 is 500. Figure 9-9 also shows a distribution tree (dotted lines) with the root as AED-1. AED1 and AED2 run the OTV IS-IS control protocol and also take part in the provider routing protocol.

- One option to forward the TRILL or FabricPath traffic is to tunnel the original TRILL or FabricPath frame across the OTV core. This method is preferable because the data center sites belong to the same IS-IS domain. Because the TRILL or FabricPath frames are tunneled, the AEDs may not decapsulate all the TRILL or FabricPath frames they receive, and therefore may not learn the end-host MAC addresses. For example, in Figure 9-9, if SW1 originates a FabricPath frame destined to SW3, AED1 just acts as a core switch and does not decapsulate the FabricPath frame to learn the end-host MAC address. The AEDs may choose to decapsulate all TRILL or FabricPath traffic to learn the end-host MAC addresses.

  Another alternative to facilitate learning without incurring the decapsulation overhead is to use a TRILL or FabricPath control protocol such as the End System Distribution Information (ESADI) protocol to distribute the end-host MAC addresses. The OTV control plane does not need to advertise the end-host reachability information. The AED just advertises its MAC address and associated IP address. If a TRILL frames arrives at an AED and forwarding lookup indicates that the next hop is the remote AED, its MAC address will be looked up in the OTV database to get the associated IP address. The TRILL or FabricPath frame is then encapsulated with an OTV header and sent to the remote AED. The remote AED decapsulates the OTV header and forwards the inner TRILL or FabricPath frame to the destination. Figure 9-9 shows a frame from H1 to H2 tunneled inside a FabricPath payload, which is further encapsulated with an OTV header.

- Yet another option to forward the TRILL or FabricPath frame is to terminate the TRILL or FabricPath frames at a border switch. This method is more suitable if the two data center sites do not belong to the same IS-IS domain. Here, OTV advertises the end-host MAC addresses and the IP address of the AED through which the end-host can be reached. More details on forwarding are provided in a subsequent section.

Independent TRILL or FabricPath Networks

In this method, each data center running TRILL or FabricPath is independent of each other and runs as a separate IS-IS domain. The IS-IS control frames are not tunneled across the data centers. The Nicknames or Switch-IDs need not be globally unique. As described in the previous section, the AEDs need to run three different instances of routing protocols. The TRILL or FabricPath frames can either be terminated at the border switch and get reconstructed at the remote data center or can be tunneled to the remote data center. Here, OTV advertises the end-host MAC addresses along with the AED's IP address. Now consider the approach in which the frames are terminated at the border switch. A sample topology is shown in Figure 9-10. As was also shown in Figure 9-9, Site-1 and Site-2 each run their intradomain IS-IS routing protocol for FabricPath. Because the IS-IS frames are not tunneled, both the sites act as independent IS-IS networks. The routing table for SW1 and SW4 is shown in Figure 9-10. The Switch-ID of each node is given in parentheses, and it can be seen that the Switch-IDs across both the sites are not unique. It is assumed that the cost of each link inside a site is 100. Figure 9-10 also shows each site having its own distribution tree (dotted lines) with the root as AED1 and AED2.

AED1 and AED2 run the OTV IS-IS control protocol and also take part in the provider routing protocol.

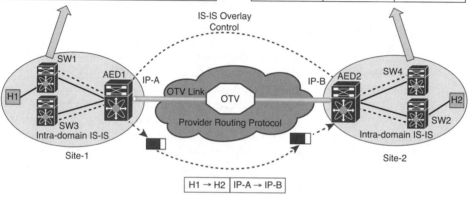

Figure 9-10   *Independent FabricPath Data Center Networks*

- The AED also acts as the border switch for the FabricPath or TRILL network. Frames that are destined to the remote data center are sent to the remote border switch or AED.

- The AED decapsulates the TRILL or FabricPath frame and does a lookup on the inner destination MAC address to get the remote AED's IP address. If the lookup results in a miss, the frame is dropped because unknown unicast frames are dropped with OTV. Otherwise, the frame is sent to the remote AED after OTV encapsulation.

- The remote AED decapsulates the OTV frame and reconstructs the TRILL or FabricPath frame to send it to the destination FabricPath switch or RBridge.

- The source Nickname or Switch-ID should be set to the AED or border switch's Nickname or Switch-ID.

- For Multitopology Routing (MTR), the FTAG or the Topology ID has to be derived based on the original frame's tag (1q or qinq).

- Similarly, the segment ID or FGL has to be derived based on the original frame's tag (1q or qinq). So it is mandatory for the inner frame to carry the 802.1q tag.

Figure 9-10 shows a frame from H1 to H2 carried within an OTV header. Note that AED1 decapsulates the FabricPath header before stamping the OTV header on the original inner payload. If the TRILL or FabricPath frames are tunneled across the OTV cloud, the following needs to be considered. This approach is not suitable for this independent network model:

- The border switches must allocate some globally unique Nicknames or Switch-ID and exchange the information with the other border switches. This information somehow needs to be piggybacked with the provider control protocol.

- For frames that are destined to the remote data center site, the source Nickname or Switch-ID of the frame should be modified to the globally unique Nickname or Switch-ID of the border switch.

- The border switches must exchange Nickname or Switch-ID reachability information with each other through the provider routing protocol. In other words, a lookup for the destination Nickname or Switch-ID should give the adjacency information containing the MAC address of the remote border switch or AED, the IP address of the AED and the interface, and MAC address of the next hop.

Interconnection of TRILL and FabricPath Data Centers

The previous sections considered the symmetric cases in which in the remote data centers that were connected through OTV were running either TRILL or FabricPath. There may be cases in which a data center running TRILL needs to be interconnected with a data center running FabricPath. When two data centers that are running TRILL and FabricPath, respectively, need to be interconnected, the two have to run the ISIS control protocol independently, as described in the previous section. The TRILL or FabricPath data frames need to be terminated at the border switch (AED) and reconstructed as appropriate FabricPath or TRILL data frames at the remote AED.

Packet Flow

This section describes a detailed step-by-step packet flow between two FabricPath data centers that are interconnected through OTV, as shown in Figure 9-11. All the various combinations described so far related to interconnecting TRILL or FabricPath data centers can be realized with some minor modifications based on the adopted methodology. For this case study, assume that the approach mentioned in the "Independent TRILL or FabricPath Network" section is employed wherein the FabricPath frames are terminated at the border switch and not tunneled across the data centers.

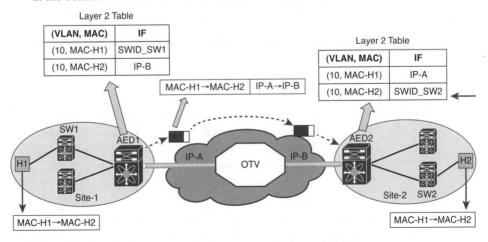

Figure 9-11 *FabricPath Data Centers Connected Through OTV*

Following are the steps involved in the traversal of a data frame from Site-1 to Site-2 using OTV:

1. Assume that a host H1 in Site-1 with MAC-H1 in VLAN 10 wants to communicate with a remote host with MAC-H2 at Site-2.

2. Switch SW1 does a lookup in its Layer 2 table, which results in a miss when the remote entry has not been learned. SW1 encapsulates the frame into a FabricPath header where the FTAG denotes the multicast tree on which the frame has to be transmitted.

3. The FabricPath frame reaches AED1 at Site-1. AED1 decapsulates the FabricPath frame. It also learns the source MAC address MAC-H1 and associates it with the Switch-ID of SW1.

4. Based on the control plane advertisement, OTV edge devices (AEDs) on Site-1 and Site-2 would have learned the remote host MACs. The AEDs can choose to distribute the remote MACs locally within the data center with the associated Switch-ID as itself. Then any frames destined to the remote hosts will be sent to the local AED (border switch). If AED1 had distributed the remote MAC addresses, the lookup in step 2 will not be a miss.

5. The OTV edge device (AED) in Site-1 will do a Layer 2 lookup for <MAC-H2, VLAN 10>. The lookup result will be IP-B, which corresponds to the AED at Site-2.

6. Consequently, AED1 on Site-1 will appropriately encapsulate the packet with an OTV header with DIP in the outer IP header set to IP-B and SIP set to IP-A and send it toward the WAN core. The original frame should have the inner tag (1q or qinq) so that the remote switch can associate the frame with the right segment/VLAN.

7. The WAN core delivers the packet to AED2 at Site-2 based on the DIP in the packet using regular IP-based forwarding. AED2 at Site-2 decapsulates the packet, strips off the OTV header, and then performs a Layer 2 lookup based on the inner payload.

8. A Layer 2 lookup is performed for (10, MAC-H2). Because the MAC address of H2 has been advertised by this AED using OTV, the lookup will not be a miss. However, assume for the sake of explaining the concept that the lookup result is a miss.

9. The AED or Border Switch at Site-2 treats this as an unknown unicast and floods it internally within Site-2. It encapsulates the original Layer 2 frame with a FabricPath header. The source Switch-ID in the frame is set to the Switch-ID of itself (AED2). The FTAG is set to the appropriate multicast tree. The outer destination MAC address is set to the reserved multicast MAC address that denotes a unicast lookup miss.

10. The FabricPath frame reaches the switch SW2, which decapsulates the frame and sends it to the attached host H2. SW2 also learns the source MAC address MAC-H1 and associates it with the Switch-ID of AED2.

11. For the reverse traffic, that is, (H2->H1), the switch SW2 constructs the FabricPath frame and sends it toward AED2 as learned in the Layer 2 table.

12. AED2 decapsulates the FabricPath frame and does a lookup for <MAC-H1, VLAN 10>. The lookup result is IP-A, which corresponds to the AED at Site-1 (AED1).

13. Consequently, the AED on Site-2 appropriately encapsulates the packet with the OTV header with DIP in the outer IP header set to IP-A and SIP set to IP-B and sends it toward the WAN core. The original frame should have the inner tag (1q or qinq) so that the remote switch can associate the frame with the right segment/VLAN.

14. The WAN core delivers the packet to the AED at Site-1 based on the DIP in the packet using regular IP-based forwarding. AED1 decapsulates the packet, strips off the OTV header, and then performs a Layer 2 lookup based on the inner payload.

15. The lookup result at AED1 yields the Switch-ID (SW1 in this example) of the FabricPath switch to which the destination host is attached. The FTAG field denotes the topology ID and is derived based on the tag (1q or qinq) carried in the frame. The destination Switch-ID is set to the Switch-ID of SW1, and the source Switch-ID to that of AED1.

16. The FabricPath frame reaches the switch SW1, which decapsulates the same and sends it to the attached host H1. SW1 also learns the source MAC address MAC-H2 and associates it with the Switch-ID of AED1.

17. The flooding due to unknown unicast is local to the data center site and not in the WAN core. If host H1 wants to communicate with a host H3 with MAC-H3, which is not known in the control plane at AED1, this packet is dropped and not sent toward the WAN core, thereby mitigating the floods due to unknown unicast traffic, which is one of the prime benefits of OTV.

Summary

This chapter takes a closer look at some multi-overlay deployment options. The chapter delves into one intra-DC case study with VXLAN connectivity from the server to the ToR switch and TRILL in the core of the data center. This case study basically focuses on how the 24-bit VXLAN VNI can be carried as Double-Q in the TRILL network. The other two case studies deal with the inter-DC deployment scenarios and use the OTV as the DCI technology. OTV enables the Layer 2 extension across any IP network by leveraging IP-encapsulated MAC address routing. These simplified Layer 2 extensions over an existing network without redesigning the core of the network enable the IT staff to move their workloads across data centers.

References

1. http://www.cisco.com/en/US/products/ps9902/prod_presentation_list.html.

2. http://www.cisco.com/en/US/prod/collateral/switches/ps9441/ps9902/guide_c07-702975.html.

3. http://www.borgcube.com/blogs/wp-content/uploads/2012/10/VXLAN-Extending-Networking-to-Fit-the-CloudFinal.pdf.

4. http://www.cisco.com/web/DK/assets/docs/presentations/A1-Scaling-the-DC-external.pdf.

5. http://www.cisco.com/en/US/docs/solutions/Enterprise/Data_Center/DCI/5.0/OTVmulticast.pdf.

6. http://www.cisco.com/en/US/docs/solutions/Enterprise/Data_Center/DCI/whitepaper/DCI3_OTV_Intro_WP.pdf.

7. http://www.cisco.com/en/US/prod/collateral/routers/ps9343/white_paper_c11-452157.html.

8. http://www.cisco.com/en/US/docs/routers/csr1000/software/configuration/csroverview.html.

9. http://www.cisco.com/en/US/docs/solutions/Enterprise/Data_Center/desguide.pdf.

10. "Multiprotocol Label Switching Architecture—RFC 3031.

11. "Encapsulation Methods for Transport of Ethernet over MPLS Networks—RFC 4448.

12. "Virtual Private LAN Service (VPLS) Using BGP for Auto-Discovery and Signaling—RFC 4761.

13. "Virtual Private LAN Service (VPLS) Using Label Distribution Protocol (LDP) Signaling—RFC 4762.

Index

Numerics

A

F

J-K-L

M

P

W-X-Y-Z

FREE
Online Edition

Your purchase of *Using TRILL, FabricPath, and VXLAN* includes access to a free online edition for 45 days through the **Safari Books Online** subscription service. Nearly every Cisco Press book is available online through **Safari Books Online**, along with thousands of books and videos from publishers such as Addison-Wesley Professional, Exam Cram, IBM Press, O'Reilly Media, Prentice Hall, Que, Sams, and VMware Press.

Safari Books Online is a digital library providing searchable, on-demand access to thousands of technology, digital media, and professional development books and videos from leading publishers. With one monthly or yearly subscription price, you get unlimited access to learning tools and information on topics including mobile app and software development, tips and tricks on using your favorite gadgets, networking, project management, graphic design, and much more.

Activate your FREE Online Edition at
informit.com/safarifree

STEP 1: Enter the coupon code: COOMMXA.

STEP 2: New Safari users, complete the brief registration form.
Safari subscribers, just log in.

If you have difficulty registering on Safari or accessing the online edition,
please e-mail customer-service@safaribooksonline.com